SHIROICHI AMAUI &
KONEKONEKO PRESENT

CHARACTER DESIGN
TAMAGONOKIMI

The HERO LIFE
of a (Self-Proclaimed) "Mediocre"
DEMON!

2

AUTHOR **SHIROICHI AMAUI**

ARTIST **KONEKONEKO**

CHARACTER
DESIGN **TAMAGONOKIMI**

🔲 CHRONO ALKON

A YOUNG JINN WITH A TREMENDOUS AMOUNT OF POTENTIAL.
HOWEVER, HE STUBBORNLY SELF-PROCLAIMS THAT HE'S
MEDIOCRE. HE CAN USE HIS POWER TO MATERIALIZE THE
"CHAINS OF DOMINATION" AND MAKE OTHERS BECOME HIS
SLAVES.

🔲 SOFIA GRAVE

THE VAMPIRE PRINCESS OF THE FAMOUS GRAVE FAMILY.
WHILE SHE'S BECOME CHRONO'S SLAVE, SHE DOESN'T SEEM ALL
THAT UNHAPPY ABOUT IT SINCE SHE LIKES HIM.
SHE'S A MEMBER OF THE "SPECIAL EXPLORATION UNIT."

STORY ←

CHRONO IS A (SELF-PROCLAIMED) "MEDIOCRE" DEMON WHO ENTERED A DEMON ACADEMY.
HOWEVER, IN THE "DUNGEON CREATION" TEST THAT DETERMINES THE CLASSES, HE DISPLAYED
EXTRAORDINARY ABILITIES.

CHRONO, WHO WAS IMMEDIATELY NOTICED BY THE DEMON KING, LIZA, WAS SCOUTED TO BE
PART OF THE "SPECIAL EXPLORATION UNIT," AND WAS ORDERED TO EXPLORE THE PREVIOUS
DEMON KINGS' DUNGEONS TO FIND THE TREASURE WITHIN.

BUT WHILE EXPLORING, CHRONO UNINTENTIONALLY DOMINATED THE VAMPIRE SOFIA AND HIS
SEMPAI, YUKINO, WITH SOME POWERFUL MAGIC, RESULTING IN THEM BECOMING HIS SLAVES.

NOW, TO RELEASE THEM FROM THEIR ENSLAVEMENT, CHRONO AND HIS FRIENDS ARE ABOUT TO
EXPLORE THE NEXT DUNGEON!

CHARACTER

🎲 Liza Malta Philanikos

THE 50TH DEMON KING. ALONG WITH CHRONO AND THE OTHERS, SHE EXPLORES DUNGEONS. SHE'S A NIGHTMARE SPECIES DEMON.

🎲 Yukino Salmard

A FEMALE LYCANTHROPE WHO'S CHRONO'S SEMPAI. SHE'S ADEPT AT CREATING DUNGEON MAPS. CHRONO'S "DOMINATION" TOOK HER OVER AND SHE'S BECOME HIS SLAVE.

🎲 Professor Dante

HE'S A BEASTMAN TEACHER IN CHARGE OF CHRONO AND HIS CLASSMATES.

🎲 Grude Vogney

A HELLHOUND. HE WAS SELECTED FOR THE SPECIAL CLASS, BUT ON EVERY OCCASION, CHRONO OVERWHELMS HIM.

🎲 Cordy

A DRAGONOID. HE WAS SELECTED TO BE IN THE SPECIAL CLASS. HE'S A NICE GUY WITH A STURDY BODY.

CONTENTS

THE HERO LIFE OF A (SELF-PROCLAIMED) "MEDIOCRE" DEMON!

The HERO LIFE of a (Self-Proclaimed) "Mediocre" DEMON!

CHAPTER 6

CHRONO GETS SOME ASSISTANCE

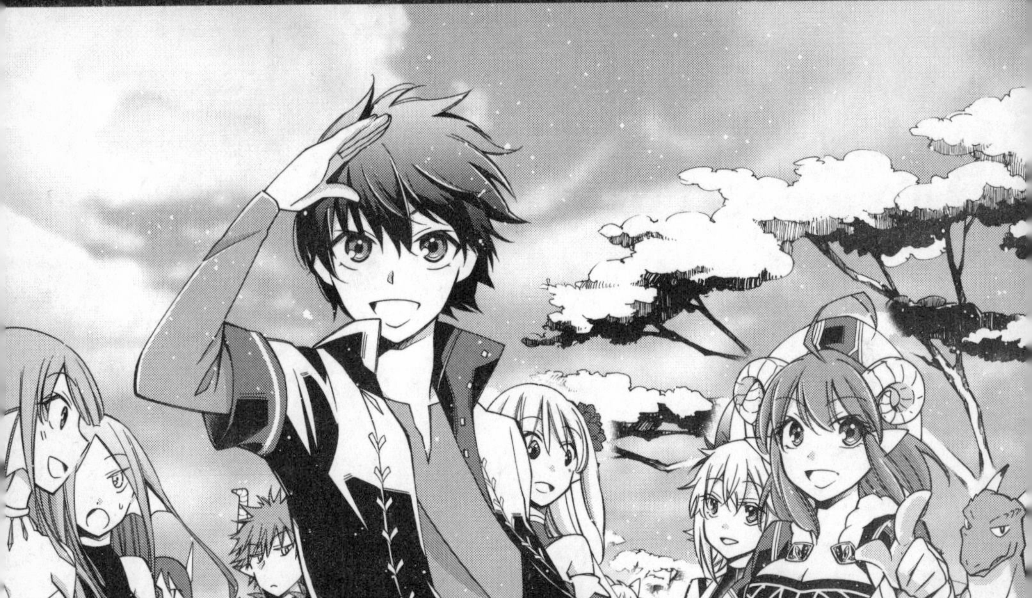

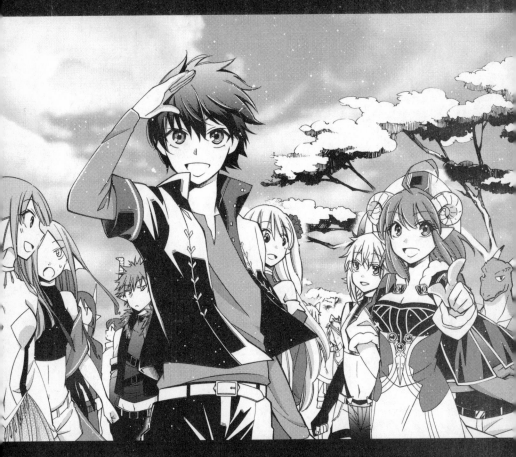

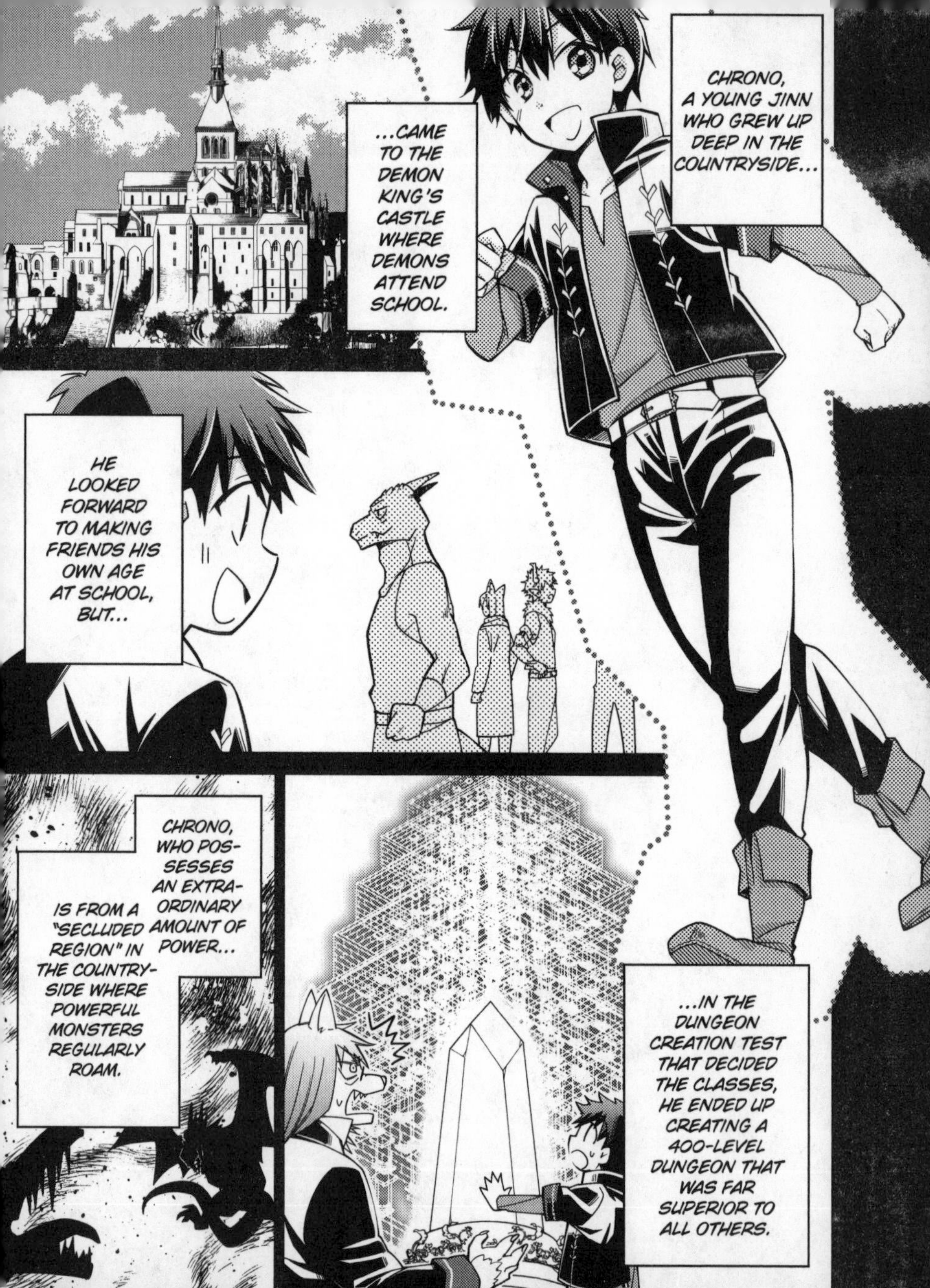
CHRONO, A YOUNG JINN WHO GREW UP DEEP IN THE COUNTRYSIDE...
...CAME TO THE DEMON KING'S CASTLE WHERE DEMONS ATTEND SCHOOL.
HE LOOKED FORWARD TO MAKING FRIENDS HIS OWN AGE AT SCHOOL, BUT...
...IN THE DUNGEON CREATION TEST THAT DECIDED THE CLASSES, HE ENDED UP CREATING A 400-LEVEL DUNGEON THAT WAS FAR SUPERIOR TO ALL OTHERS.
CHRONO, WHO POSSESSES AN EXTRAORDINARY AMOUNT OF POWER...
IS FROM A "SECLUDED REGION" IN THE COUNTRYSIDE WHERE POWERFUL MONSTERS REGULARLY ROAM.

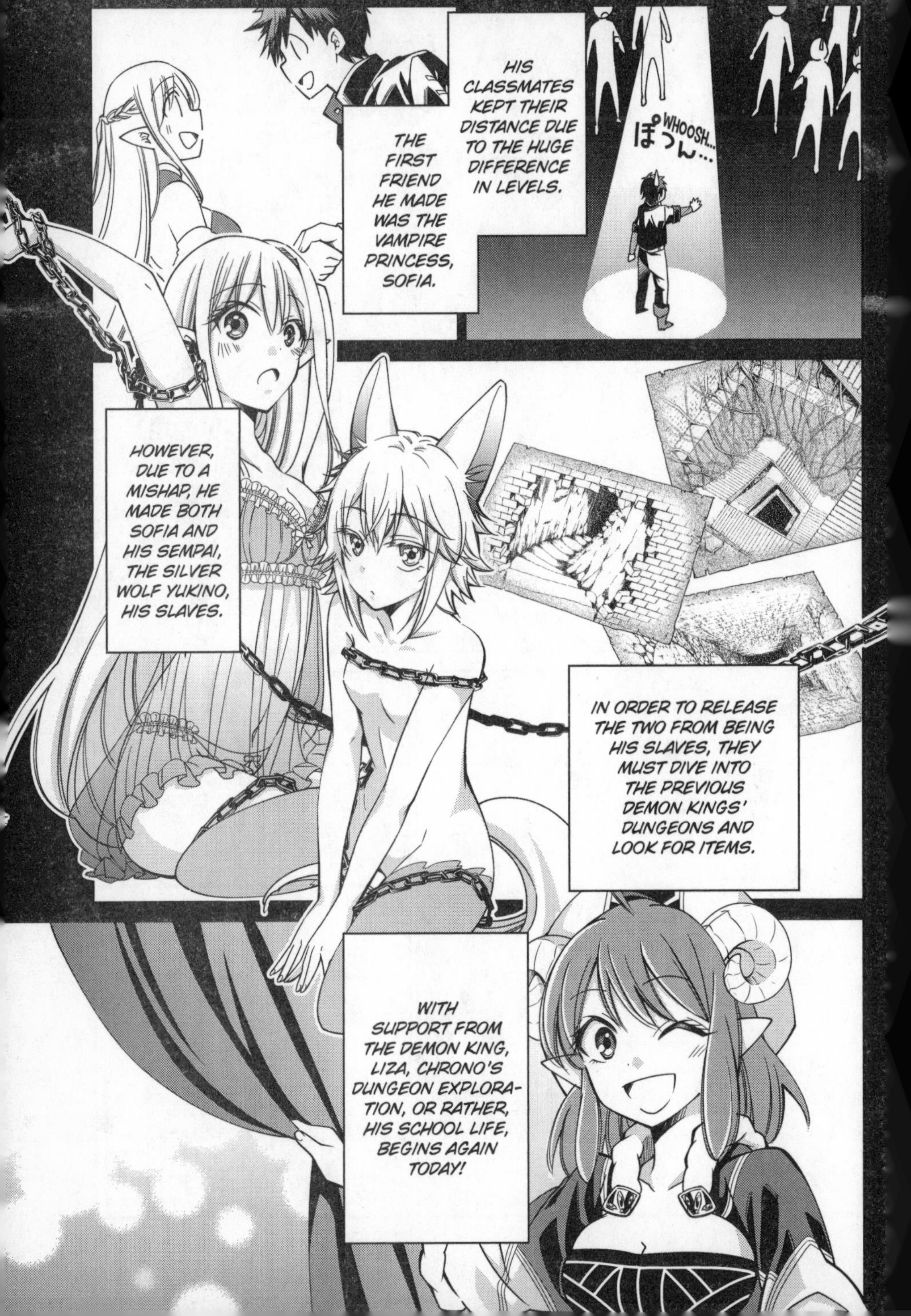
HIS CLASSMATES KEPT THEIR DISTANCE DUE TO THE HUGE DIFFERENCE IN LEVELS.
WHOOSH...
ぽつん...
THE FIRST FRIEND HE MADE WAS THE VAMPIRE PRINCESS, SOFIA.
HOWEVER, DUE TO A MISHAP, HE MADE BOTH SOFIA AND HIS SEMPAI, THE SILVER WOLF YUKINO, HIS SLAVES.
IN ORDER TO RELEASE THE TWO FROM BEING HIS SLAVES, THEY MUST DIVE INTO THE PREVIOUS DEMON KINGS' DUNGEONS AND LOOK FOR ITEMS.
WITH SUPPORT FROM THE DEMON KING, LIZA, CHRONO'S DUNGEON EXPLORATION, OR RATHER, HIS SCHOOL LIFE, BEGINS AGAIN TODAY!

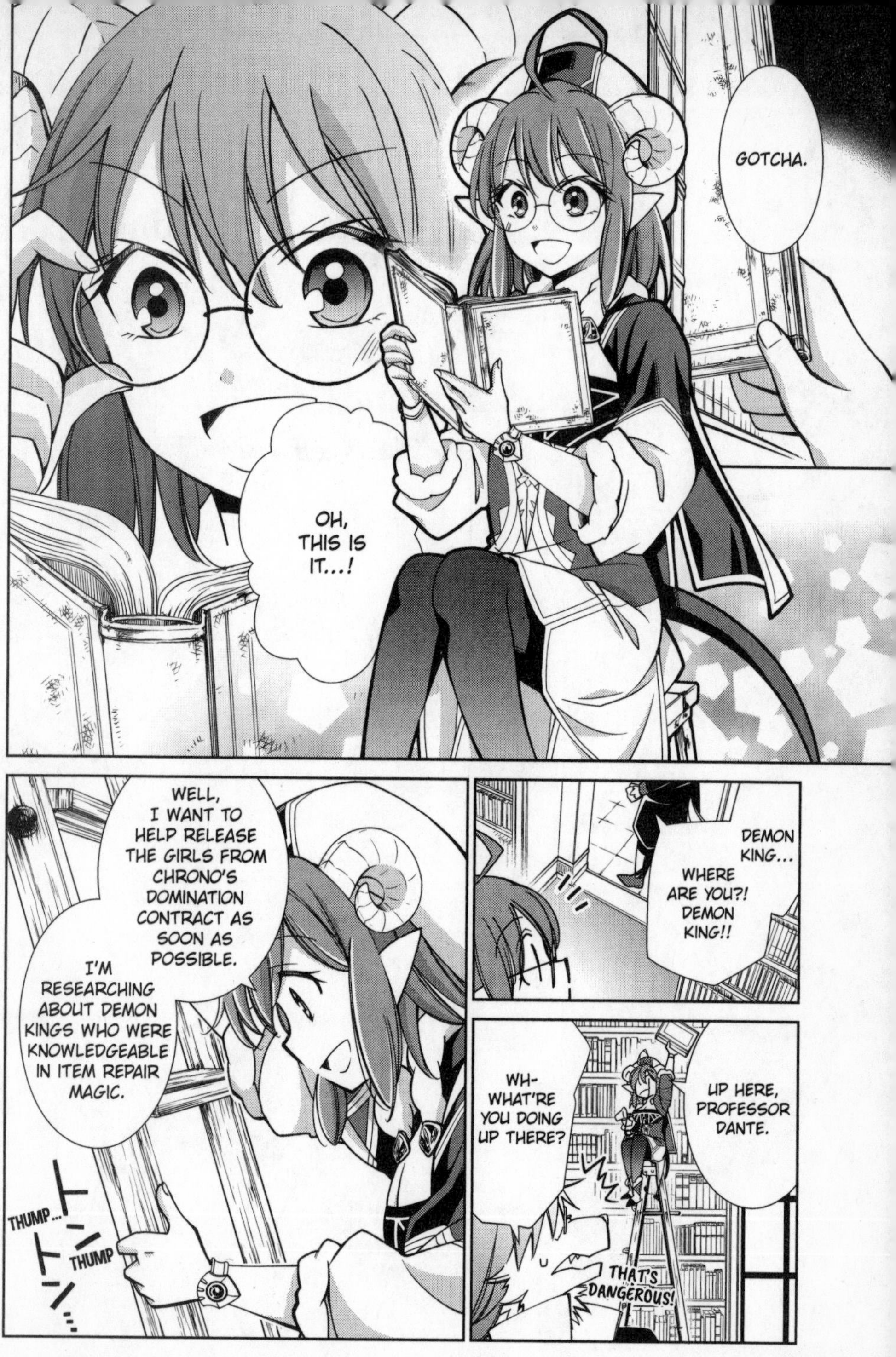

GOTCHA.
OH, THIS IS IT...!
DEMON KING... WHERE ARE YOU?! DEMON KING!!
UP HERE, PROFESSOR DANTE.
WH- WHAT'RE YOU DOING UP THERE?
THAT'S DANGEROUS!
WELL, I WANT TO HELP RELEASE THE GIRLS FROM CHRONO'S DOMINATION CONTRACT AS SOON AS POSSIBLE.
I'M RESEARCHING ABOUT DEMON KINGS WHO WERE KNOWLEDGEABLE IN ITEM REPAIR MAGIC.
THUMP...
THUMP

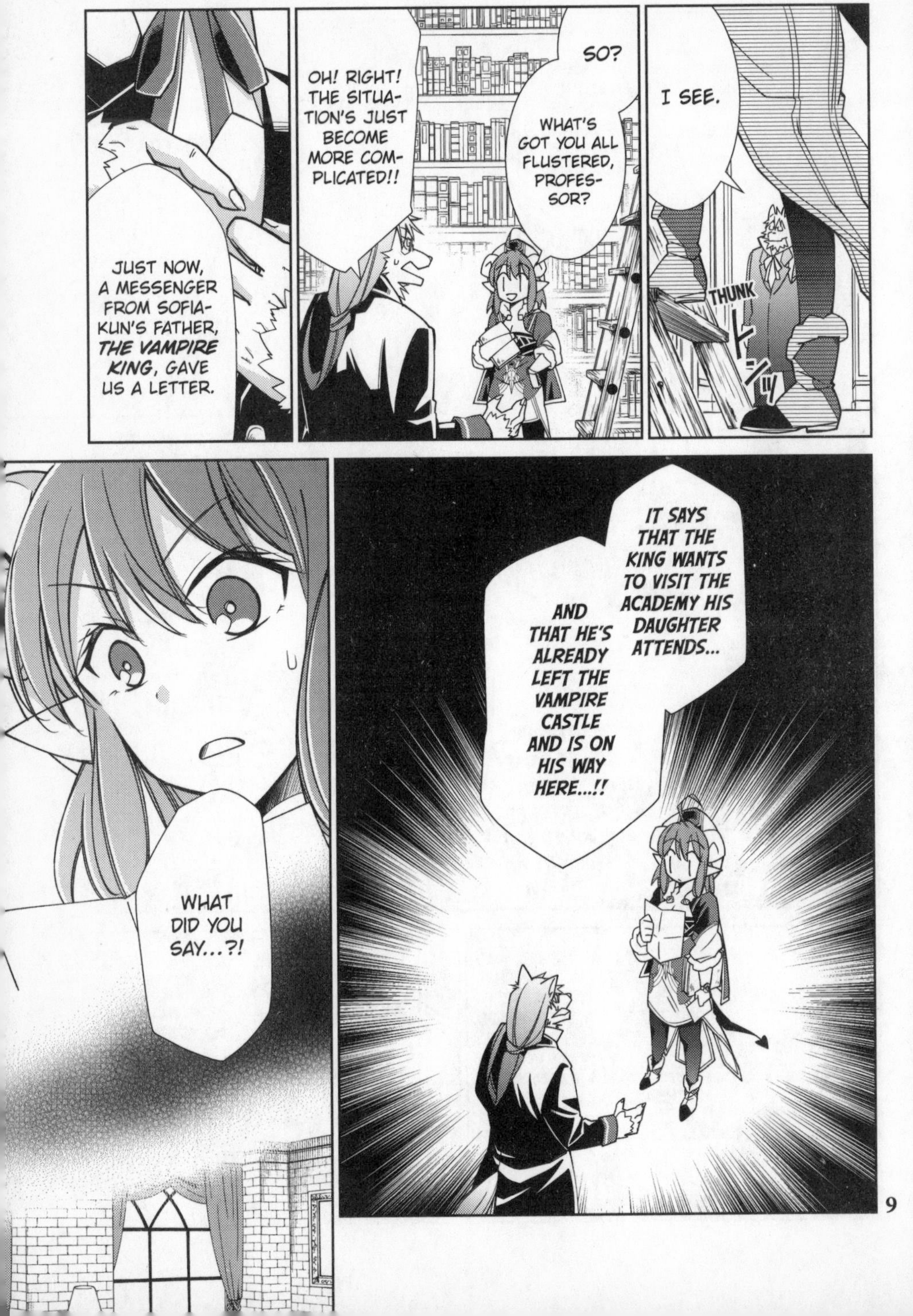
I SEE.
THUNK
SO?
WHAT'S GOT YOU ALL FLUSTERED, PROFESSOR?
OH! RIGHT! THE SITUATION'S JUST BECOME MORE COMPLICATED!!
JUST NOW, A MESSENGER FROM SOFIA-KUN'S FATHER, ***THE VAMPIRE KING***, GAVE US A LETTER.
IT SAYS THAT THE KING WANTS TO VISIT THE ACADEMY HIS DAUGHTER ATTENDS...
AND THAT HE'S ALREADY LEFT THE VAMPIRE CASTLE AND IS ON HIS WAY HERE...!!
WHAT DID YOU SAY...?!

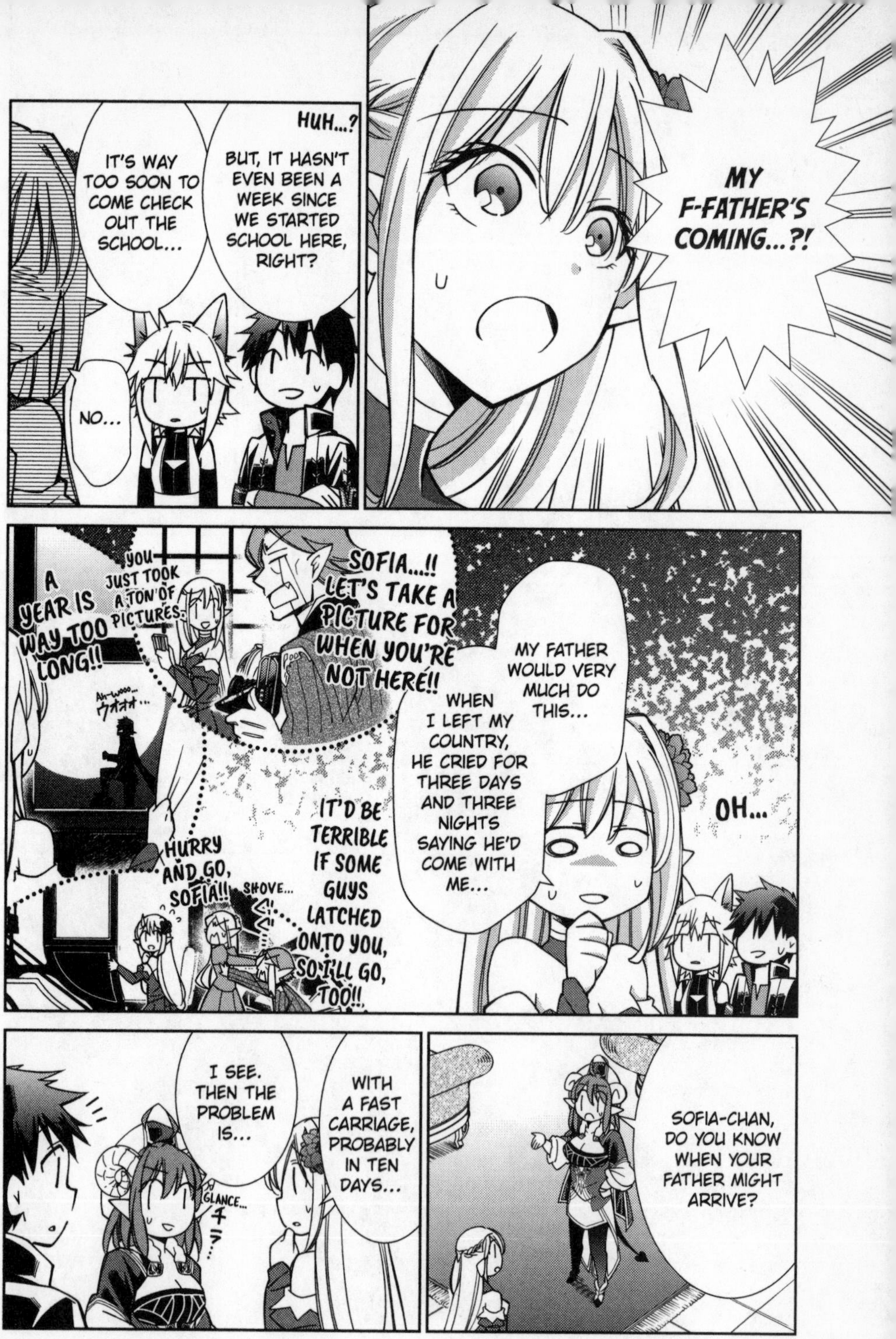
MY F-FATHER'S COMING...?!
HUH...?
BUT, IT HASN'T EVEN BEEN A WEEK SINCE WE STARTED SCHOOL HERE, RIGHT?
IT'S WAY TOO SOON TO COME CHECK OUT THE SCHOOL...
NO...
OH...
MY FATHER WOULD VERY MUCH DO THIS...
WHEN I LEFT MY COUNTRY, HE CRIED FOR THREE DAYS AND THREE NIGHTS SAYING HE'D COME WITH ME...
SOFIA...!! LET'S TAKE A PICTURE FOR WHEN YOU'RE NOT HERE!!
YOU JUST TOOK A TON OF PICTURES.
A YEAR IS WAY TOO LONG!!
Ah-wooo... ウオオオ...
IT'D BE TERRIBLE IF SOME GUYS LATCHED ON TO YOU, SO I'LL GO, TOO!!
SHOVE...
HURRY AND GO, SOFIA!!
SOFIA-CHAN, DO YOU KNOW WHEN YOUR FATHER MIGHT ARRIVE?
WITH A FAST CARRIAGE, PROBABLY IN TEN DAYS...
I SEE. THEN THE PROBLEM IS...
GLANCE... チラ...

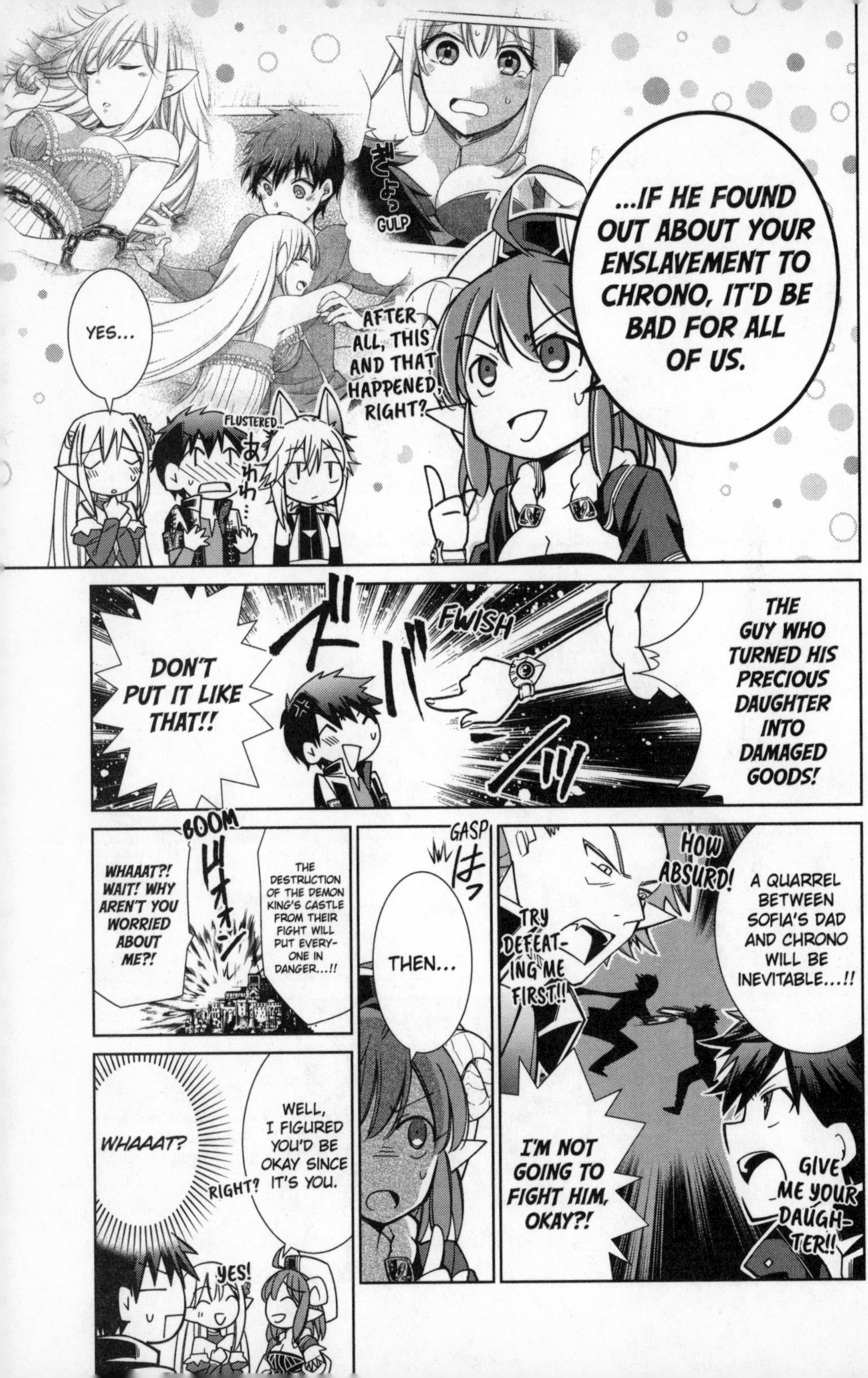
...IF HE FOUND OUT ABOUT YOUR ENSLAVEMENT TO CHRONO, IT'D BE BAD FOR ALL OF US.
ぎょっ
GULP
AFTER ALL, THIS AND THAT HAPPENED, RIGHT?
YES...
FLUSTERED...
あわわ...
THE GUY WHO TURNED HIS PRECIOUS DAUGHTER INTO DAMAGED GOODS!
FWISH
DON'T PUT IT LIKE THAT!!
A QUARREL BETWEEN SOFIA'S DAD AND CHRONO WILL BE INEVITABLE...!!
HOW ABSURD!
TRY DEFEATING ME FIRST!!
GIVE ME YOUR DAUGHTER!!
I'M NOT GOING TO FIGHT HIM, OKAY?!
GASP
はっ
THEN...
THE DESTRUCTION OF THE DEMON KING'S CASTLE FROM THEIR FIGHT WILL PUT EVERYONE IN DANGER...!!
BOOM
WHAAAT?! WAIT! WHY AREN'T YOU WORRIED ABOUT ME?!
WELL, I FIGURED YOU'D BE OKAY SINCE IT'S YOU.
RIGHT?
WHAAAT?
YES!

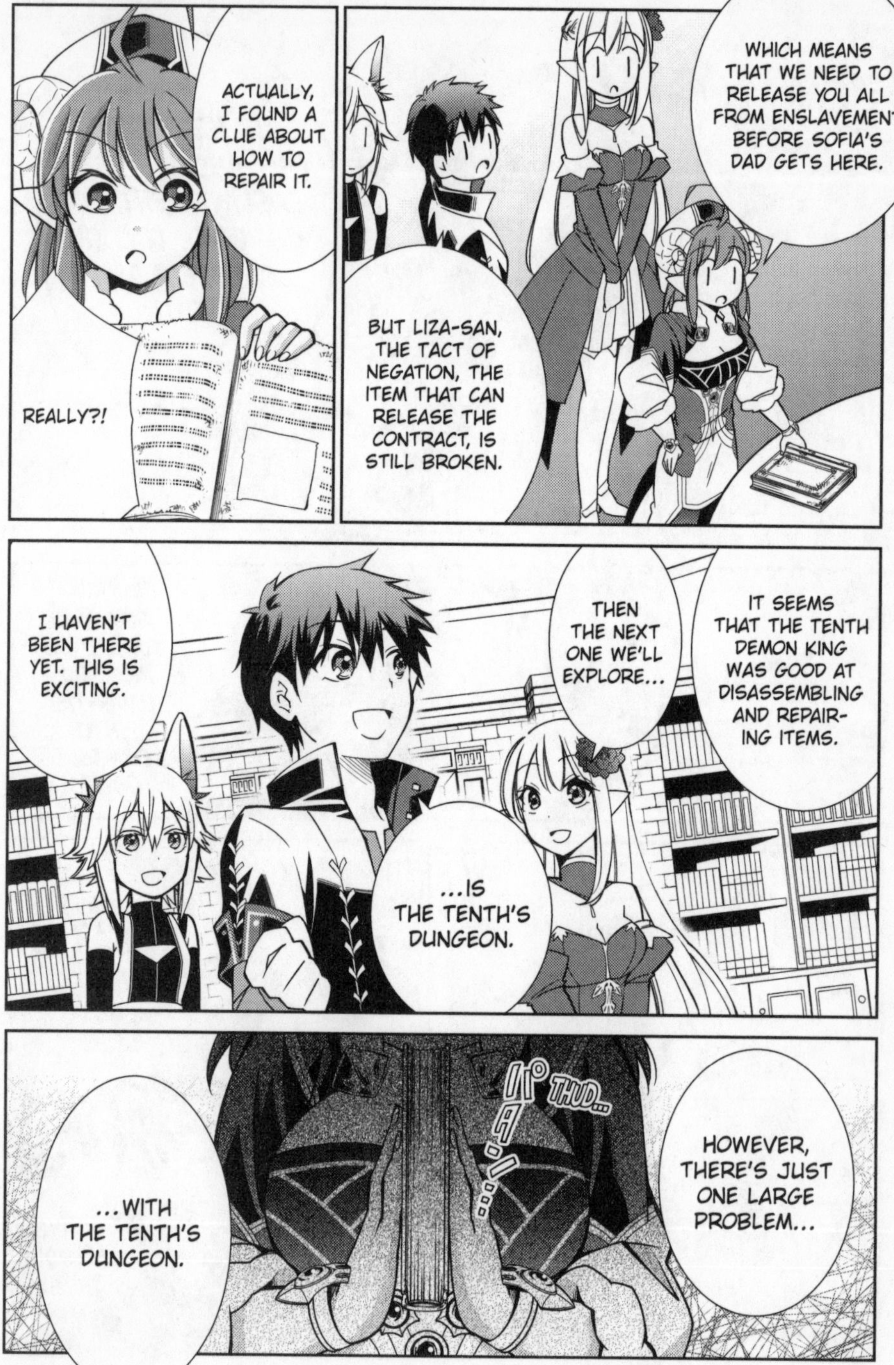
WHICH MEANS THAT WE NEED TO RELEASE YOU ALL FROM ENSLAVEMENT BEFORE SOFIA'S DAD GETS HERE.
BUT LIZA-SAN, THE TACT OF NEGATION, THE ITEM THAT CAN RELEASE THE CONTRACT, IS STILL BROKEN.
ACTUALLY, I FOUND A CLUE ABOUT HOW TO REPAIR IT.
REALLY?!
IT SEEMS THAT THE TENTH DEMON KING WAS GOOD AT DISASSEMBLING AND REPAIR-ING ITEMS.
THEN THE NEXT ONE WE'LL EXPLORE...
...IS THE TENTH'S DUNGEON.
I HAVEN'T BEEN THERE YET. THIS IS EXCITING.
HOWEVER, THERE'S JUST ONE LARGE PROBLEM...
THUD...
...WITH THE TENTH'S DUNGEON.

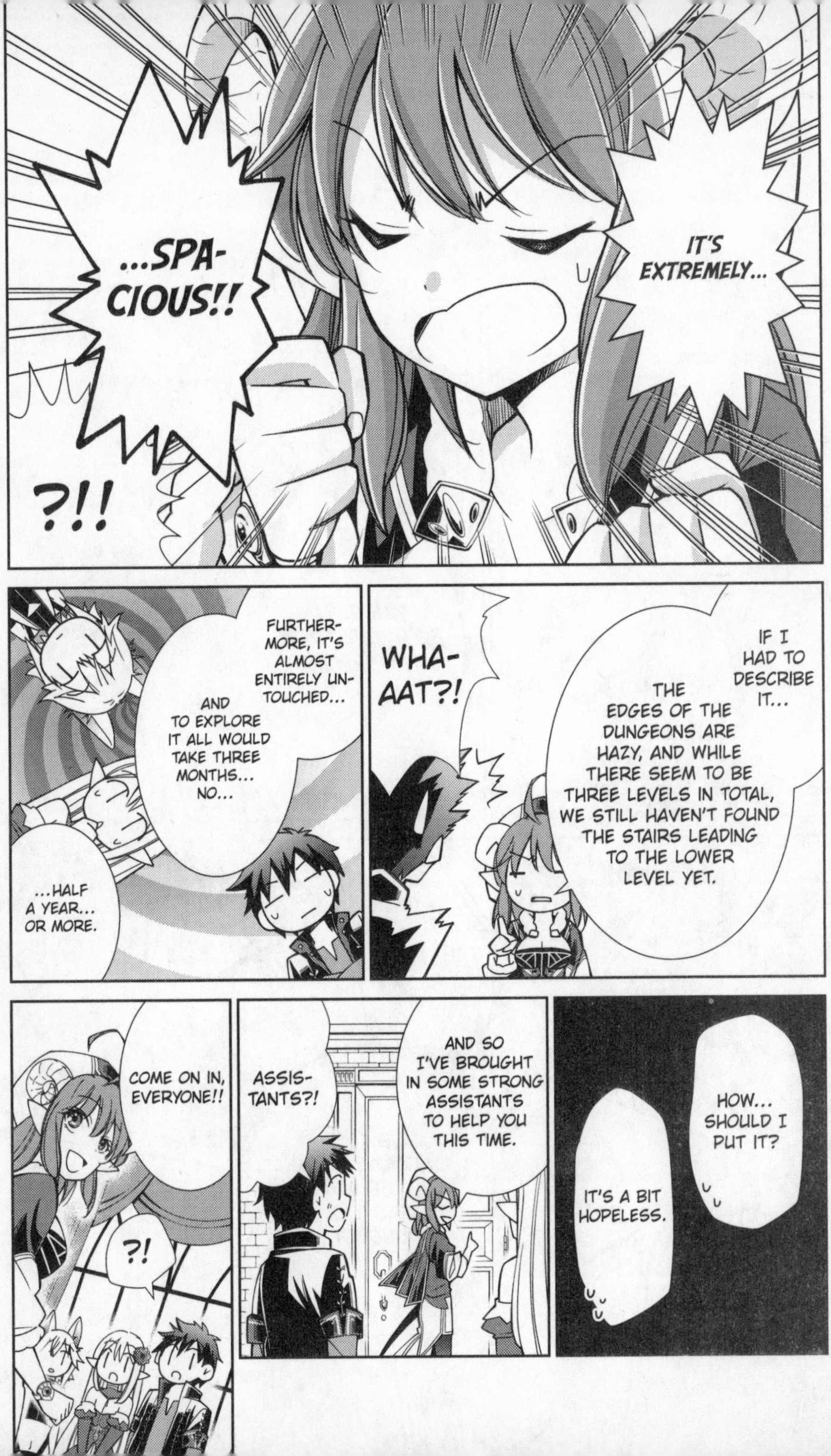
IT'S EXTREMELY...
...SPA-CIOUS!!
?!!
IF I HAD TO DESCRIBE IT...
THE EDGES OF THE DUNGEONS ARE HAZY, AND WHILE THERE SEEM TO BE THREE LEVELS IN TOTAL, WE STILL HAVEN'T FOUND THE STAIRS LEADING TO THE LOWER LEVEL YET.
WHA-AAT?!
FURTHER-MORE, IT'S ALMOST ENTIRELY UN-TOUCHED...
AND TO EXPLORE IT ALL WOULD TAKE THREE MONTHS... NO...
...HALF A YEAR... OR MORE.
HOW... SHOULD I PUT IT?
IT'S A BIT HOPELESS.
AND SO I'VE BROUGHT IN SOME STRONG ASSISTANTS TO HELP YOU THIS TIME.
ASSIS-TANTS?!
COME ON IN, EVERYONE!!
?!

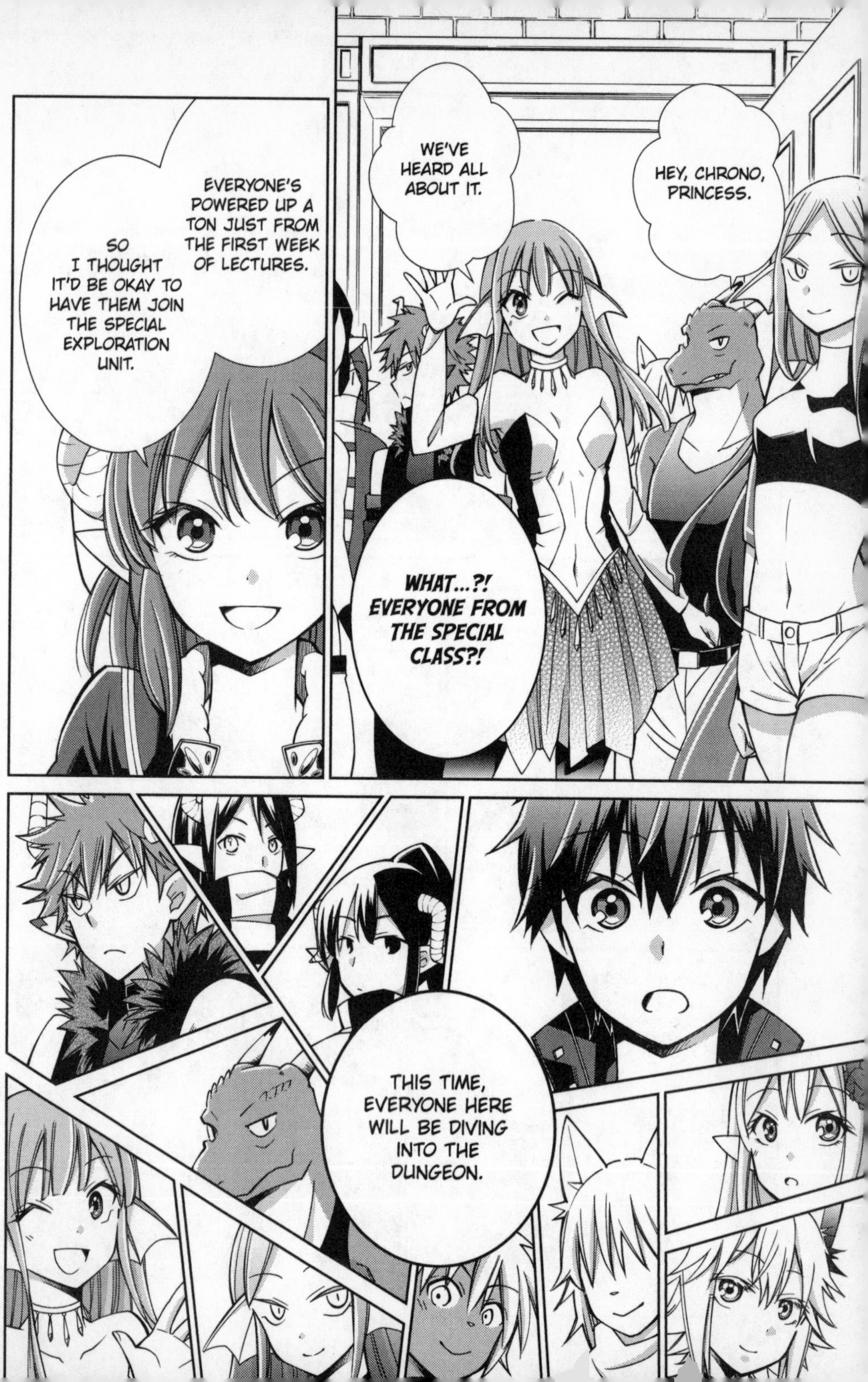
HEY, CHRONO, PRINCESS.
WE'VE HEARD ALL ABOUT IT.
WHAT...?! EVERYONE FROM THE SPECIAL CLASS?!
EVERYONE'S POWERED UP A TON JUST FROM THE FIRST WEEK OF LECTURES.
SO I THOUGHT IT'D BE OKAY TO HAVE THEM JOIN THE SPECIAL EXPLORATION UNIT.
THIS TIME, EVERYONE HERE WILL BE DIVING INTO THE DUNGEON.

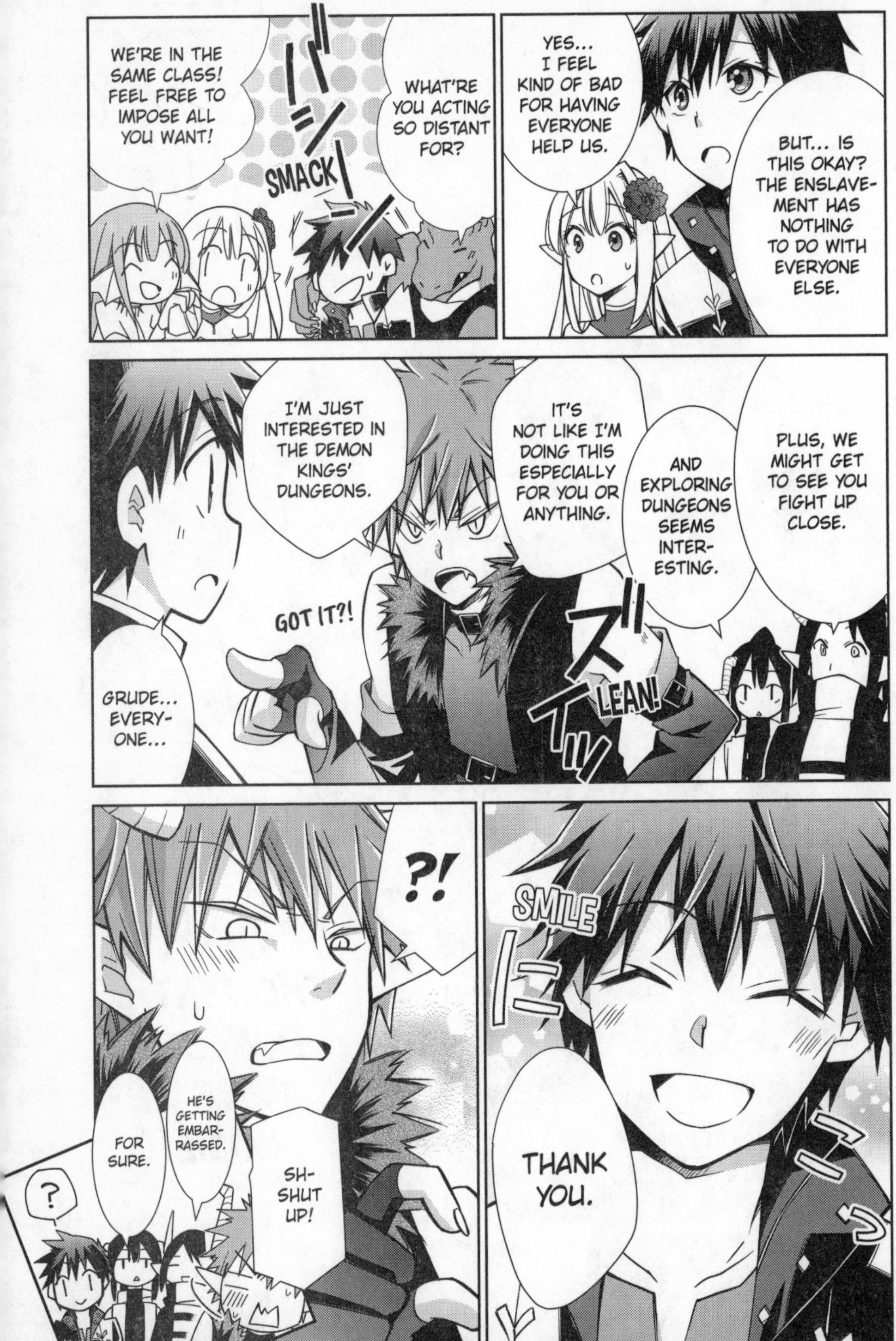
BUT... IS THIS OKAY? THE ENSLAVEMENT HAS NOTHING TO DO WITH EVERYONE ELSE.
YES... I FEEL KIND OF BAD FOR HAVING EVERYONE HELP US.
WHAT'RE YOU ACTING SO DISTANT FOR?
SMACK
WE'RE IN THE SAME CLASS! FEEL FREE TO IMPOSE ALL YOU WANT!
PLUS, WE MIGHT GET TO SEE YOU FIGHT UP CLOSE.
AND EXPLORING DUNGEONS SEEMS INTERESTING.
LEAN!
IT'S NOT LIKE I'M DOING THIS ESPECIALLY FOR YOU OR ANYTHING.
I'M JUST INTERESTED IN THE DEMON KINGS' DUNGEONS.
GOT IT?!
GRUDE... EVERYONE...
SMILE
THANK YOU.
?!
SH-SHUT UP!
HE'S GETTING EMBARRASSED.
FOR SURE.
?

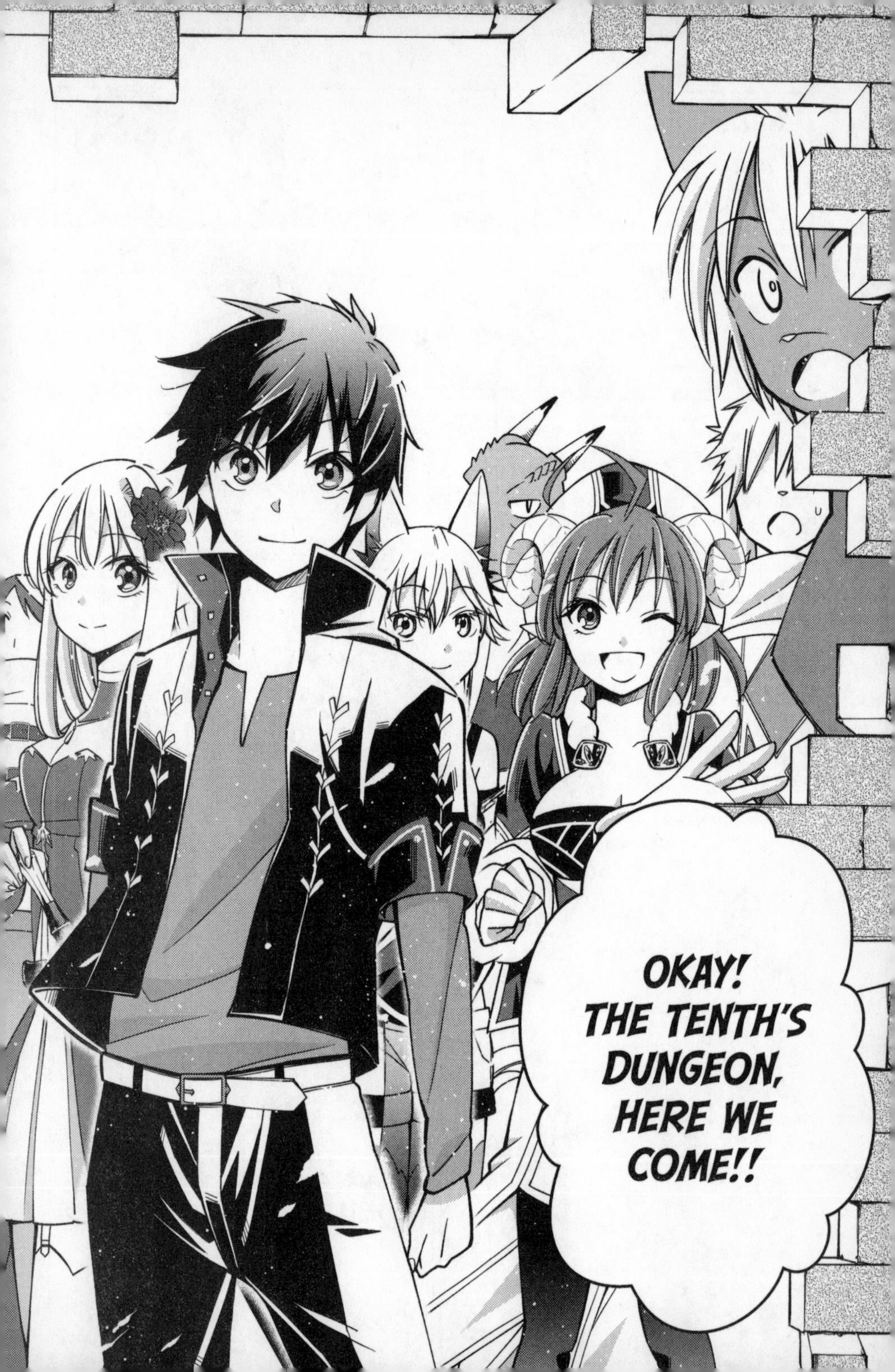
OKAY! THE TENTH'S DUNGEON, HERE WE COME!!

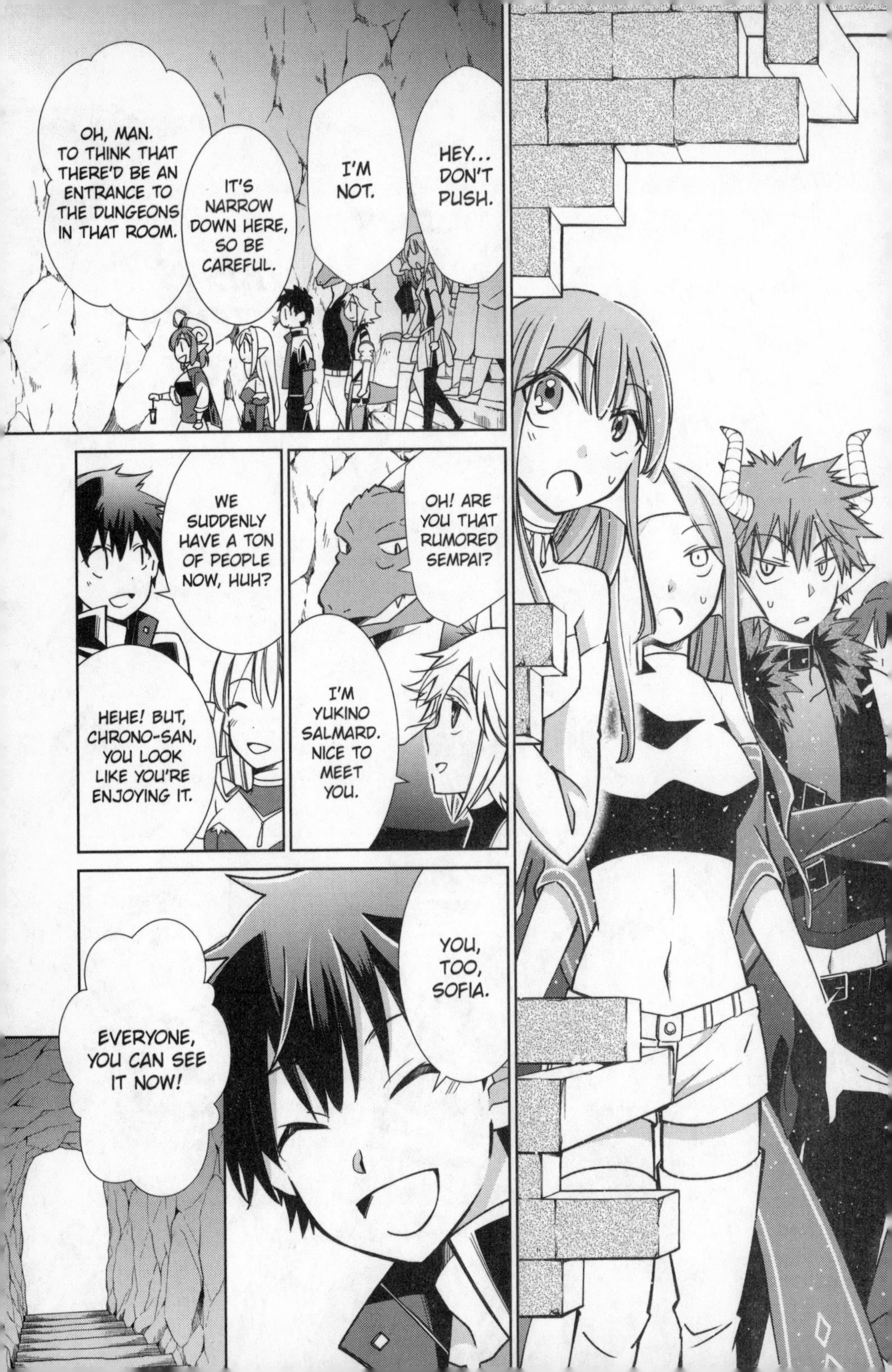
HEY... DON'T PUSH.
I'M NOT.
IT'S NARROW DOWN HERE, SO BE CAREFUL.
OH, MAN. TO THINK THAT THERE'D BE AN ENTRANCE TO THE DUNGEONS IN THAT ROOM.
OH! ARE YOU THAT RUMORED SEMPAI?
I'M YUKINO SALMARD. NICE TO MEET YOU.
WE SUDDENLY HAVE A TON OF PEOPLE NOW, HUH?
HEHE! BUT, CHRONO-SAN, YOU LOOK LIKE YOU'RE ENJOYING IT.
YOU, TOO, SOFIA.
EVERYONE, YOU CAN SEE IT NOW!

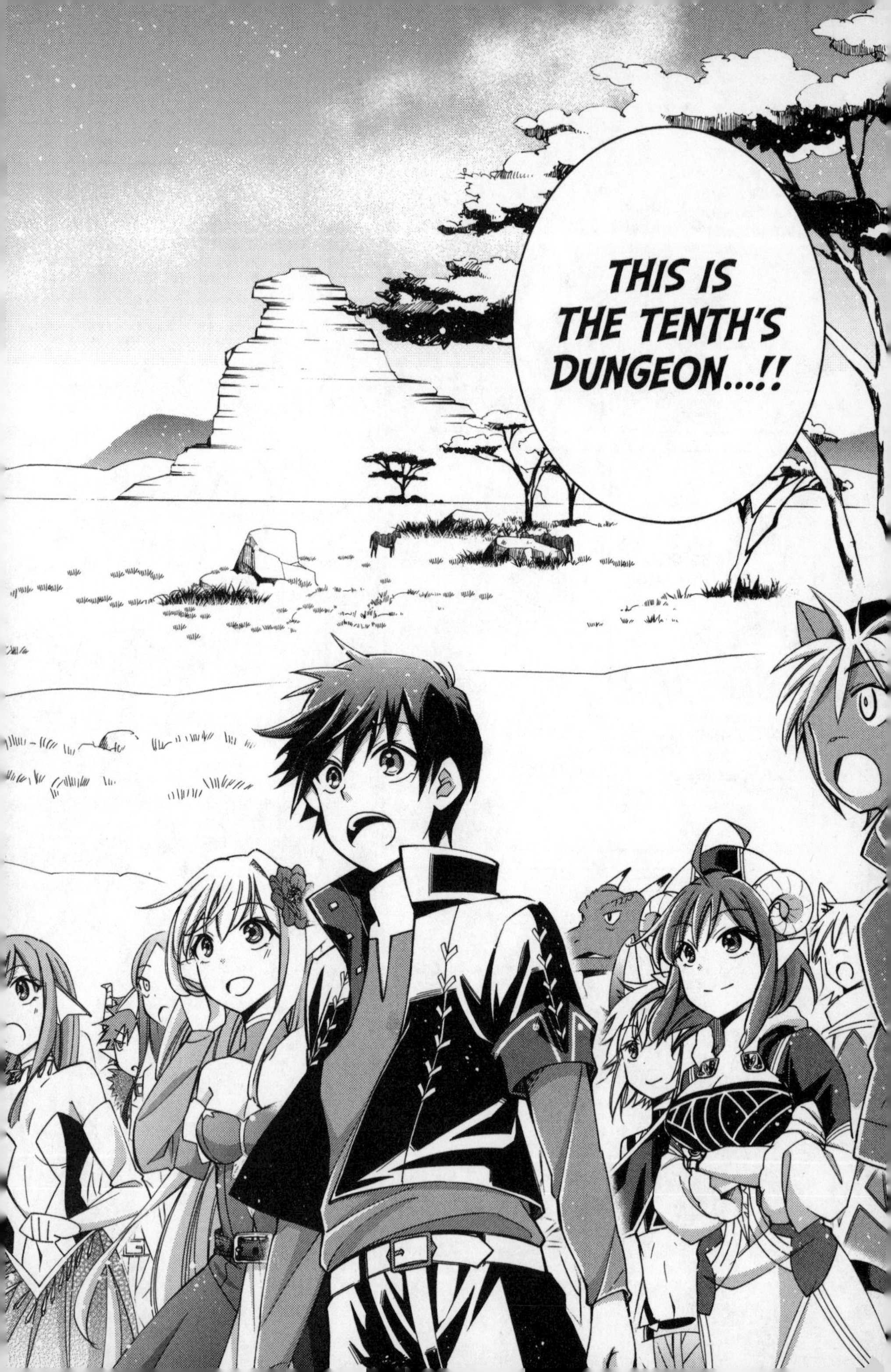
THIS IS THE TENTH'S DUNGEON...!!

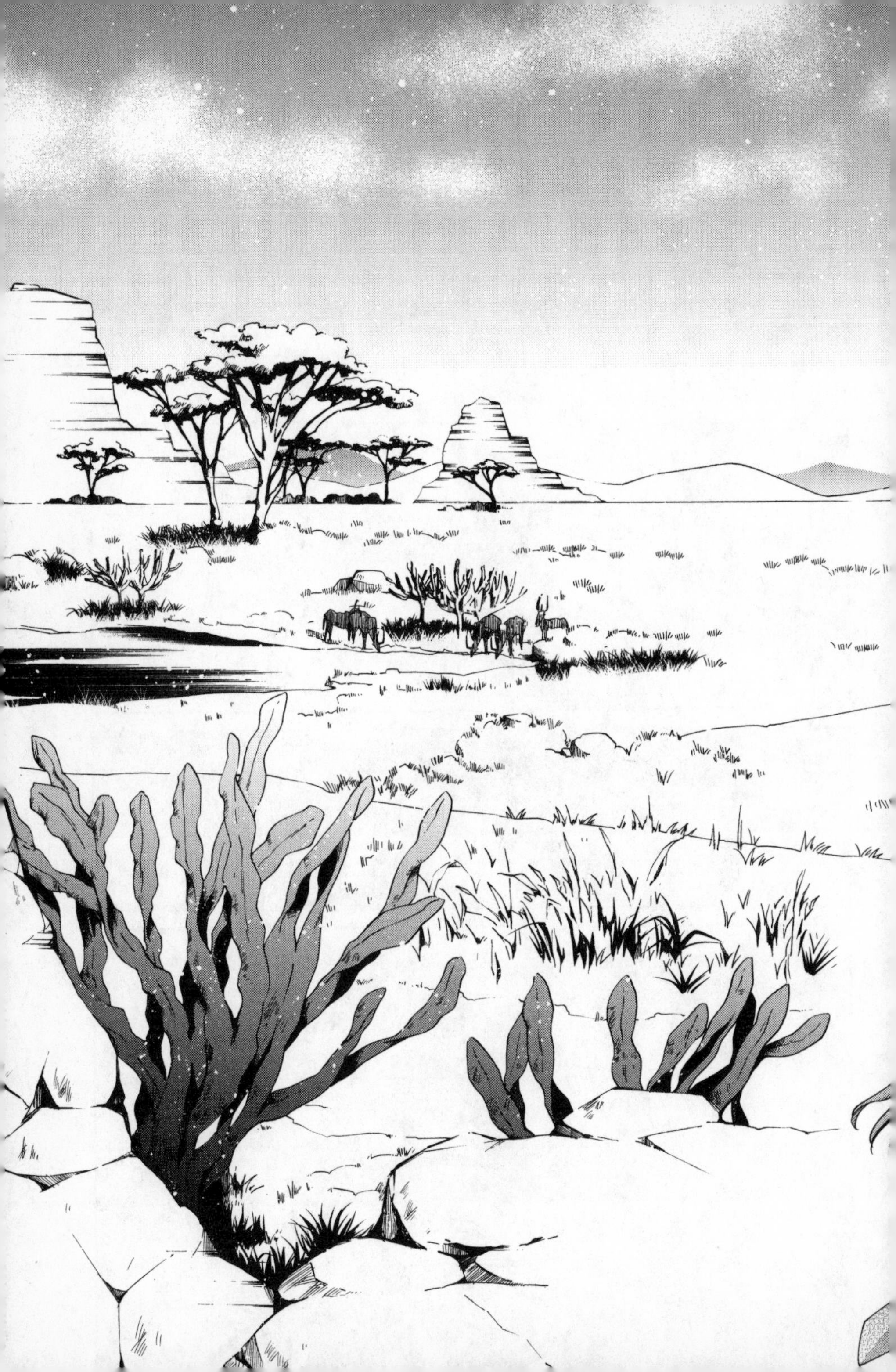

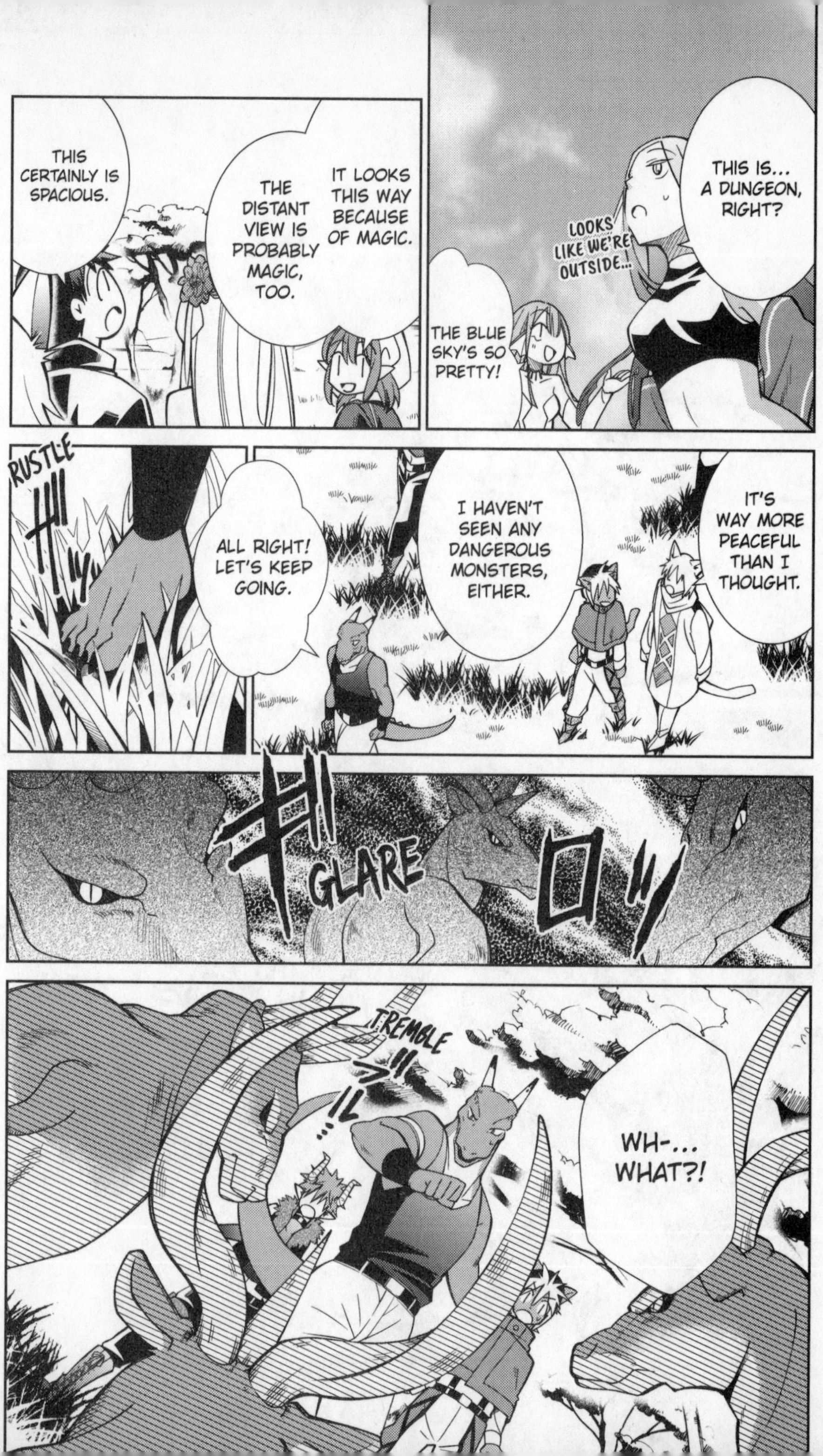
THIS IS... A DUNGEON, RIGHT?
LOOKS LIKE WE'RE OUTSIDE...
THE BLUE SKY'S SO PRETTY!
IT LOOKS THIS WAY BECAUSE OF MAGIC.
THE DISTANT VIEW IS PROBABLY MAGIC, TOO.
THIS CERTAINLY IS SPACIOUS.
IT'S WAY MORE PEACEFUL THAN I THOUGHT.
I HAVEN'T SEEN ANY DANGEROUS MONSTERS, EITHER.
ALL RIGHT! LET'S KEEP GOING.
RUSTLE
GLARE
WH-... WHAT?!
TREMBLE

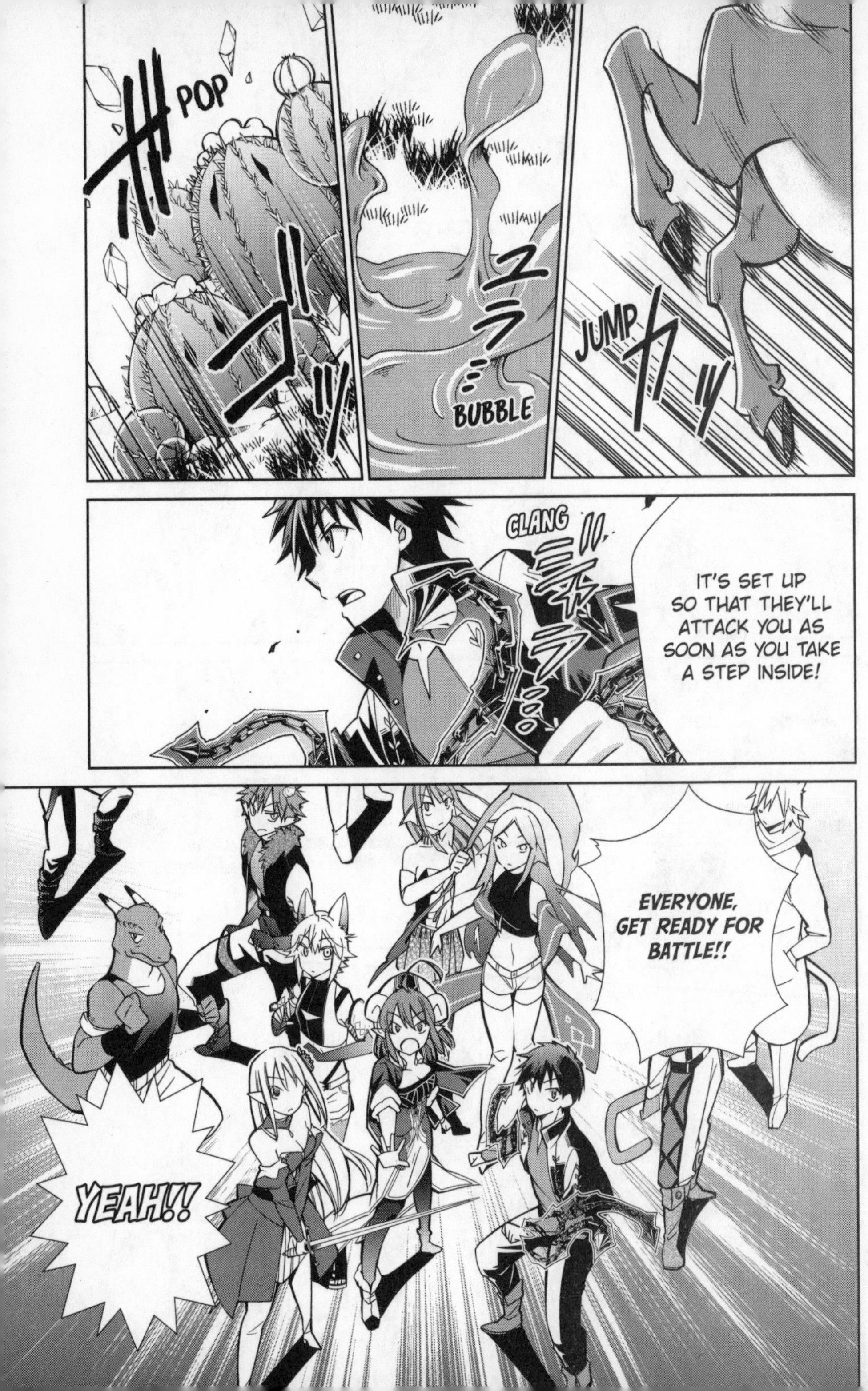
JUMP
BUBBLE
POP
CLANG
IT'S SET UP SO THAT THEY'LL ATTACK YOU AS SOON AS YOU TAKE A STEP INSIDE!
EVERYONE, GET READY FOR BATTLE!!
YEAH!!

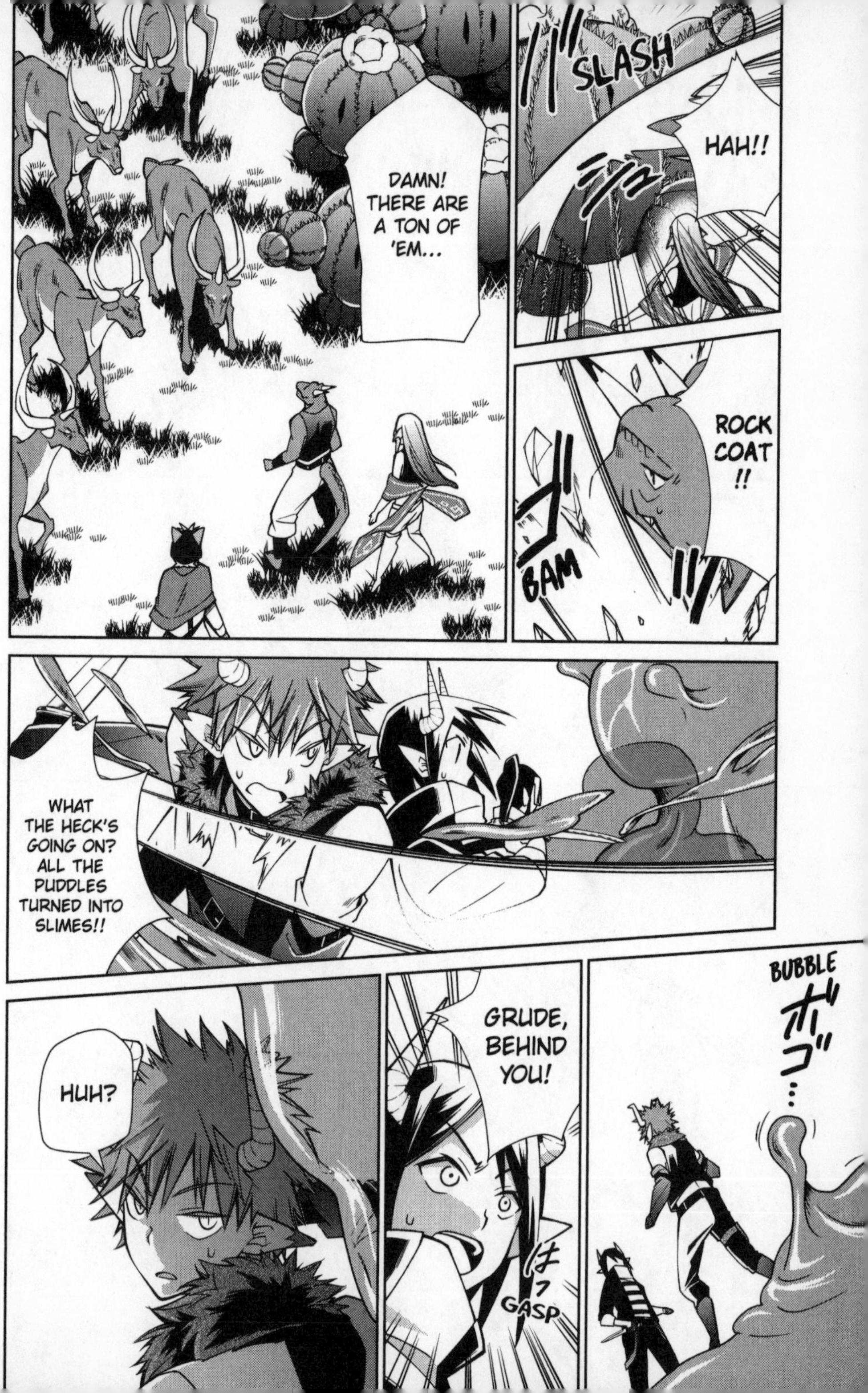
SLASH
HAH!!
ROCK COAT!!
BAM
DAMN! THERE ARE A TON OF 'EM...
WHAT THE HECK'S GOING ON? ALL THE PUDDLES TURNED INTO SLIMES!!
BUBBLE
ボゴ…
GRUDE, BEHIND YOU!
はっ
GASP
HUH?

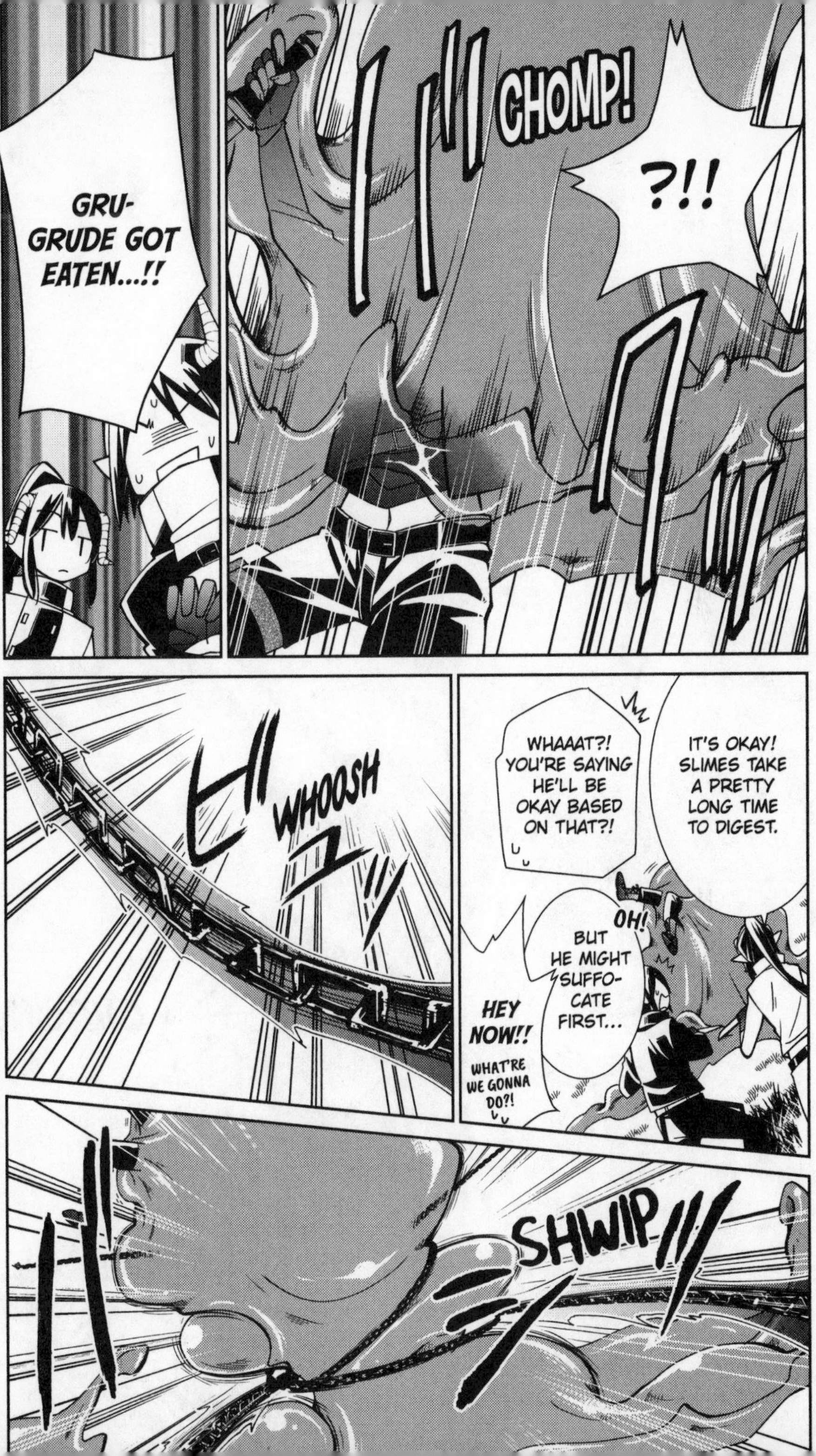
CHOMP!
?!!
GRU-GRUDE GOT EATEN...!!
IT'S OKAY! SLIMES TAKE A PRETTY LONG TIME TO DIGEST.
WHAAAT?! YOU'RE SAYING HE'LL BE OKAY BASED ON THAT?!
OH!
BUT HE MIGHT SUFFO-CATE FIRST...
HEY NOW!!
WHAT'RE WE GONNA DO?!
WHOOSH
SHWIP!!!

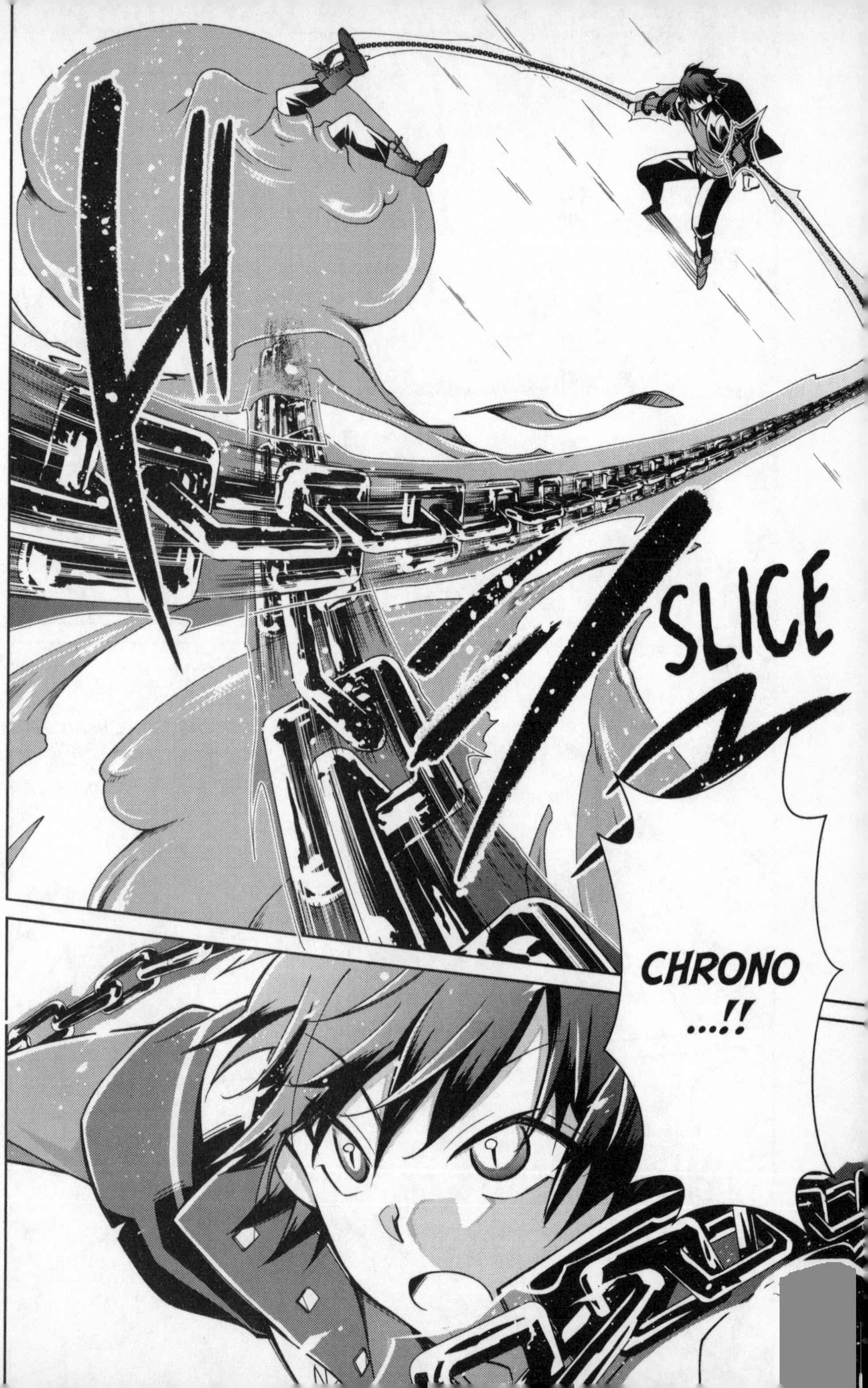
SLICE
CHRONO ...!!

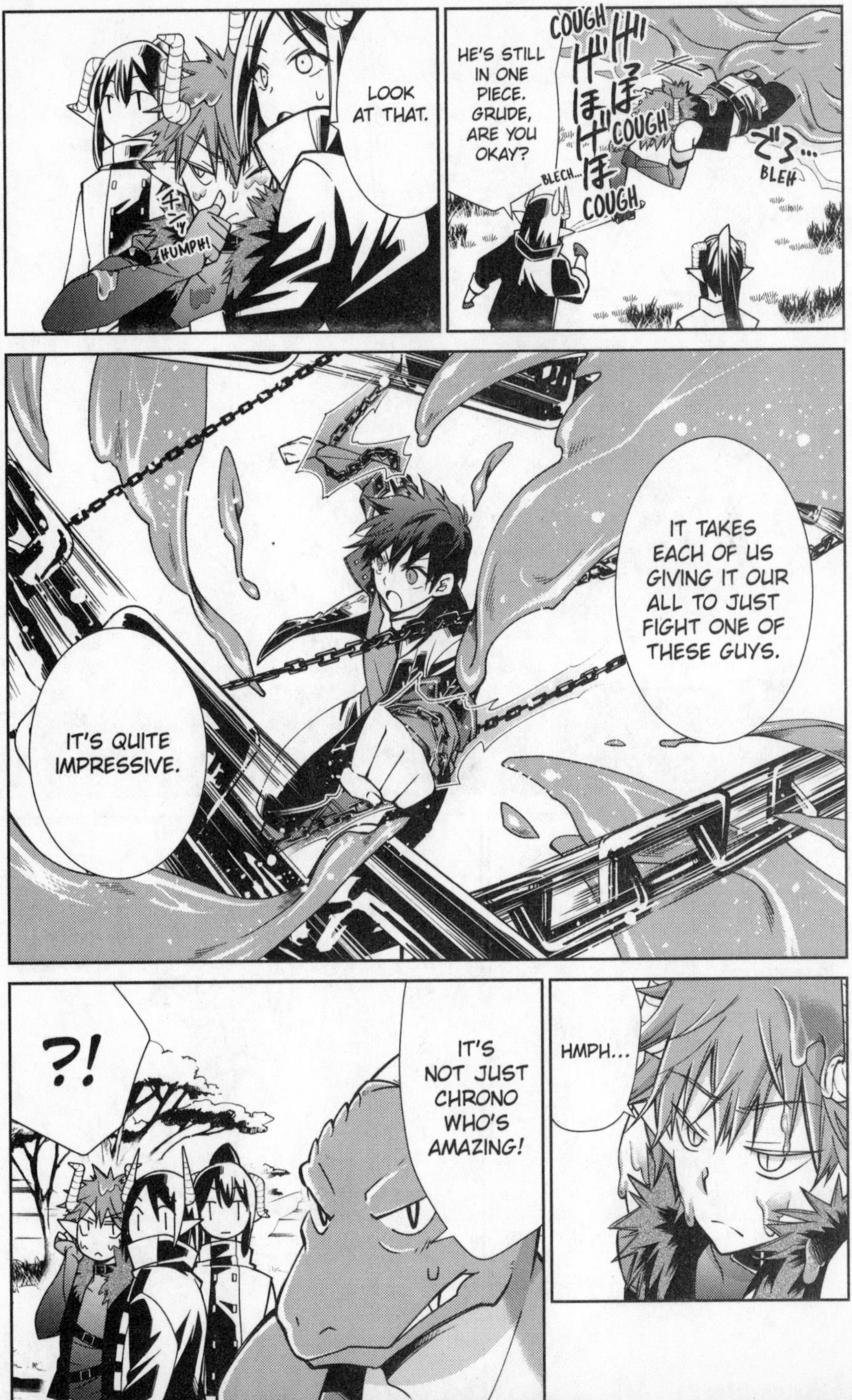
COUGH
COUGH
COUGH
HE'S STILL IN ONE PIECE. GRUDE, ARE YOU OKAY?
BLEH
BLECH...
LOOK AT THAT.
HUMPH!
IT TAKES EACH OF US GIVING IT OUR ALL TO JUST FIGHT ONE OF THESE GUYS.
IT'S QUITE IMPRESSIVE.
HMPH...
IT'S NOT JUST CHRONO WHO'S AMAZING!
?!

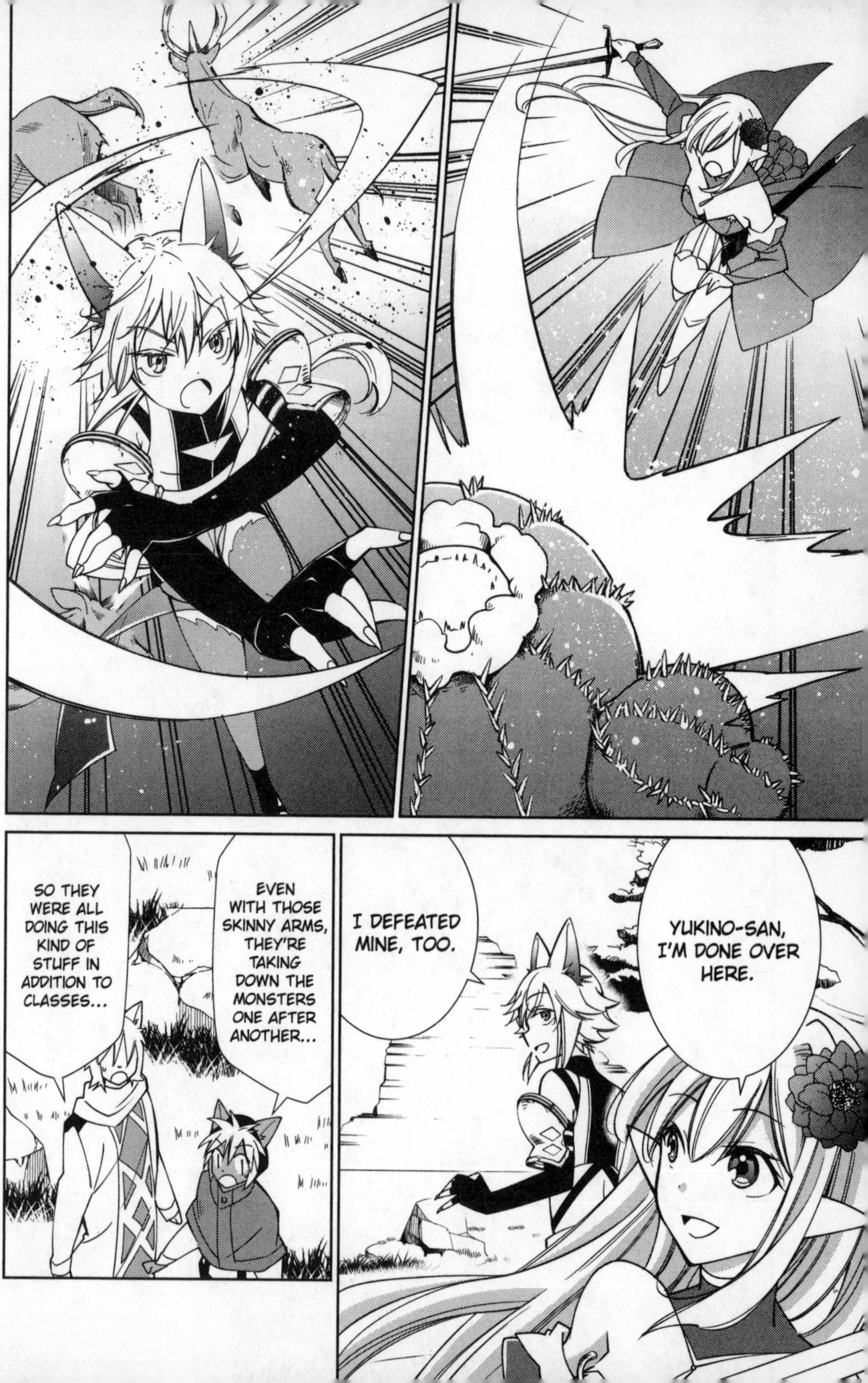
YUKINO-SAN, I'M DONE OVER HERE.
I DEFEATED MINE, TOO.
EVEN WITH THOSE SKINNY ARMS, THEY'RE TAKING DOWN THE MONSTERS ONE AFTER ANOTHER...
SO THEY WERE ALL DOING THIS KIND OF STUFF IN ADDITION TO CLASSES...

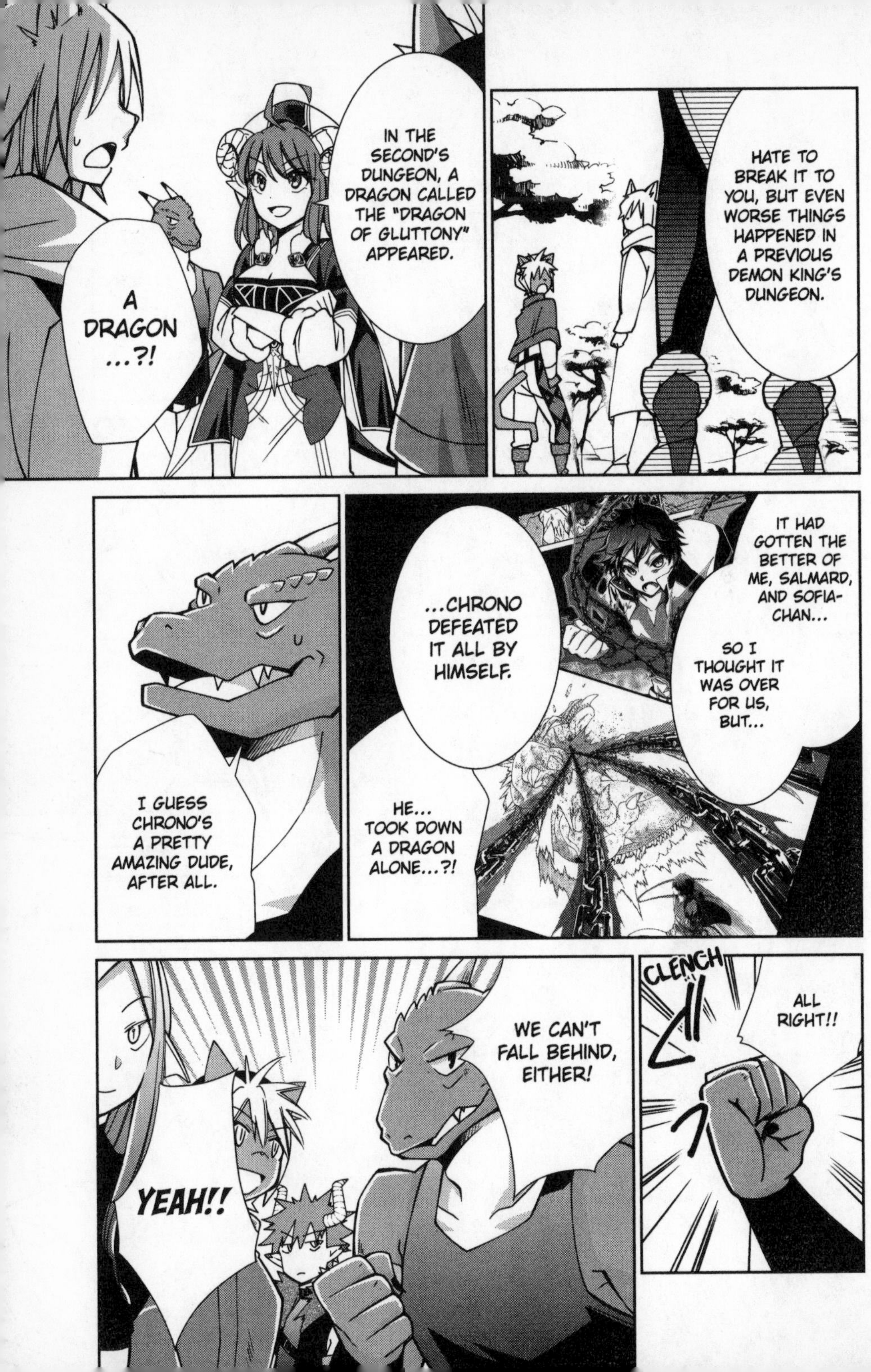
HATE TO BREAK IT TO YOU, BUT EVEN WORSE THINGS HAPPENED IN A PREVIOUS DEMON KING'S DUNGEON.
IN THE SECOND'S DUNGEON, A DRAGON CALLED THE "DRAGON OF GLUTTONY" APPEARED.
A DRAGON ...?!
IT HAD GOTTEN THE BETTER OF ME, SALMARD, AND SOFIA-CHAN...
SO I THOUGHT IT WAS OVER FOR US, BUT...
...CHRONO DEFEATED IT ALL BY HIMSELF.
HE... TOOK DOWN A DRAGON ALONE...?!
I GUESS CHRONO'S A PRETTY AMAZING DUDE, AFTER ALL.
CLENCH
ALL RIGHT!!
WE CAN'T FALL BEHIND, EITHER!
YEAH!!

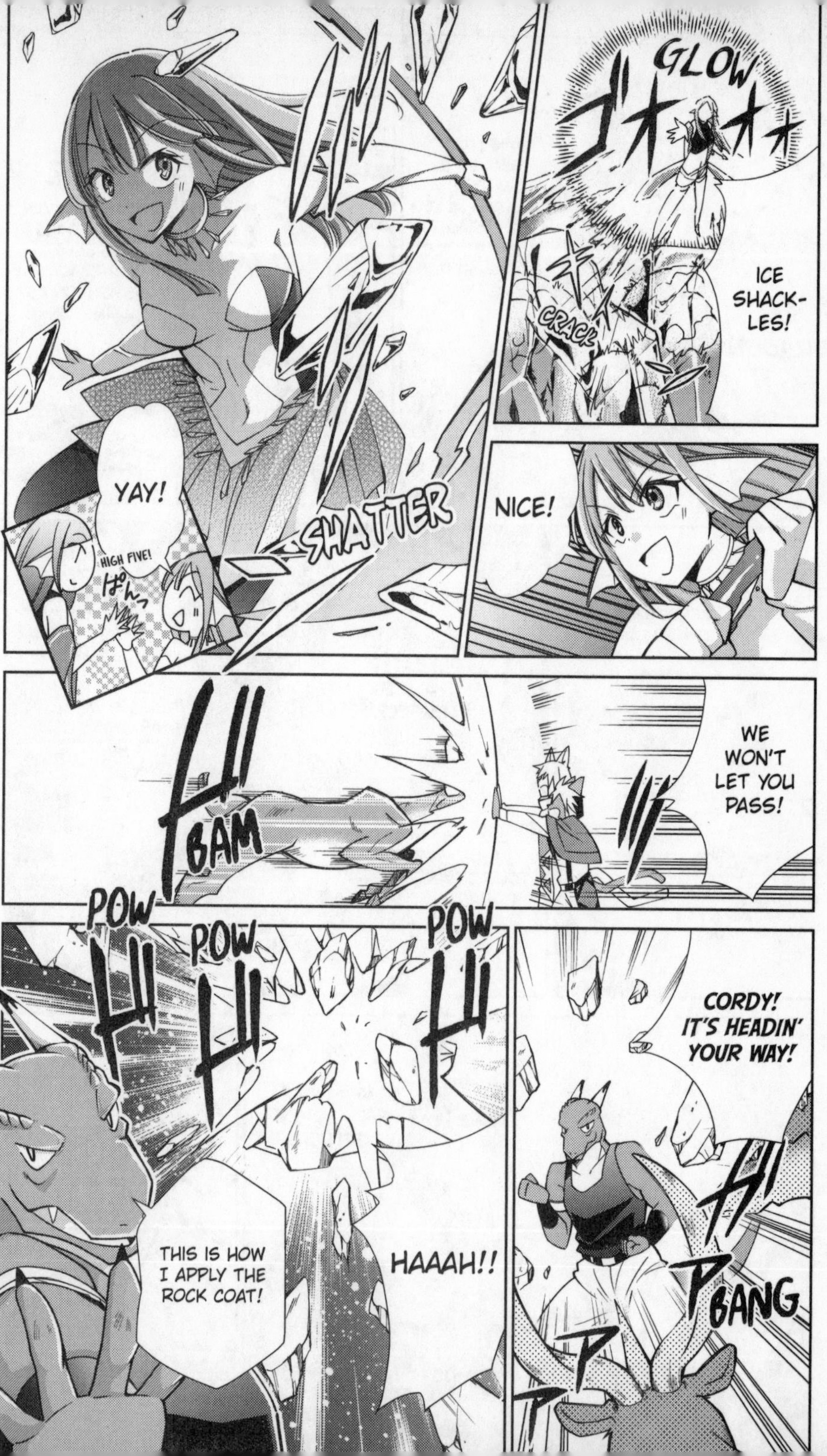
GLOW
ゴオオオ
CRACK
ICE SHACKLES!
NICE!
SHATTER
YAY!
HIGH FIVE!
ぱんっ
WE WON'T LET YOU PASS!
BAM
CORDY! IT'S HEADIN' YOUR WAY!
BANG
POW
POW
POW
HAAAH!!
THIS IS HOW I APPLY THE ROCK COAT!

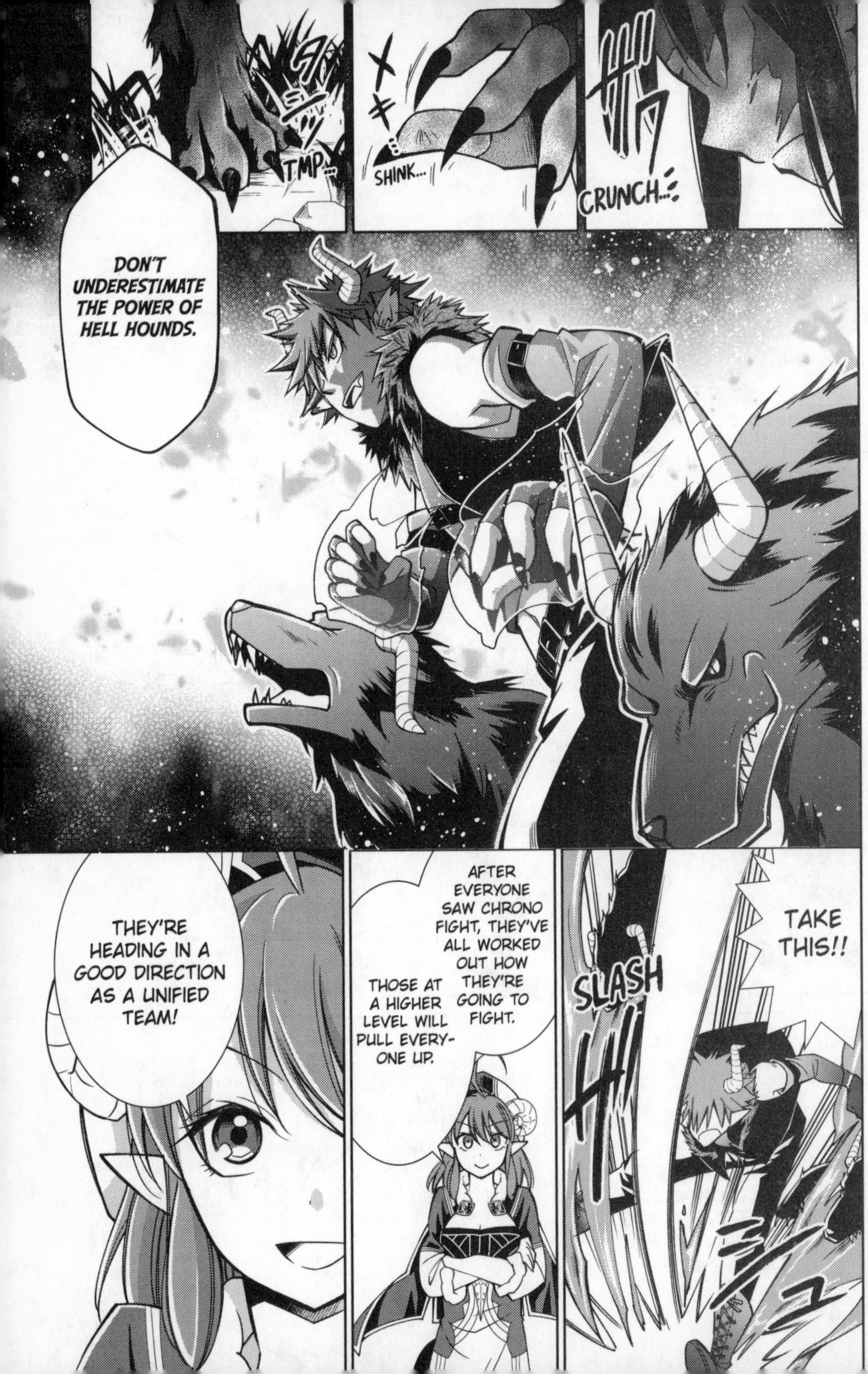
CRUNCH...
SHINK...
TMP...
DON'T UNDERESTIMATE THE POWER OF HELL HOUNDS.
TAKE THIS!!
SLASH
AFTER EVERYONE SAW CHRONO FIGHT, THEY'VE ALL WORKED OUT HOW THEY'RE GOING TO FIGHT.
THOSE AT A HIGHER LEVEL WILL PULL EVERY-ONE UP.
THEY'RE HEADING IN A GOOD DIRECTION AS A UNIFIED TEAM!

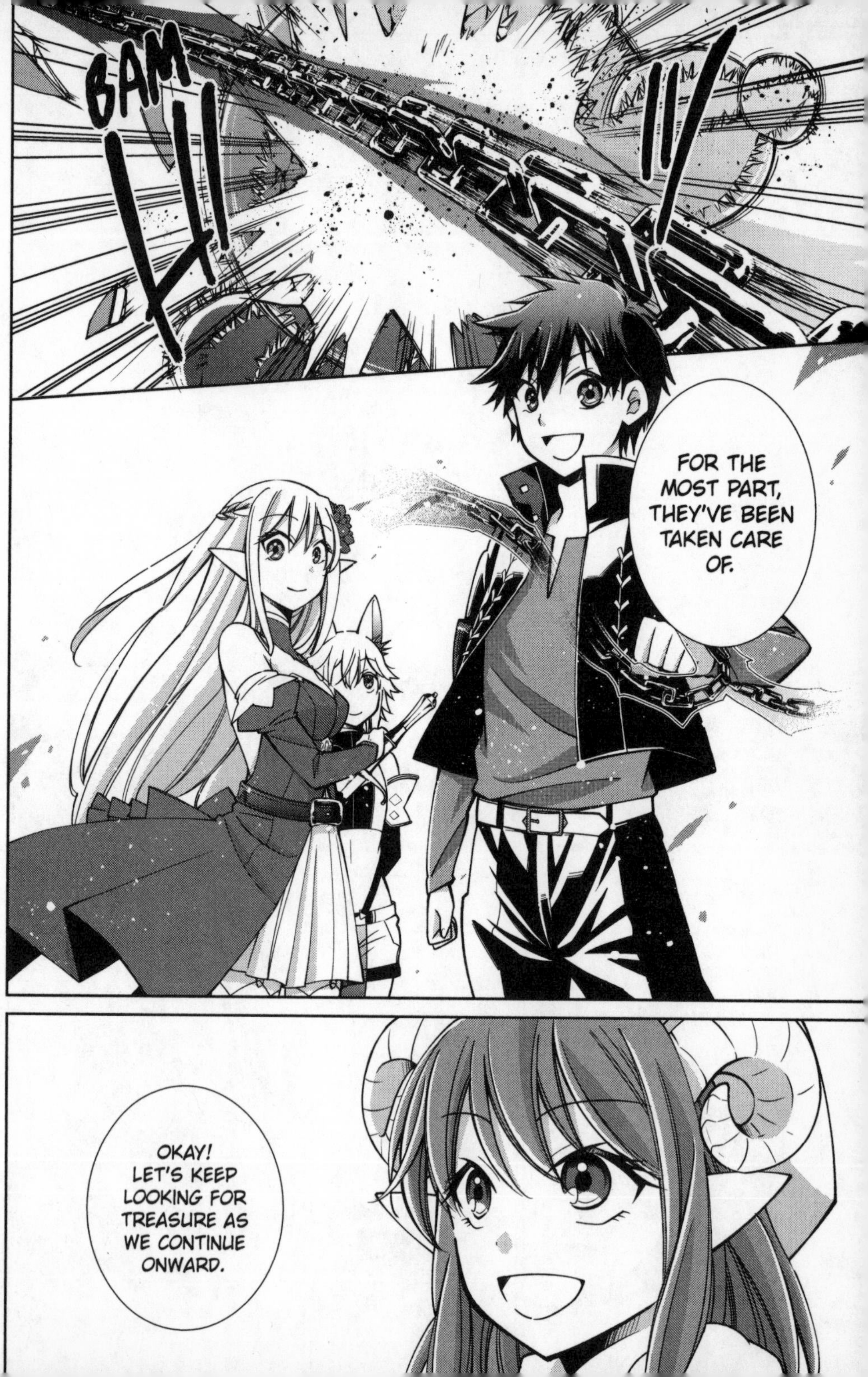
BAM!!
FOR THE MOST PART, THEY'VE BEEN TAKEN CARE OF.
OKAY! LET'S KEEP LOOKING FOR TREASURE AS WE CONTINUE ONWARD.

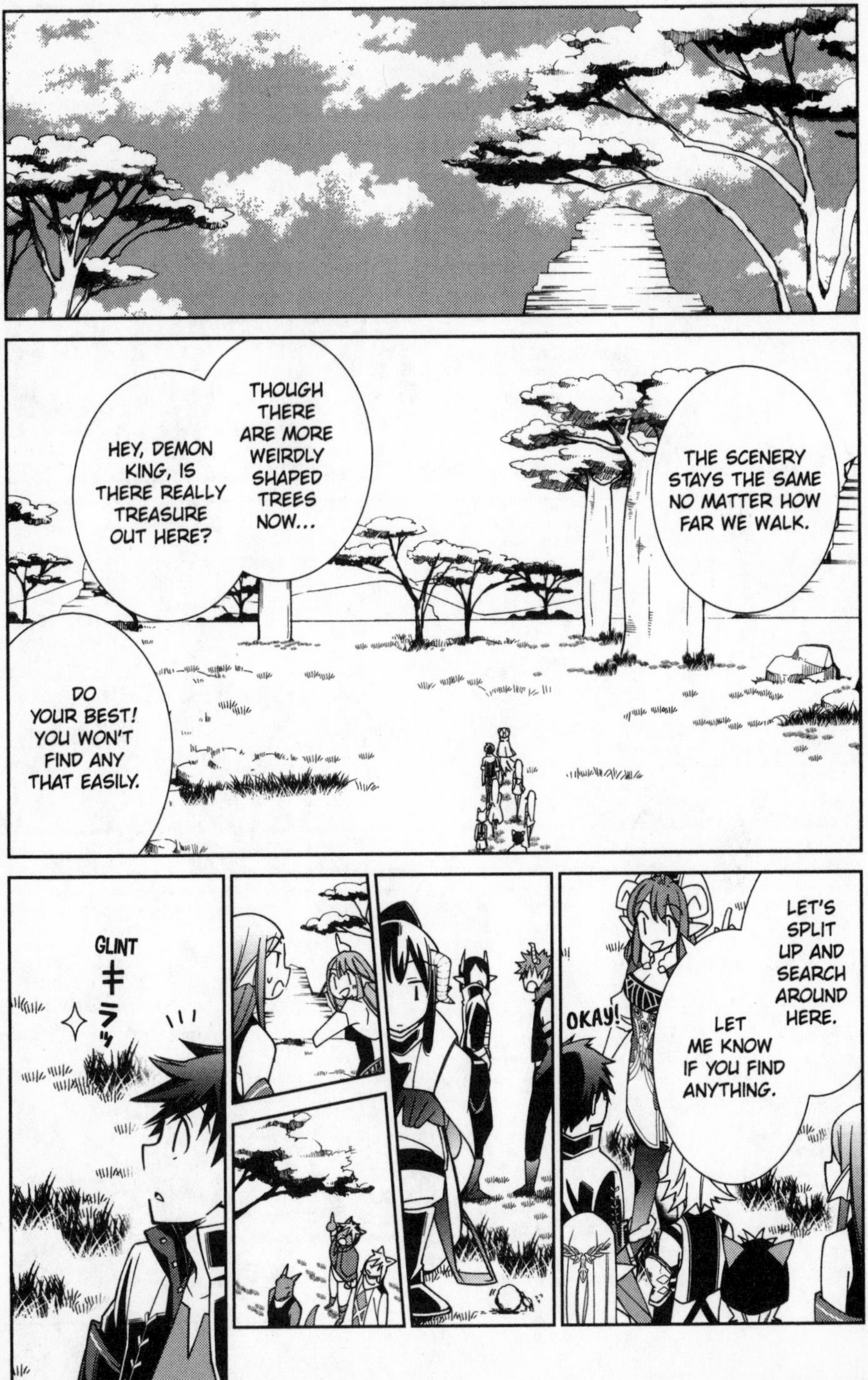
THE SCENERY STAYS THE SAME NO MATTER HOW FAR WE WALK.
THOUGH THERE ARE MORE WEIRDLY SHAPED TREES NOW...
HEY, DEMON KING, IS THERE REALLY TREASURE OUT HERE?
DO YOUR BEST! YOU WON'T FIND ANY THAT EASILY.
LET'S SPLIT UP AND SEARCH AROUND HERE.
LET ME KNOW IF YOU FIND ANYTHING.
OKAY!
GLINT
キラッ

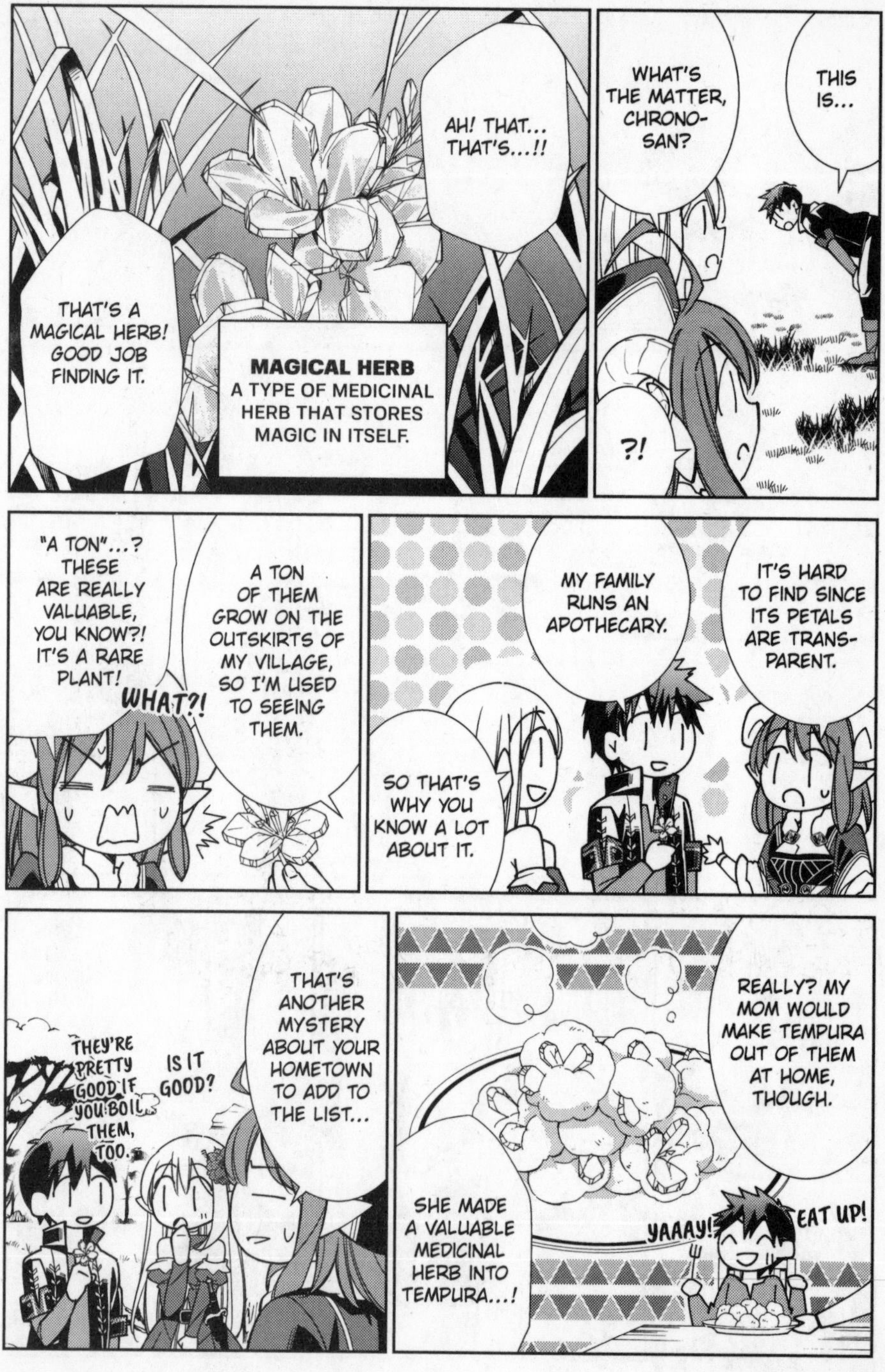
THIS IS...
WHAT'S THE MATTER, CHRONO-SAN?
?!
AH! THAT... THAT'S...!!
MAGICAL HERB A TYPE OF MEDICINAL HERB THAT STORES MAGIC IN ITSELF.
THAT'S A MAGICAL HERB! GOOD JOB FINDING IT.
IT'S HARD TO FIND SINCE ITS PETALS ARE TRANS-PARENT.
MY FAMILY RUNS AN APOTHECARY.
SO THAT'S WHY YOU KNOW A LOT ABOUT IT.
A TON OF THEM GROW ON THE OUTSKIRTS OF MY VILLAGE, SO I'M USED TO SEEING THEM.
WHAT?!
"A TON"...? THESE ARE REALLY VALUABLE, YOU KNOW?! IT'S A RARE PLANT!
REALLY? MY MOM WOULD MAKE TEMPURA OUT OF THEM AT HOME, THOUGH.
EAT UP!
YAAAY!
SHE MADE A VALUABLE MEDICINAL HERB INTO TEMPURA...!
THAT'S ANOTHER MYSTERY ABOUT YOUR HOMETOWN TO ADD TO THE LIST...
IS IT GOOD?
THEY'RE PRETTY GOOD IF YOU BOIL THEM, TOO.

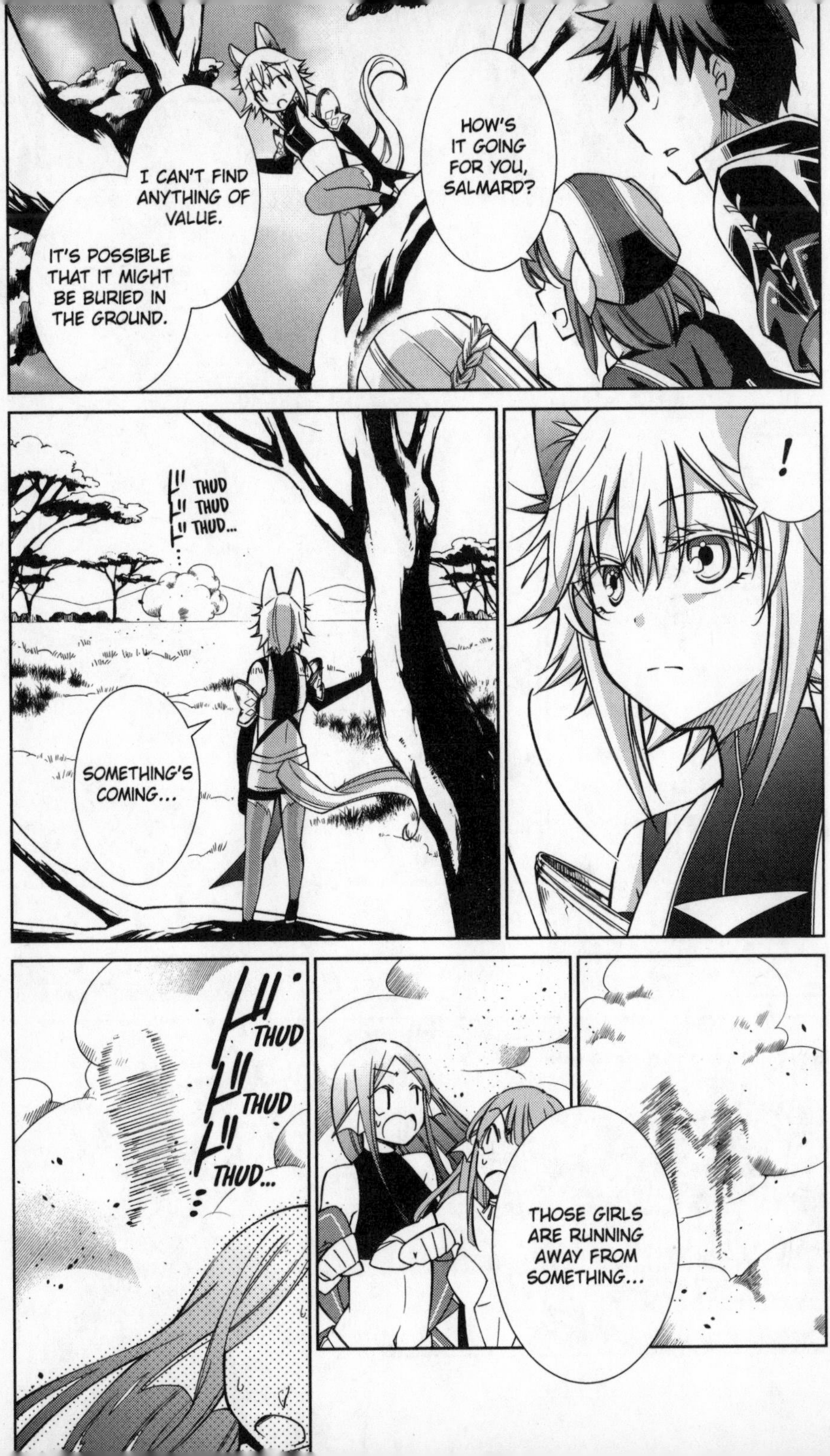
HOW'S IT GOING FOR YOU, SALMARD?
I CAN'T FIND ANYTHING OF VALUE.
IT'S POSSIBLE THAT IT MIGHT BE BURIED IN THE GROUND.
!
THUD THUD THUD...
SOMETHING'S COMING...
THOSE GIRLS ARE RUNNING AWAY FROM SOMETHING...
THUD THUD THUD...

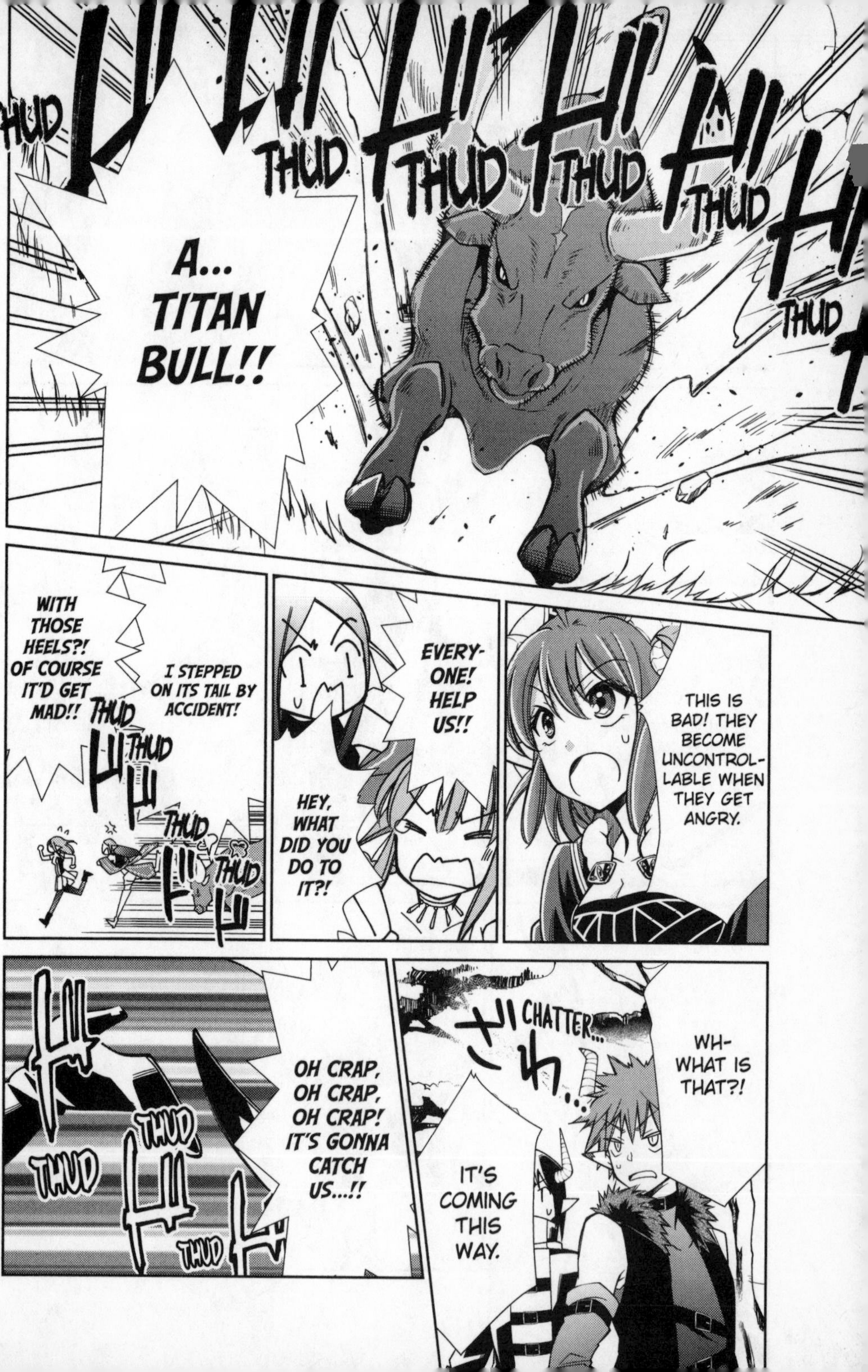
THUD
THUD
THUD
THUD
THUD
THUD
A... TITAN BULL!!
THIS IS BAD! THEY BECOME UNCONTROL-LABLE WHEN THEY GET ANGRY.
EVERY-ONE! HELP US!!
HEY, WHAT DID YOU DO TO IT?!
I STEPPED ON ITS TAIL BY ACCIDENT!
WITH THOSE HEELS?! OF COURSE IT'D GET MAD!!
THUD
THUD
THUD
THUD
CHATTER...
WH- WHAT IS THAT?!
IT'S COMING THIS WAY.
OH CRAP, OH CRAP, OH CRAP! IT'S GONNA CATCH US...!!
THUD
THUD
THUD

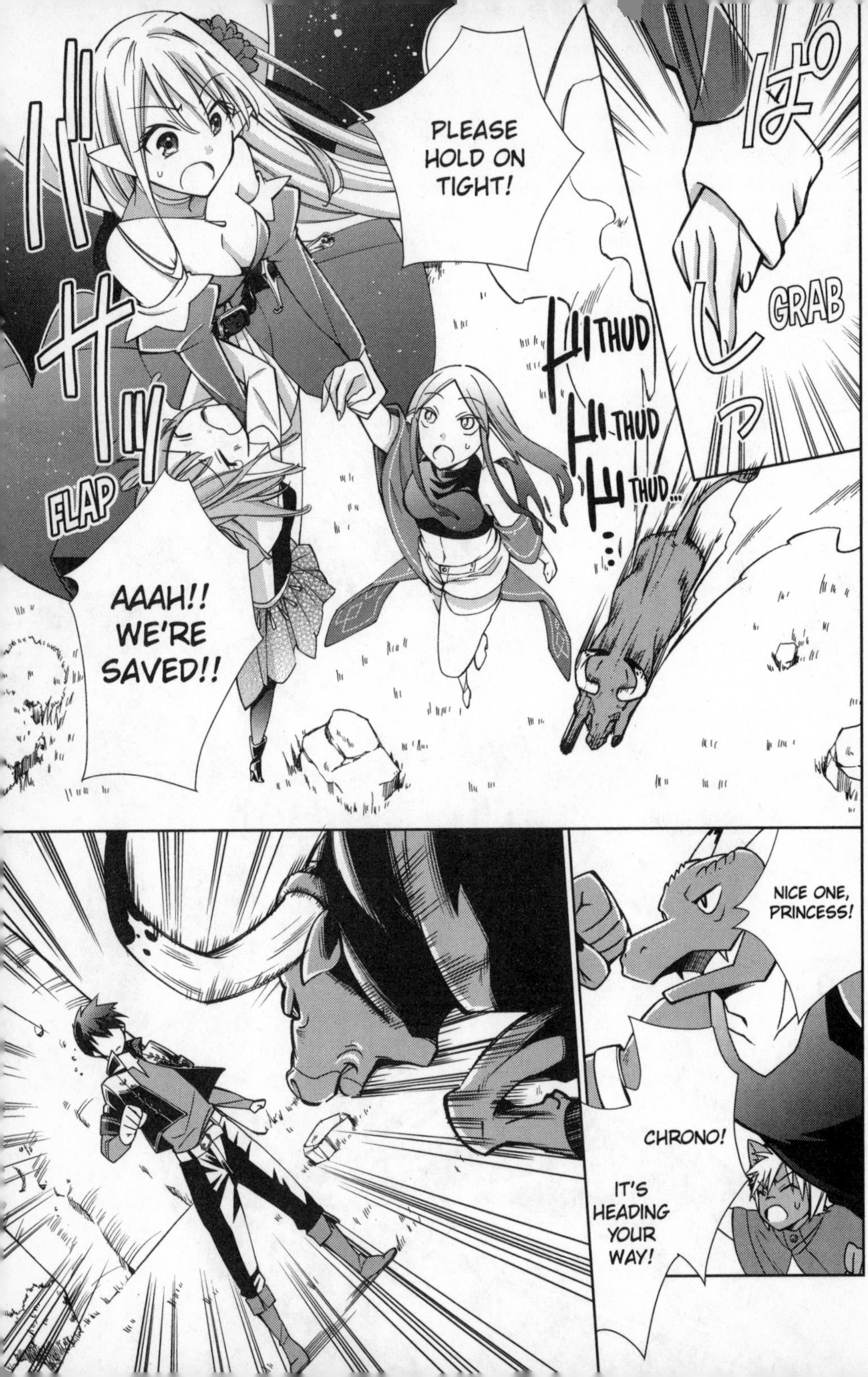
GRAB
PLEASE HOLD ON TIGHT!
THUD
THUD
THUD...
...
FLAP
AAAH!! WE'RE SAVED!!
NICE ONE, PRINCESS!
CHRONO!
IT'S HEADING YOUR WAY!

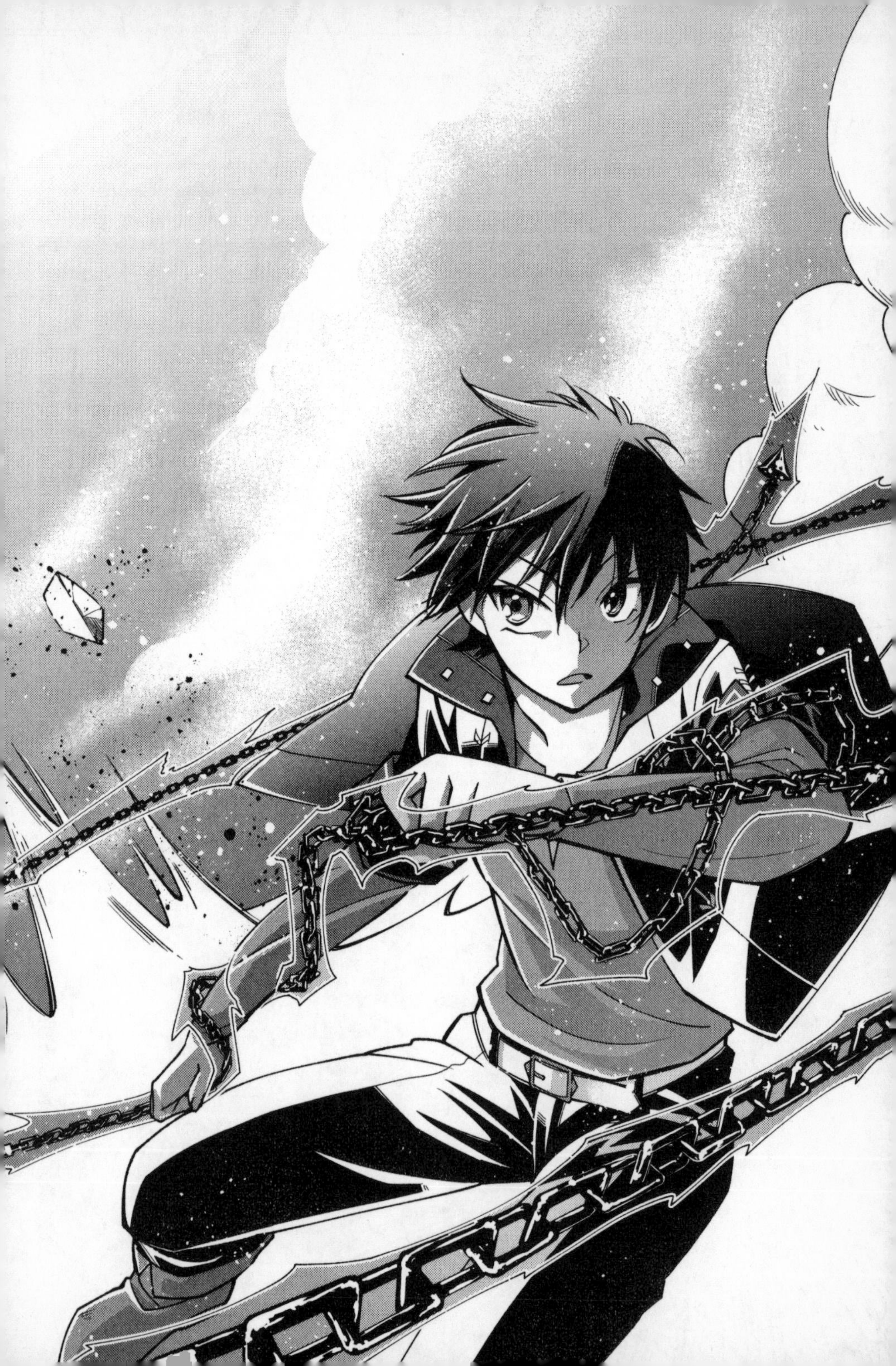

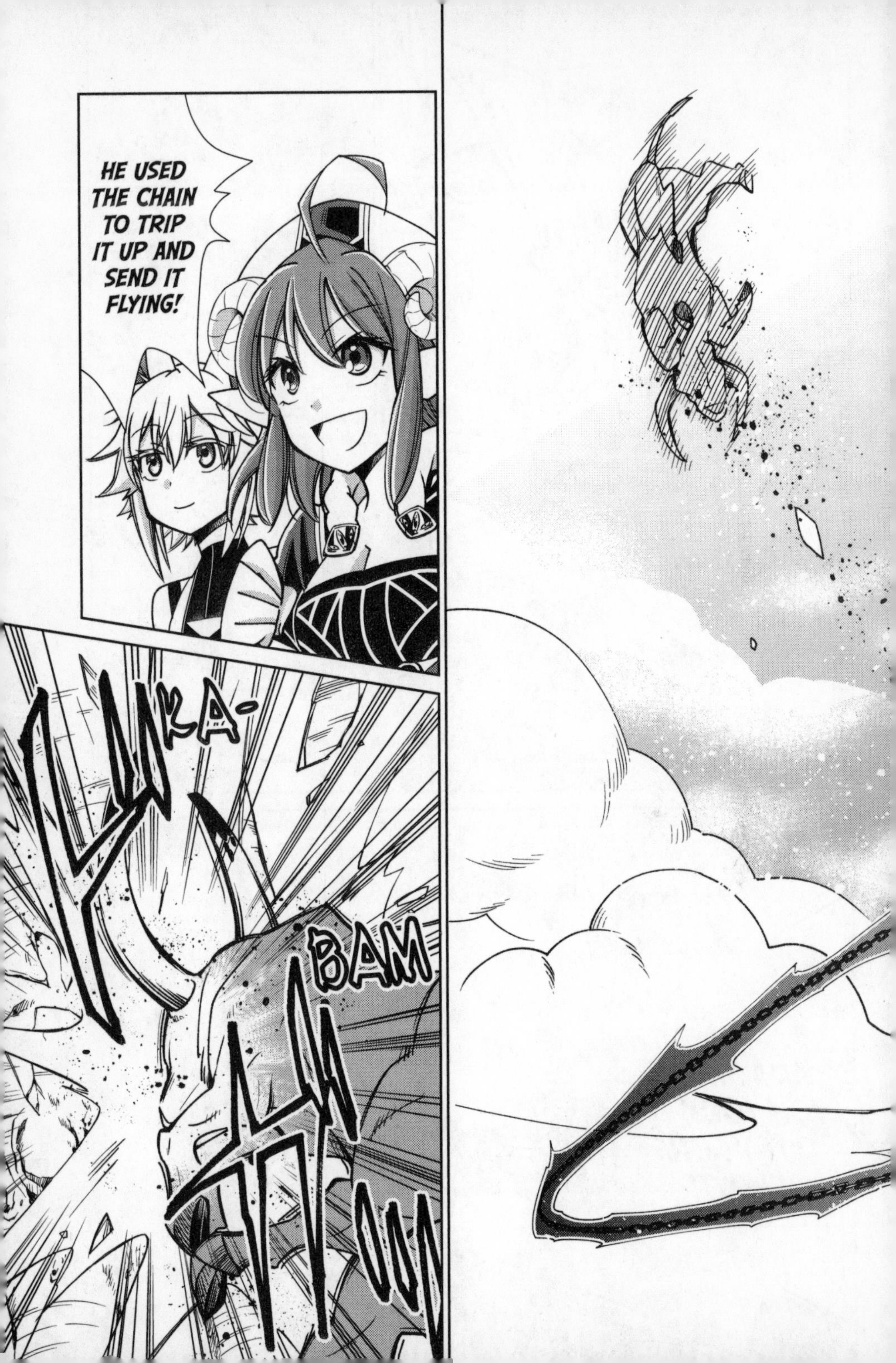
HE USED THE CHAIN TO TRIP IT UP AND SEND IT FLYING!
KA-
BAM

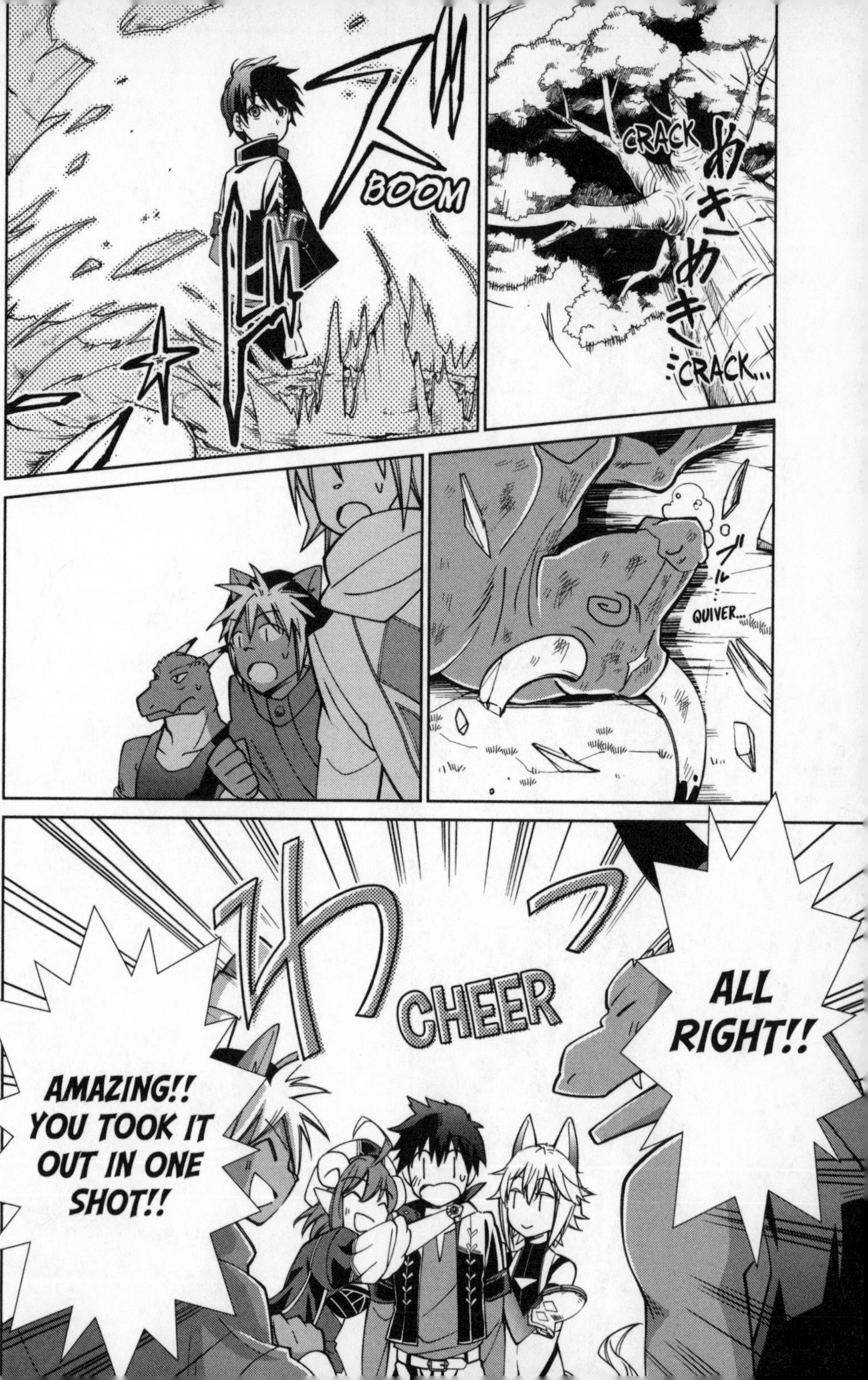
CRACK
CRACK...
BOOM
QUIVER...
ALL RIGHT!!
CHEER
AMAZING!! YOU TOOK IT OUT IN ONE SHOT!!

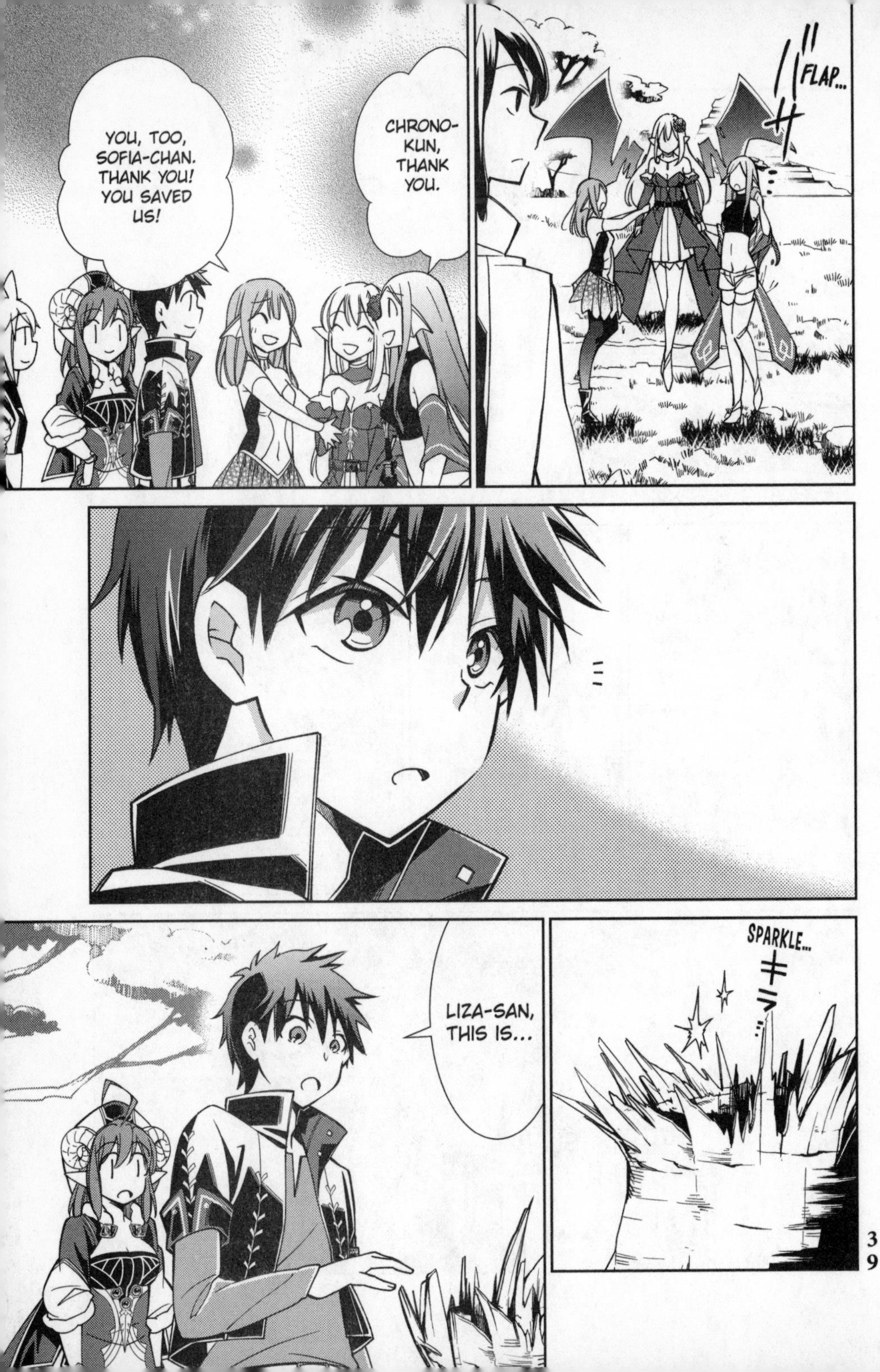
FLAP...
CHRONO-KUN, THANK YOU.
YOU, TOO, SOFIA-CHAN. THANK YOU! YOU SAVED US!
SPARKLE...
LIZA-SAN, THIS IS...

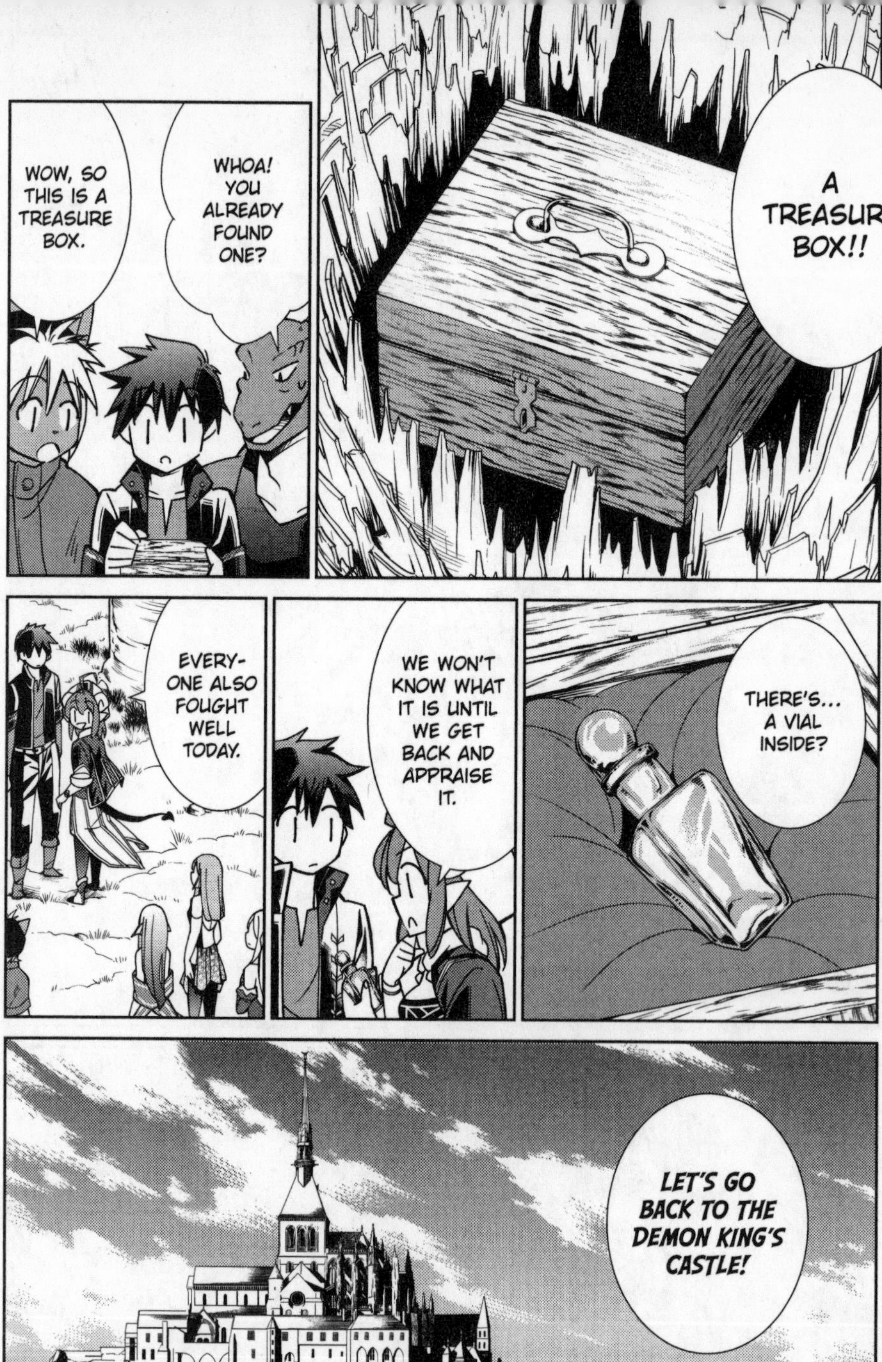
A TREASURE BOX!!
WHOA! YOU ALREADY FOUND ONE?
WOW, SO THIS IS A TREASURE BOX.
THERE'S... A VIAL INSIDE?
WE WON'T KNOW WHAT IT IS UNTIL WE GET BACK AND APPRAISE IT.
EVERY-ONE ALSO FOUGHT WELL TODAY.
LET'S GO BACK TO THE DEMON KING'S CASTLE!

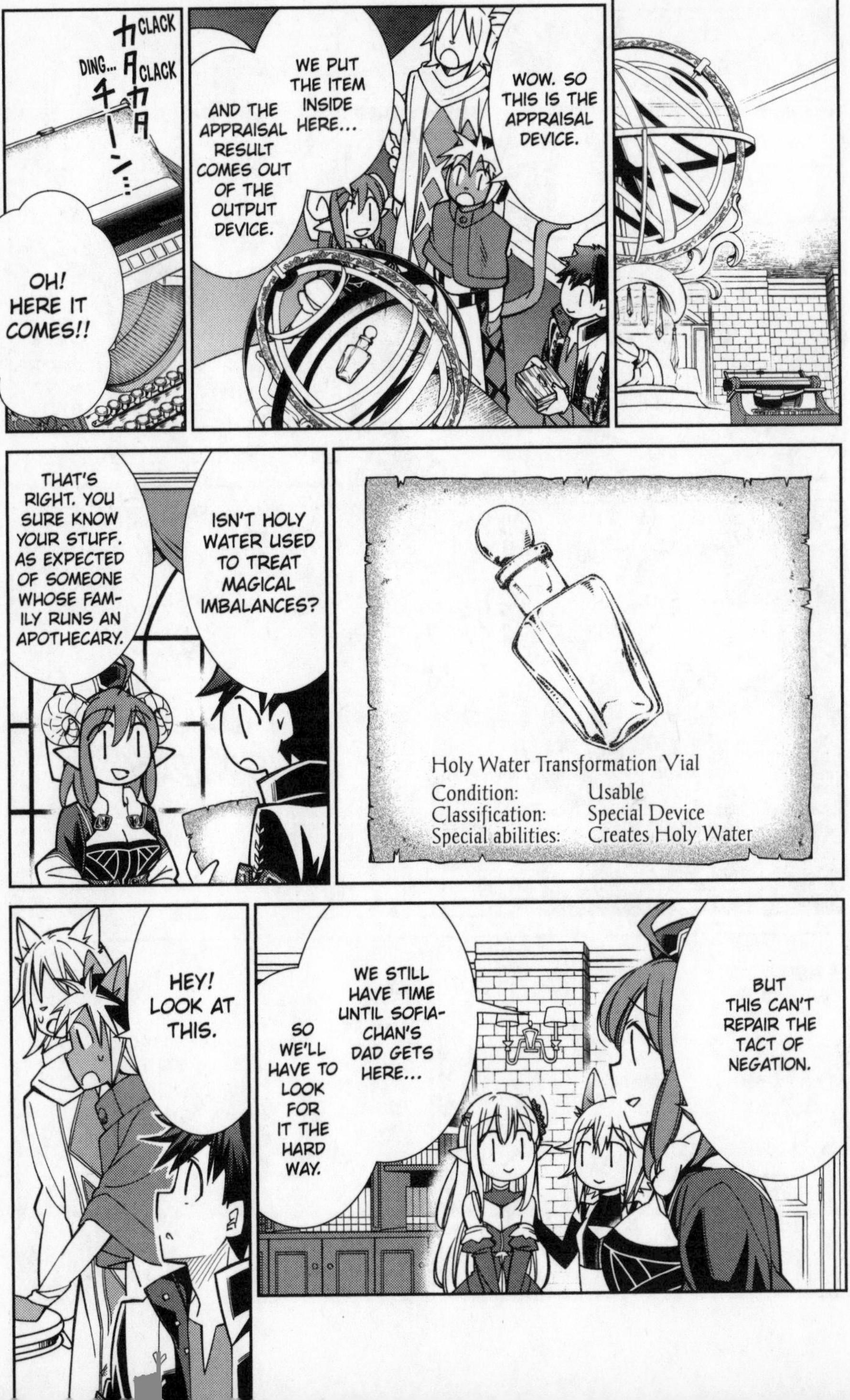
WOW. SO THIS IS THE APPRAISAL DEVICE.
WE PUT THE ITEM INSIDE HERE...
AND THE APPRAISAL RESULT COMES OUT OF THE OUTPUT DEVICE.
カタカタ CLACK CLACK
チーン DING...
OH! HERE IT COMES!!
Holy Water Transformation Vial
Condition: Usable
Classification: Special Device
Special abilities: Creates Holy Water
ISN'T HOLY WATER USED TO TREAT MAGICAL IMBALANCES?
THAT'S RIGHT. YOU SURE KNOW YOUR STUFF. AS EXPECTED OF SOMEONE WHOSE FAMILY RUNS AN APOTHECARY.
BUT THIS CAN'T REPAIR THE TACT OF NEGATION.
WE STILL HAVE TIME UNTIL SOFIA-CHAN'S DAD GETS HERE...
SO WE'LL HAVE TO LOOK FOR IT THE HARD WAY.
HEY! LOOK AT THIS.

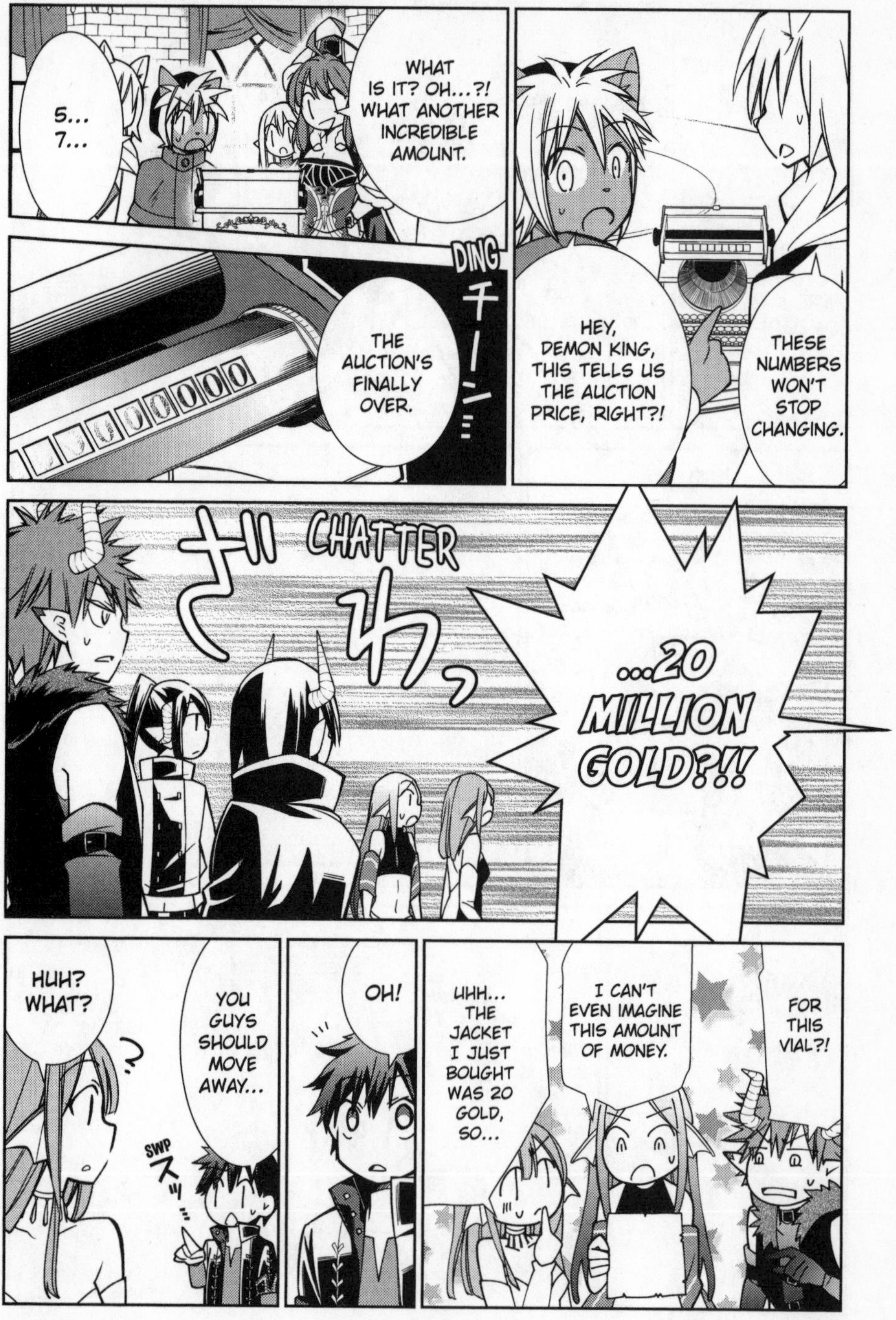
THESE NUMBERS WON'T STOP CHANGING.
HEY, DEMON KING, THIS TELLS US THE AUCTION PRICE, RIGHT?!
WHAT IS IT? OH...?! WHAT ANOTHER INCREDIBLE AMOUNT.
5... 7...
DING
チーン
THE AUCTION'S FINALLY OVER.
...20 MILLION GOLD?!!
CHATTER
さわっ
FOR THIS VIAL?!
I CAN'T EVEN IMAGINE THIS AMOUNT OF MONEY.
UHH... THE JACKET I JUST BOUGHT WAS 20 GOLD, SO...
OH!
YOU GUYS SHOULD MOVE AWAY...
SWP
スッ
HUH? WHAT?

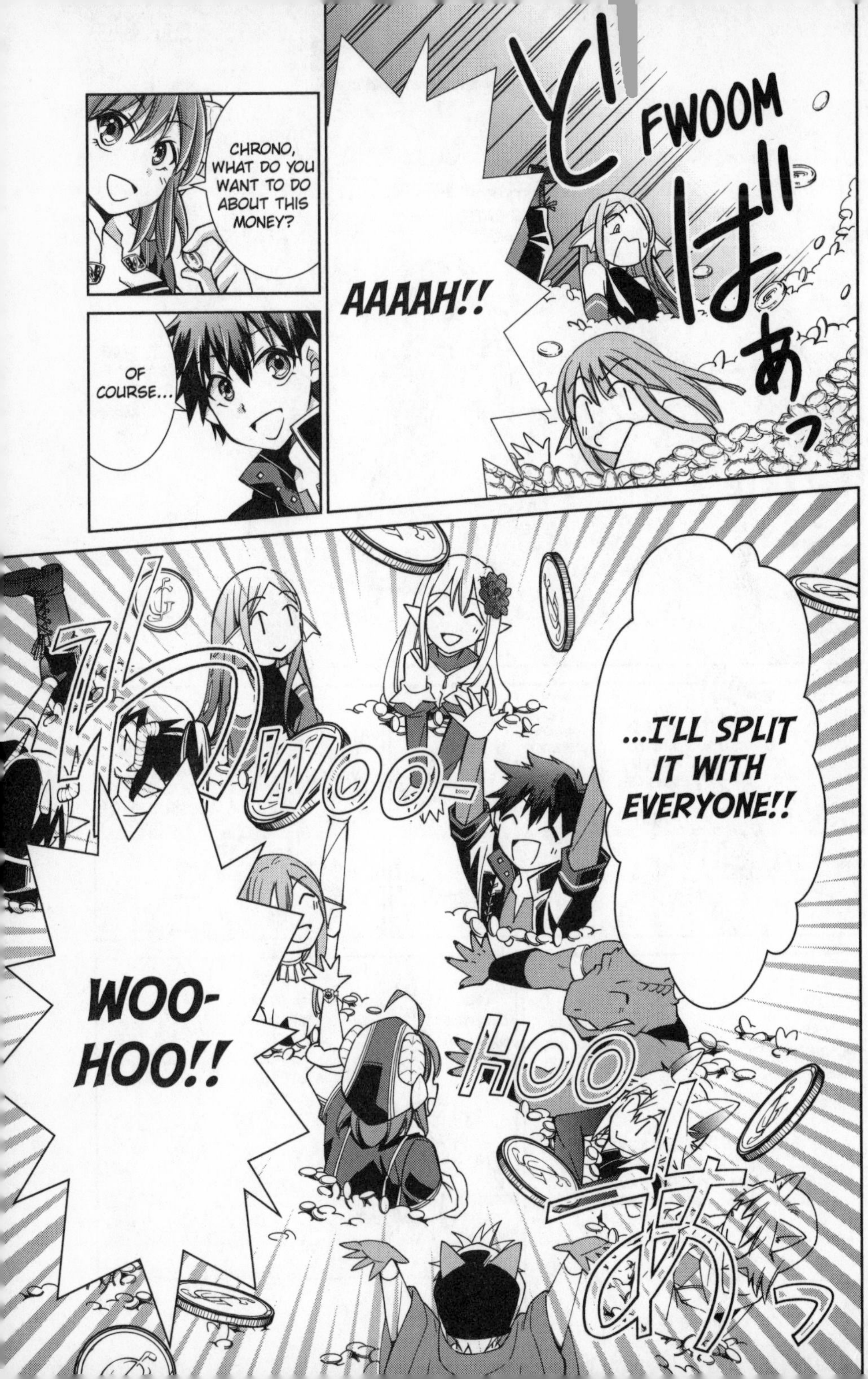
どばあっ
FWOOM
AAAAH!!
CHRONO, WHAT DO YOU WANT TO DO ABOUT THIS MONEY?
OF COURSE...
...I'LL SPLIT IT WITH EVERYONE!!
WOO-HOO
WOO-HOO!!

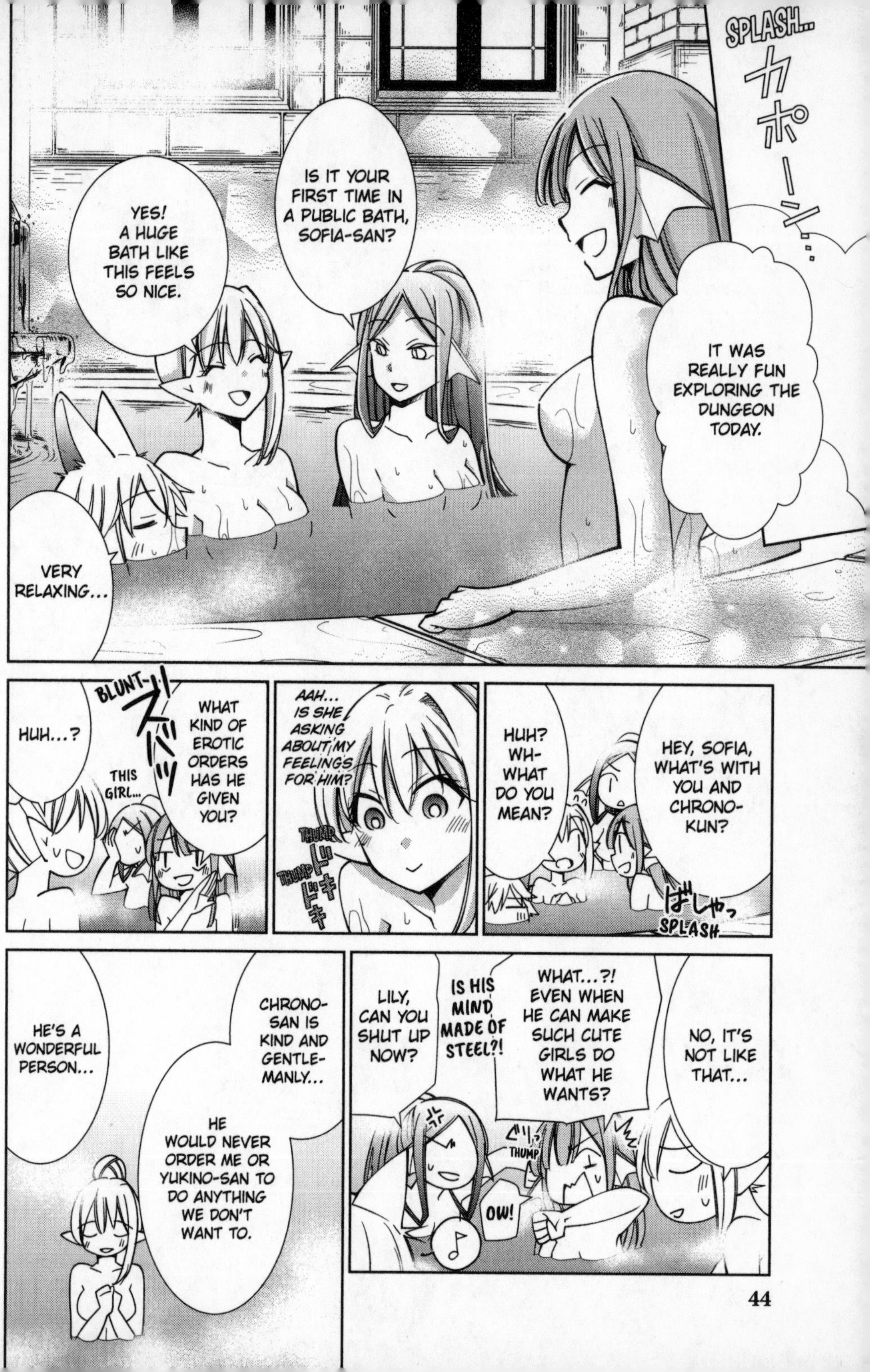
SPLASH...
カポーン…
IT WAS REALLY FUN EXPLORING THE DUNGEON TODAY.
IS IT YOUR FIRST TIME IN A PUBLIC BATH, SOFIA-SAN?
YES! A HUGE BATH LIKE THIS FEELS SO NICE.
VERY RELAXING...
HEY, SOFIA, WHAT'S WITH YOU AND CHRONO-KUN?
ばしゃっ
SPLASH
HUH? WH-WHAT DO YOU MEAN?
AAH... IS SHE ASKING ABOUT MY FEELINGS FOR HIM?
THUMP THUMP
ドキドキ
BLUNT
ズバッ
WHAT KIND OF EROTIC ORDERS HAS HE GIVEN YOU?
THIS GIRL...
HUH...?
NO, IT'S NOT LIKE THAT...
WHAT...?! EVEN WHEN HE CAN MAKE SUCH CUTE GIRLS DO WHAT HE WANTS?
IS HIS MIND MADE OF STEEL?!
LILY, CAN YOU SHUT UP NOW?
ぐりっ
THUMP
OW!
CHRONO-SAN IS KIND AND GENTLE-MANLY...
HE'S A WONDERFUL PERSON...
HE WOULD NEVER ORDER ME OR YUKINO-SAN TO DO ANYTHING WE DON'T WANT TO.

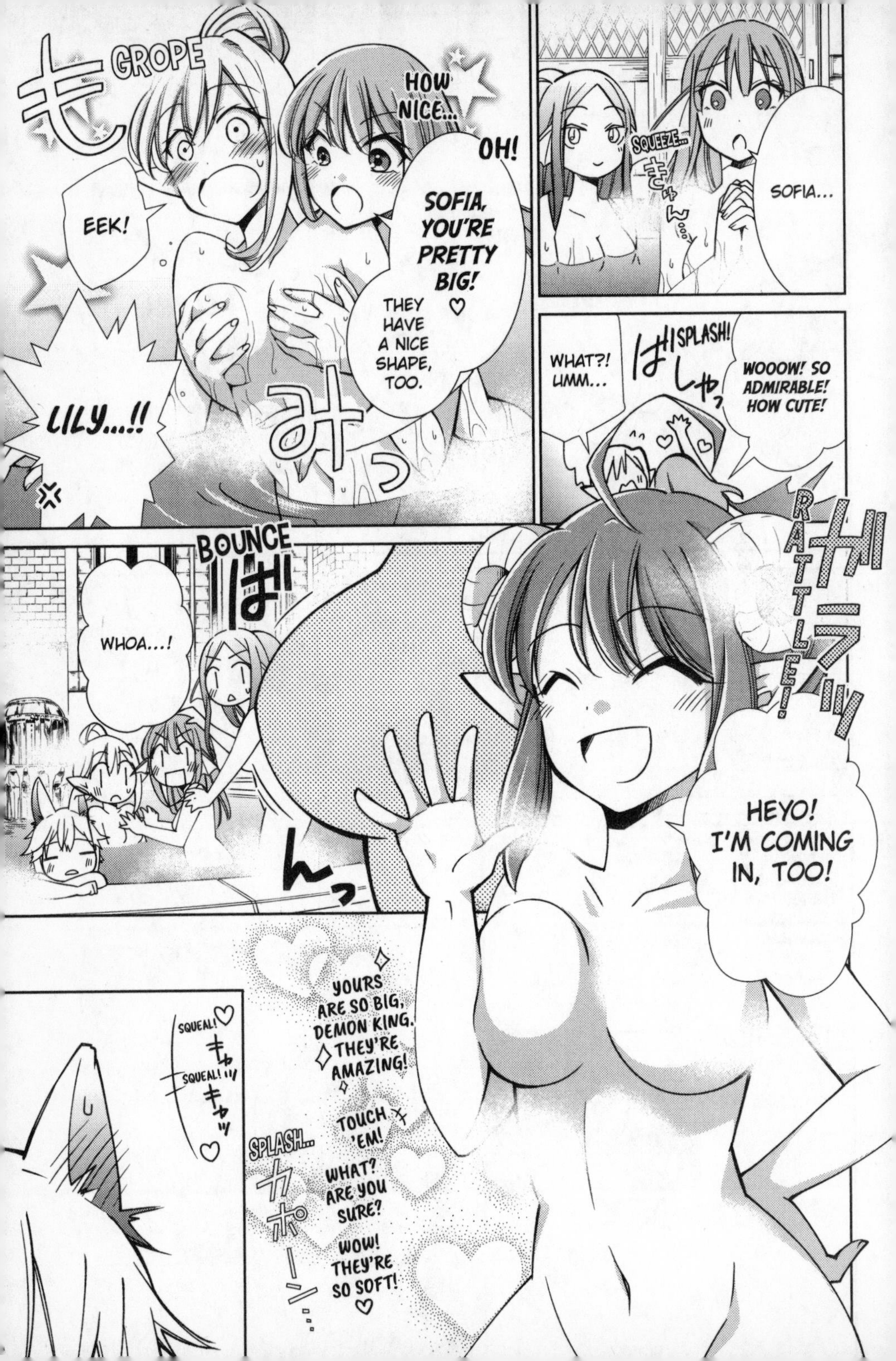
SQUEEZE... きゅん...
SOFIA...
WOOOW! SO ADMIRABLE! HOW CUTE!
SPLASH! ばしゃっ
WHAT?! UMM...
HOW NICE...
OH!
SOFIA, YOU'RE PRETTY BIG! ♡
THEY HAVE A NICE SHAPE, TOO.
GROPE も
EEK!
みっ
LILY...!!
RATTLE! ガラッ
HEYO! I'M COMING IN, TOO!
BOUNCE ばっ
WHOA...!
んっ
YOURS ARE SO BIG, DEMON KING. THEY'RE AMAZING!
TOUCH 'EM!
WHAT? ARE YOU SURE?
WOW! THEY'RE SO SOFT! ♡
SPLASH... カポーン...
SQUEAL! キャ
SQUEAL! キャッ ♡

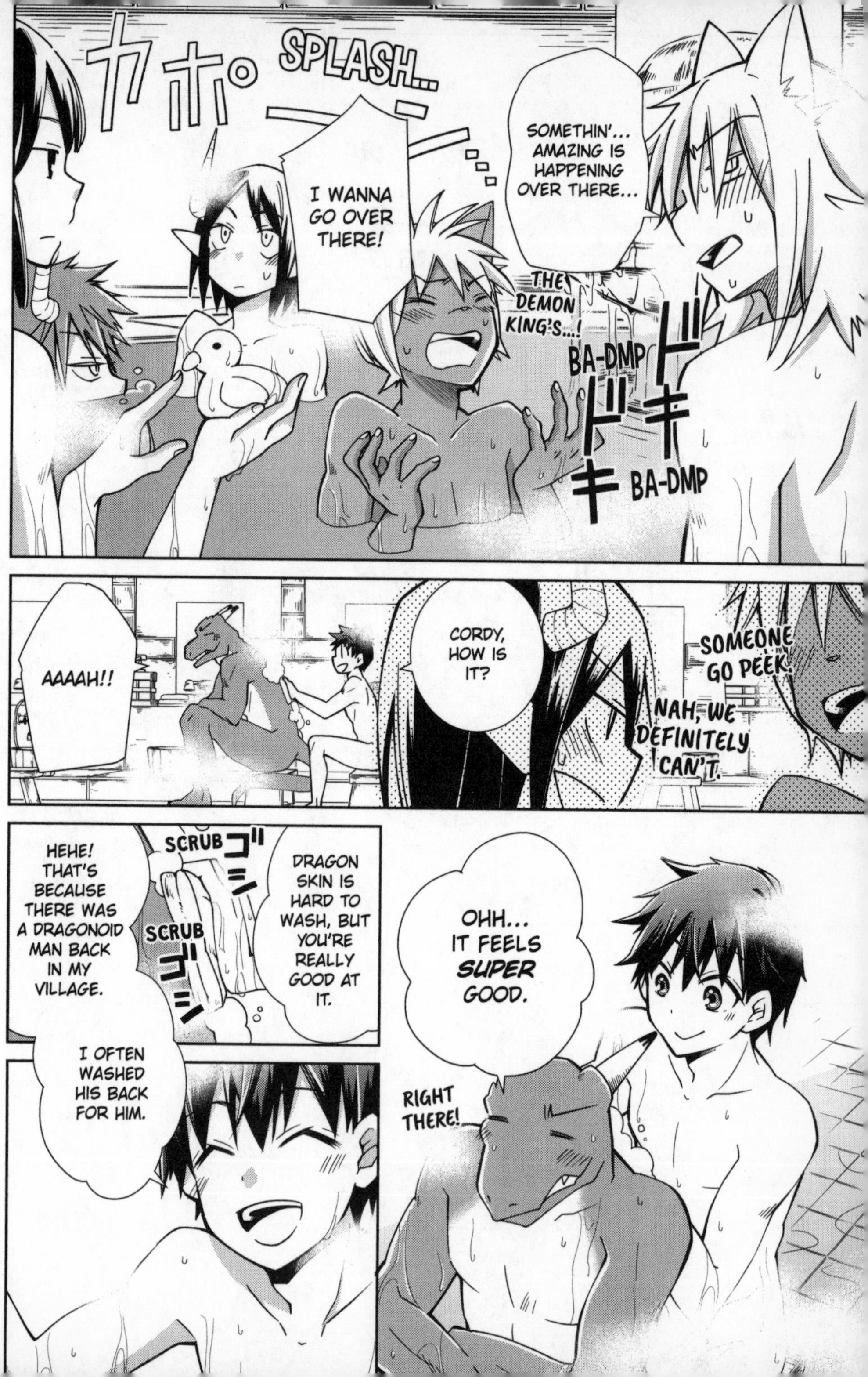
SOMETHIN'... AMAZING IS HAPPENING OVER THERE...
THE DEMON KING'S...!
BA-DMP
ドキドキ
BA-DMP
I WANNA GO OVER THERE!
SPLASH...
カポ。
SOMEONE GO PEEK.
NAH, WE DEFINITELY CAN'T.
CORDY, HOW IS IT?
AAAAH!!
OHH... IT FEELS SUPER GOOD.
RIGHT THERE!
DRAGON SKIN IS HARD TO WASH, BUT YOU'RE REALLY GOOD AT IT.
SCRUB
ゴシ
SCRUB
ゴシ
HEHE! THAT'S BECAUSE THERE WAS A DRAGONOID MAN BACK IN MY VILLAGE.
I OFTEN WASHED HIS BACK FOR HIM.

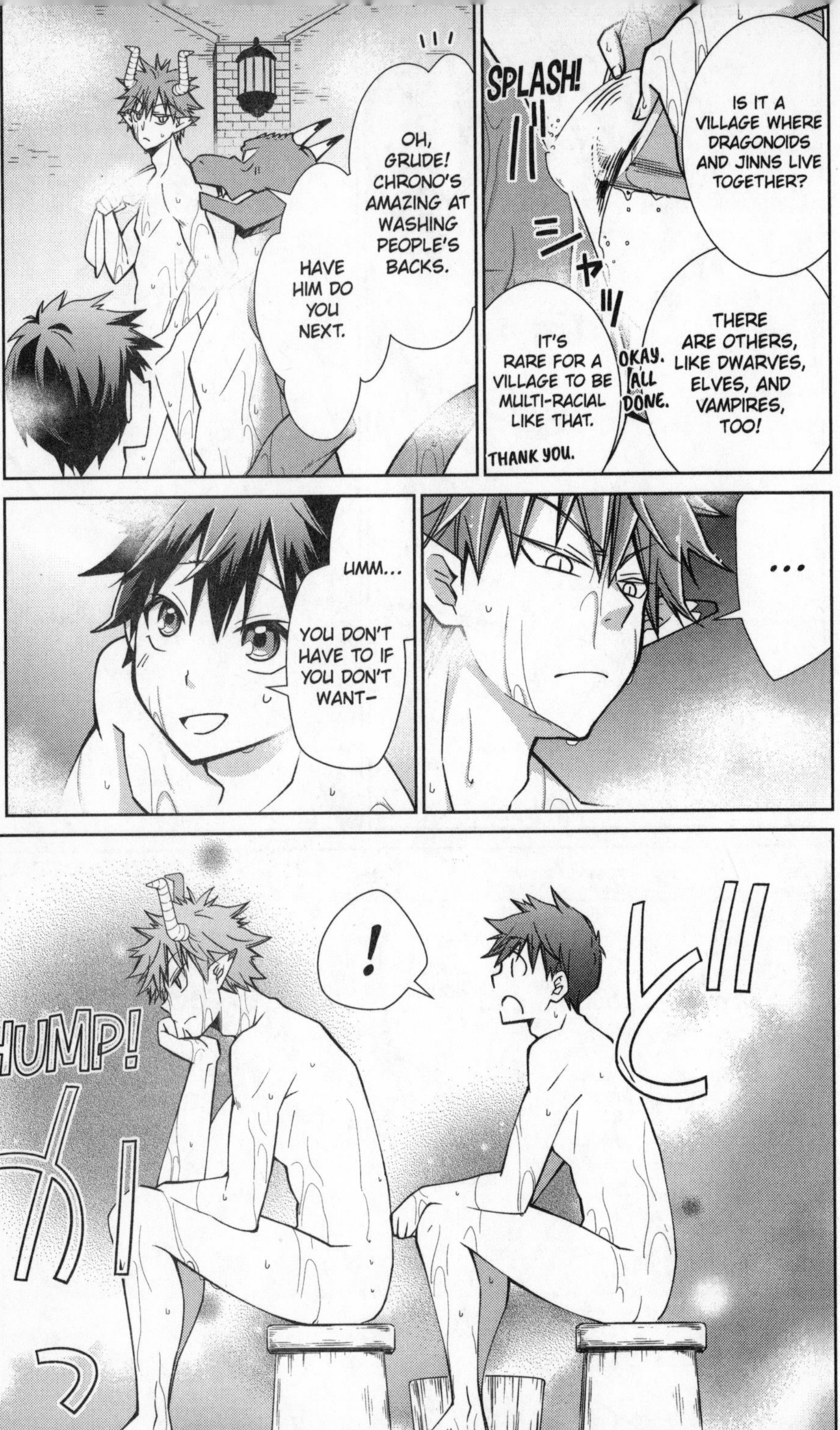
SPLASH!
IS IT A VILLAGE WHERE DRAGONOIDS AND JINNS LIVE TOGETHER?
THERE ARE OTHERS, LIKE DWARVES, ELVES, AND VAMPIRES, TOO!
OKAY. ALL DONE.
IT'S RARE FOR A VILLAGE TO BE MULTI-RACIAL LIKE THAT.
THANK YOU.
OH, GRUDE! CHRONO'S AMAZING AT WASHING PEOPLE'S BACKS.
HAVE HIM DO YOU NEXT.
...
UMM...
YOU DON'T HAVE TO IF YOU DON'T WANT—
!
THUMP!

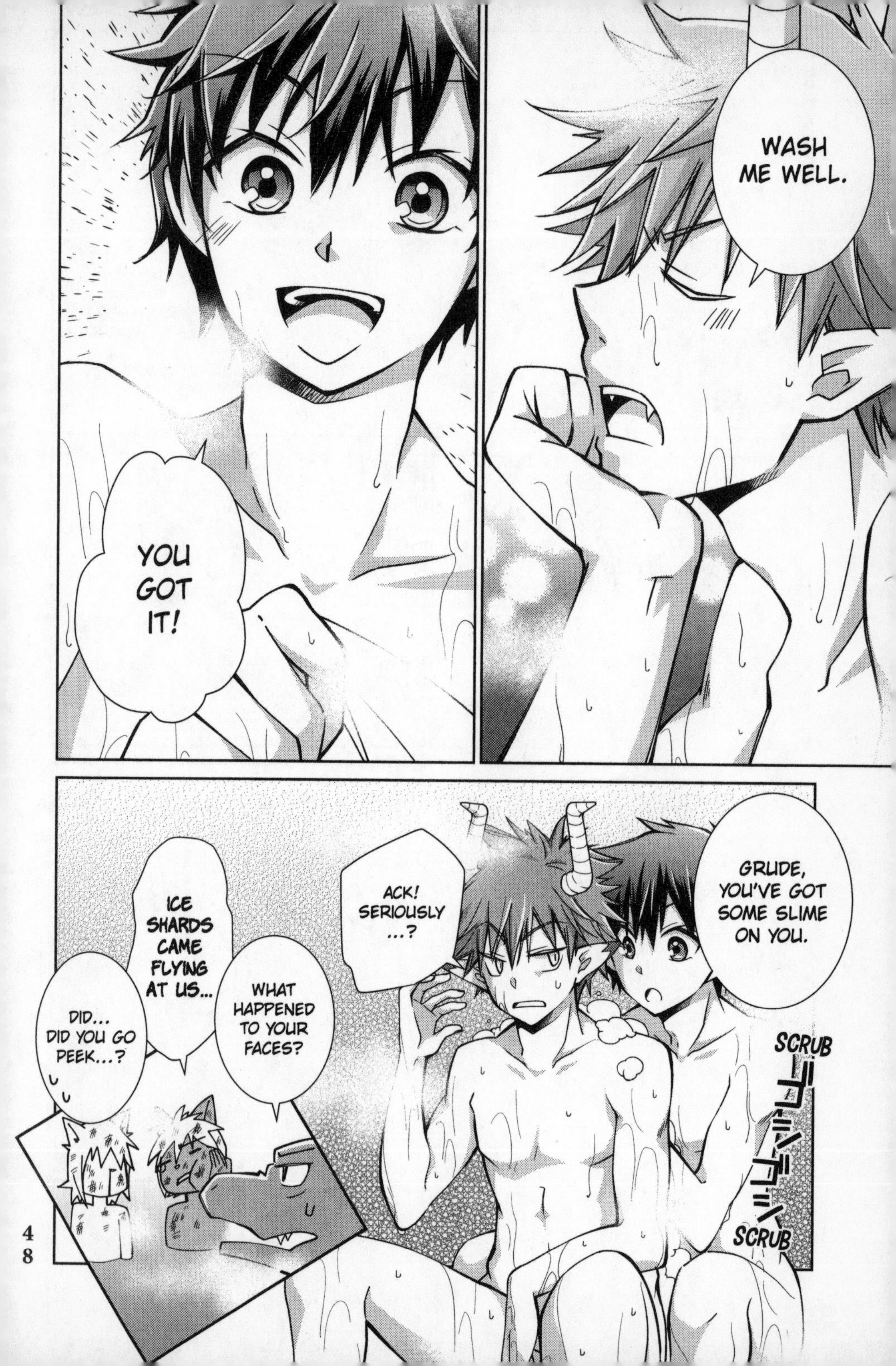
WASH ME WELL.
YOU GOT IT!
GRUDE, YOU'VE GOT SOME SLIME ON YOU.
SCRUB
SCRUB
ACK! SERIOUSLY ...?
WHAT HAPPENED TO YOUR FACES?
ICE SHARDS CAME FLYING AT US...
DID... DID YOU GO PEEK...?

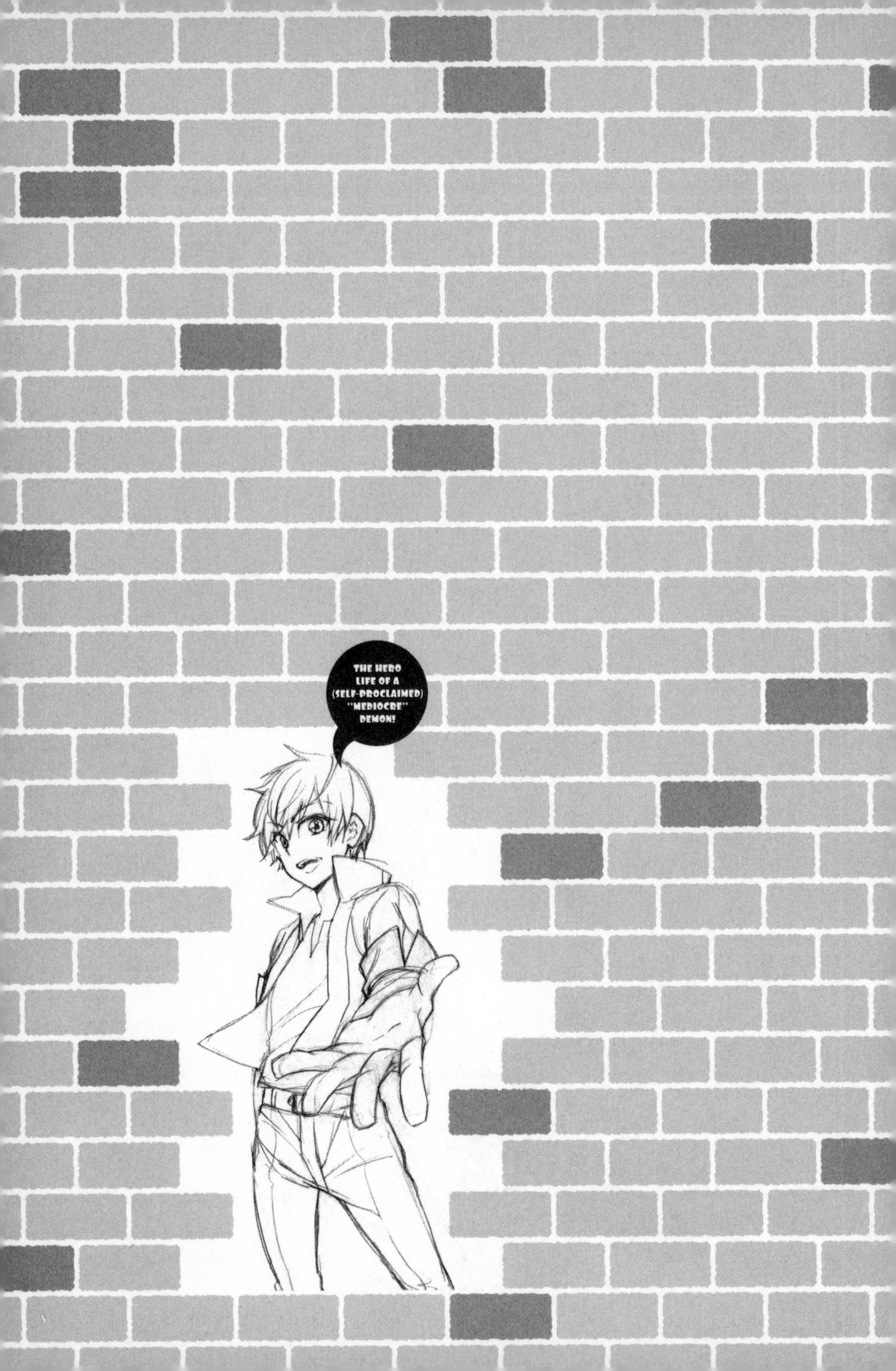
THE HERO LIFE OF A (SELF-PROCLAIMED) "MEDIOCRE" DEMON!

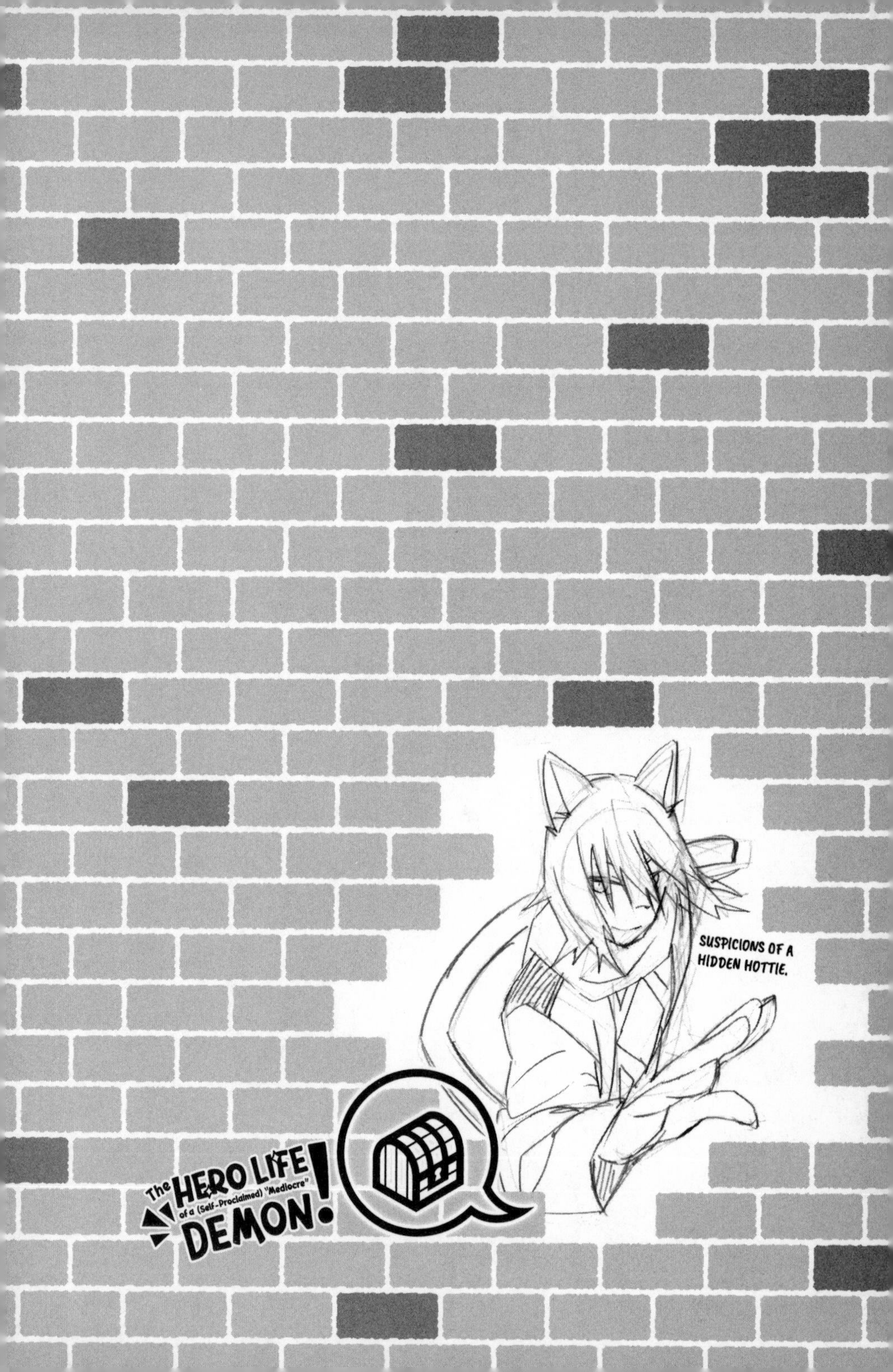
SUSPICIONS OF A HIDDEN HOTTIE.
The HERO LIFE of a (Self-Proclaimed) "Mediocre" DEMON!

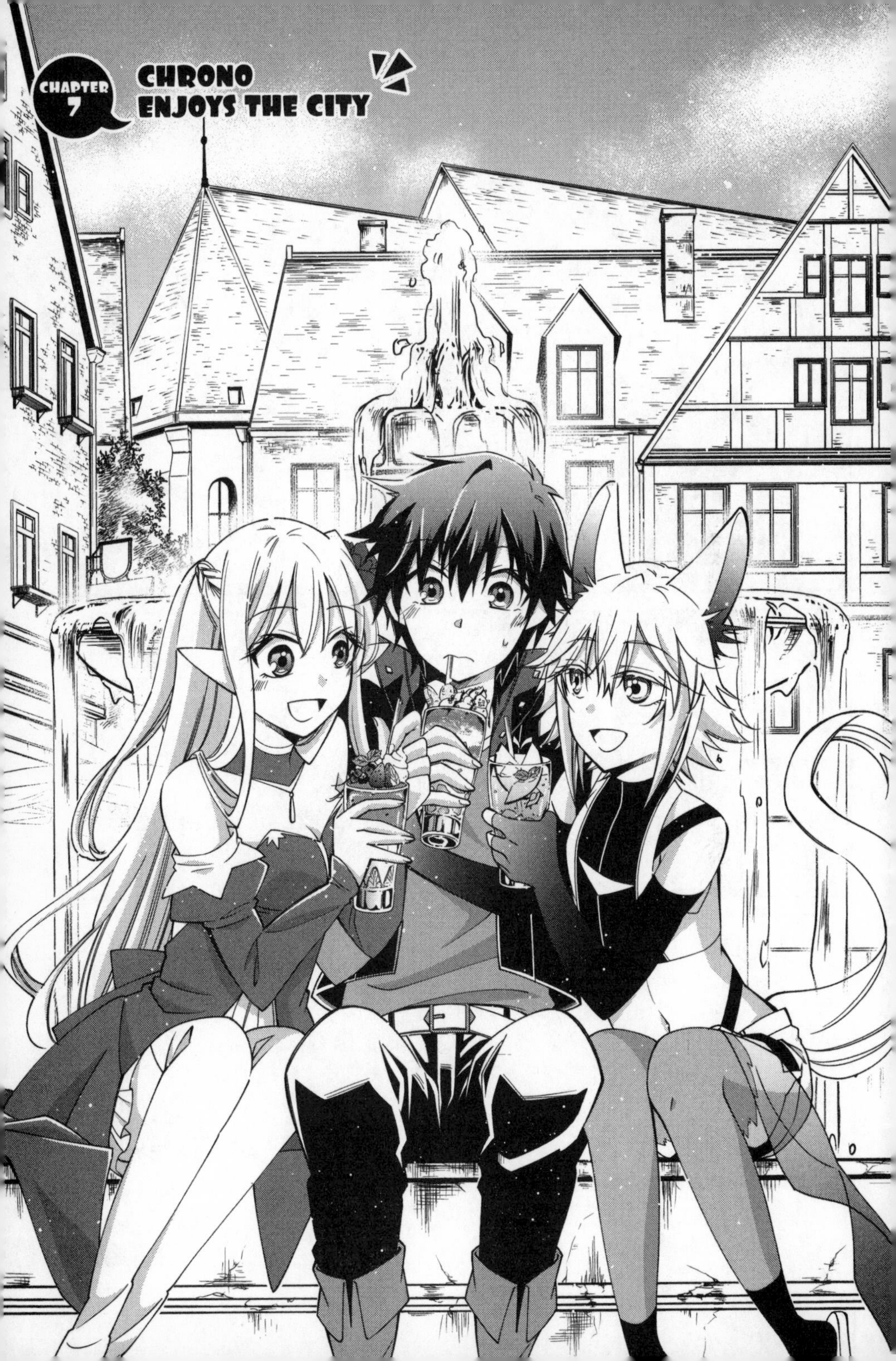
CHAPTER 7
CHRONO
ENJOYS THE CITY

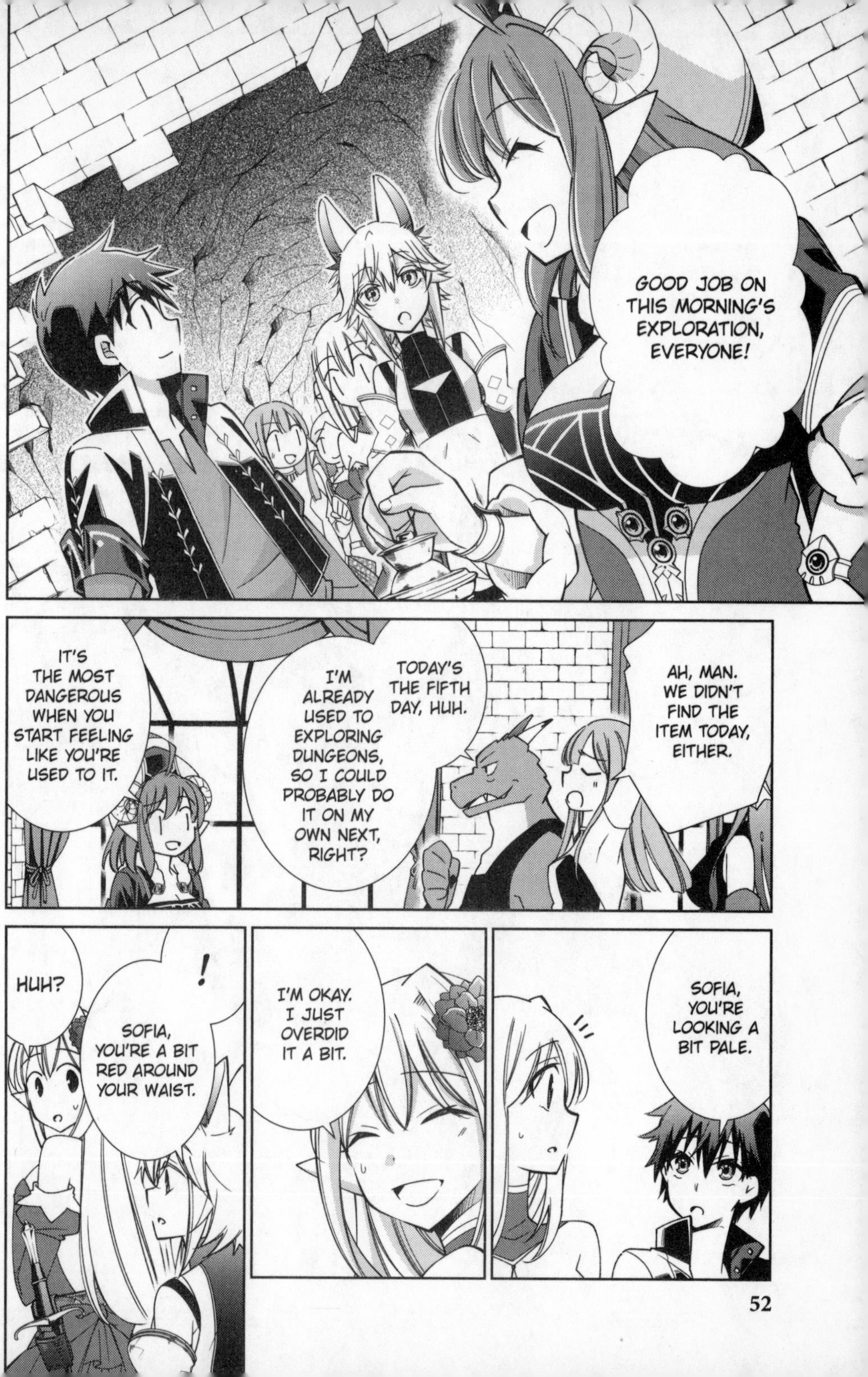
GOOD JOB ON THIS MORNING'S EXPLORATION, EVERYONE!
AH, MAN. WE DIDN'T FIND THE ITEM TODAY, EITHER.
TODAY'S THE FIFTH DAY, HUH.
I'M ALREADY USED TO EXPLORING DUNGEONS, SO I COULD PROBABLY DO IT ON MY OWN NEXT, RIGHT?
IT'S THE MOST DANGEROUS WHEN YOU START FEELING LIKE YOU'RE USED TO IT.
SOFIA, YOU'RE LOOKING A BIT PALE.
I'M OKAY. I JUST OVERDID IT A BIT.
!
SOFIA, YOU'RE A BIT RED AROUND YOUR WAIST.
HUH?

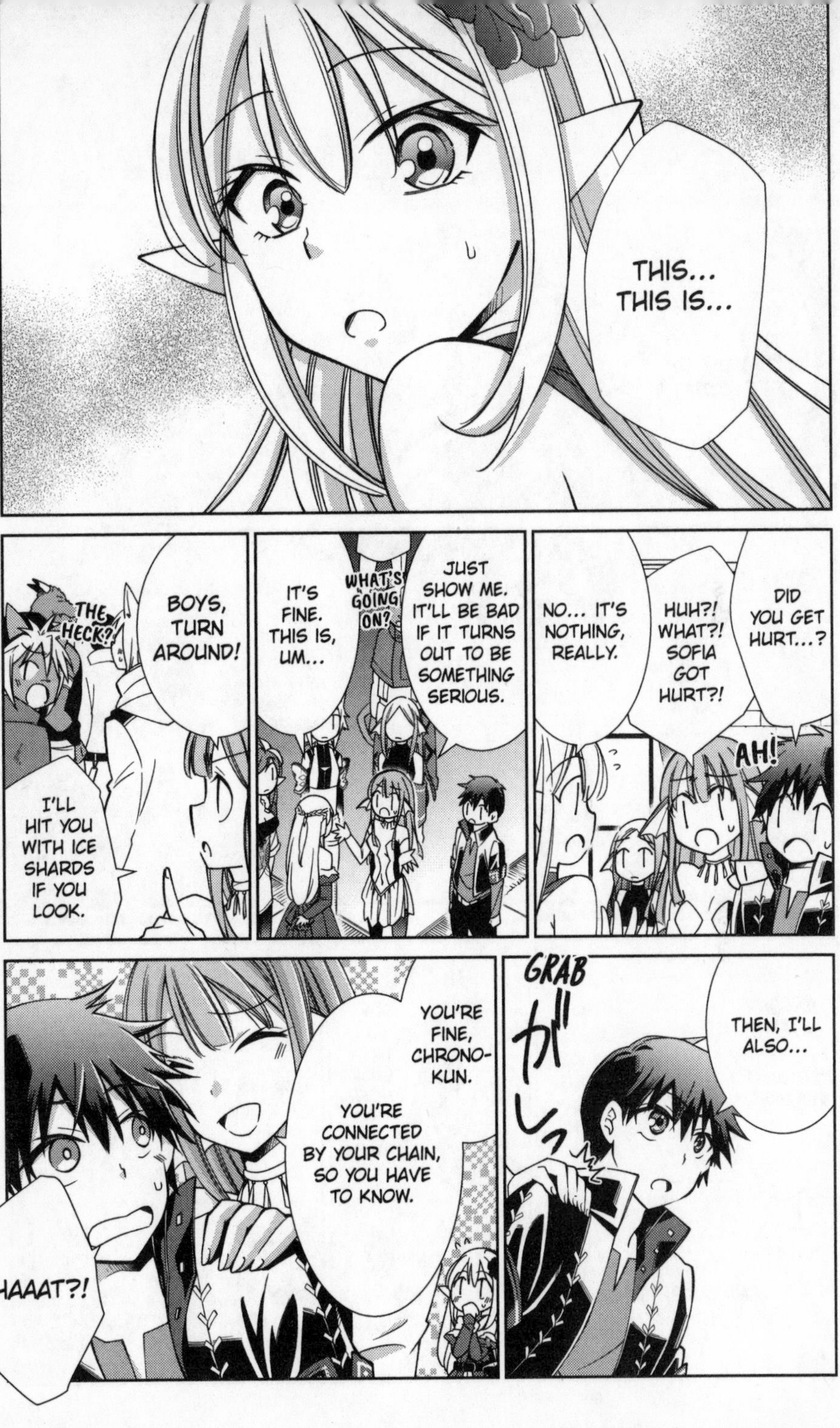
THIS... THIS IS...
DID YOU GET HURT...?
AH!
HUH?! WHAT?! SOFIA GOT HURT?!
NO... IT'S NOTHING, REALLY.
JUST SHOW ME. IT'LL BE BAD IF IT TURNS OUT TO BE SOMETHING SERIOUS.
WHAT'S GOING ON?
IT'S FINE. THIS IS, UM...
BOYS, TURN AROUND!
THE HECK?!
I'LL HIT YOU WITH ICE SHARDS IF YOU LOOK.
THEN, I'LL ALSO...
GRAB
がしっ
YOU'RE FINE, CHRONO-KUN.
YOU'RE CONNECTED BY YOUR CHAIN, SO YOU HAVE TO KNOW.
WHAAAT?!

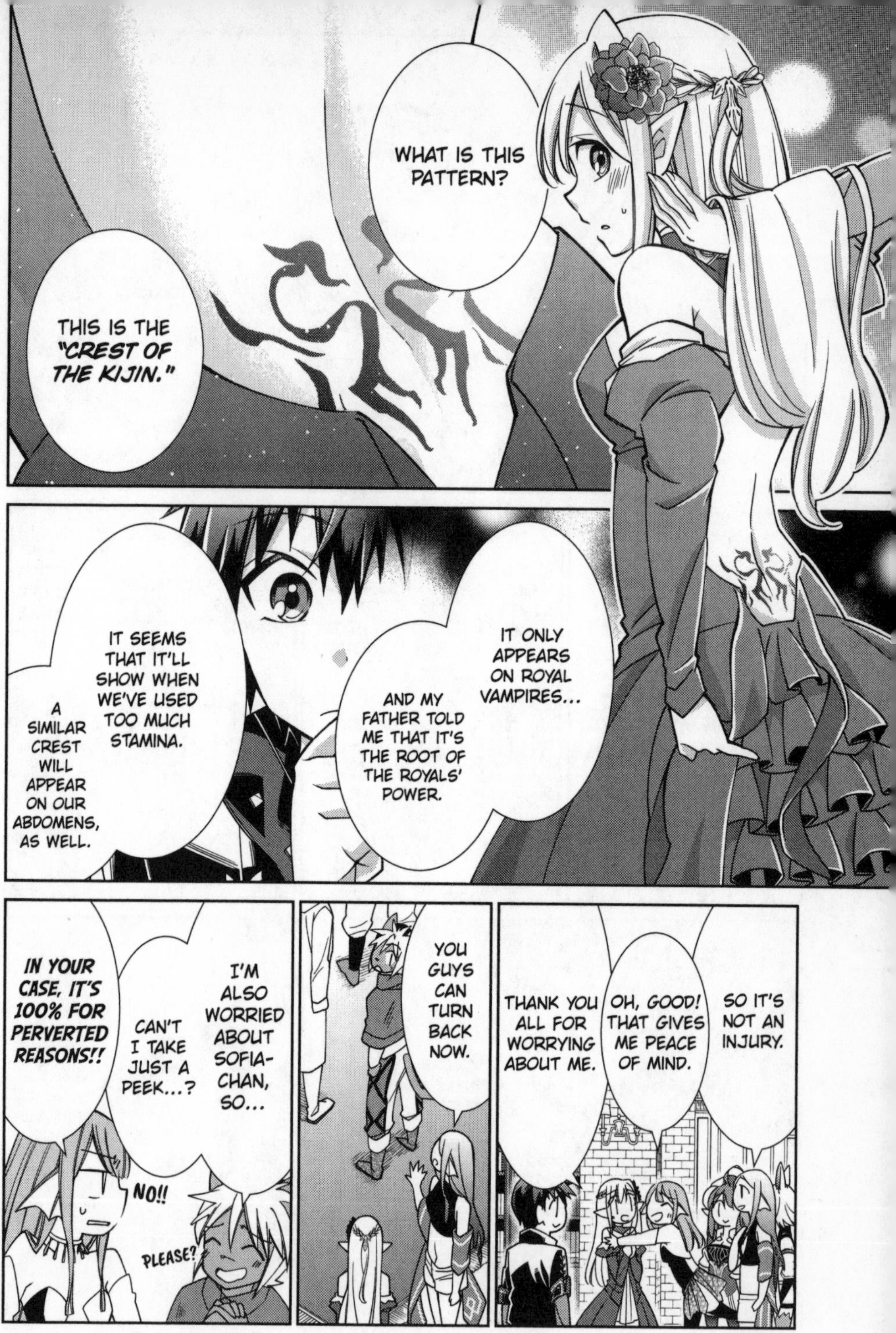
WHAT IS THIS PATTERN?
THIS IS THE *"CREST OF THE KIJIN."*
IT ONLY APPEARS ON ROYAL VAMPIRES...
AND MY FATHER TOLD ME THAT IT'S THE ROOT OF THE ROYALS' POWER.
IT SEEMS THAT IT'LL SHOW WHEN WE'VE USED TOO MUCH STAMINA.
A SIMILAR CREST WILL APPEAR ON OUR ABDOMENS, AS WELL.
SO IT'S NOT AN INJURY.
OH, GOOD! THAT GIVES ME PEACE OF MIND.
THANK YOU ALL FOR WORRYING ABOUT ME.
YOU GUYS CAN TURN BACK NOW.
I'M ALSO WORRIED ABOUT SOFIA-CHAN, SO...
CAN'T I TAKE JUST A PEEK...?
IN YOUR CASE, IT'S 100% FOR PERVERTED REASONS!!
NO!!
PLEASE?

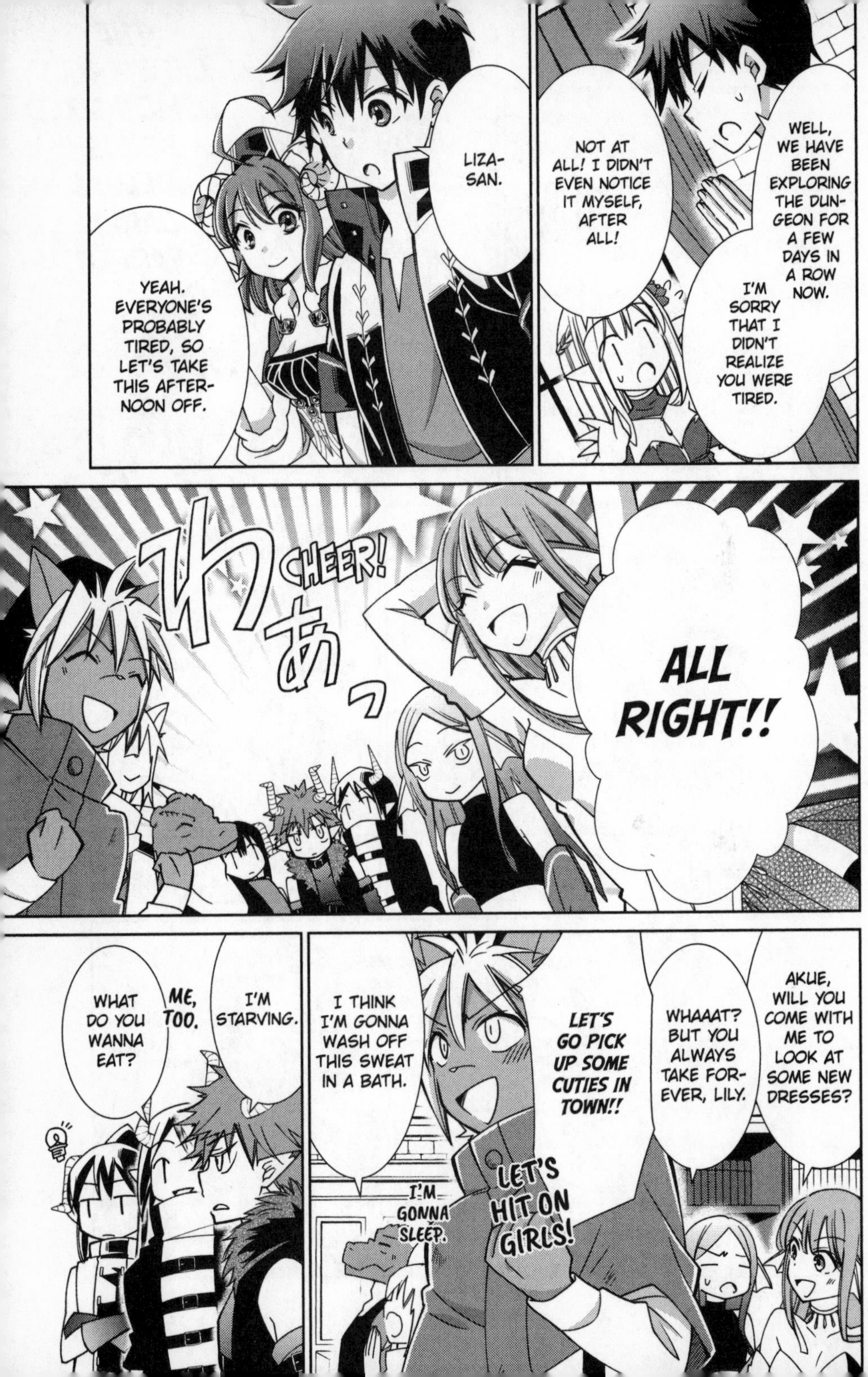
WELL, WE HAVE BEEN EXPLORING THE DUN-GEON FOR A FEW DAYS IN A ROW NOW.
I'M SORRY THAT I DIDN'T REALIZE YOU WERE TIRED.
NOT AT ALL! I DIDN'T EVEN NOTICE IT MYSELF, AFTER ALL!
LIZA-SAN.
YEAH. EVERYONE'S PROBABLY TIRED, SO LET'S TAKE THIS AFTER-NOON OFF.
ALL RIGHT!!
わあっ
CHEER!
AKUE, WILL YOU COME WITH ME TO LOOK AT SOME NEW DRESSES?
WHAAAT? BUT YOU ALWAYS TAKE FOR-EVER, LILY.
LET'S GO PICK UP SOME CUTIES IN TOWN!!
LET'S HIT ON GIRLS!
I THINK I'M GONNA WASH OFF THIS SWEAT IN A BATH.
I'M GONNA SLEEP.
I'M STARVING.
ME, TOO.
WHAT DO YOU WANNA EAT?

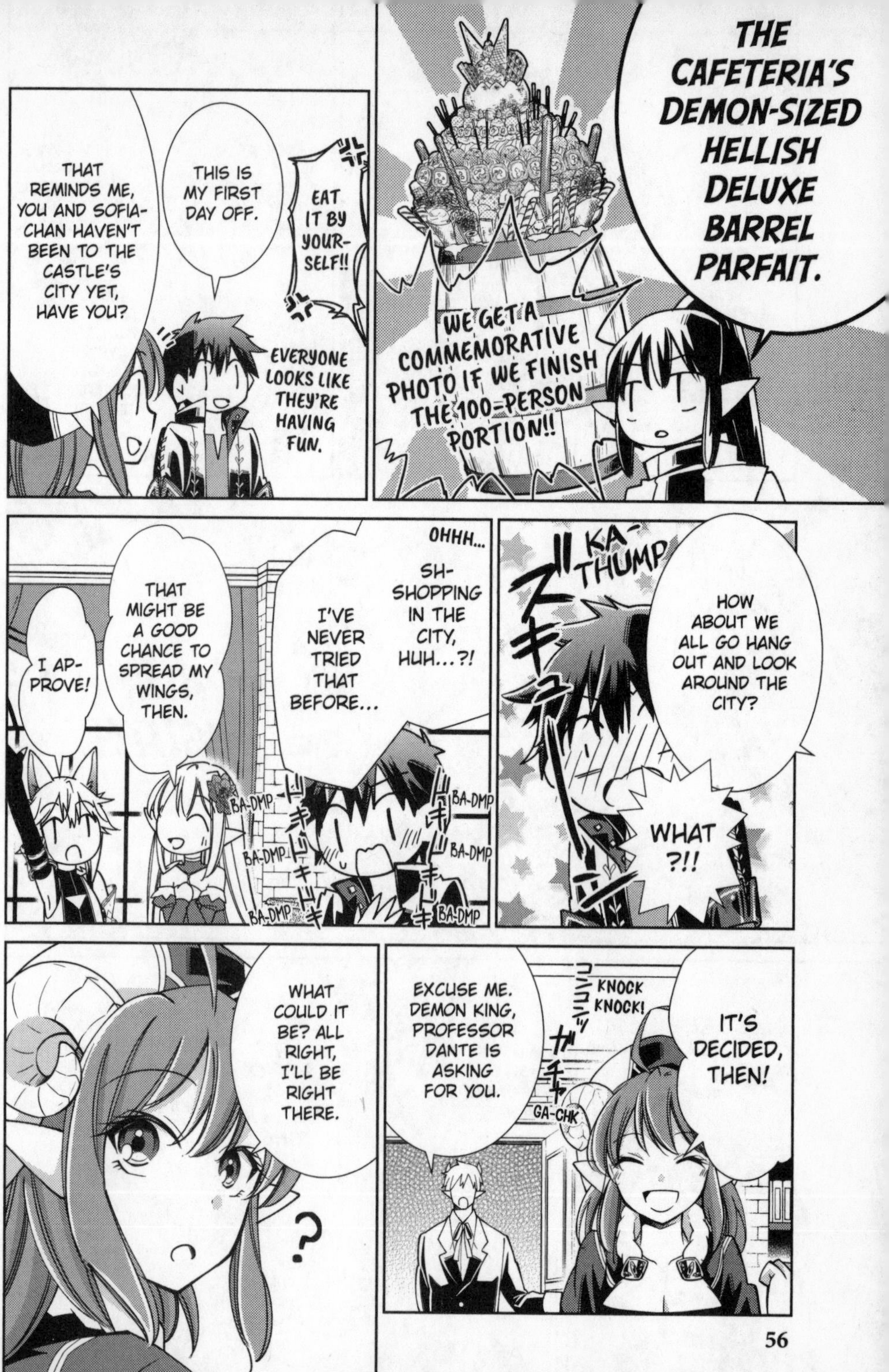
THE CAFETERIA'S DEMON-SIZED HELLISH DELUXE BARREL PARFAIT.
WE GET A COMMEMORATIVE PHOTO IF WE FINISH THE 100-PERSON PORTION!!
EAT IT BY YOURSELF!!
THIS IS MY FIRST DAY OFF.
THAT REMINDS ME, YOU AND SOFIA-CHAN HAVEN'T BEEN TO THE CASTLE'S CITY YET, HAVE YOU?
EVERYONE LOOKS LIKE THEY'RE HAVING FUN.
KA-THUMP
HOW ABOUT WE ALL GO HANG OUT AND LOOK AROUND THE CITY?
WHAT ?!!
OHHH...
SH-SHOPPING IN THE CITY, HUH...?!
I'VE NEVER TRIED THAT BEFORE...
BA-DMP
BA-DMP
BA-DMP
BA-DMP
BA-DMP
BA-DMP
THAT MIGHT BE A GOOD CHANCE TO SPREAD MY WINGS, THEN.
I AP-PROVE!
IT'S DECIDED, THEN!
KNOCK KNOCK!
GA-CHK
EXCUSE ME. DEMON KING, PROFESSOR DANTE IS ASKING FOR YOU.
WHAT COULD IT BE? ALL RIGHT, I'LL BE RIGHT THERE.
?

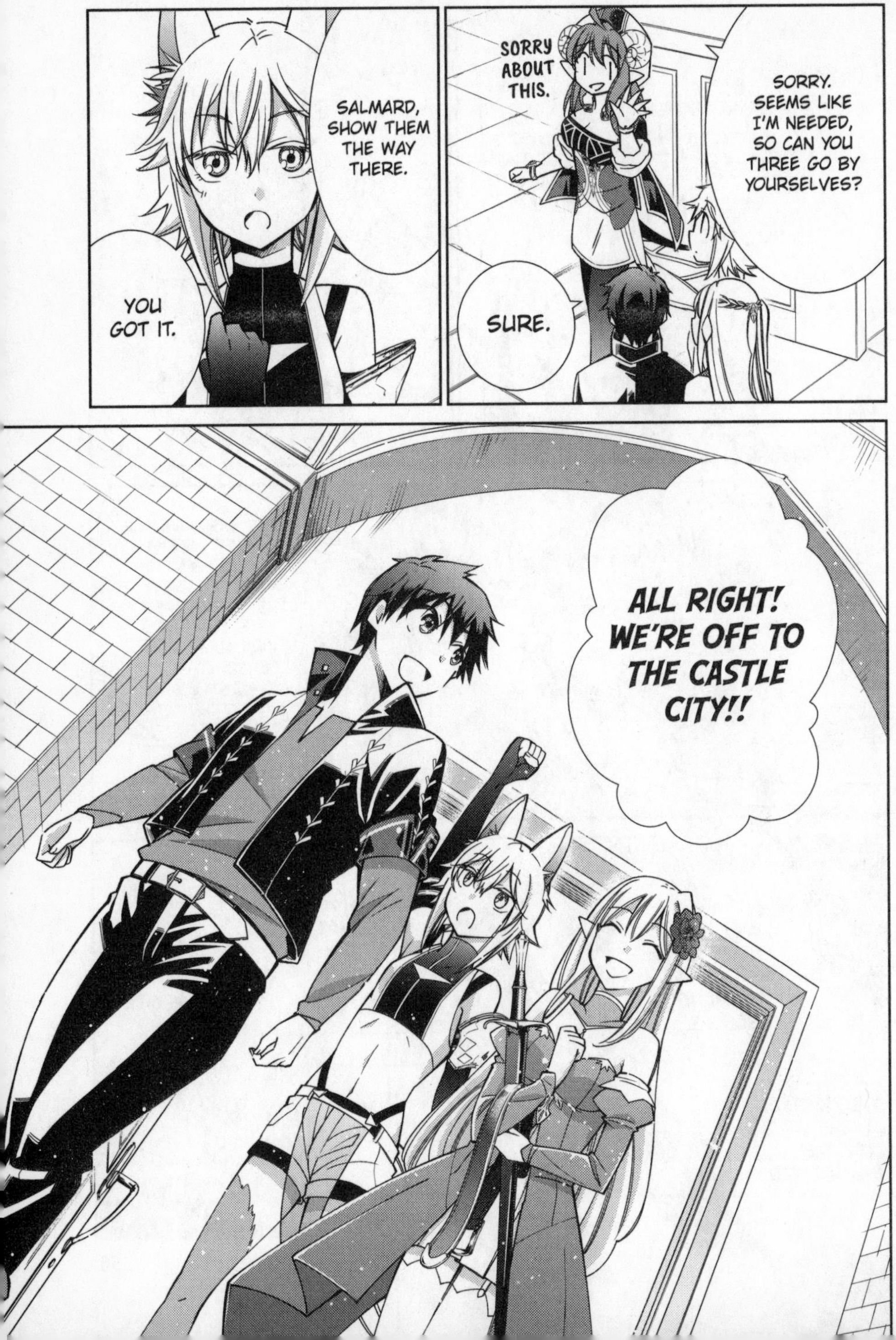
SORRY. SEEMS LIKE I'M NEEDED, SO CAN YOU THREE GO BY YOURSELVES?
SORRY ABOUT THIS.
SURE.
SALMARD, SHOW THEM THE WAY THERE.
YOU GOT IT.
ALL RIGHT! WE'RE OFF TO THE CASTLE CITY!!

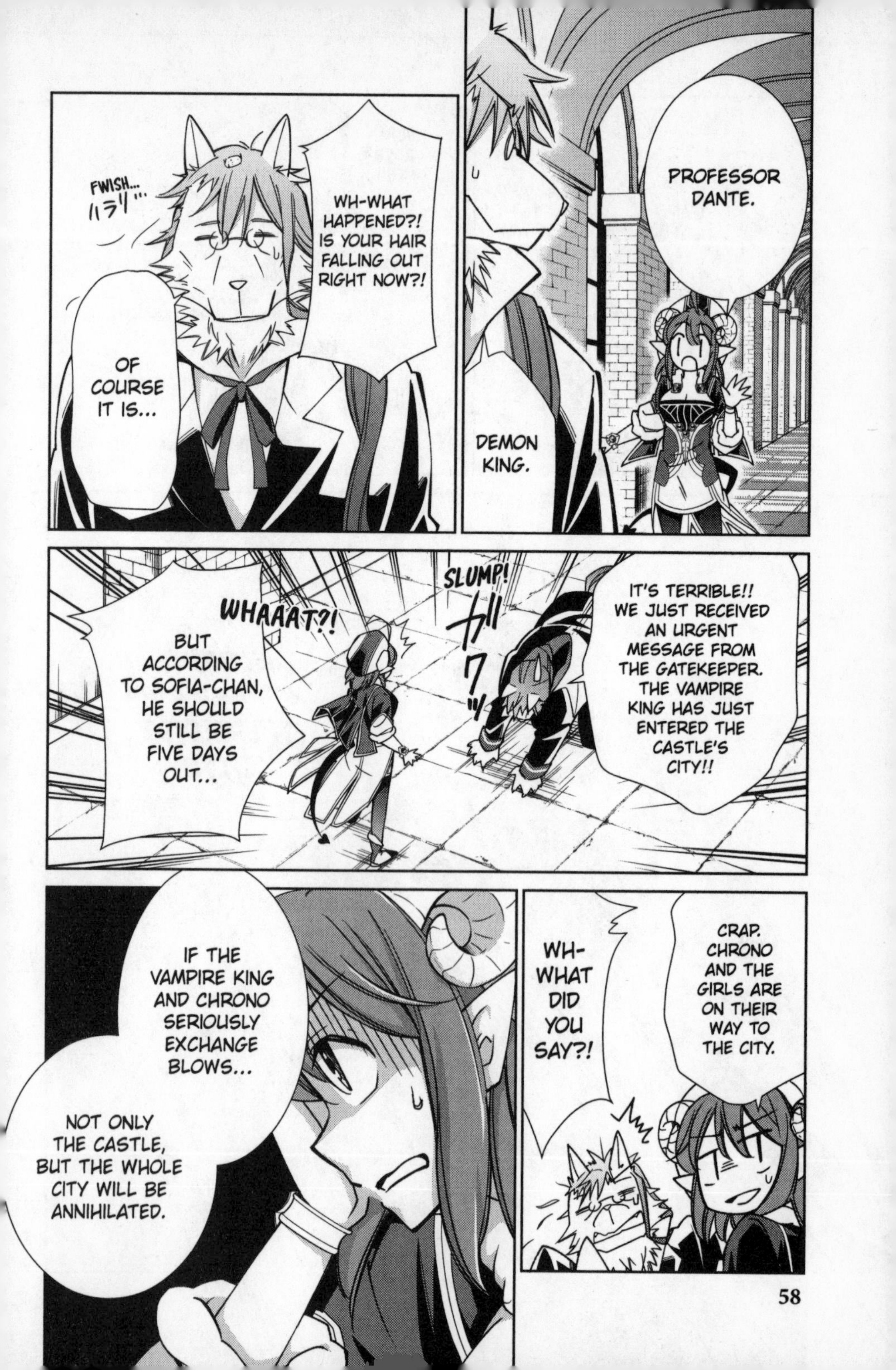
PROFESSOR DANTE.
DEMON KING.
WH-WHAT HAPPENED?! IS YOUR HAIR FALLING OUT RIGHT NOW?!
FWISH... ハラリ...
OF COURSE IT IS...
IT'S TERRIBLE!! WE JUST RECEIVED AN URGENT MESSAGE FROM THE GATEKEEPER. THE VAMPIRE KING HAS JUST ENTERED THE CASTLE'S CITY!!
SLUMP! ガクッ
WHAAAT?!
BUT ACCORDING TO SOFIA-CHAN, HE SHOULD STILL BE FIVE DAYS OUT...
CRAP. CHRONO AND THE GIRLS ARE ON THEIR WAY TO THE CITY.
WH-WHAT DID YOU SAY?!
IF THE VAMPIRE KING AND CHRONO SERIOUSLY EXCHANGE BLOWS...
NOT ONLY THE CASTLE, BUT THE WHOLE CITY WILL BE ANNIHILATED.

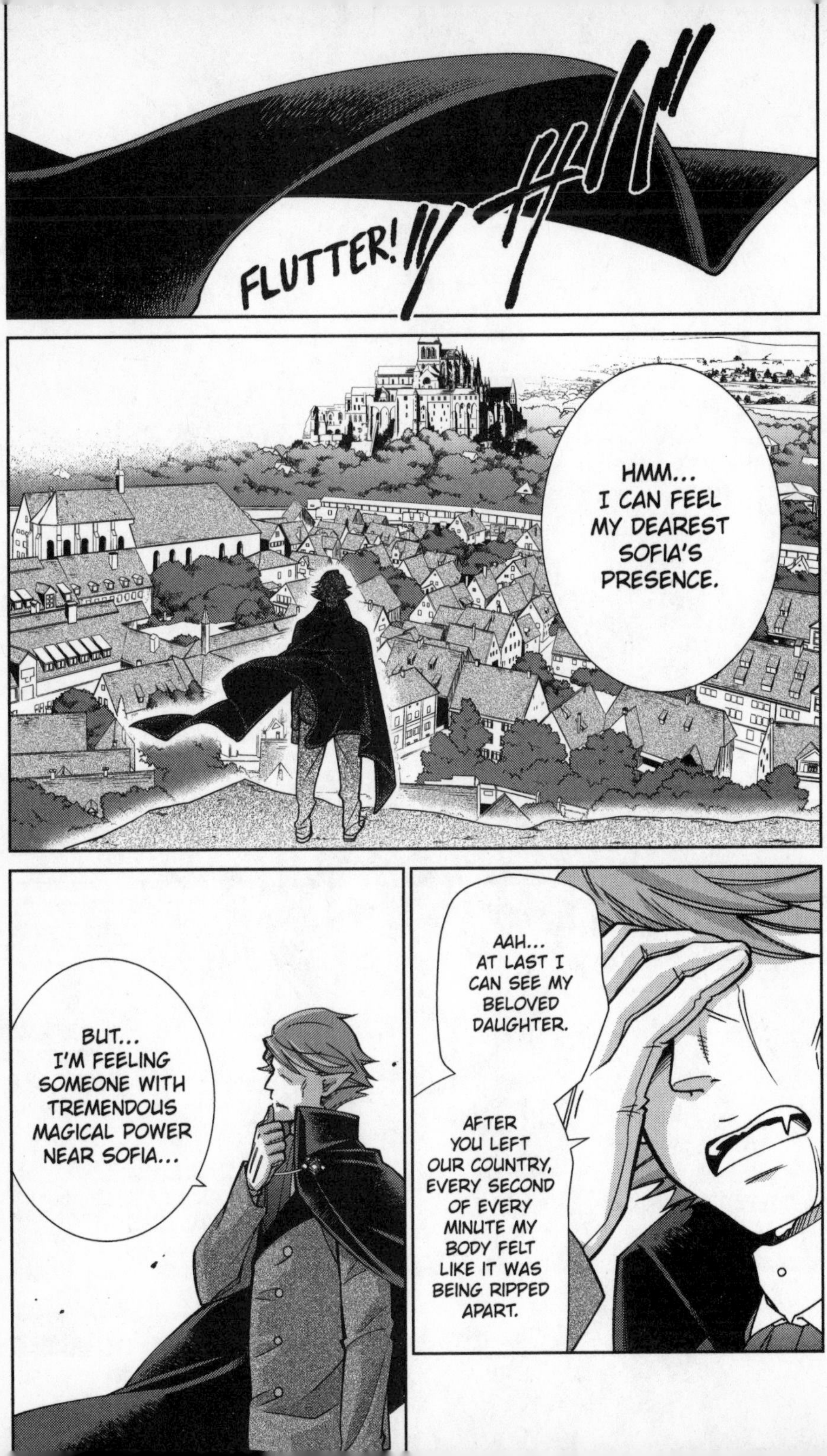
FLUTTER!
HMM... I CAN FEEL MY DEAREST SOFIA'S PRESENCE.
AAH... AT LAST I CAN SEE MY BELOVED DAUGHTER.
AFTER YOU LEFT OUR COUNTRY, EVERY SECOND OF EVERY MINUTE MY BODY FELT LIKE IT WAS BEING RIPPED APART.
BUT... I'M FEELING SOMEONE WITH TREMENDOUS MAGICAL POWER NEAR SOFIA...

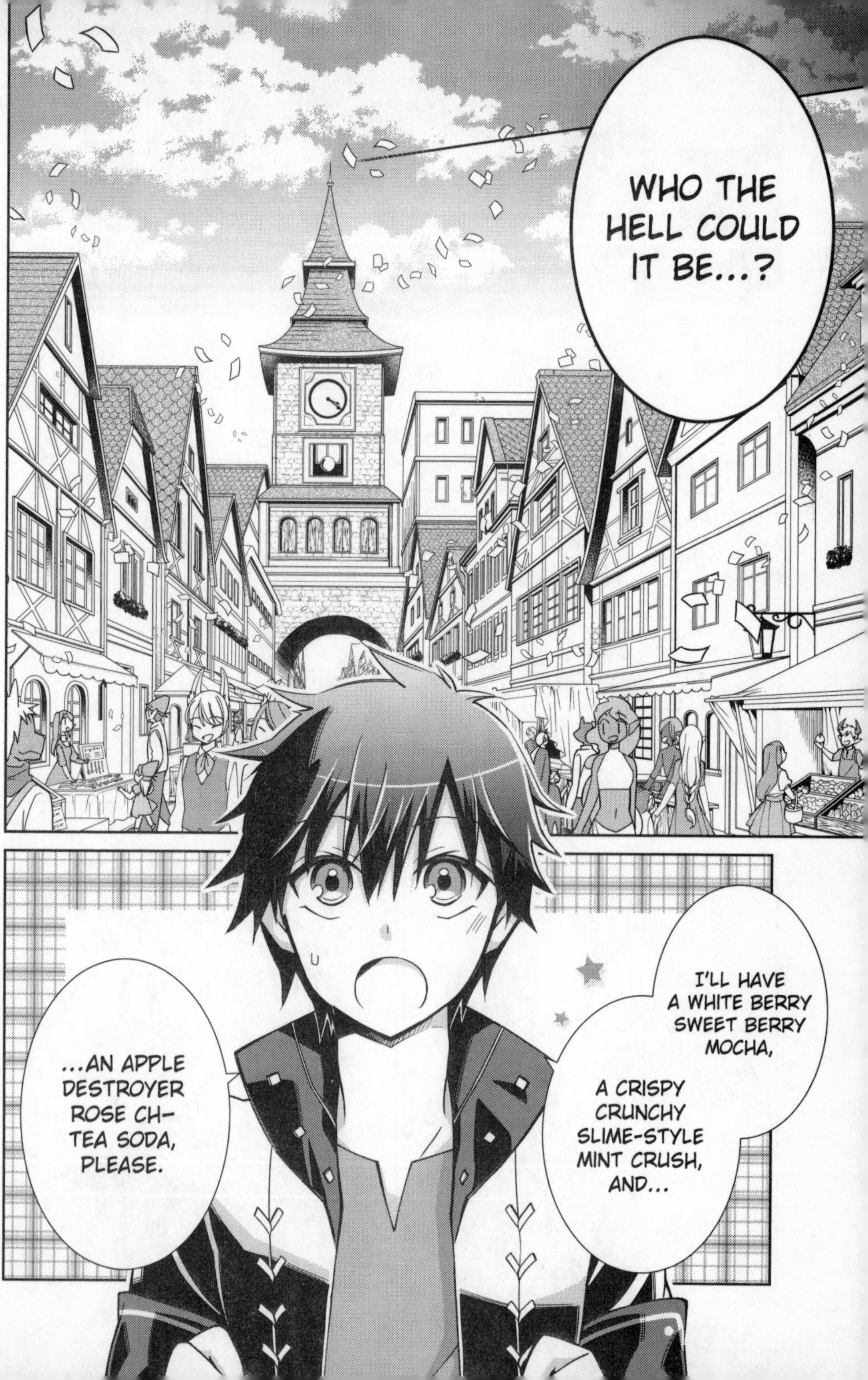
WHO THE HELL COULD IT BE...?
I'LL HAVE A WHITE BERRY SWEET BERRY MOCHA,
A CRISPY CRUNCHY SLIME-STYLE MINT CRUSH, AND...
...AN APPLE DESTROYER ROSE CH-TEA SODA, PLEASE.

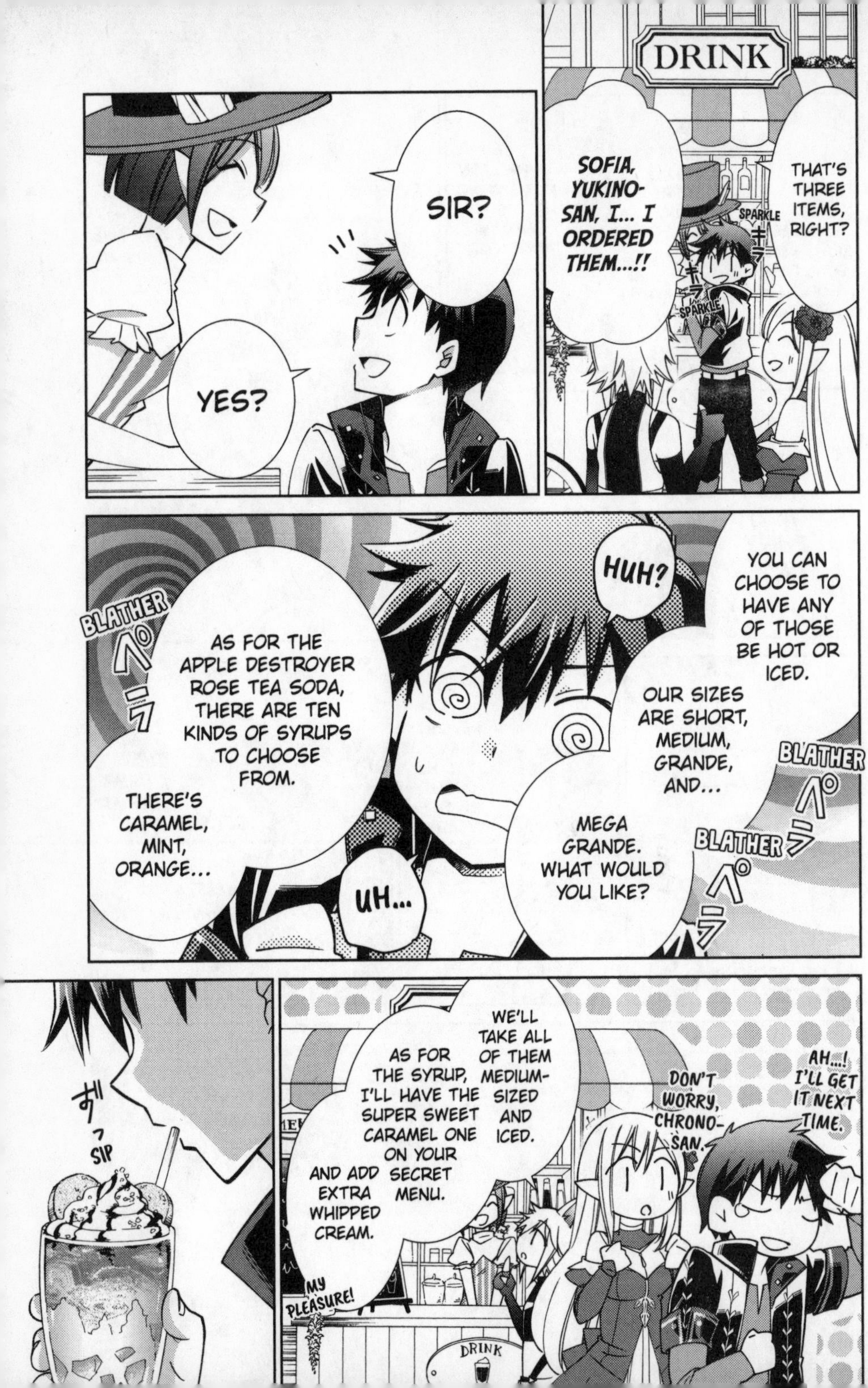
DRINK
THAT'S THREE ITEMS, RIGHT?
SPARKLE
SPARKLE
SOFIA, YUKINO-SAN, I... I ORDERED THEM...!!
SIR?
YES?
YOU CAN CHOOSE TO HAVE ANY OF THOSE BE HOT OR ICED.
HUH?
OUR SIZES ARE SHORT, MEDIUM, GRANDE, AND...
BLATHER
BLATHER
MEGA GRANDE. WHAT WOULD YOU LIKE?
BLATHER
AS FOR THE APPLE DESTROYER ROSE TEA SODA, THERE ARE TEN KINDS OF SYRUPS TO CHOOSE FROM.
THERE'S CARAMEL, MINT, ORANGE...
UH...
AH...! I'LL GET IT NEXT TIME.
DON'T WORRY, CHRONO-SAN.
WE'LL TAKE ALL OF THEM MEDIUM-SIZED AND ICED.
AS FOR THE SYRUP, I'LL HAVE THE SUPER SWEET CARAMEL ONE ON YOUR SECRET MENU.
AND ADD EXTRA WHIPPED CREAM.
MY PLEASURE!
DRINK
SIP

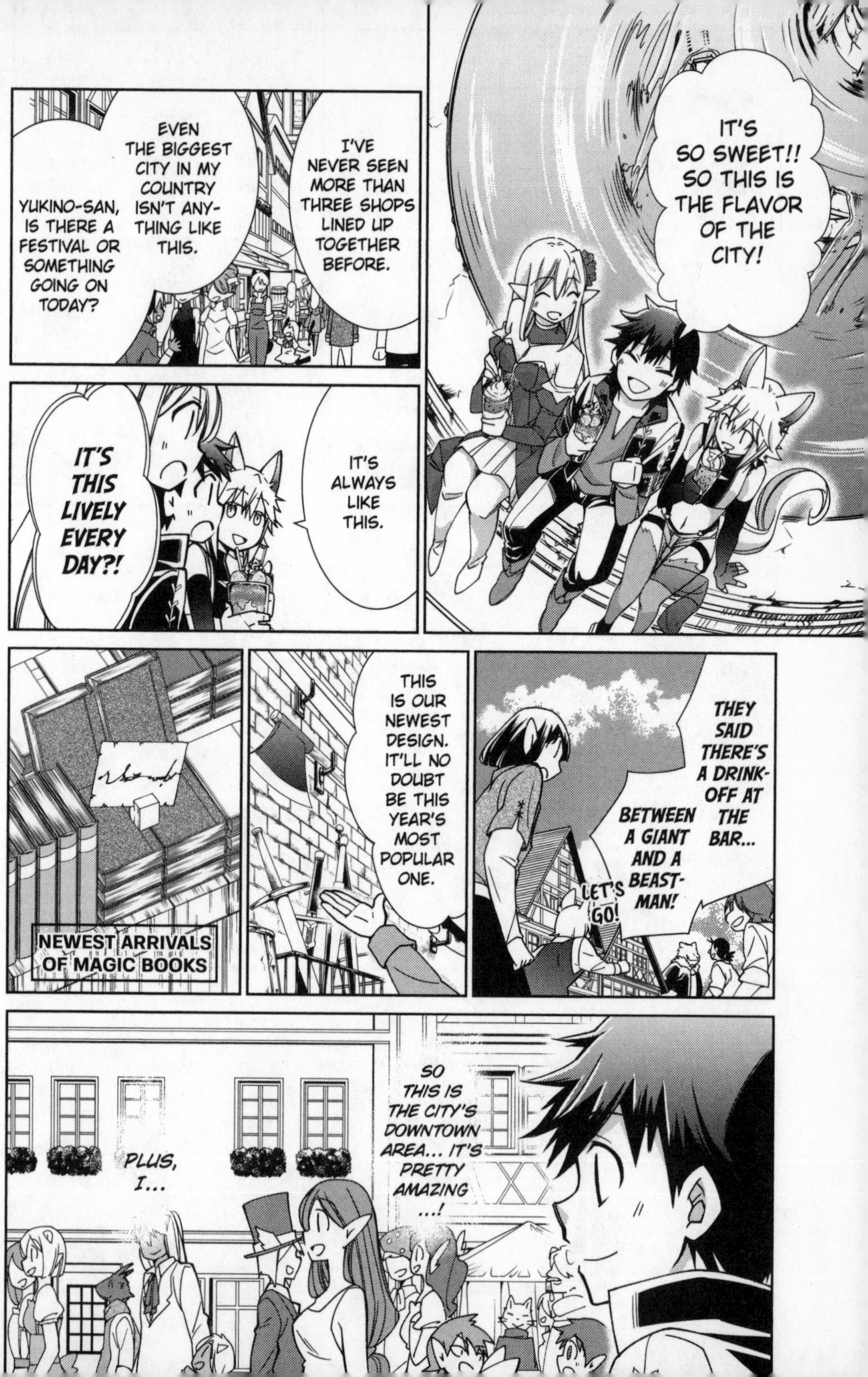
IT'S SO SWEET!! SO THIS IS THE FLAVOR OF THE CITY!
I'VE NEVER SEEN MORE THAN THREE SHOPS LINED UP TOGETHER BEFORE.
EVEN THE BIGGEST CITY IN MY COUNTRY ISN'T ANYTHING LIKE THIS.
YUKINO-SAN, IS THERE A FESTIVAL OR SOMETHING GOING ON TODAY?
IT'S ALWAYS LIKE THIS.
IT'S THIS LIVELY EVERY DAY?!
THEY SAID THERE'S A DRINK-OFF AT THE BAR...
BETWEEN A GIANT AND A BEAST-MAN!
LET'S GO!
THIS IS OUR NEWEST DESIGN. IT'LL NO DOUBT BE THIS YEAR'S MOST POPULAR ONE.
NEWEST ARRIVALS OF MAGIC BOOKS
SO THIS IS THE CITY'S DOWNTOWN AREA... IT'S PRETTY AMAZING ...!
PLUS, I...

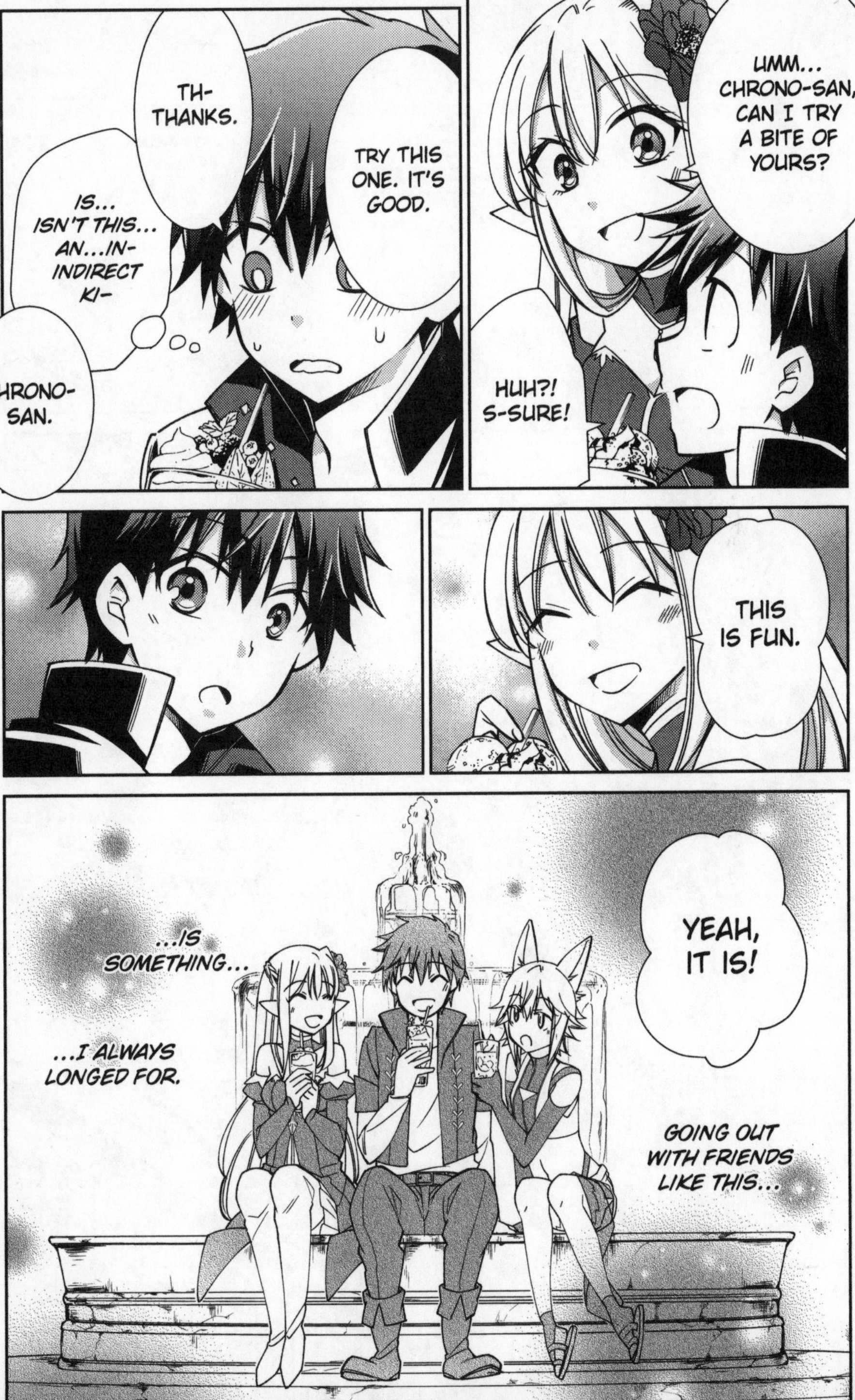
UMM... CHRONO-SAN, CAN I TRY A BITE OF YOURS?
HUH?! S-SURE!
TRY THIS ONE. IT'S GOOD.
TH- THANKS.
IS... ISN'T THIS... AN...IN- INDIRECT KI-
CHRONO-SAN.
THIS IS FUN.
YEAH, IT IS!
GOING OUT WITH FRIENDS LIKE THIS...
...IS SOMETHING...
...I ALWAYS LONGED FOR.

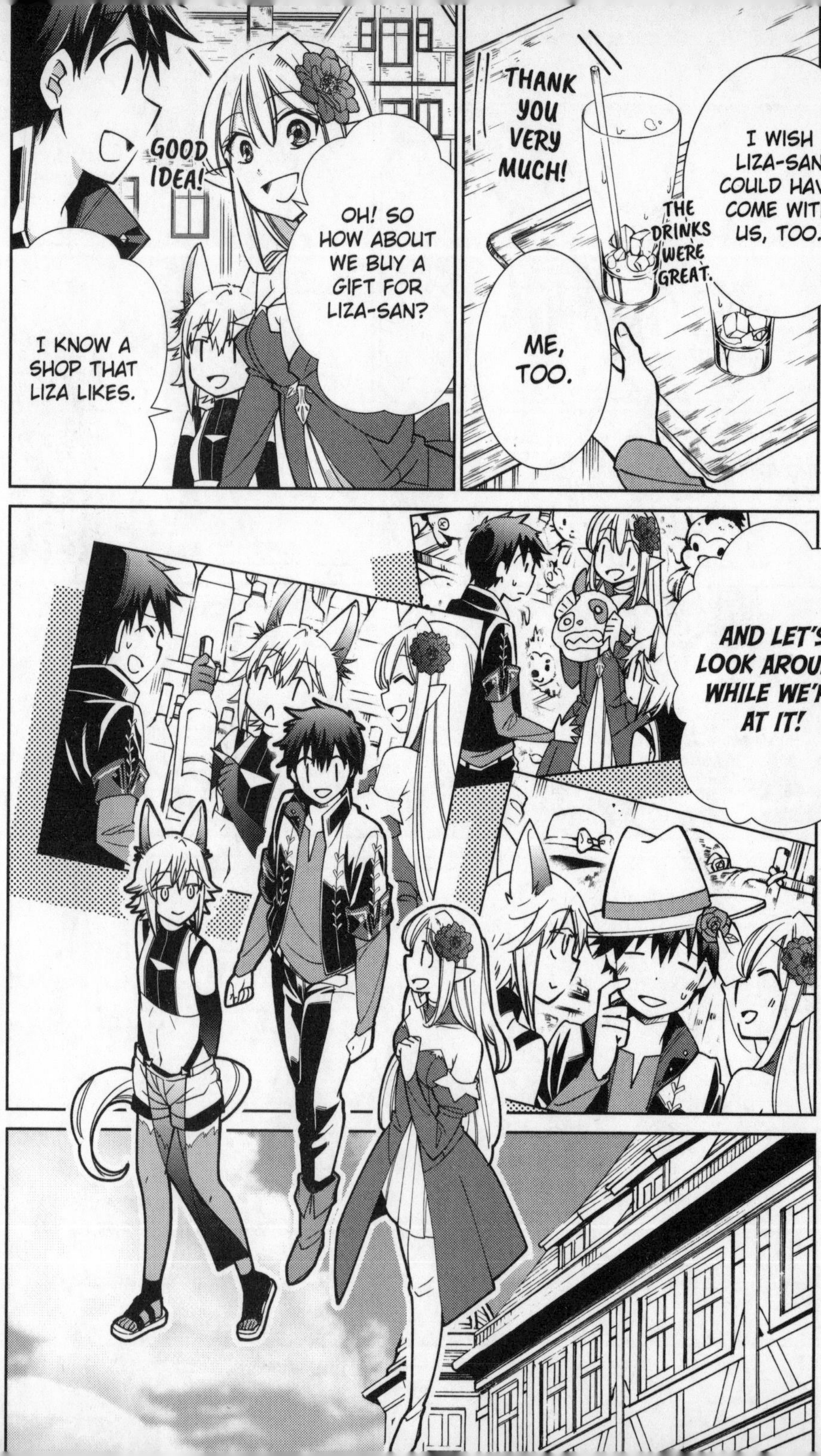
THANK YOU VERY MUCH!
THE DRINKS WERE GREAT.
I WISH LIZA-SAN COULD HAVE COME WITH US, TOO.
ME, TOO.
OH! SO HOW ABOUT WE BUY A GIFT FOR LIZA-SAN?
GOOD IDEA!
I KNOW A SHOP THAT LIZA LIKES.
AND LET'S LOOK AROUND WHILE WE'RE AT IT!

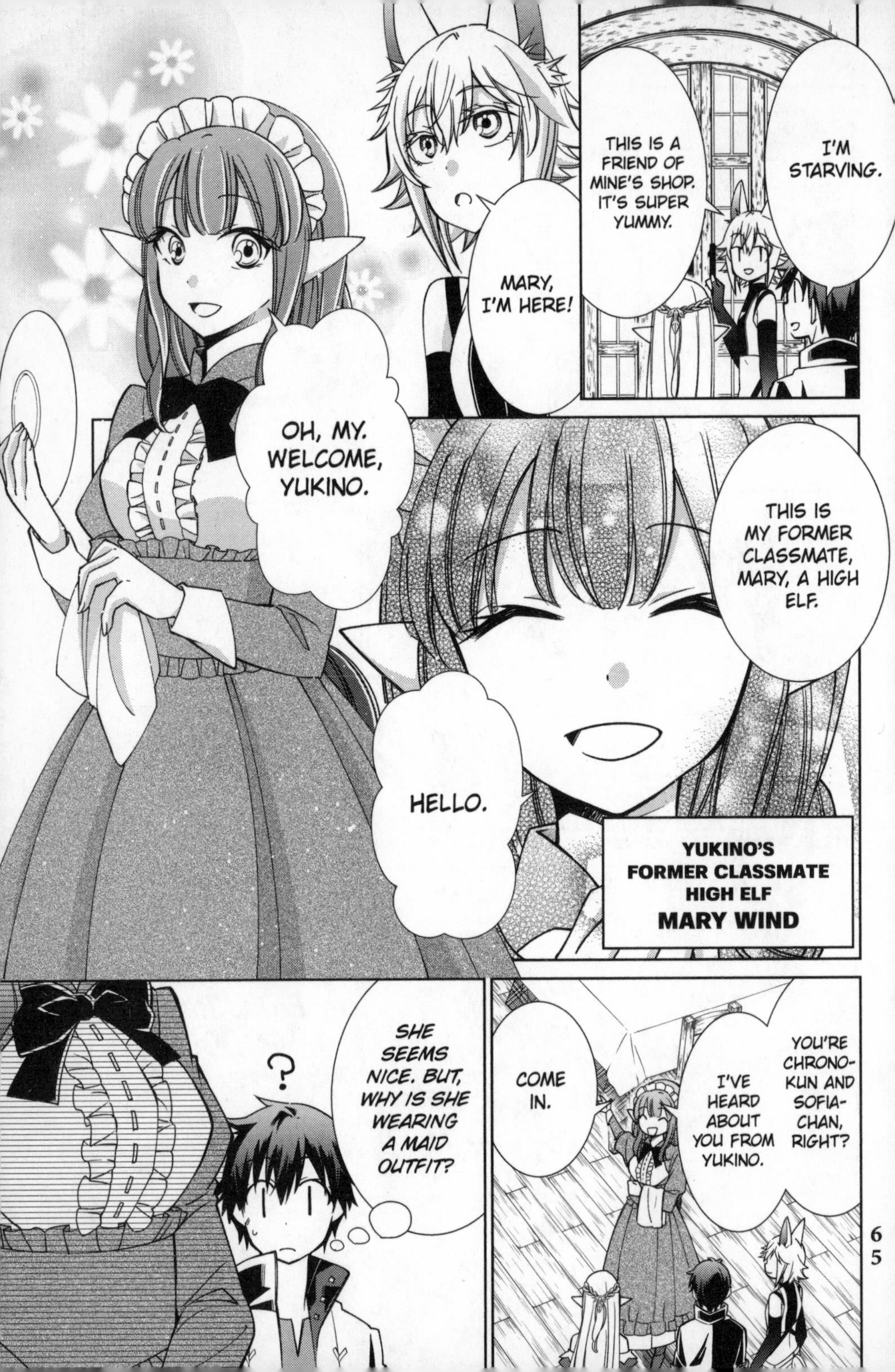
I'M STARVING.
THIS IS A FRIEND OF MINE'S SHOP. IT'S SUPER YUMMY.
MARY, I'M HERE!
OH, MY. WELCOME, YUKINO.
THIS IS MY FORMER CLASSMATE, MARY, A HIGH ELF.
HELLO.
YUKINO'S FORMER CLASSMATE HIGH ELF MARY WIND
YOU'RE CHRONO-KUN AND SOFIA-CHAN, RIGHT?
I'VE HEARD ABOUT YOU FROM YUKINO.
COME IN.
?
SHE SEEMS NICE. BUT, WHY IS SHE WEARING A MAID OUTFIT?

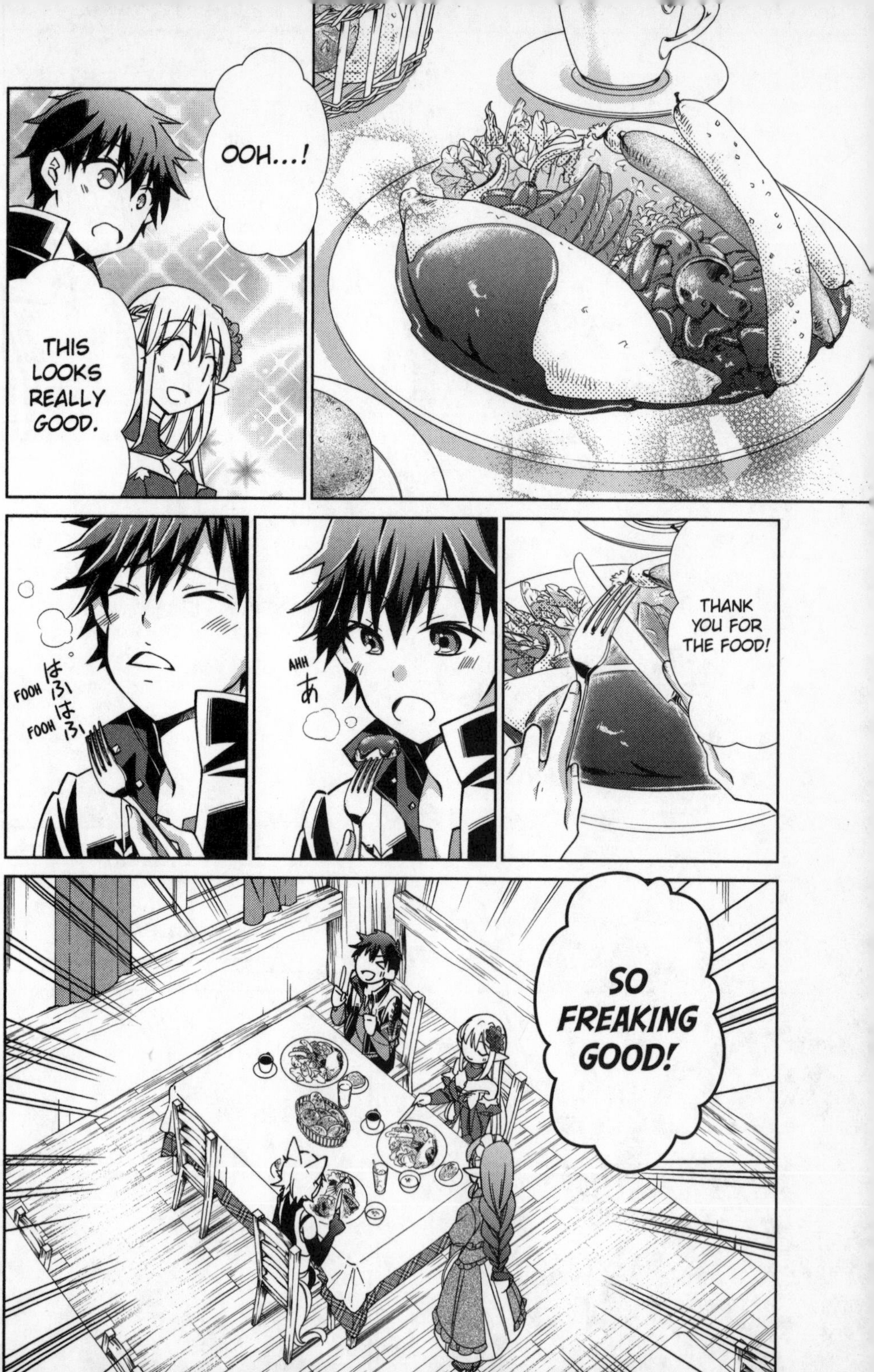
OOH...!
THIS LOOKS REALLY GOOD.
THANK YOU FOR THE FOOD!
AHH あ
FOOH はふ
FOOH はふ
SO FREAKING GOOD!

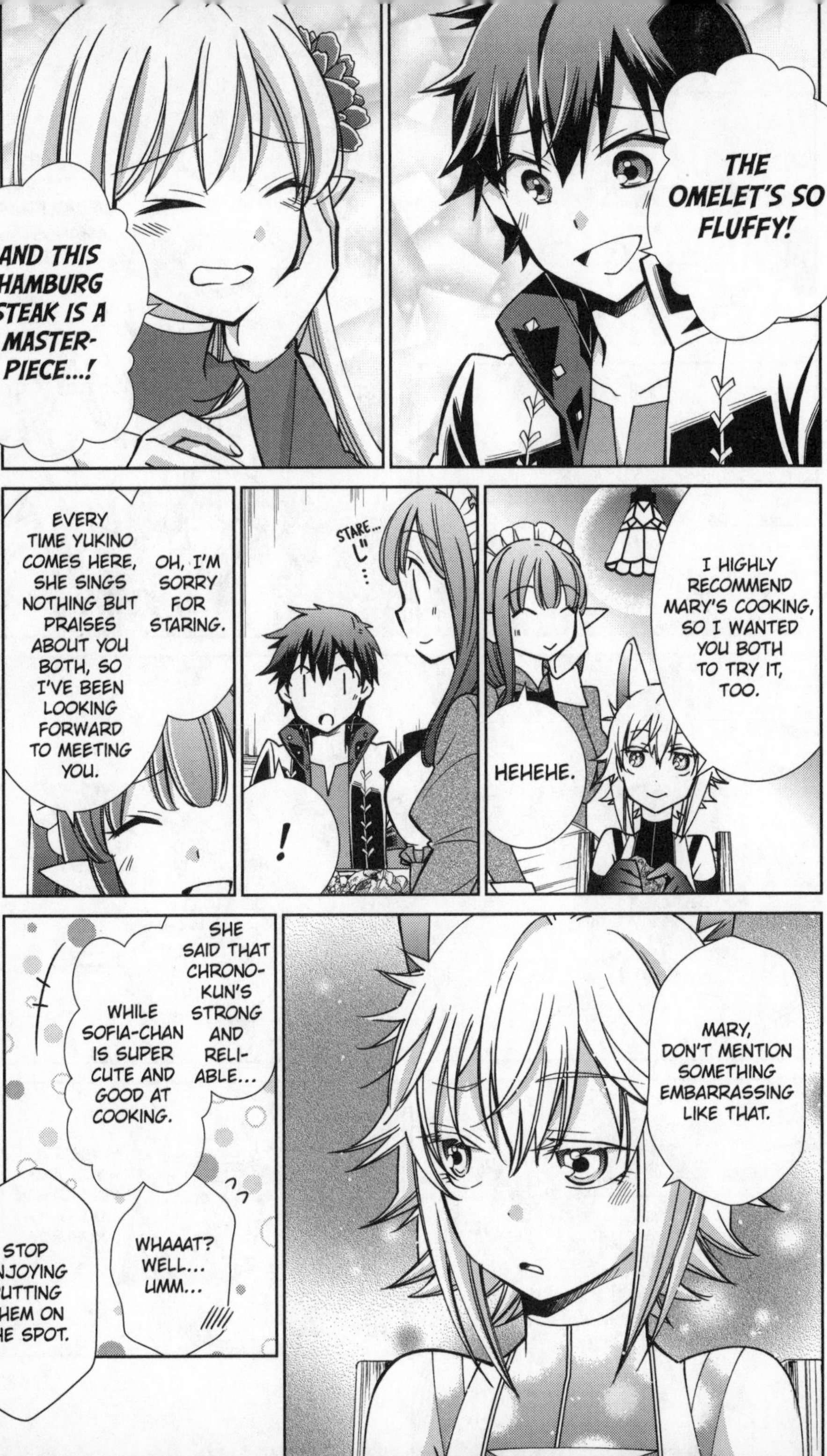
THE OMELET'S SO FLUFFY!
AND THIS HAMBURG STEAK IS A MASTER-PIECE...!
I HIGHLY RECOMMEND MARY'S COOKING, SO I WANTED YOU BOTH TO TRY IT, TOO.
HEHEHE.
STARE...
!
OH, I'M SORRY FOR STARING.
EVERY TIME YUKINO COMES HERE, SHE SINGS NOTHING BUT PRAISES ABOUT YOU BOTH, SO I'VE BEEN LOOKING FORWARD TO MEETING YOU.
MARY, DON'T MENTION SOMETHING EMBARRASSING LIKE THAT.
SHE SAID THAT CHRONO-KUN'S STRONG AND RELI-ABLE...
WHILE SOFIA-CHAN IS SUPER CUTE AND GOOD AT COOKING.
WHAAAT? WELL... UMM...
STOP ENJOYING PUTTING THEM ON THE SPOT.

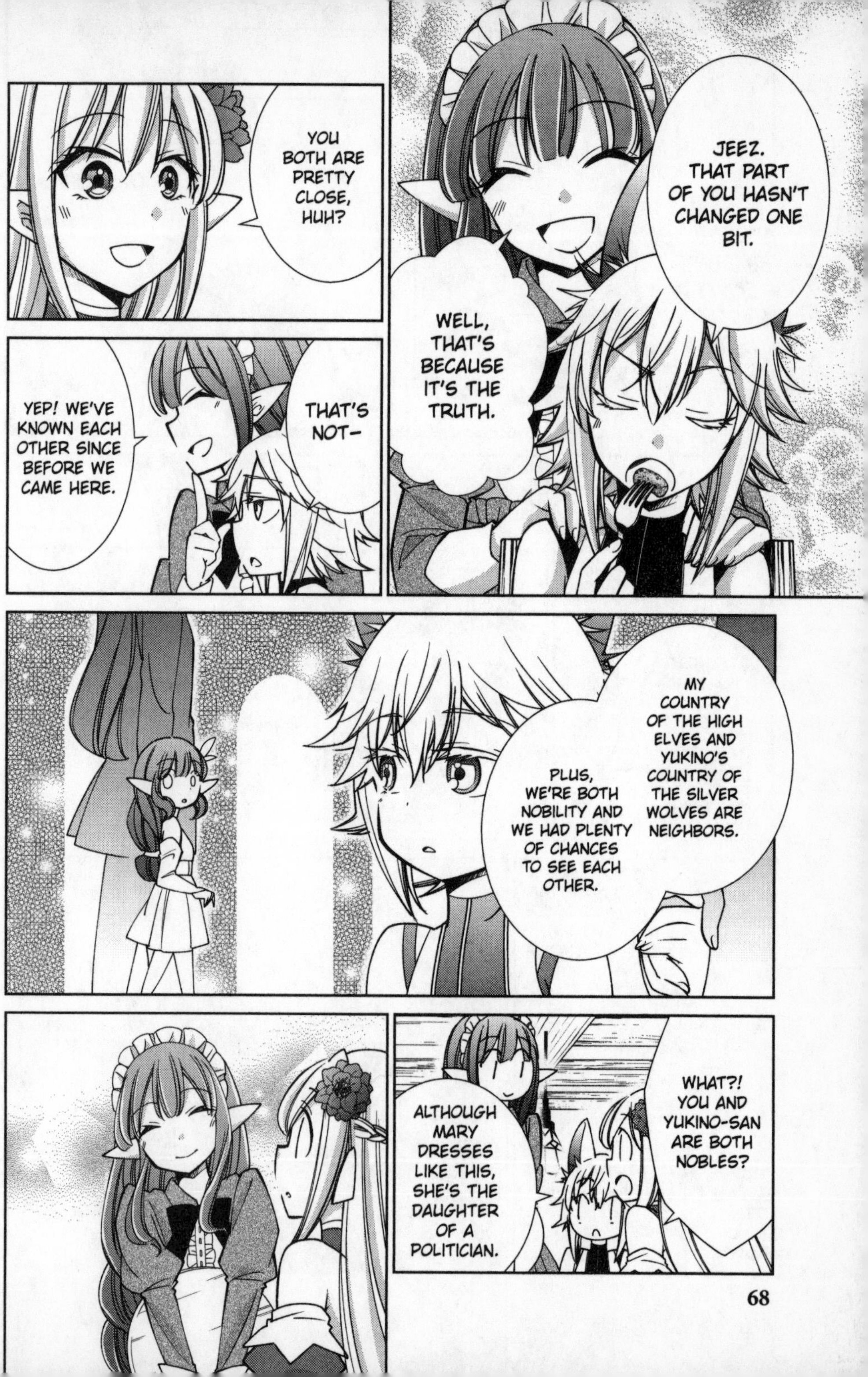
YOU BOTH ARE PRETTY CLOSE, HUH?
YEP! WE'VE KNOWN EACH OTHER SINCE BEFORE WE CAME HERE.
THAT'S NOT-
JEEZ. THAT PART OF YOU HASN'T CHANGED ONE BIT.
WELL, THAT'S BECAUSE IT'S THE TRUTH.
MY COUNTRY OF THE HIGH ELVES AND YUKINO'S COUNTRY OF THE SILVER WOLVES ARE NEIGHBORS.
PLUS, WE'RE BOTH NOBILITY AND WE HAD PLENTY OF CHANCES TO SEE EACH OTHER.
WHAT?! YOU AND YUKINO-SAN ARE BOTH NOBLES?
ALTHOUGH MARY DRESSES LIKE THIS, SHE'S THE DAUGHTER OF A POLITICIAN.

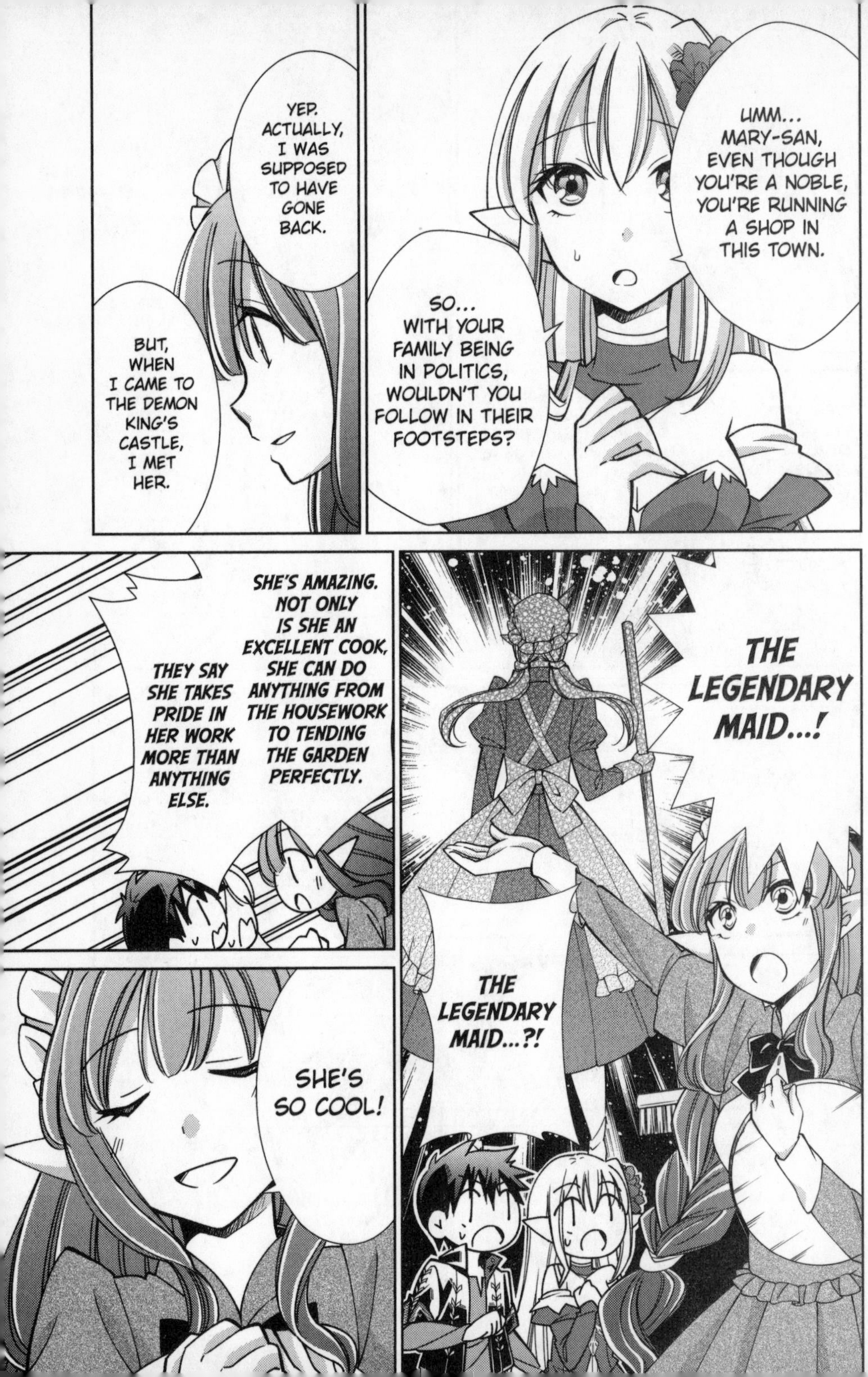
UMM... MARY-SAN, EVEN THOUGH YOU'RE A NOBLE, YOU'RE RUNNING A SHOP IN THIS TOWN.
SO... WITH YOUR FAMILY BEING IN POLITICS, WOULDN'T YOU FOLLOW IN THEIR FOOTSTEPS?
YEP. ACTUALLY, I WAS SUPPOSED TO HAVE GONE BACK.
BUT, WHEN I CAME TO THE DEMON KING'S CASTLE, I MET HER.
THE LEGENDARY MAID...!
THE LEGENDARY MAID...?!
SHE'S AMAZING. NOT ONLY IS SHE AN EXCELLENT COOK, SHE CAN DO ANYTHING FROM THE HOUSEWORK TO TENDING THE GARDEN PERFECTLY.
THEY SAY SHE TAKES PRIDE IN HER WORK MORE THAN ANYTHING ELSE.
SHE'S SO COOL!

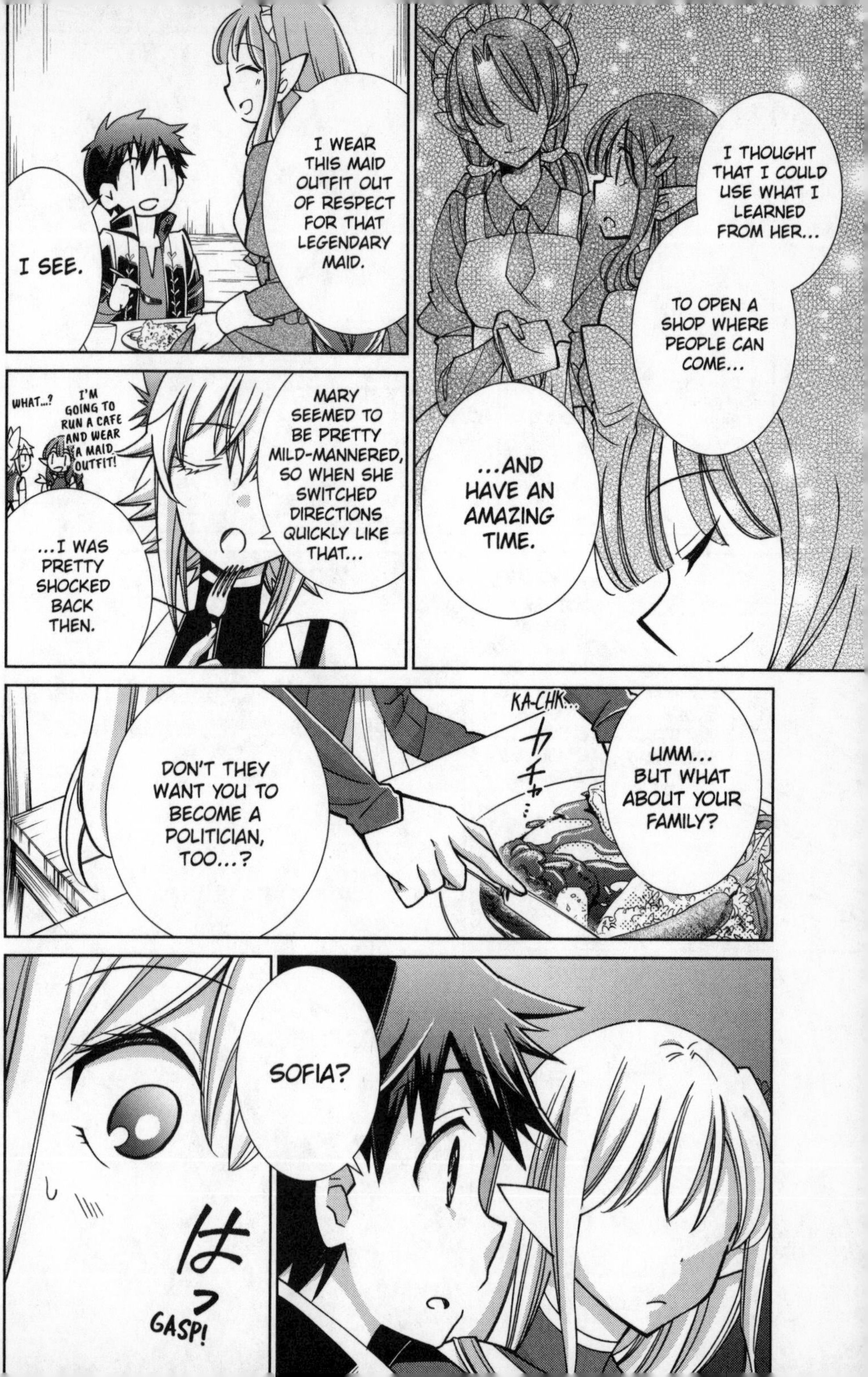
I THOUGHT THAT I COULD USE WHAT I LEARNED FROM HER...
TO OPEN A SHOP WHERE PEOPLE CAN COME...
...AND HAVE AN AMAZING TIME.
I WEAR THIS MAID OUTFIT OUT OF RESPECT FOR THAT LEGENDARY MAID.
I SEE.
MARY SEEMED TO BE PRETTY MILD-MANNERED, SO WHEN SHE SWITCHED DIRECTIONS QUICKLY LIKE THAT...
I'M GOING TO RUN A CAFE AND WEAR A MAID OUTFIT!
WHAT...?
...I WAS PRETTY SHOCKED BACK THEN.
UMM... BUT WHAT ABOUT YOUR FAMILY?
KA-CHK...
カチャ
DON'T THEY WANT YOU TO BECOME A POLITICIAN, TOO...?
SOFIA?
はっ
GASP!

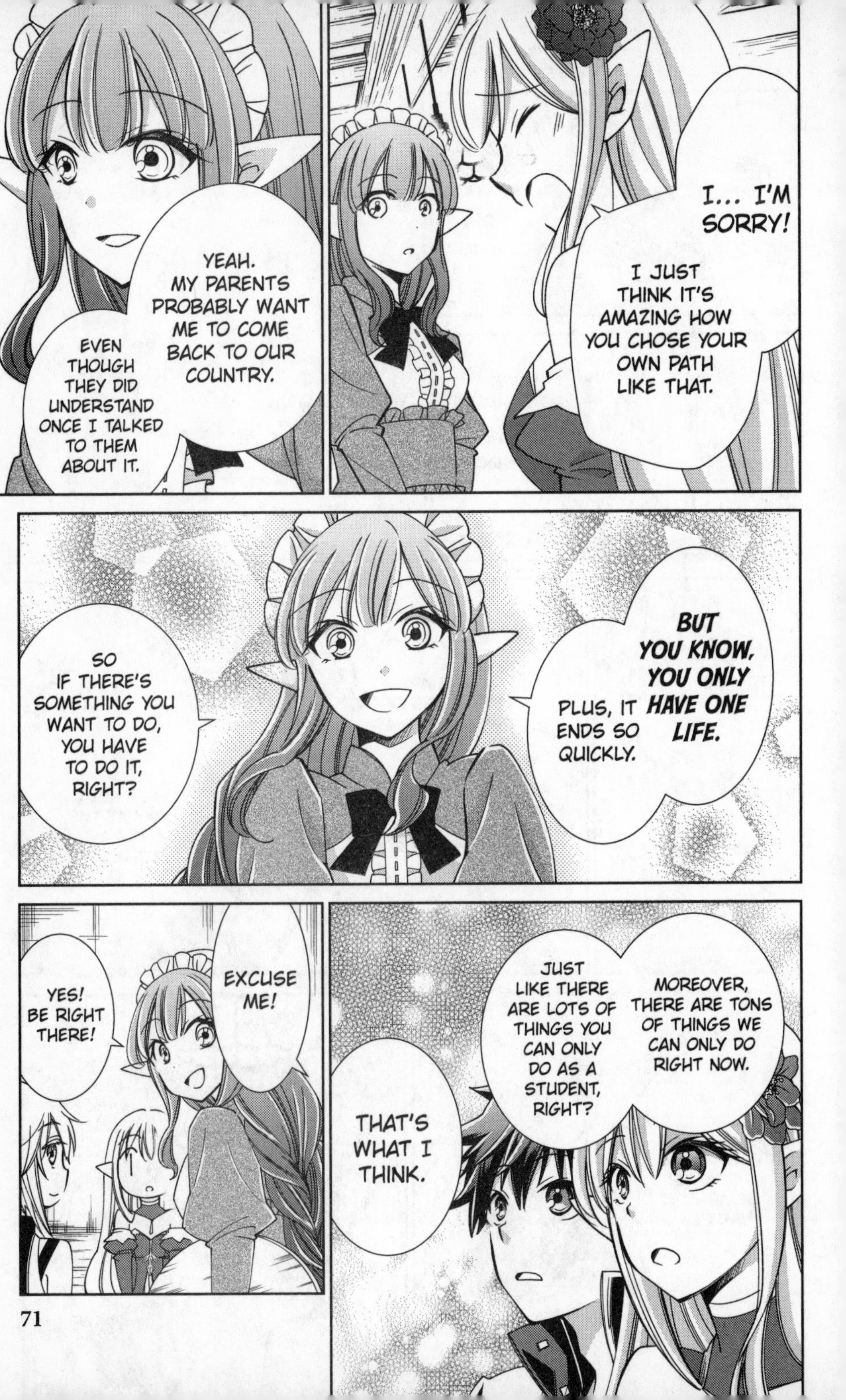
I… I'M SORRY!
I JUST THINK IT'S AMAZING HOW YOU CHOSE YOUR OWN PATH LIKE THAT.
YEAH. MY PARENTS PROBABLY WANT ME TO COME BACK TO OUR COUNTRY.
EVEN THOUGH THEY DID UNDERSTAND ONCE I TALKED TO THEM ABOUT IT.
BUT YOU KNOW, YOU ONLY HAVE ONE LIFE.
PLUS, IT ENDS SO QUICKLY.
SO IF THERE'S SOMETHING YOU WANT TO DO, YOU HAVE TO DO IT, RIGHT?
MOREOVER, THERE ARE TONS OF THINGS WE CAN ONLY DO RIGHT NOW.
JUST LIKE THERE ARE LOTS OF THINGS YOU CAN ONLY DO AS A STUDENT, RIGHT?
THAT'S WHAT I THINK.
EXCUSE ME!
YES! BE RIGHT THERE!

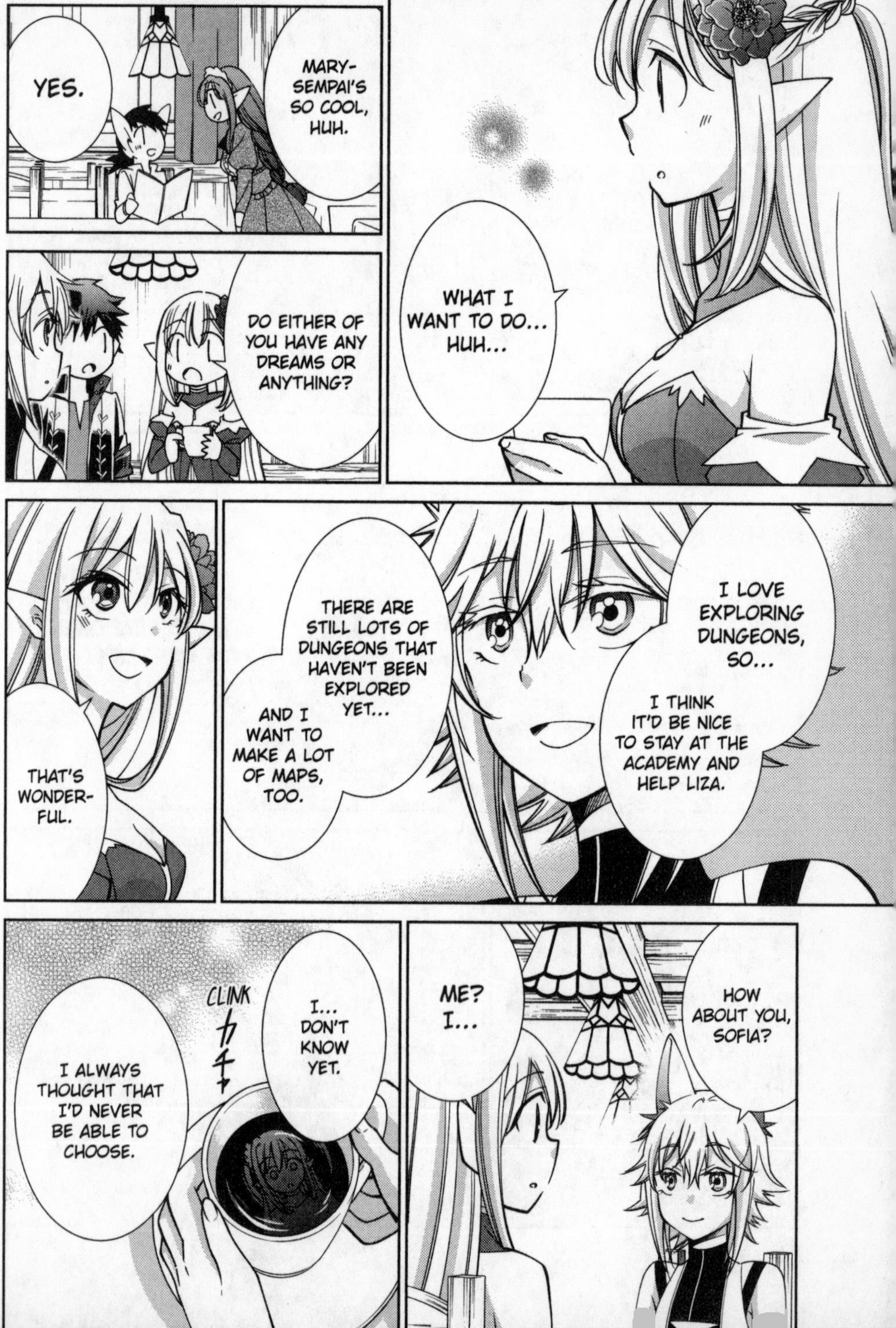
WHAT I WANT TO DO... HUH...
MARY-SEMPAI'S SO COOL, HUH.
YES.
DO EITHER OF YOU HAVE ANY DREAMS OR ANYTHING?
I LOVE EXPLORING DUNGEONS, SO...
I THINK IT'D BE NICE TO STAY AT THE ACADEMY AND HELP LIZA.
THERE ARE STILL LOTS OF DUNGEONS THAT HAVEN'T BEEN EXPLORED YET...
AND I WANT TO MAKE A LOT OF MAPS, TOO.
THAT'S WONDERFUL.
HOW ABOUT YOU, SOFIA?
ME? I...
I... DON'T KNOW YET.
CLINK
カチャ
I ALWAYS THOUGHT THAT I'D NEVER BE ABLE TO CHOOSE.

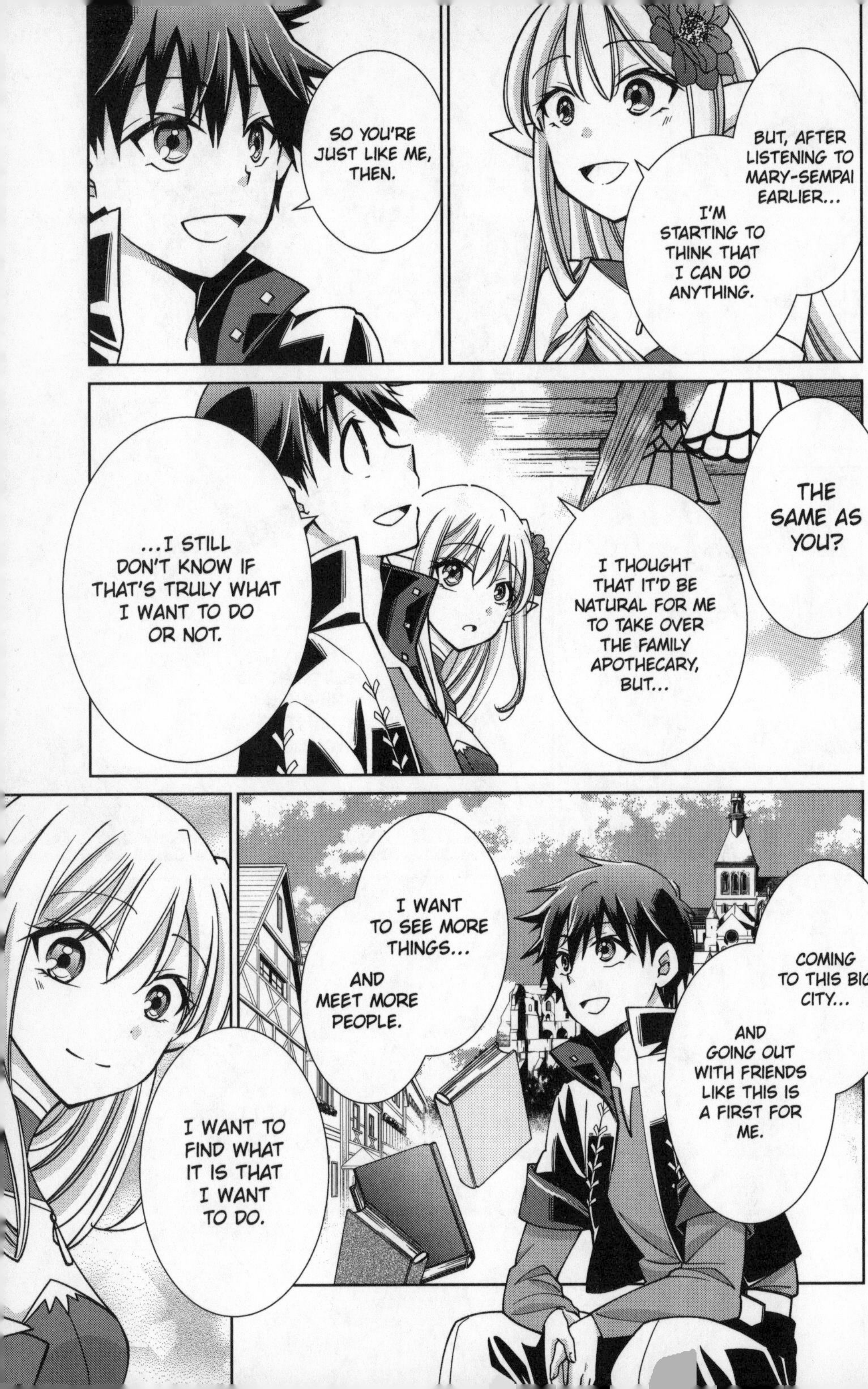
BUT, AFTER LISTENING TO MARY-SEMPAI EARLIER...
I'M STARTING TO THINK THAT I CAN DO ANYTHING.
SO YOU'RE JUST LIKE ME, THEN.
THE SAME AS YOU?
I THOUGHT THAT IT'D BE NATURAL FOR ME TO TAKE OVER THE FAMILY APOTHECARY, BUT...
...I STILL DON'T KNOW IF THAT'S TRULY WHAT I WANT TO DO OR NOT.
COMING TO THIS BIG CITY...
AND GOING OUT WITH FRIENDS LIKE THIS IS A FIRST FOR ME.
I WANT TO SEE MORE THINGS...
AND MEET MORE PEOPLE.
I WANT TO FIND WHAT IT IS THAT I WANT TO DO.

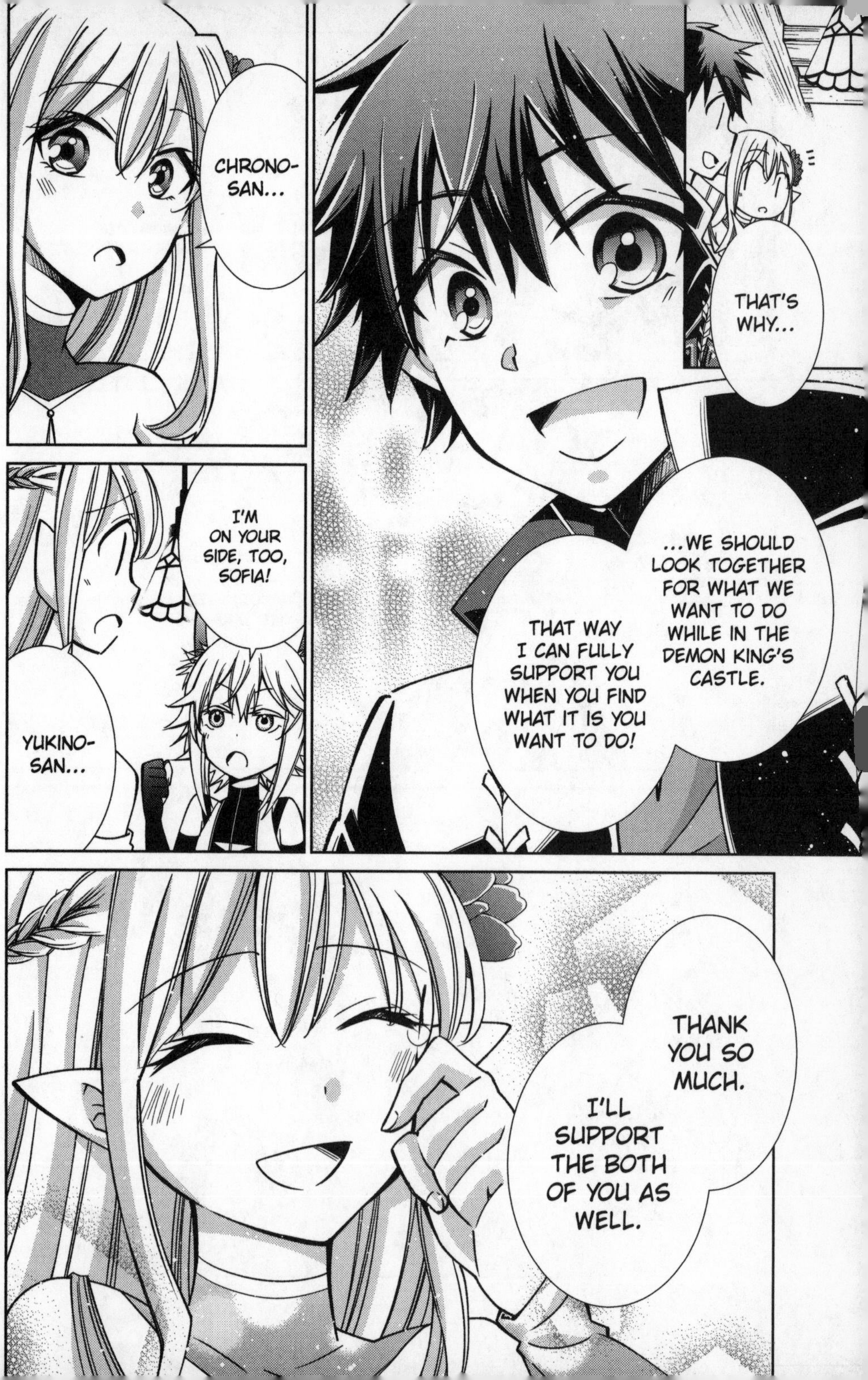
THAT'S WHY...
...WE SHOULD LOOK TOGETHER FOR WHAT WE WANT TO DO WHILE IN THE DEMON KING'S CASTLE.
THAT WAY I CAN FULLY SUPPORT YOU WHEN YOU FIND WHAT IT IS YOU WANT TO DO!
CHRONO-SAN...
I'M ON YOUR SIDE, TOO, SOFIA!
YUKINO-SAN...
THANK YOU SO MUCH.
I'LL SUPPORT THE BOTH OF YOU AS WELL.

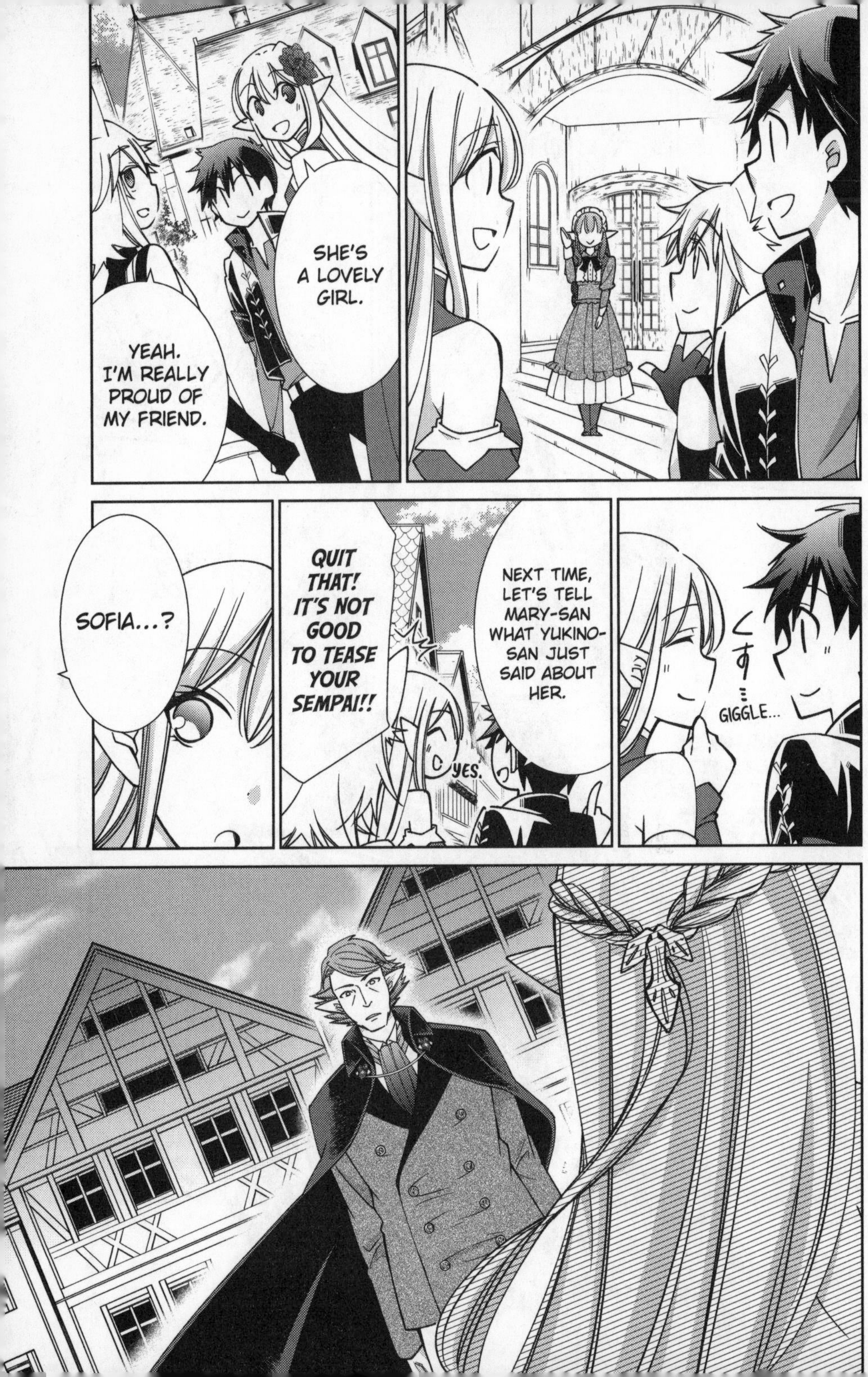

SHE'S A LOVELY GIRL.
YEAH. I'M REALLY PROUD OF MY FRIEND.
くすっ
GIGGLE...
NEXT TIME, LET'S TELL MARY-SAN WHAT YUKINO-SAN JUST SAID ABOUT HER.
QUIT THAT! IT'S NOT GOOD TO TEASE YOUR SEMPAI!!
YES.
SOFIA...?

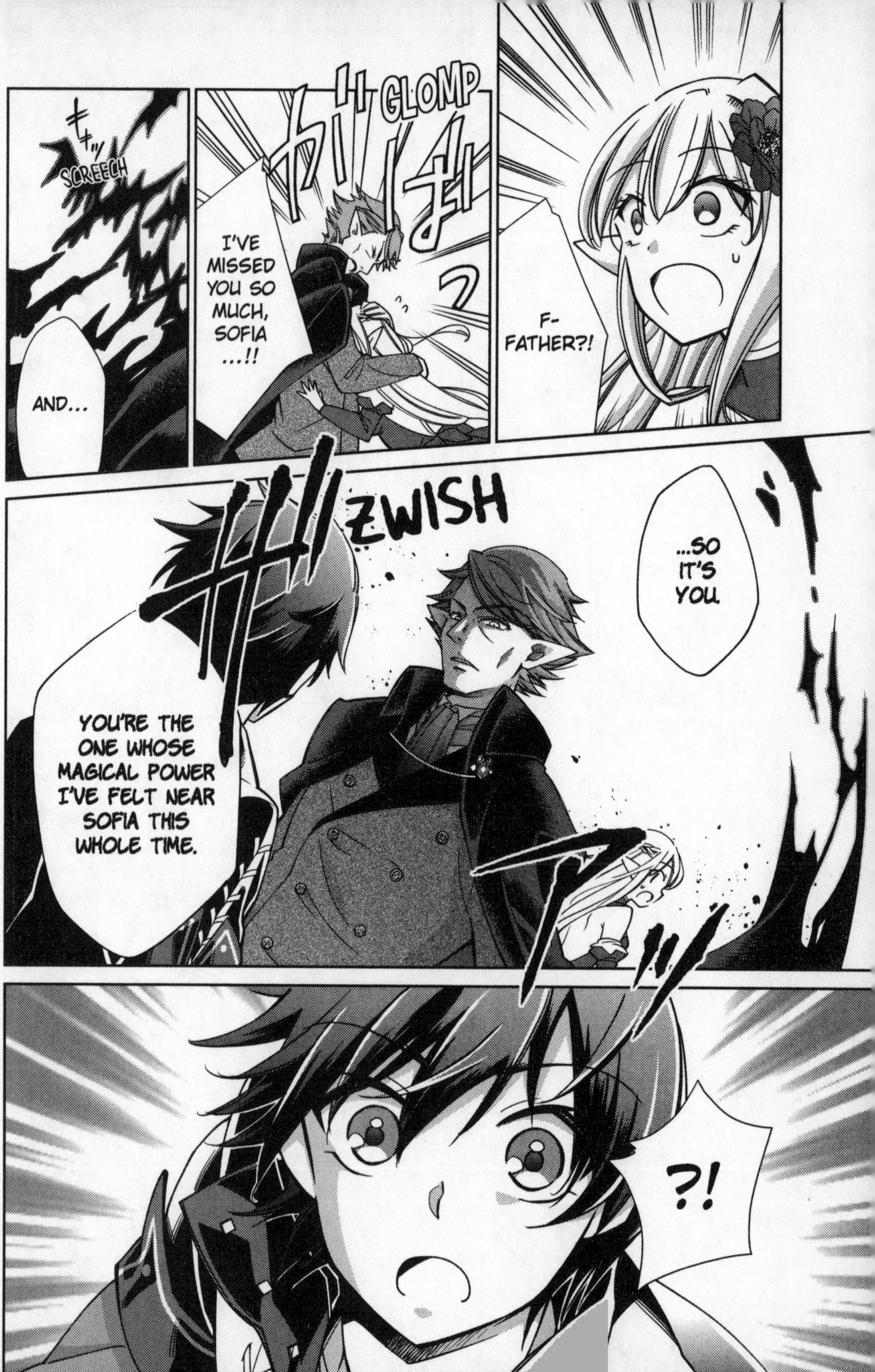
F-
FATHER?!
GLOMP
I'VE MISSED YOU SO MUCH, SOFIA ...!!
SCREECH
AND...
...SO IT'S YOU.
ZWISH
YOU'RE THE ONE WHOSE MAGICAL POWER I'VE FELT NEAR SOFIA THIS WHOLE TIME.
?!

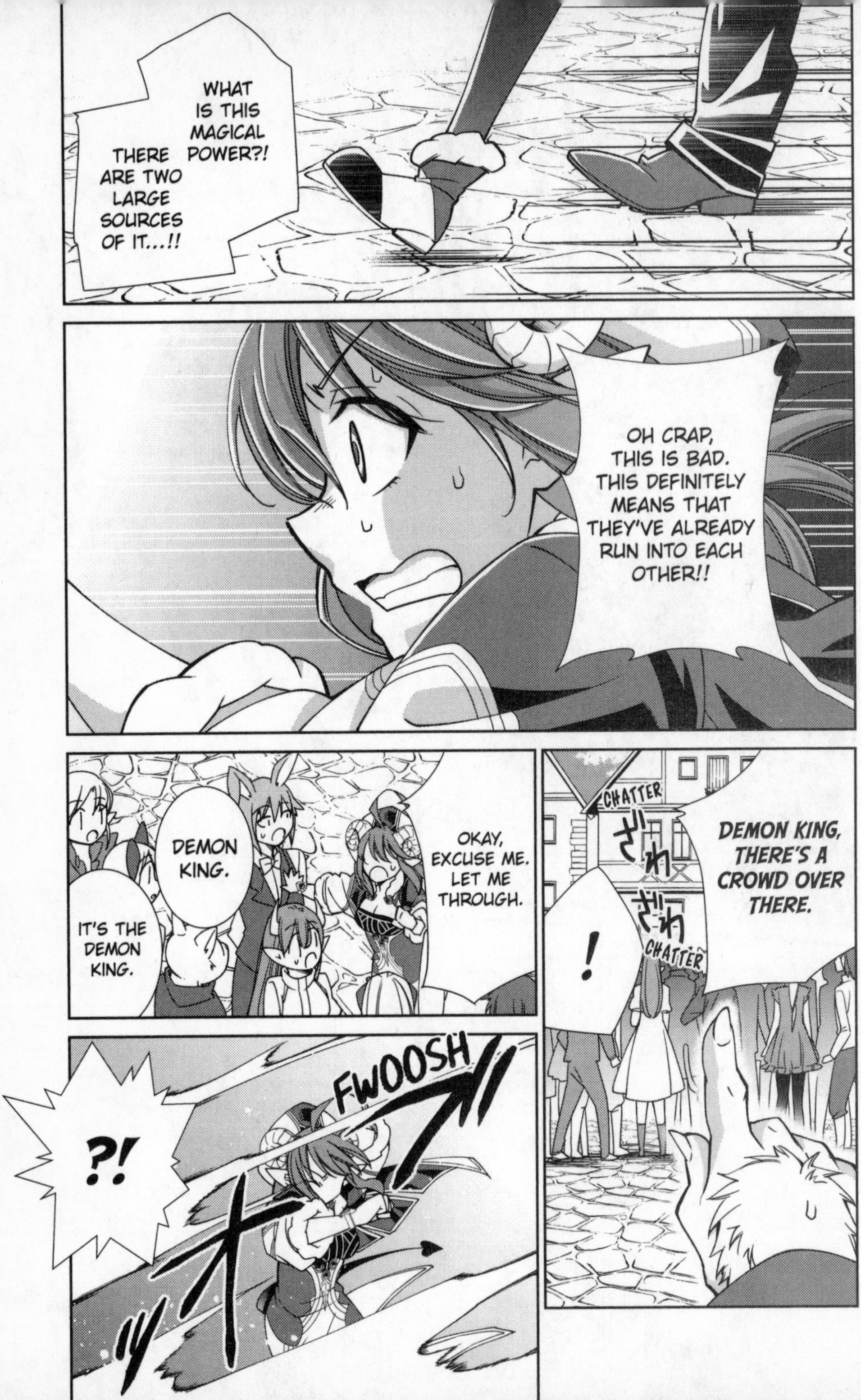
WHAT IS THIS MAGICAL POWER?!
THERE ARE TWO LARGE SOURCES OF IT...!!
OH CRAP, THIS IS BAD. THIS DEFINITELY MEANS THAT THEY'VE ALREADY RUN INTO EACH OTHER!!
CHATTER
ざわ
ざわ
CHATTER
DEMON KING, THERE'S A CROWD OVER THERE.
!
OKAY, EXCUSE ME. LET ME THROUGH.
DEMON KING.
IT'S THE DEMON KING.
FWOOSH
?!

SMACK

SMACK

SMACK

SMACK

SMACK

SMACK

...I-I WAS TOO LATE...

SO-SOFIA-CHAN, I'M SORRY. I CAME HERE AS QUICKLY AS POSSIBLE, BUT...

LIZA-SAN! PROFESSOR DANTE!!

THOSE... TWO ARE SOMETHING ELSE...

WHAT'S GOING ON?!

CHATTER

CHATTER

SLUMP

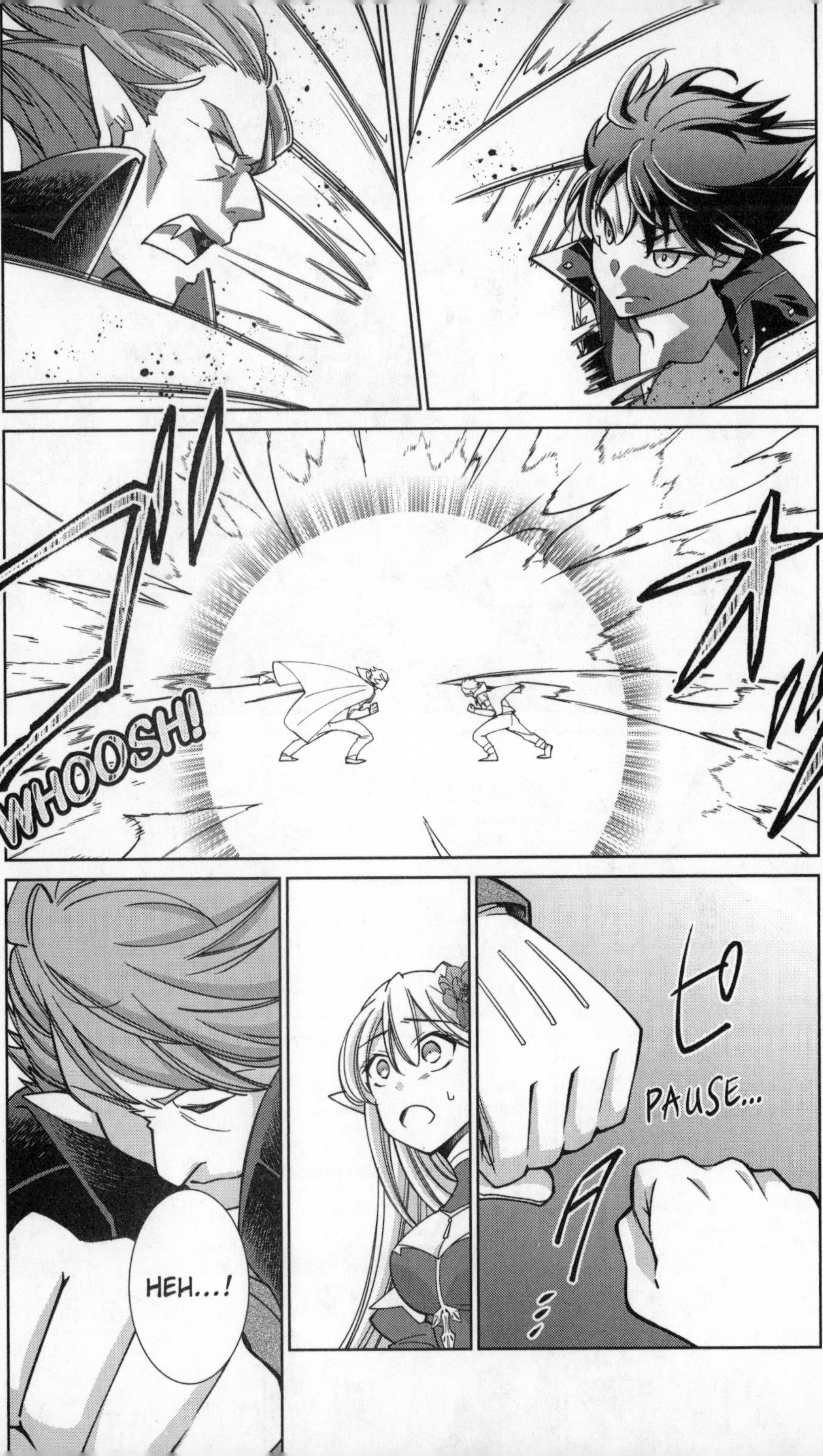
WHOOSH!
PAUSE...
HEH...!

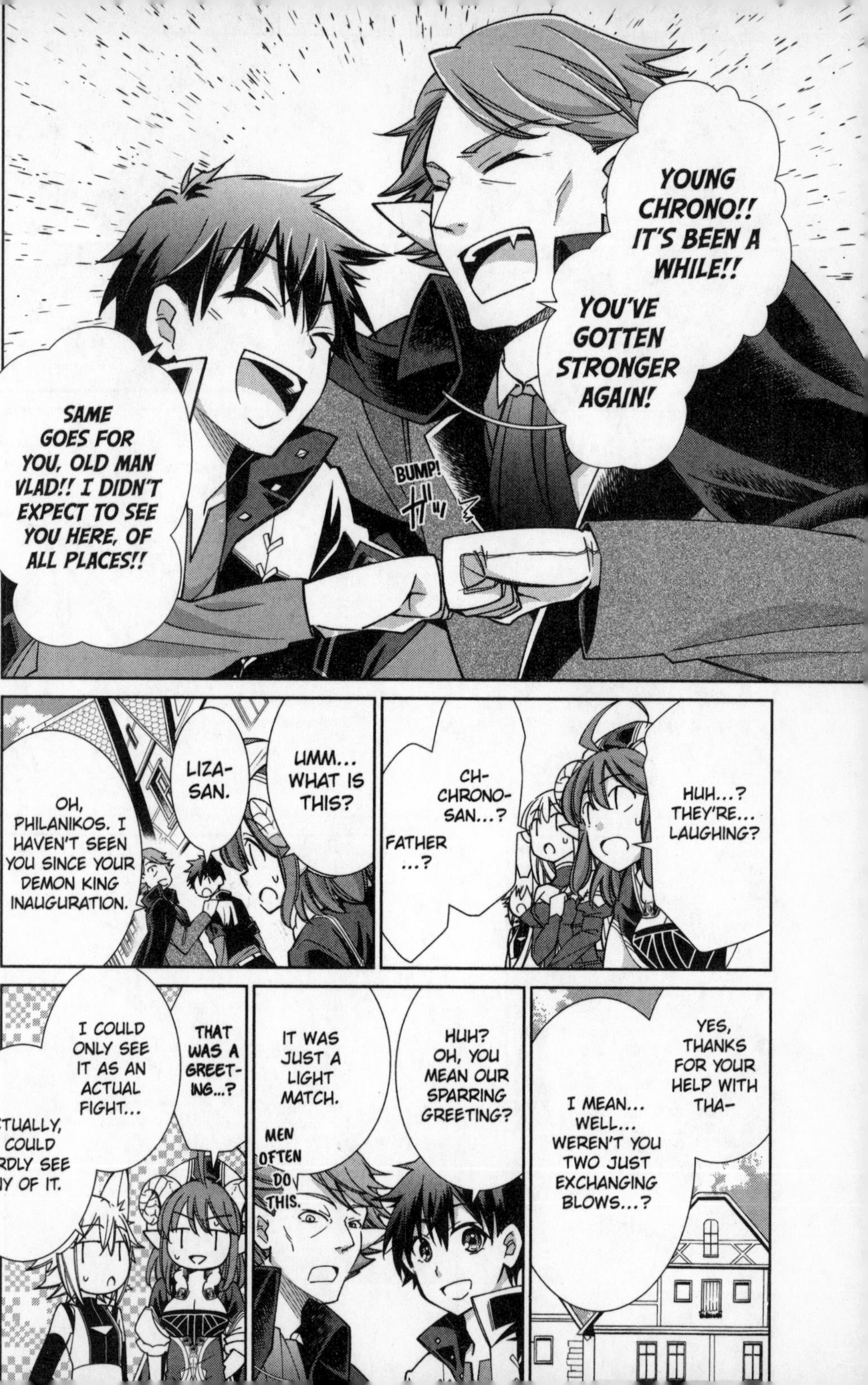
YOUNG CHRONO!! IT'S BEEN A WHILE!!
YOU'VE GOTTEN STRONGER AGAIN!
BUMP!
ガッ
SAME GOES FOR YOU, OLD MAN VLAD!! I DIDN'T EXPECT TO SEE YOU HERE, OF ALL PLACES!!
HUH...? THEY'RE... LAUGHING?
CH-CHRONO-SAN...?
FATHER...?
UMM... WHAT IS THIS?
LIZA-SAN.
OH, PHILANIKOS. I HAVEN'T SEEN YOU SINCE YOUR DEMON KING INAUGURATION.
YES, THANKS FOR YOUR HELP WITH THA-
I MEAN... WELL... WEREN'T YOU TWO JUST EXCHANGING BLOWS...?
HUH? OH, YOU MEAN OUR SPARRING GREETING?
IT WAS JUST A LIGHT MATCH.
MEN OFTEN DO THIS.
THAT WAS A GREETING...?
I COULD ONLY SEE IT AS AN ACTUAL FIGHT...
ACTUALLY, I COULD HARDLY SEE ANY OF IT.

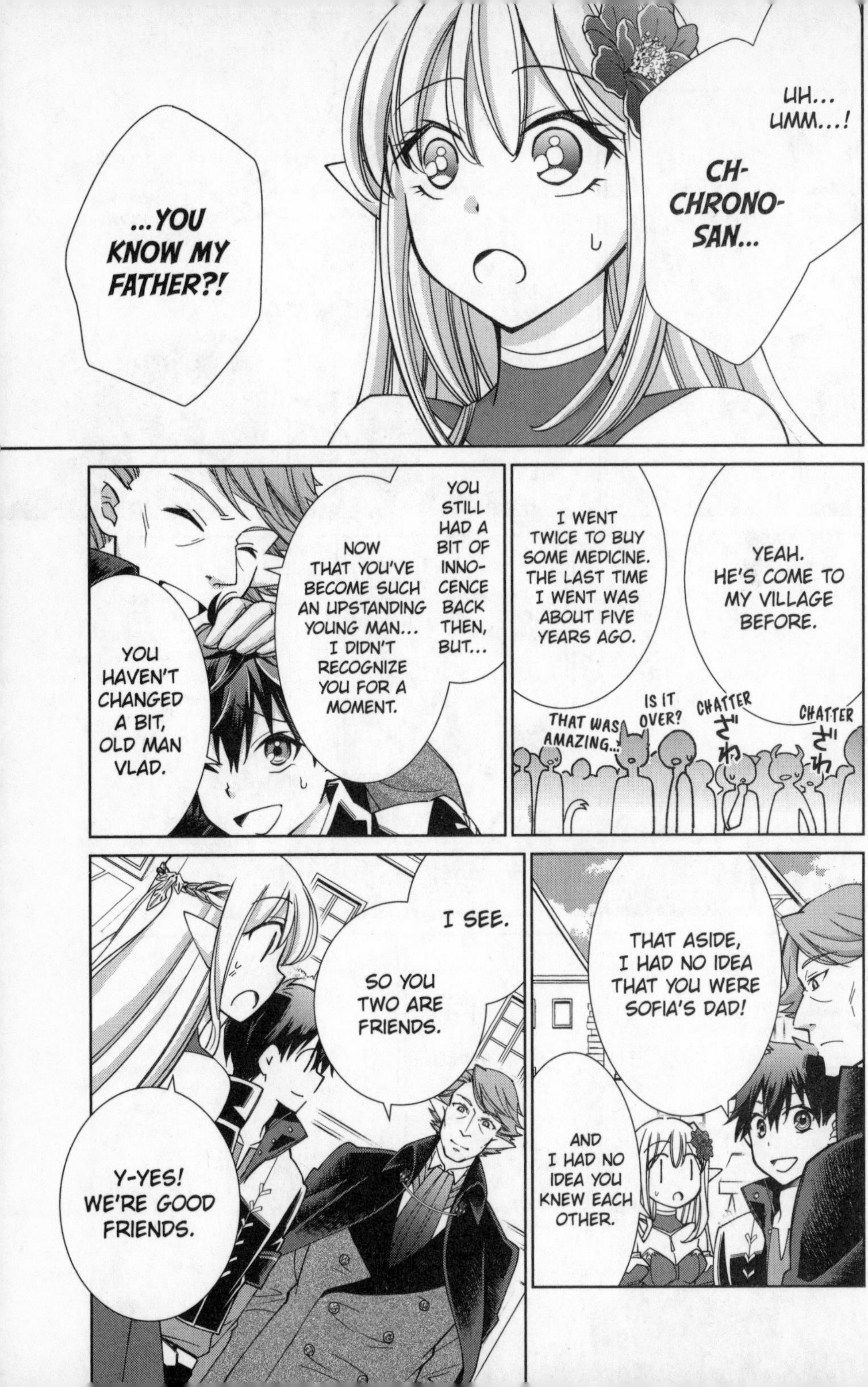
UH... UMM...!
CH-CHRONO-SAN...
...YOU KNOW MY FATHER?!
YEAH. HE'S COME TO MY VILLAGE BEFORE.
I WENT TWICE TO BUY SOME MEDICINE. THE LAST TIME I WENT WAS ABOUT FIVE YEARS AGO.
CHATTER ざわ
CHATTER ざわ
IS IT OVER?
THAT WAS AMAZING...
YOU STILL HAD A BIT OF INNO-CENCE BACK THEN, BUT...
NOW THAT YOU'VE BECOME SUCH AN UPSTANDING YOUNG MAN... I DIDN'T RECOGNIZE YOU FOR A MOMENT.
YOU HAVEN'T CHANGED A BIT, OLD MAN VLAD.
THAT ASIDE, I HAD NO IDEA THAT YOU WERE SOFIA'S DAD!
AND I HAD NO IDEA YOU KNEW EACH OTHER.
I SEE.
SO YOU TWO ARE FRIENDS.
Y-YES! WE'RE GOOD FRIENDS.

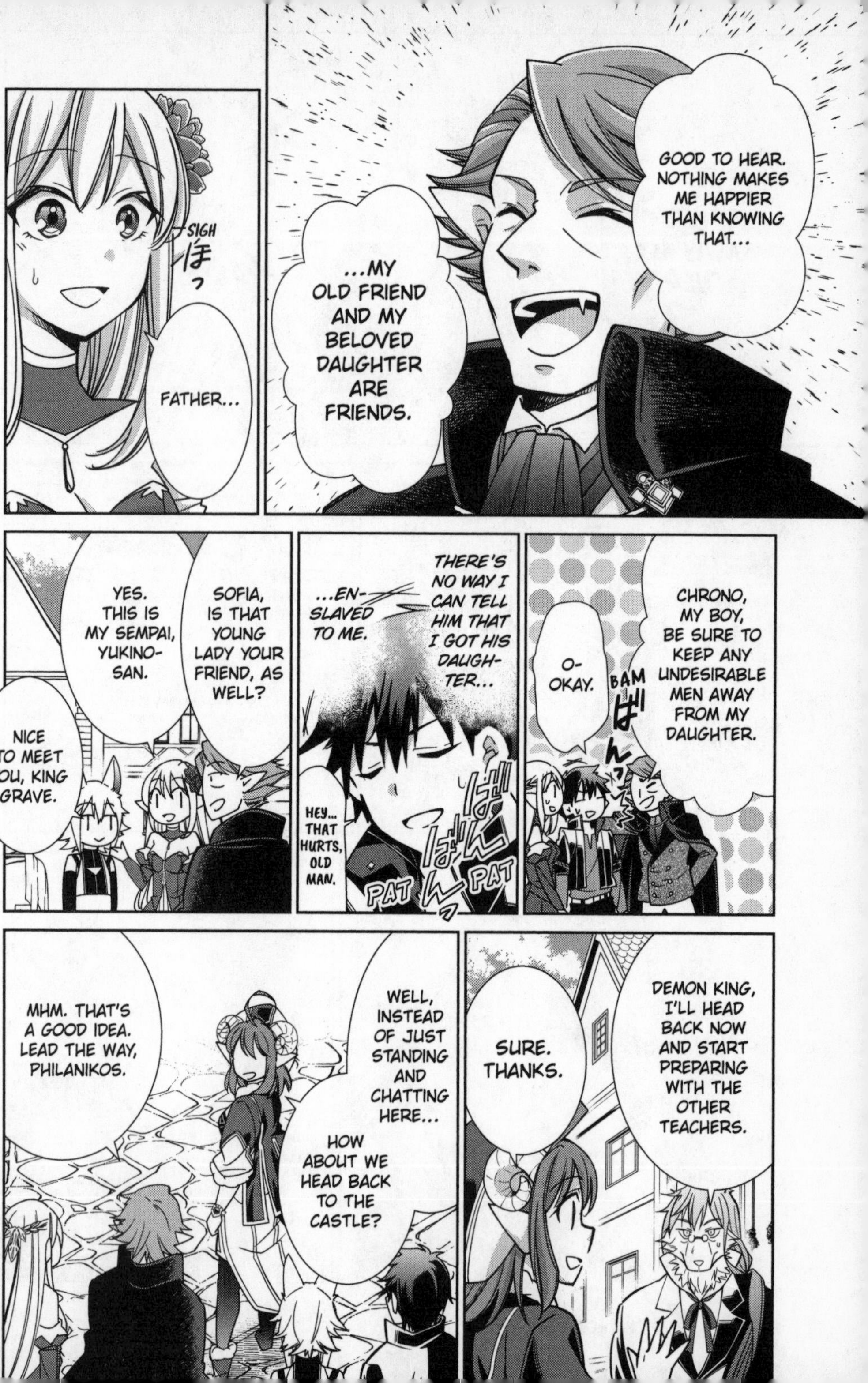
GOOD TO HEAR. NOTHING MAKES ME HAPPIER THAN KNOWING THAT...
...MY OLD FRIEND AND MY BELOVED DAUGHTER ARE FRIENDS.
SIGH
FATHER...
CHRONO, MY BOY, BE SURE TO KEEP ANY UNDESIRABLE MEN AWAY FROM MY DAUGHTER.
BAM
O-OKAY.
THERE'S NO WAY I CAN TELL HIM THAT I GOT HIS DAUGHTER...
...EN-SLAVED TO ME.
HEY... THAT HURTS, OLD MAN.
PAT
PAT
SOFIA, IS THAT YOUNG LADY YOUR FRIEND, AS WELL?
YES. THIS IS MY SEMPAI, YUKINO-SAN.
NICE TO MEET YOU, KING GRAVE.
DEMON KING, I'LL HEAD BACK NOW AND START PREPARING WITH THE OTHER TEACHERS.
SURE. THANKS.
WELL, INSTEAD OF JUST STANDING AND CHATTING HERE...
HOW ABOUT WE HEAD BACK TO THE CASTLE?
MHM. THAT'S A GOOD IDEA. LEAD THE WAY, PHILANIKOS.

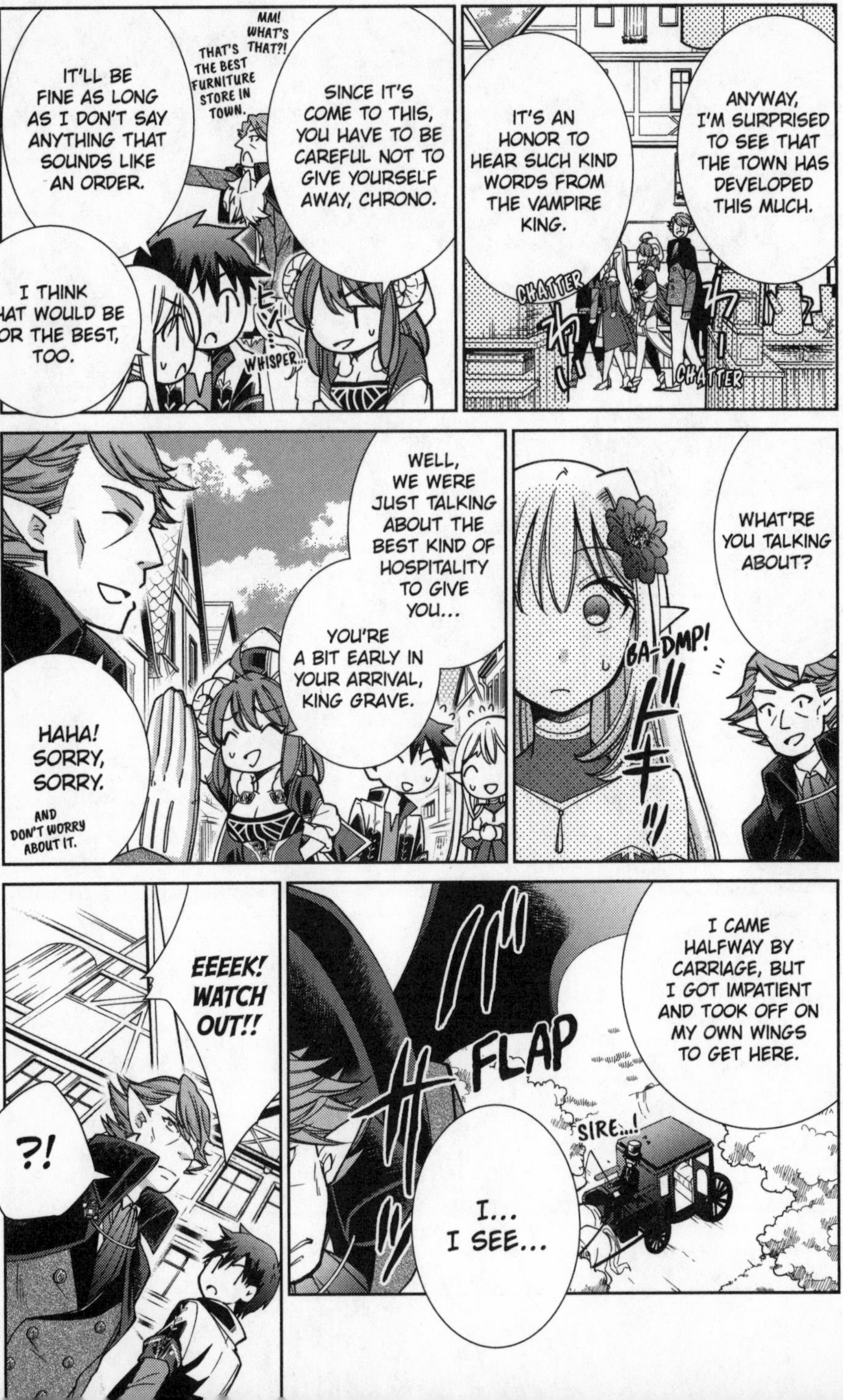
ANYWAY, I'M SURPRISED TO SEE THAT THE TOWN HAS DEVELOPED THIS MUCH.
IT'S AN HONOR TO HEAR SUCH KIND WORDS FROM THE VAMPIRE KING.
CHATTER
CHATTER
SINCE IT'S COME TO THIS, YOU HAVE TO BE CAREFUL NOT TO GIVE YOURSELF AWAY, CHRONO.
MM! WHAT'S THAT?!
THAT'S THE BEST FURNITURE STORE IN TOWN.
IT'LL BE FINE AS LONG AS I DON'T SAY ANYTHING THAT SOUNDS LIKE AN ORDER.
I THINK THAT WOULD BE FOR THE BEST, TOO.
WHISPER...
WHAT'RE YOU TALKING ABOUT?
BA-DMP!
WELL, WE WERE JUST TALKING ABOUT THE BEST KIND OF HOSPITALITY TO GIVE YOU...
YOU'RE A BIT EARLY IN YOUR ARRIVAL, KING GRAVE.
HAHA! SORRY, SORRY.
AND DON'T WORRY ABOUT IT.
I CAME HALFWAY BY CARRIAGE, BUT I GOT IMPATIENT AND TOOK OFF ON MY OWN WINGS TO GET HERE.
FLAP
SIRE...!
I... I SEE...
EEEEK! WATCH OUT!!
?!

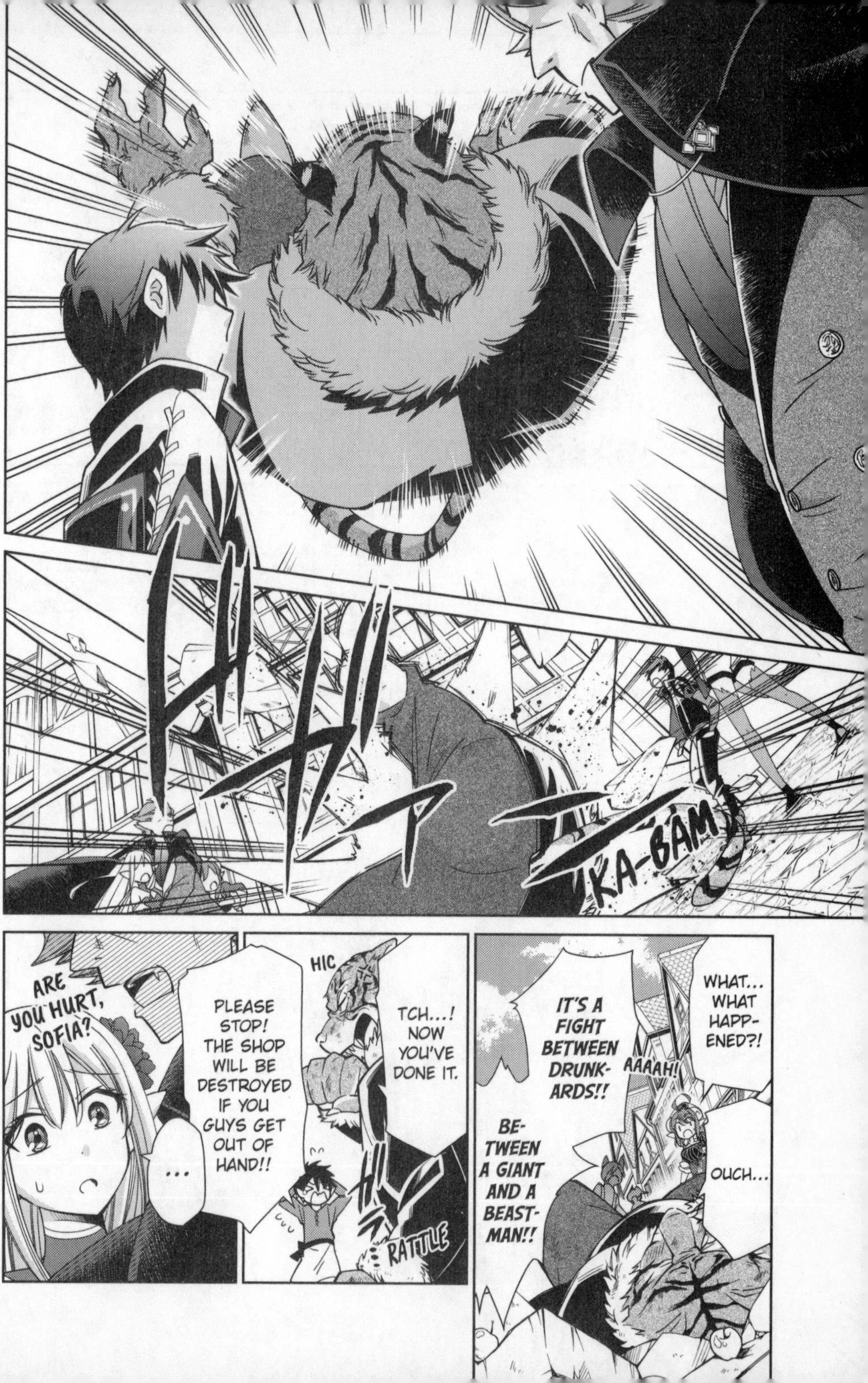
KA-BAM
WHAT... WHAT HAPPENED?!
AAAAH!
IT'S A FIGHT BETWEEN DRUNKARDS!!
BETWEEN A GIANT AND A BEASTMAN!!
OUCH...
HIC
TCH...! NOW YOU'VE DONE IT.
PLEASE STOP! THE SHOP WILL BE DESTROYED IF YOU GUYS GET OUT OF HAND!!
RATTLE
ARE YOU HURT, SOFIA?
...

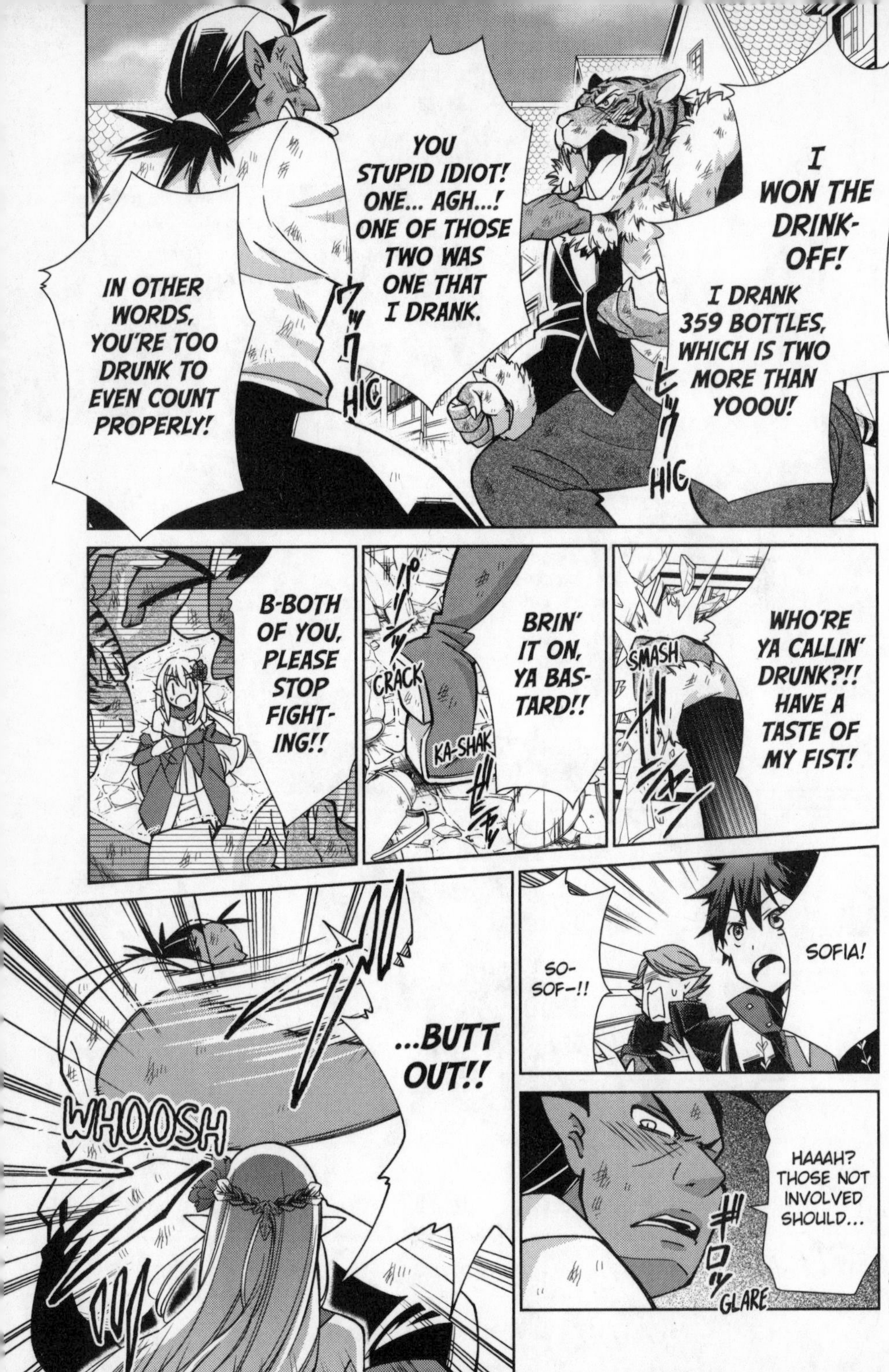
I WON THE DRINK-OFF!
I DRANK 359 BOTTLES, WHICH IS TWO MORE THAN YOOOU!
HIC
YOU STUPID IDIOT! ONE... AGH...! ONE OF THOSE TWO WAS ONE THAT I DRANK.
HIC
IN OTHER WORDS, YOU'RE TOO DRUNK TO EVEN COUNT PROPERLY!
WHO'RE YA CALLIN' DRUNK?!! HAVE A TASTE OF MY FIST!
SMASH
BRIN' IT ON, YA BASTARD!!
CRACK
KA-SHAK
B-BOTH OF YOU, PLEASE STOP FIGHTING!!
SOFIA!
SO- SOF-!!
HAAAH? THOSE NOT INVOLVED SHOULD...
GLARE
...BUTT OUT!!
WHOOSH

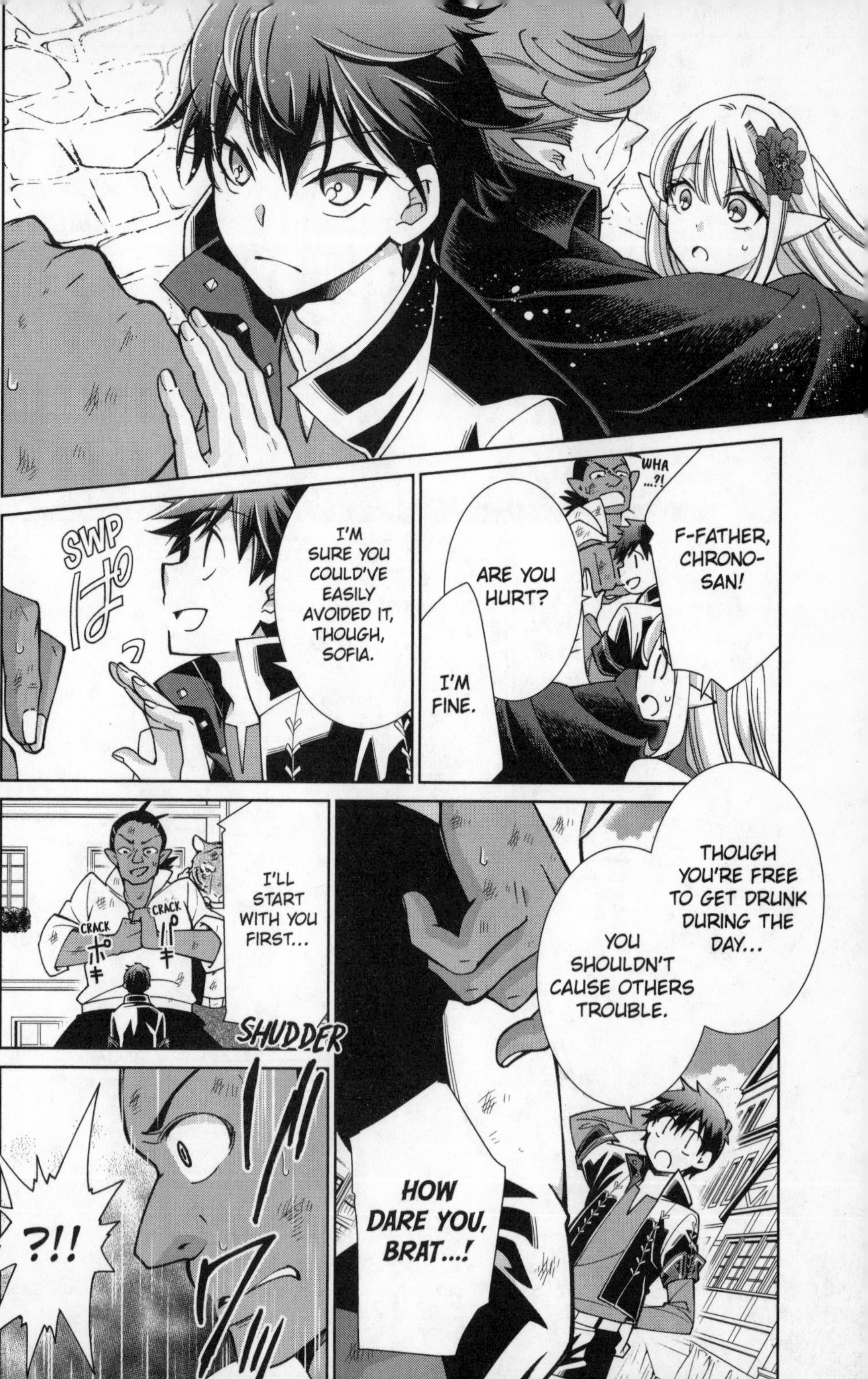
WHA ...?!
F-FATHER, CHRONO-SAN!
ARE YOU HURT?
I'M FINE.
SWP
ぱっ
I'M SURE YOU COULD'VE EASILY AVOIDED IT, THOUGH, SOFIA.
THOUGH YOU'RE FREE TO GET DRUNK DURING THE DAY...
YOU SHOULDN'T CAUSE OTHERS TROUBLE.
I'LL START WITH YOU FIRST...
CRACK
パキ
CRACK
ポキ
SHUDDER
HOW DARE YOU, BRAT...!
?!!

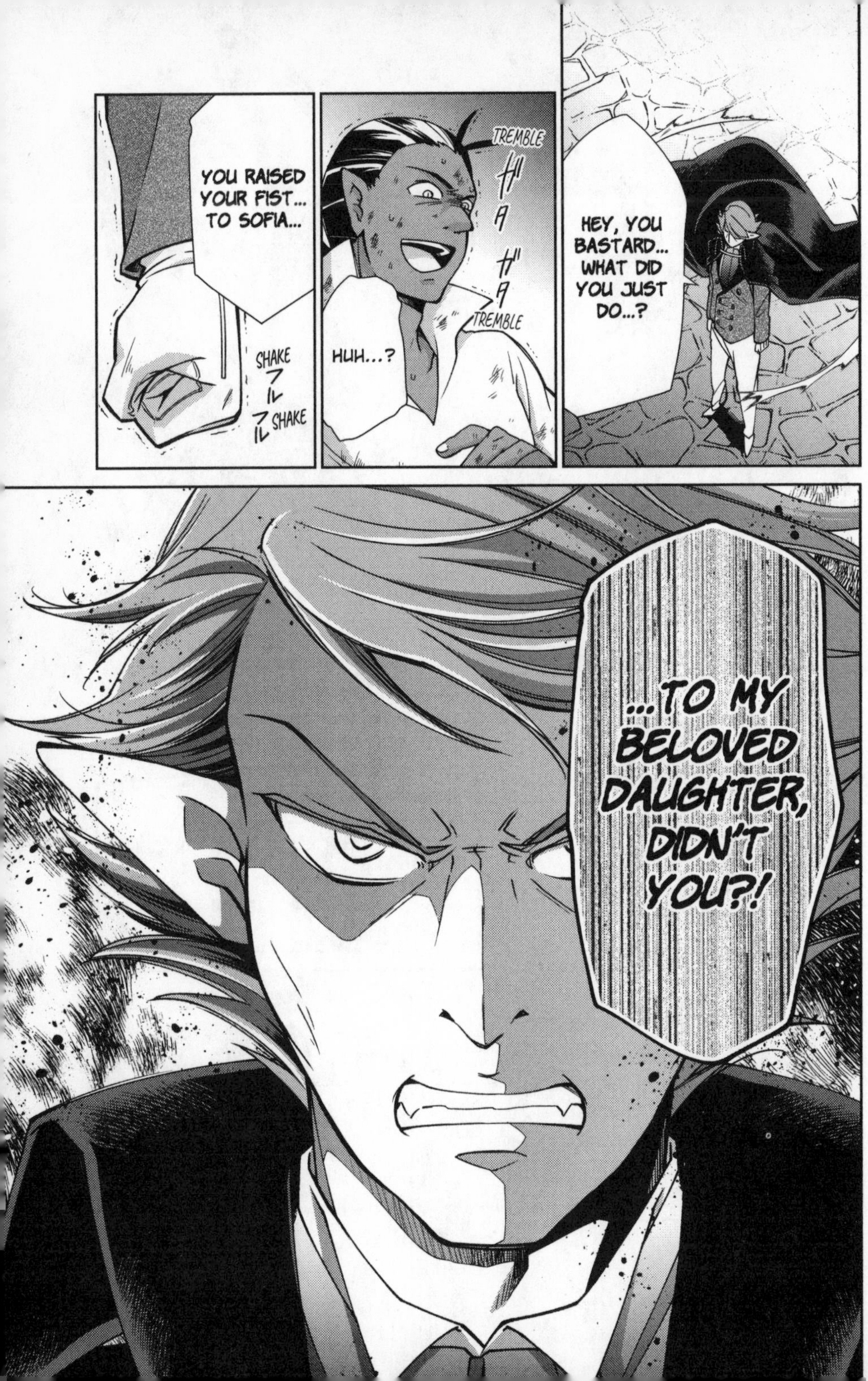
HEY, YOU BASTARD... WHAT DID YOU JUST DO...?
TREMBLE
ガタ
ガタ
TREMBLE
HUH...?
YOU RAISED YOUR FIST... TO SOFIA...
SHAKE
フル
フル
SHAKE
...TO MY BELOVED DAUGHTER, DIDN'T YOU?!

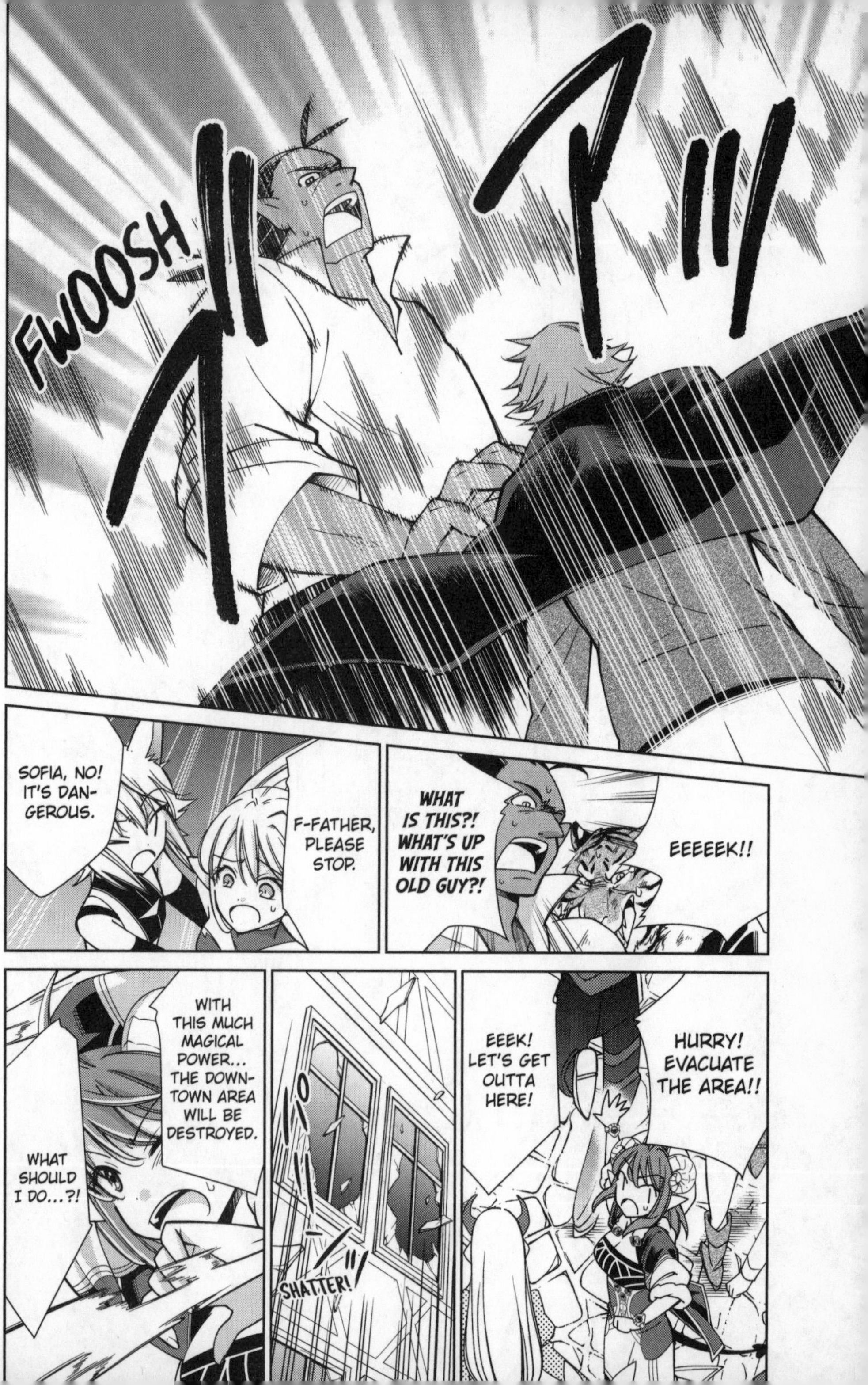
FWOOSH
EEEEEK!!
WHAT IS THIS?! WHAT'S UP WITH THIS OLD GUY?!
F-FATHER, PLEASE STOP.
SOFIA, NO! IT'S DAN-GEROUS.
HURRY! EVACUATE THE AREA!!
EEEK! LET'S GET OUTTA HERE!
SHATTER!
WITH THIS MUCH MAGICAL POWER... THE DOWN-TOWN AREA WILL BE DESTROYED.
WHAT SHOULD I DO...?!

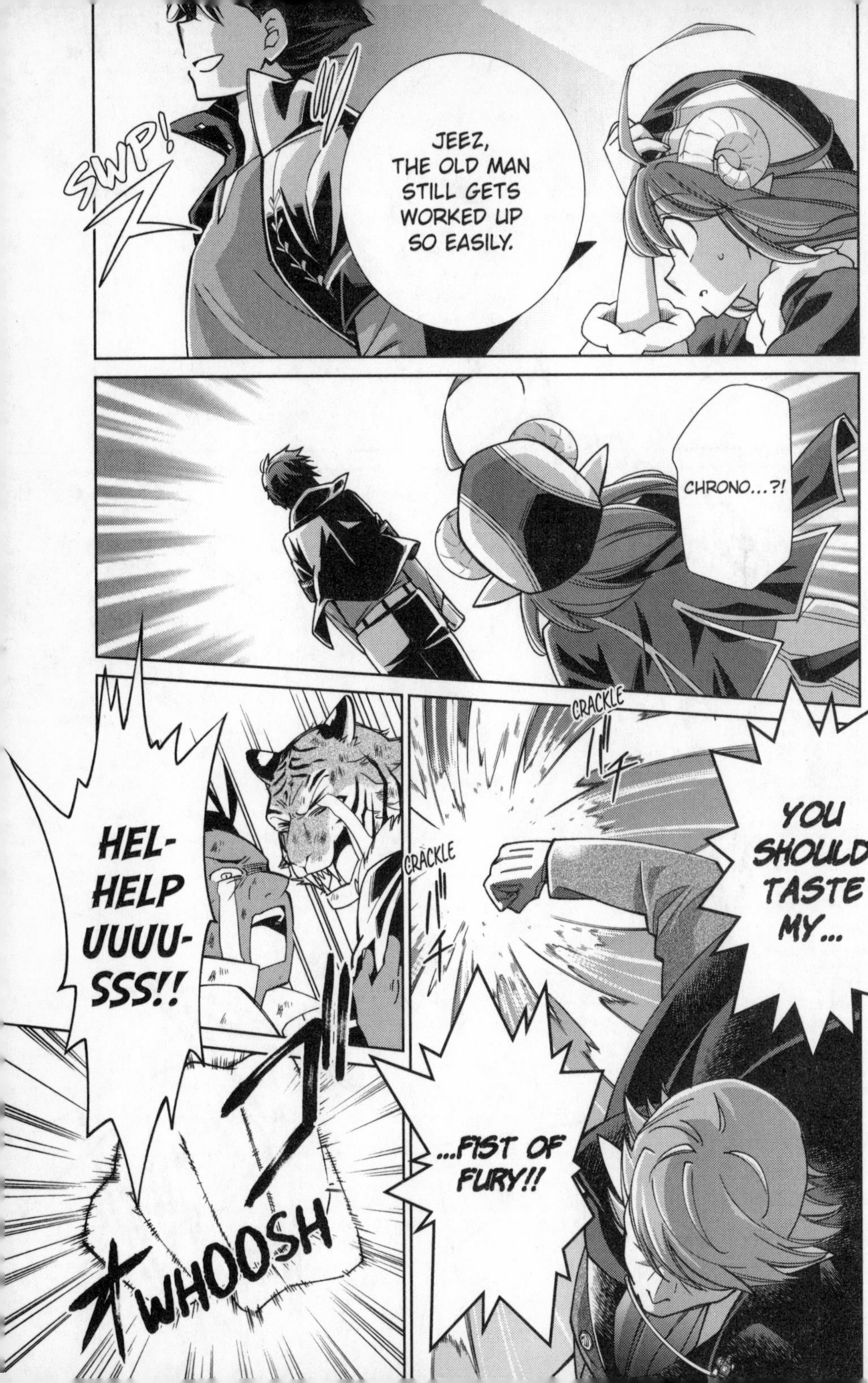
JEEZ, THE OLD MAN STILL GETS WORKED UP SO EASILY.
SWP!
CHRONO...?!
CRACKLE
YOU SHOULD TASTE MY...
CRACKLE
...FIST OF FURY!!
HEL- HELP UUUU-SSS!!
WHOOSH

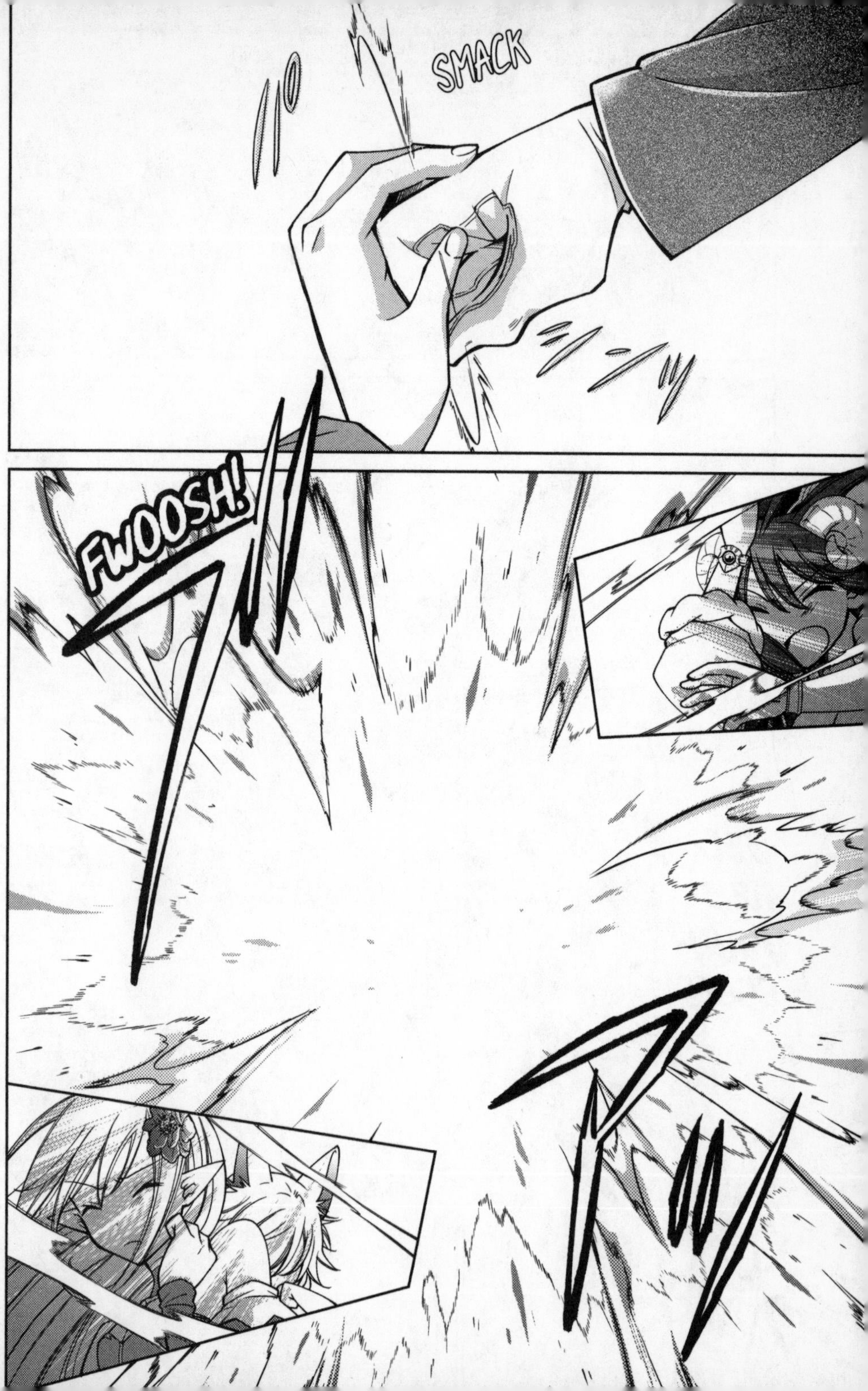
SMACK
FWOOSH!

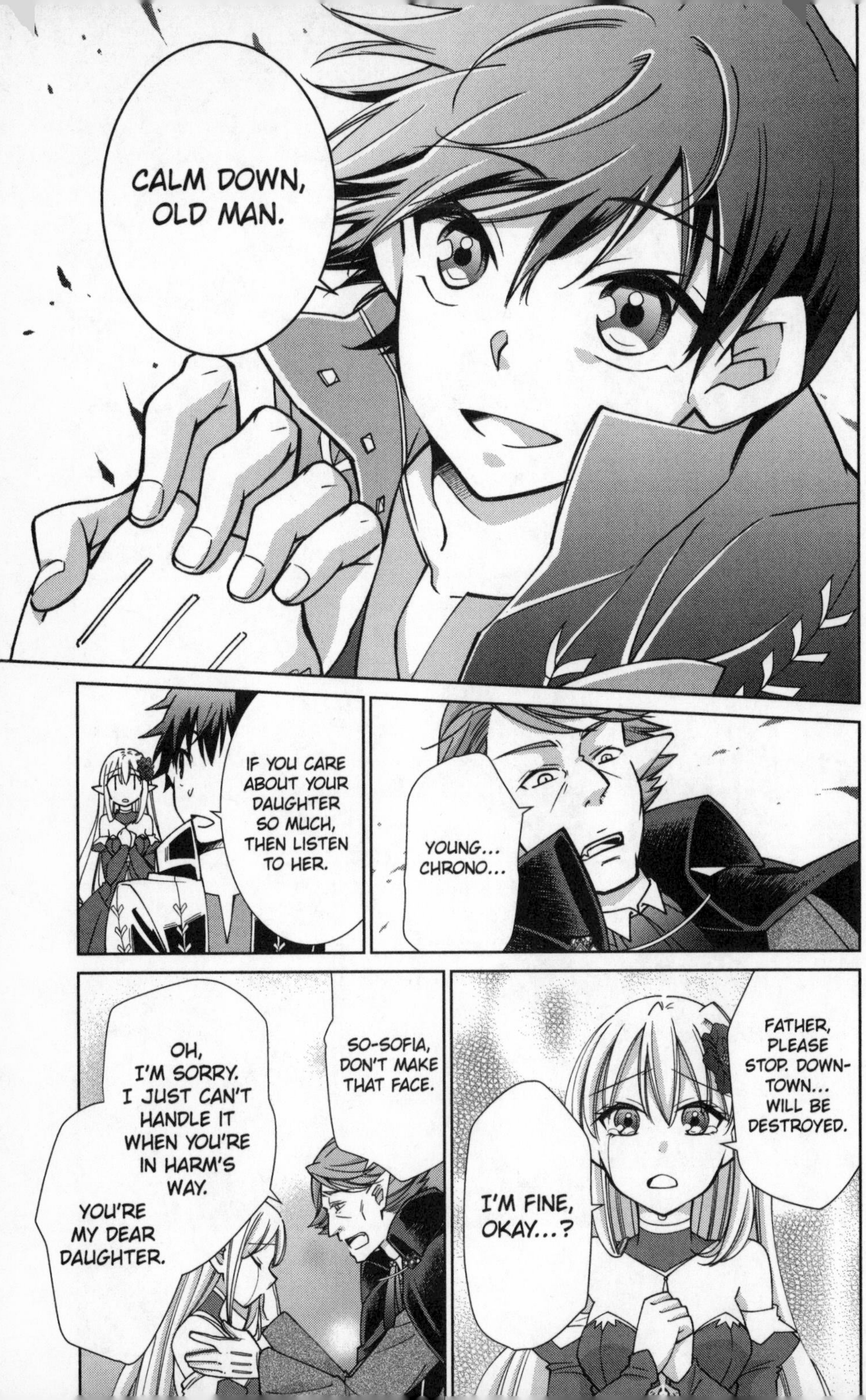
CALM DOWN, OLD MAN.
YOUNG... CHRONO...
IF YOU CARE ABOUT YOUR DAUGHTER SO MUCH, THEN LISTEN TO HER.
FATHER, PLEASE STOP. DOWN-TOWN... WILL BE DESTROYED.
I'M FINE, OKAY...?
SO-SOFIA, DON'T MAKE THAT FACE.
OH, I'M SORRY. I JUST CAN'T HANDLE IT WHEN YOU'RE IN HARM'S WAY.
YOU'RE MY DEAR DAUGHTER.

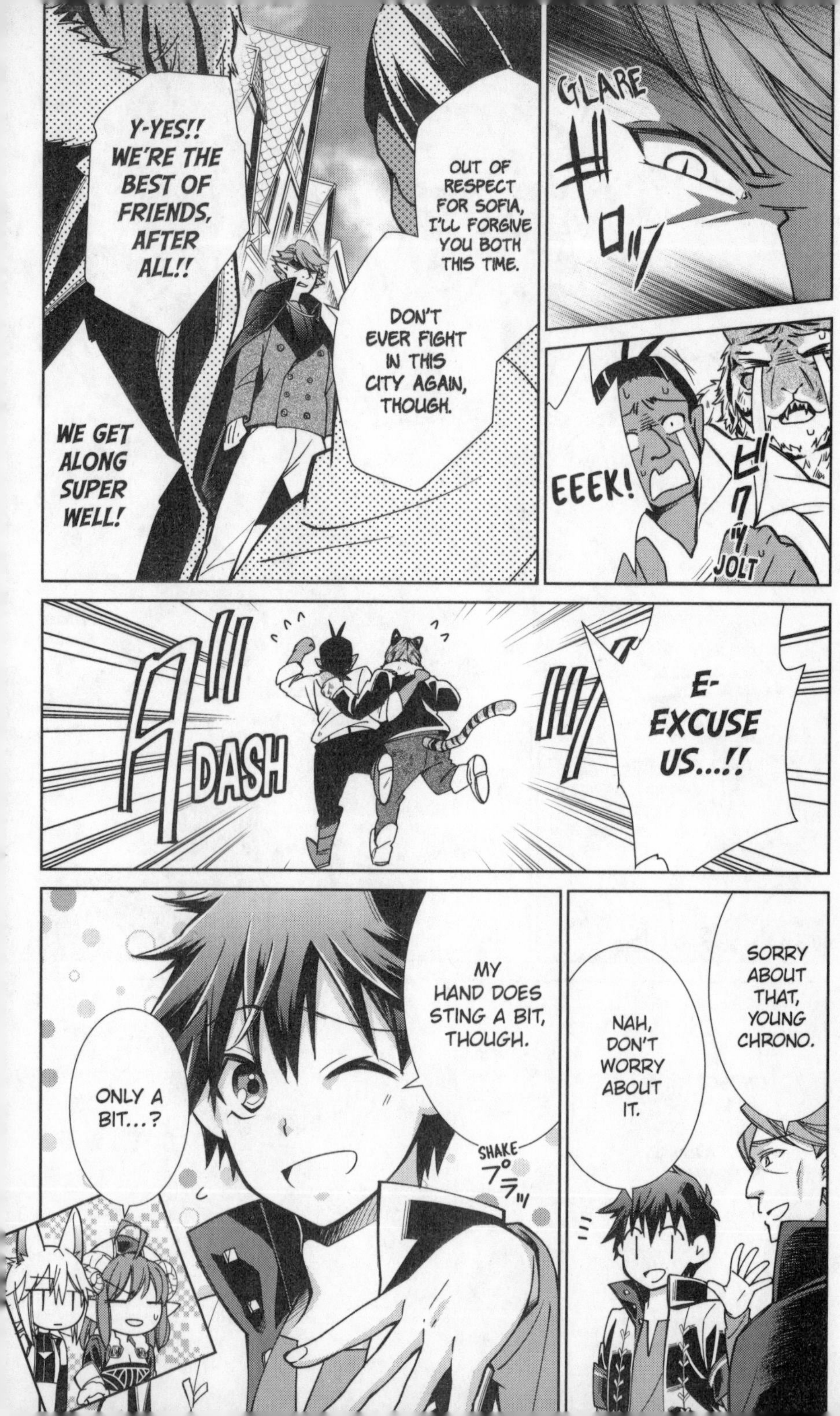
GLARE
EEEK!
JOLT
OUT OF RESPECT FOR SOFIA, I'LL FORGIVE YOU BOTH THIS TIME.
DON'T EVER FIGHT IN THIS CITY AGAIN, THOUGH.
Y-YES!! WE'RE THE BEST OF FRIENDS, AFTER ALL!!
WE GET ALONG SUPER WELL!
E-EXCUSE US...!!
DASH
SORRY ABOUT THAT, YOUNG CHRONO.
NAH, DON'T WORRY ABOUT IT.
MY HAND DOES STING A BIT, THOUGH.
SHAKE
ONLY A BIT...?

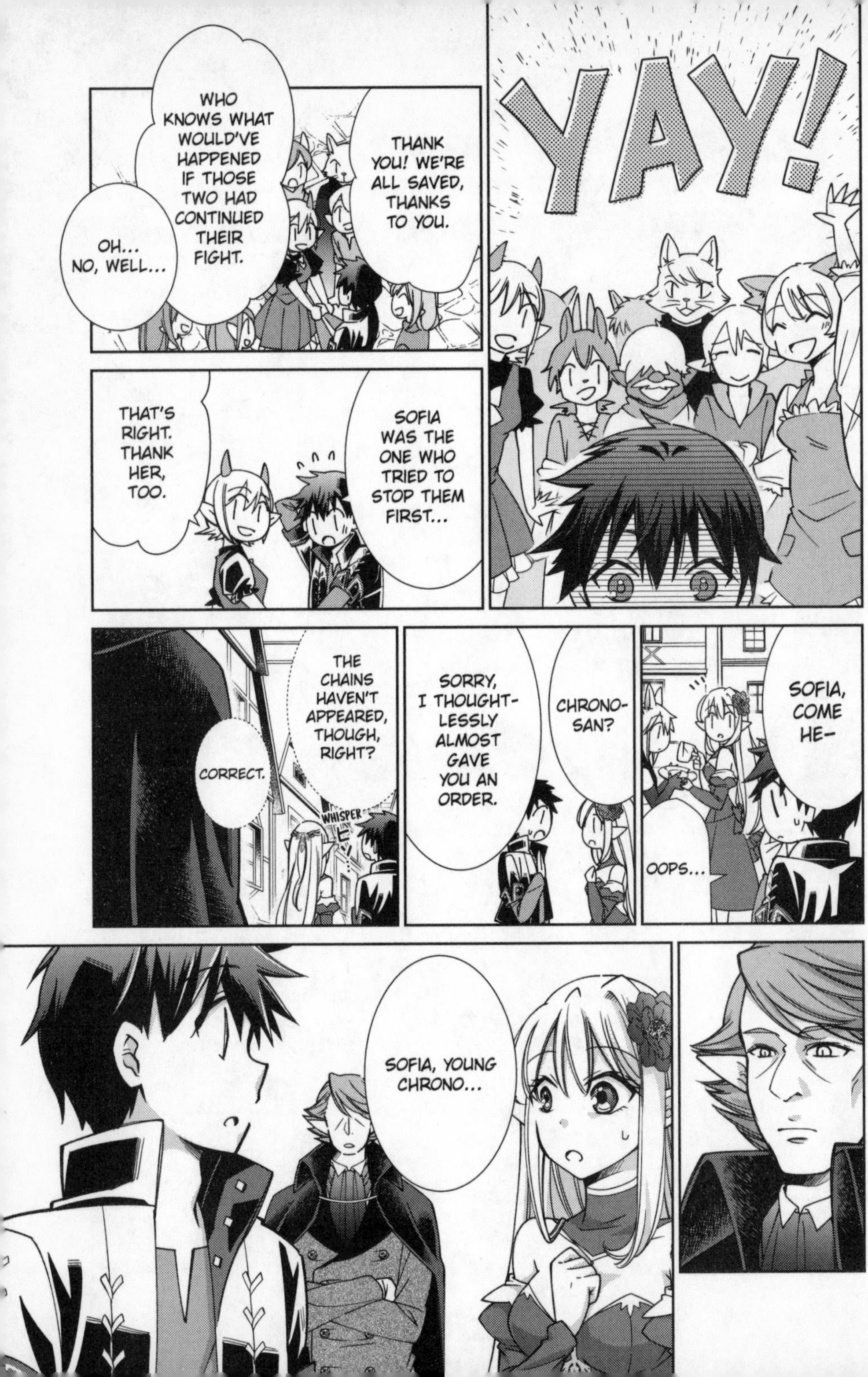
YAY!
THANK YOU! WE'RE ALL SAVED, THANKS TO YOU.
WHO KNOWS WHAT WOULD'VE HAPPENED IF THOSE TWO HAD CONTINUED THEIR FIGHT.
OH... NO, WELL...
SOFIA WAS THE ONE WHO TRIED TO STOP THEM FIRST...
THAT'S RIGHT. THANK HER, TOO.
SOFIA, COME HE-
OOPS...
CHRONO-SAN?
SORRY, I THOUGHTLESSLY ALMOST GAVE YOU AN ORDER.
THE CHAINS HAVEN'T APPEARED, THOUGH, RIGHT?
WHISPER
CORRECT.
SOFIA, YOUNG CHRONO...

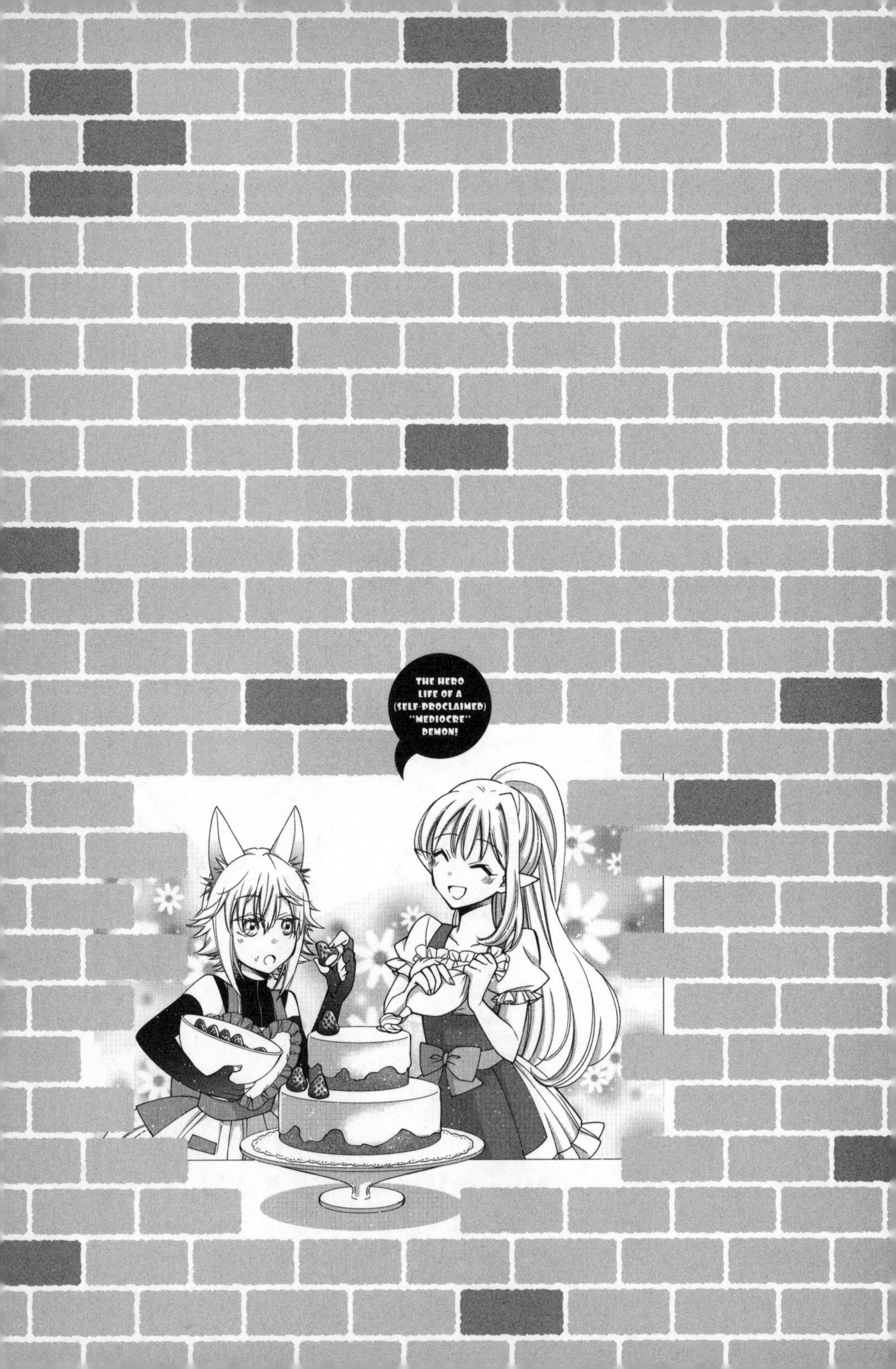
THE HERO LIFE OF A (SELF-PROCLAIMED) "MEDIOCRE" DEMON!

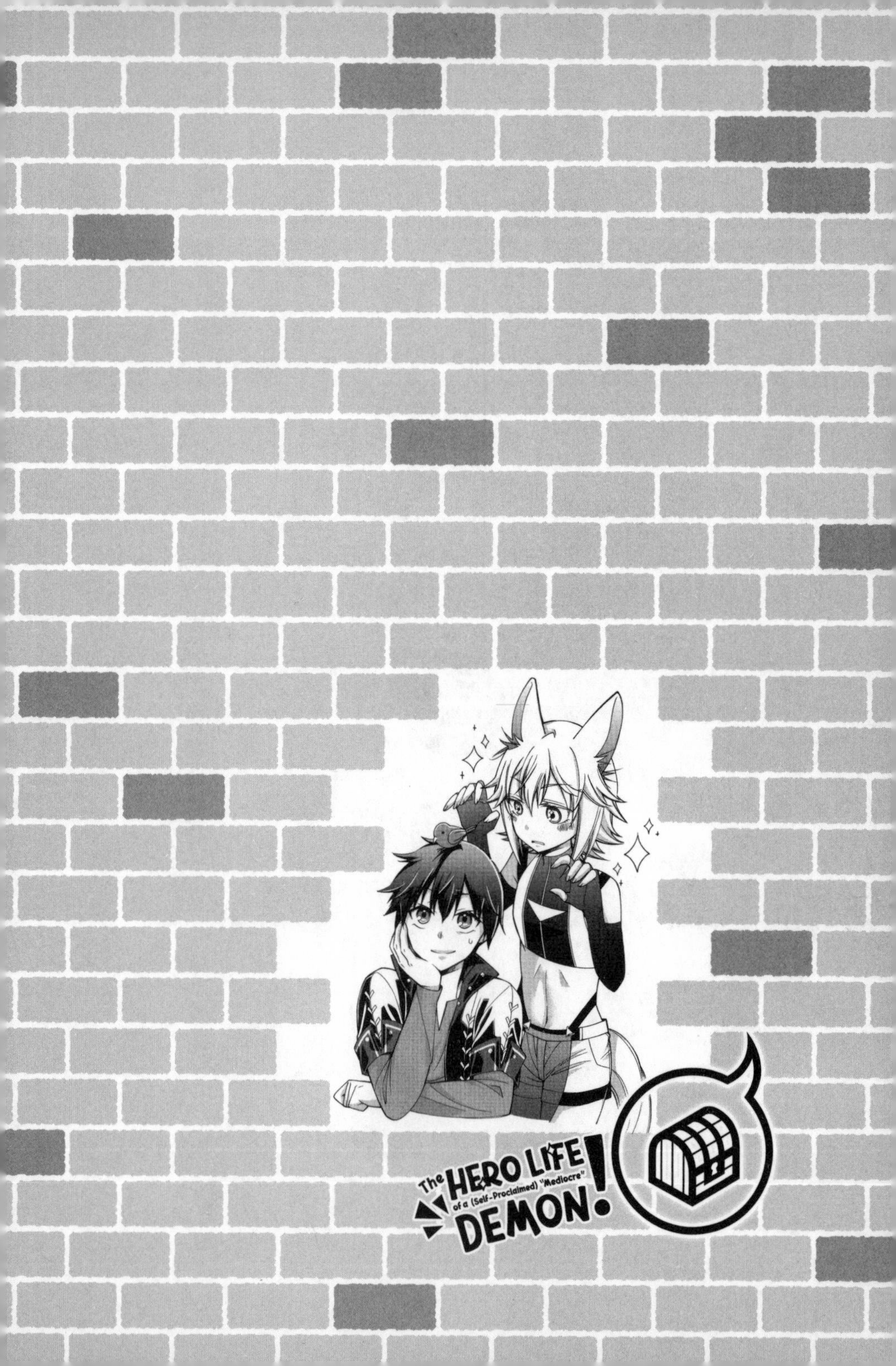

The HERO LIFE of a (Self-Proclaimed) "Mediocre" DEMON!

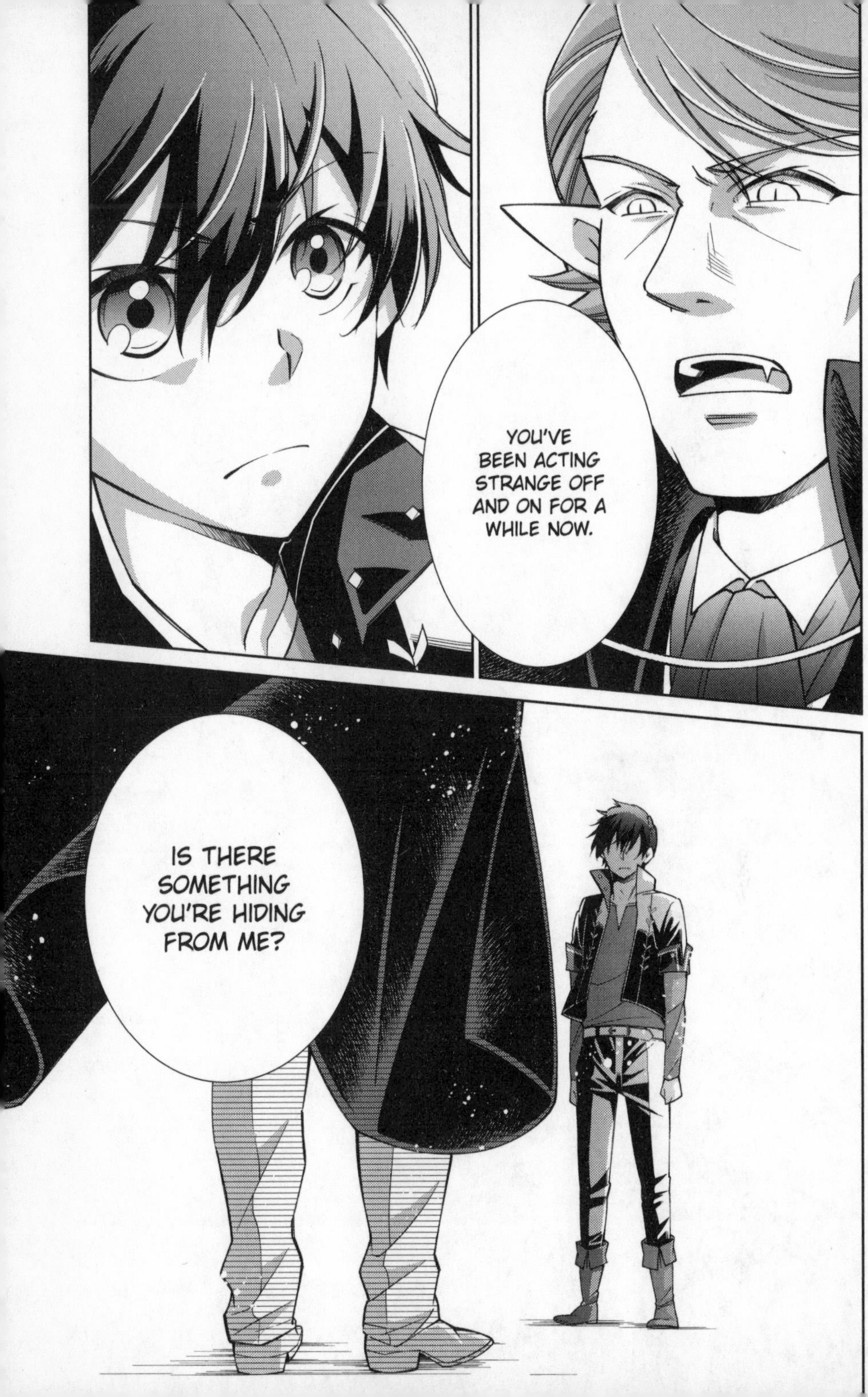
YOU'VE BEEN ACTING STRANGE OFF AND ON FOR A WHILE NOW.
IS THERE SOMETHING YOU'RE HIDING FROM ME?

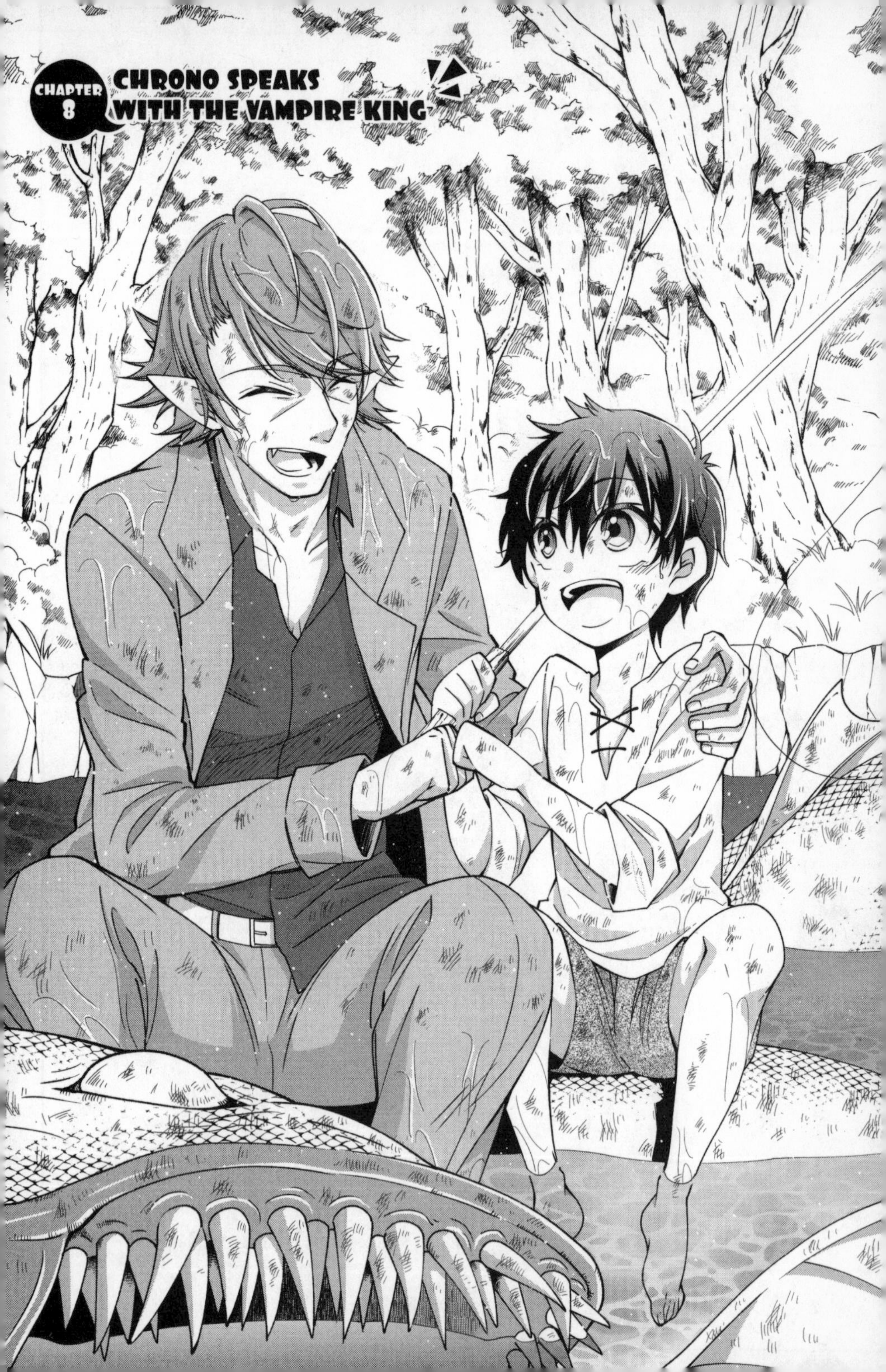
CHAPTER 8
CHRONO SPEAKS WITH THE VAMPIRE KING

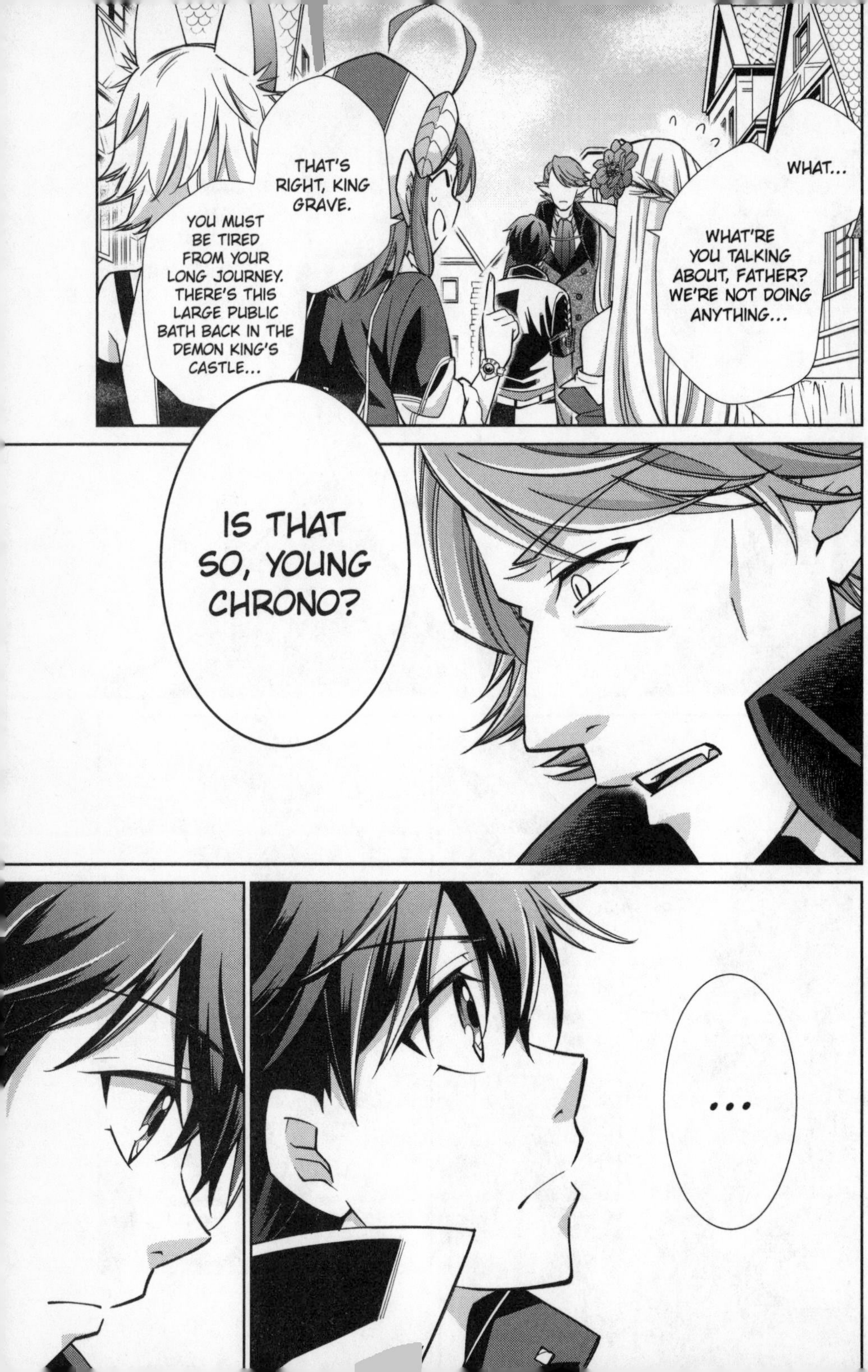
WHAT...
WHAT'RE YOU TALKING ABOUT, FATHER? WE'RE NOT DOING ANYTHING...
THAT'S RIGHT, KING GRAVE.
YOU MUST BE TIRED FROM YOUR LONG JOURNEY. THERE'S THIS LARGE PUBLIC BATH BACK IN THE DEMON KING'S CASTLE...
IS THAT SO, YOUNG CHRONO?
...

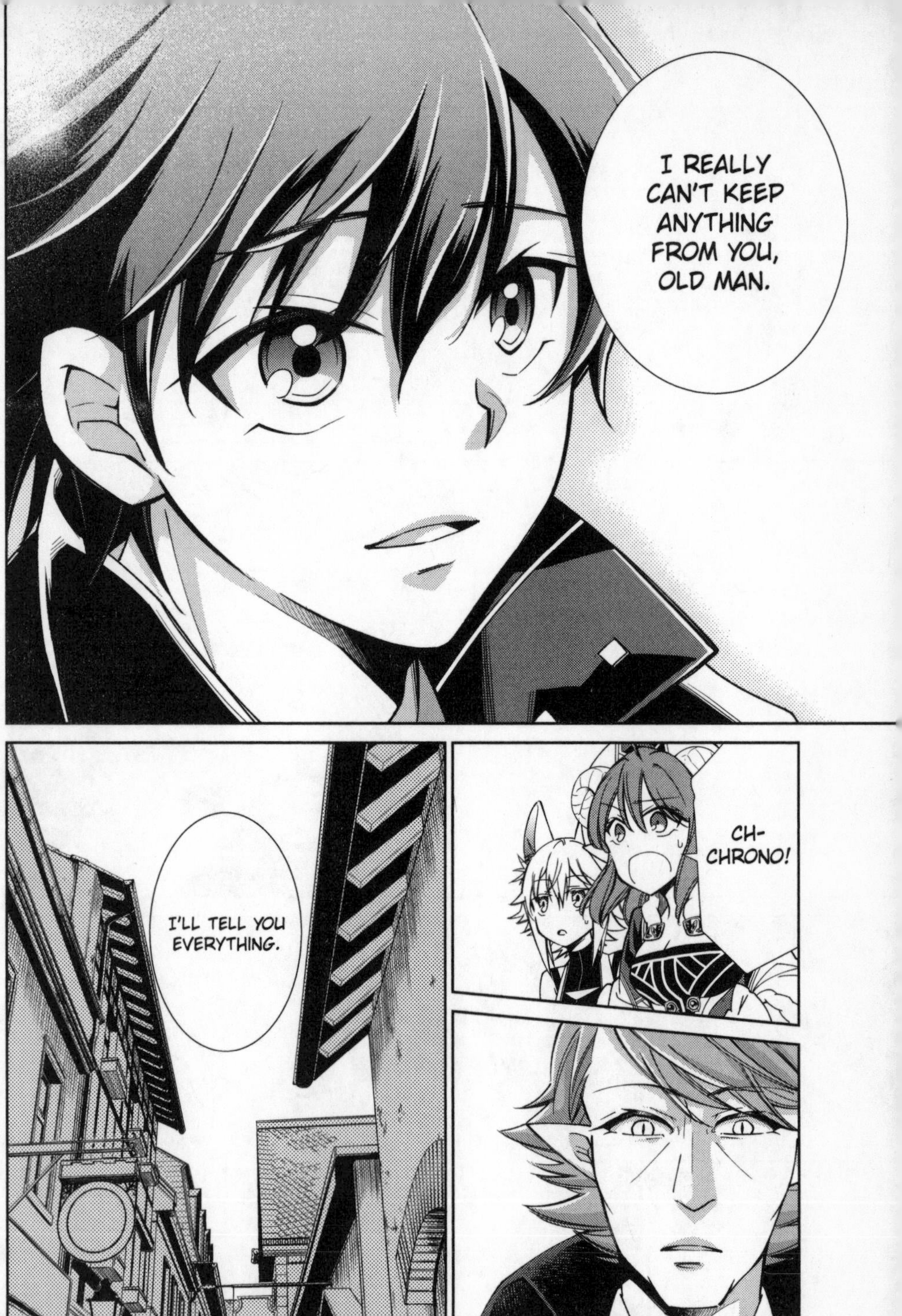
I REALLY CAN'T KEEP ANYTHING FROM YOU, OLD MAN.
CH- CHRONO!
I'LL TELL YOU EVERYTHING.

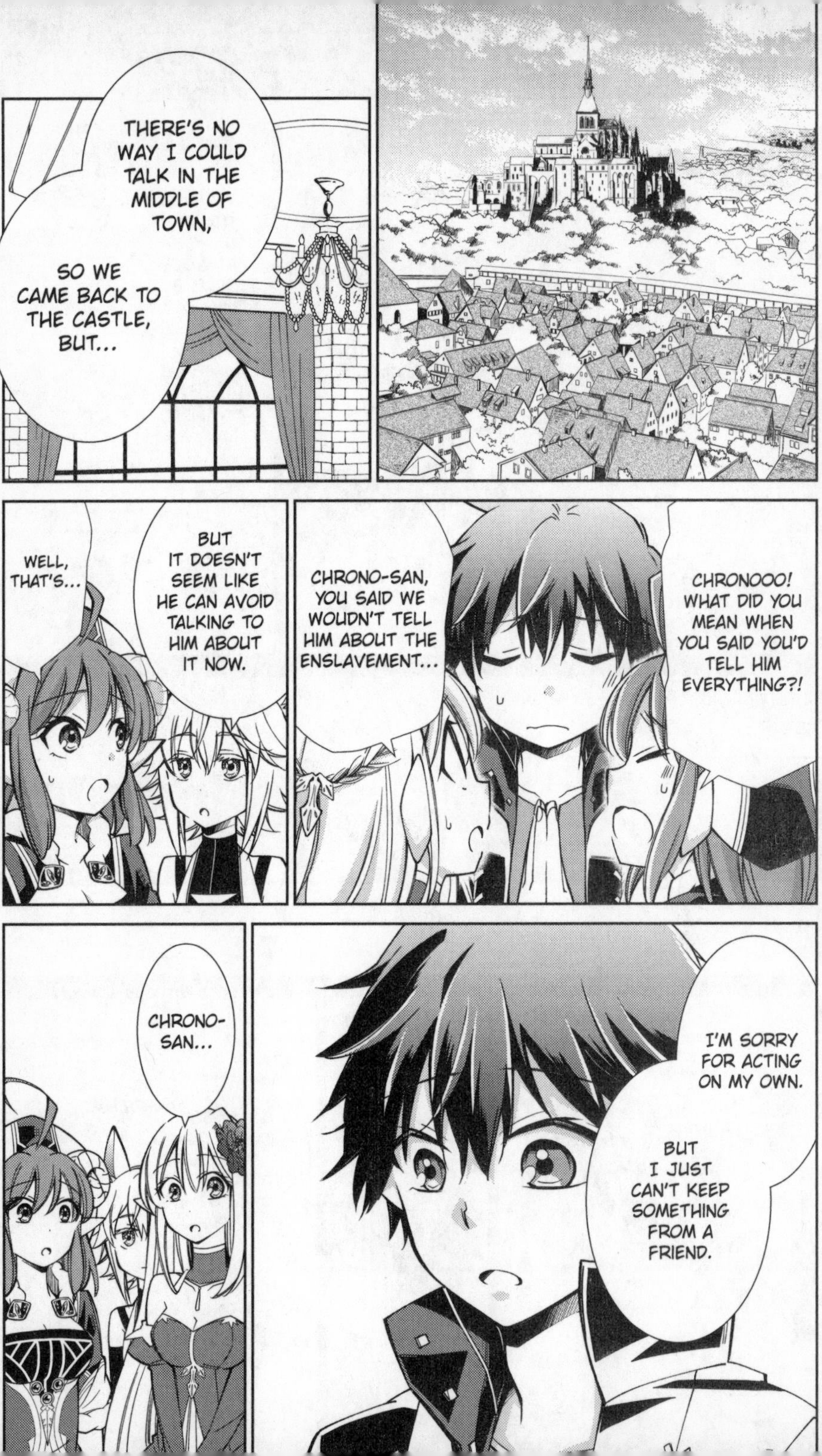
THERE'S NO WAY I COULD TALK IN THE MIDDLE OF TOWN,
SO WE CAME BACK TO THE CASTLE, BUT...
CHRONOOO! WHAT DID YOU MEAN WHEN YOU SAID YOU'D TELL HIM EVERYTHING?!
CHRONO-SAN, YOU SAID WE WOUDN'T TELL HIM ABOUT THE ENSLAVEMENT...
BUT IT DOESN'T SEEM LIKE HE CAN AVOID TALKING TO HIM ABOUT IT NOW.
WELL, THAT'S...
I'M SORRY FOR ACTING ON MY OWN.
BUT I JUST CAN'T KEEP SOMETHING FROM A FRIEND.
CHRONO-SAN...

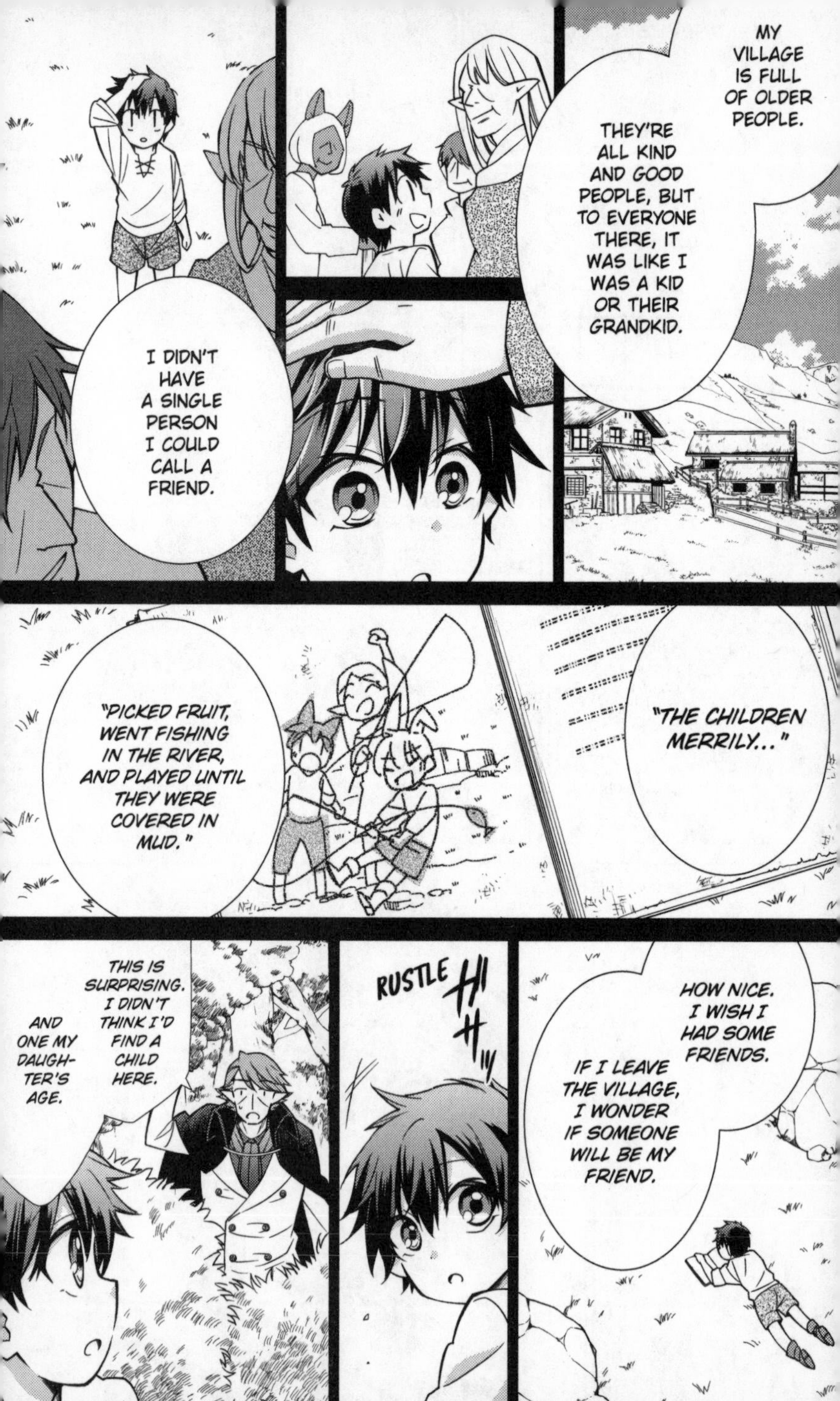
MY VILLAGE IS FULL OF OLDER PEOPLE.
THEY'RE ALL KIND AND GOOD PEOPLE, BUT TO EVERYONE THERE, IT WAS LIKE I WAS A KID OR THEIR GRANDKID.
I DIDN'T HAVE A SINGLE PERSON I COULD CALL A FRIEND.
"THE CHILDREN MERRILY..."
"PICKED FRUIT, WENT FISHING IN THE RIVER, AND PLAYED UNTIL THEY WERE COVERED IN MUD."
HOW NICE. I WISH I HAD SOME FRIENDS.
IF I LEAVE THE VILLAGE, I WONDER IF SOMEONE WILL BE MY FRIEND.
RUSTLE
THIS IS SURPRISING. I DIDN'T THINK I'D FIND A CHILD HERE.
AND ONE MY DAUGHTER'S AGE.

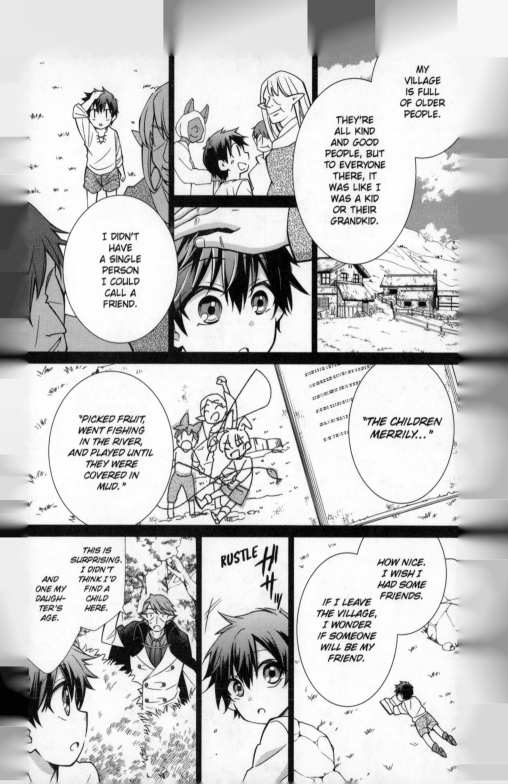

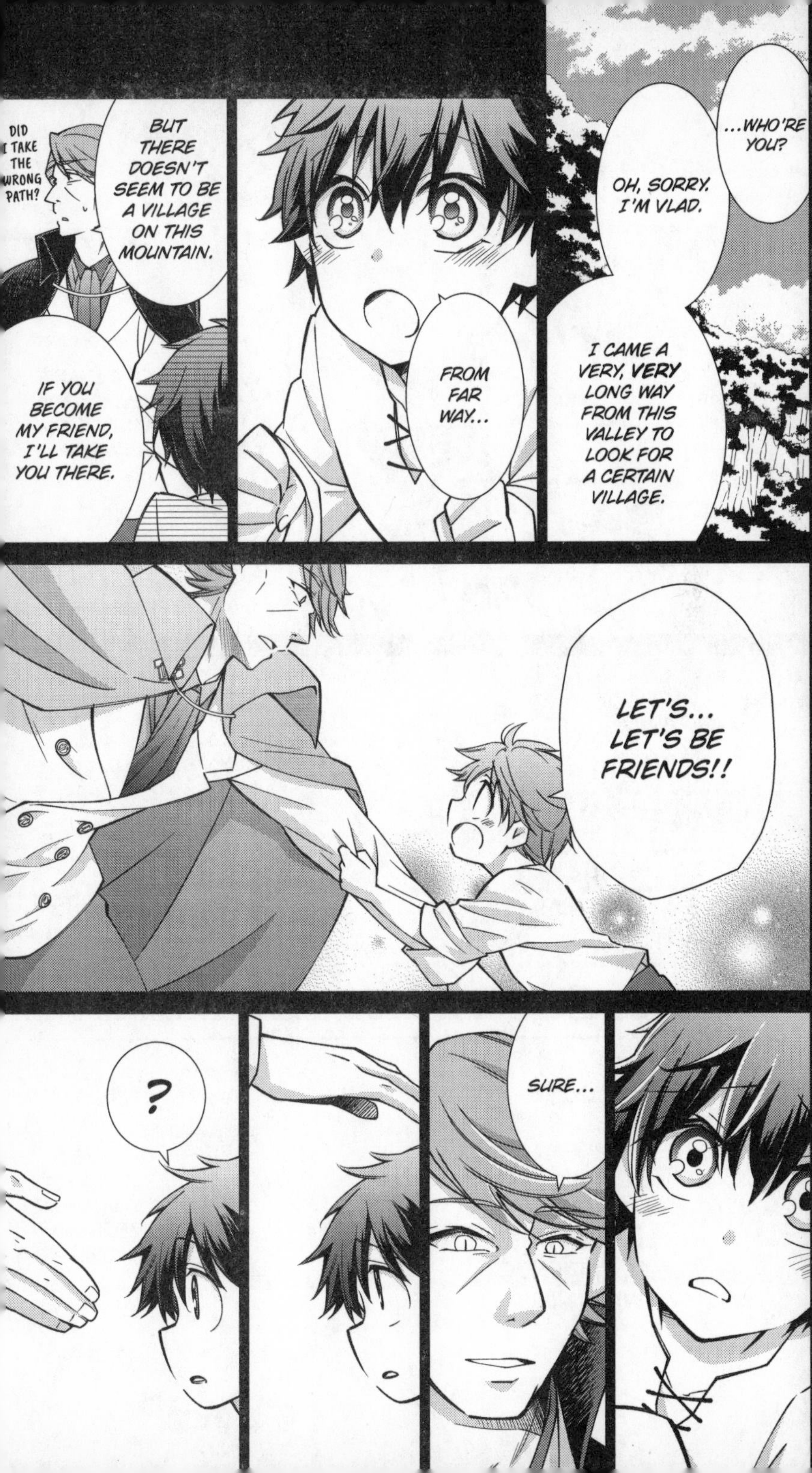
...WHO'RE YOU?
OH, SORRY. I'M VLAD.
I CAME A VERY, VERY LONG WAY FROM THIS VALLEY TO LOOK FOR A CERTAIN VILLAGE.
FROM FAR WAY...
BUT THERE DOESN'T SEEM TO BE A VILLAGE ON THIS MOUNTAIN.
DID I TAKE THE WRONG PATH?
IF YOU BECOME MY FRIEND, I'LL TAKE YOU THERE.
LET'S... LET'S BE FRIENDS!!
SURE...
?

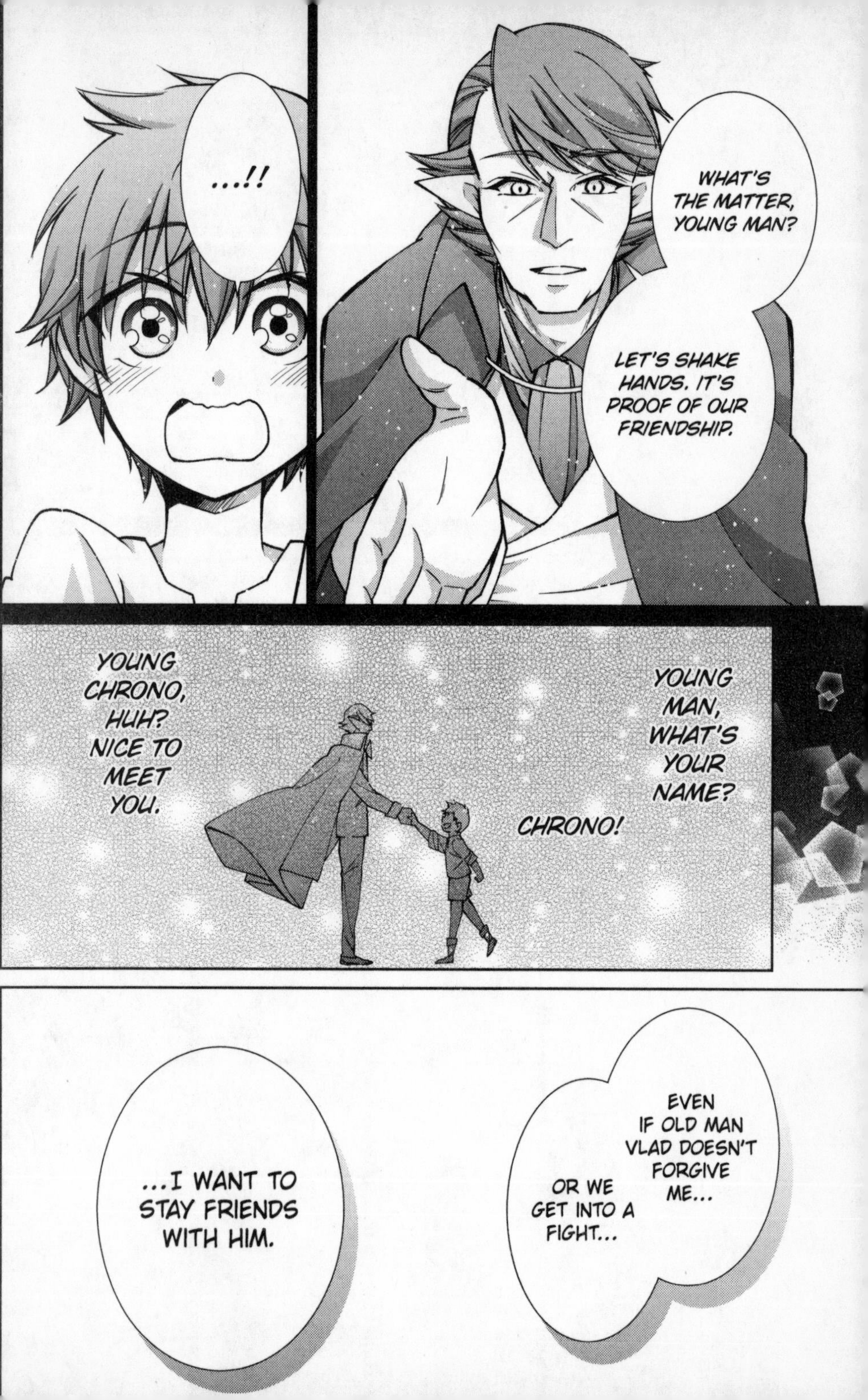
WHAT'S THE MATTER, YOUNG MAN?
LET'S SHAKE HANDS. IT'S PROOF OF OUR FRIENDSHIP.
...!!
YOUNG MAN, WHAT'S YOUR NAME?
CHRONO!
YOUNG CHRONO, HUH? NICE TO MEET YOU.
EVEN IF OLD MAN VLAD DOESN'T FORGIVE ME...
OR WE GET INTO A FIGHT...
...I WANT TO STAY FRIENDS WITH HIM.

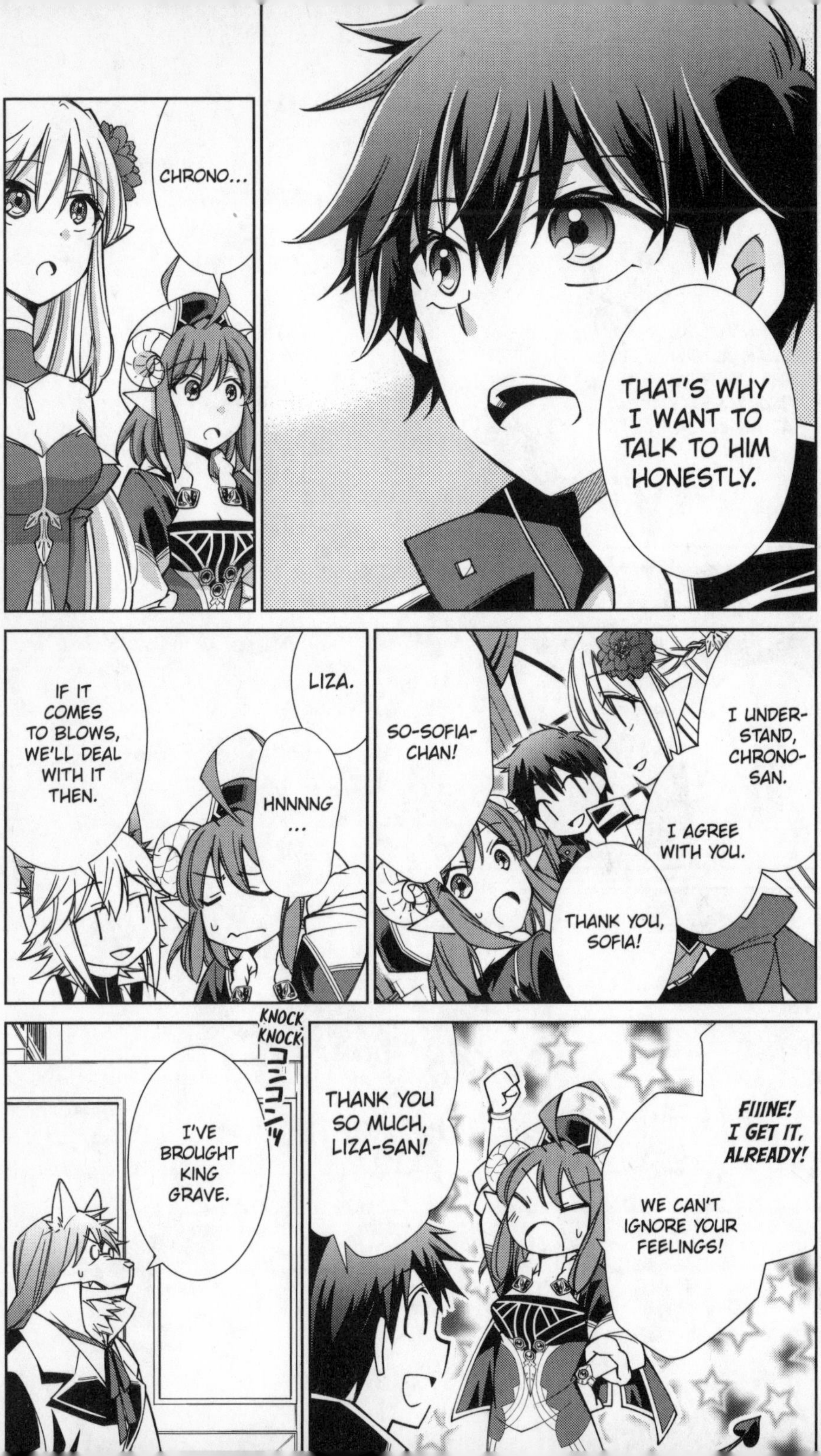
THAT'S WHY I WANT TO TALK TO HIM HONESTLY.
CHRONO...
I UNDER-STAND, CHRONO-SAN.
I AGREE WITH YOU.
THANK YOU, SOFIA!
SO-SOFIA-CHAN!
LIZA.
HNNNNG ...
IF IT COMES TO BLOWS, WE'LL DEAL WITH IT THEN.
FIIINE! I GET IT, ALREADY!
WE CAN'T IGNORE YOUR FEELINGS!
THANK YOU SO MUCH, LIZA-SAN!
KNOCK KNOCK
I'VE BROUGHT KING GRAVE.

PHILANIKOS, EVEN THOUGH I'M EARLY IN MY VISITATION, IT'S A WONDERFUL ROOM. I GIVE YOU MY GRATITUDE.

IT'S NOT LIKE I CAN ALLOW THE VAMPIRE KING TO STAY AT AN INN IN TOWN.

SORRY FOR MAKING YOU WAIT EVEN THOUGH I DIDN'T HAVE MUCH LUGGAGE.

NOW, THEN, LET'S HEAR IT.

YOUNG CHRONO, SOFIA.

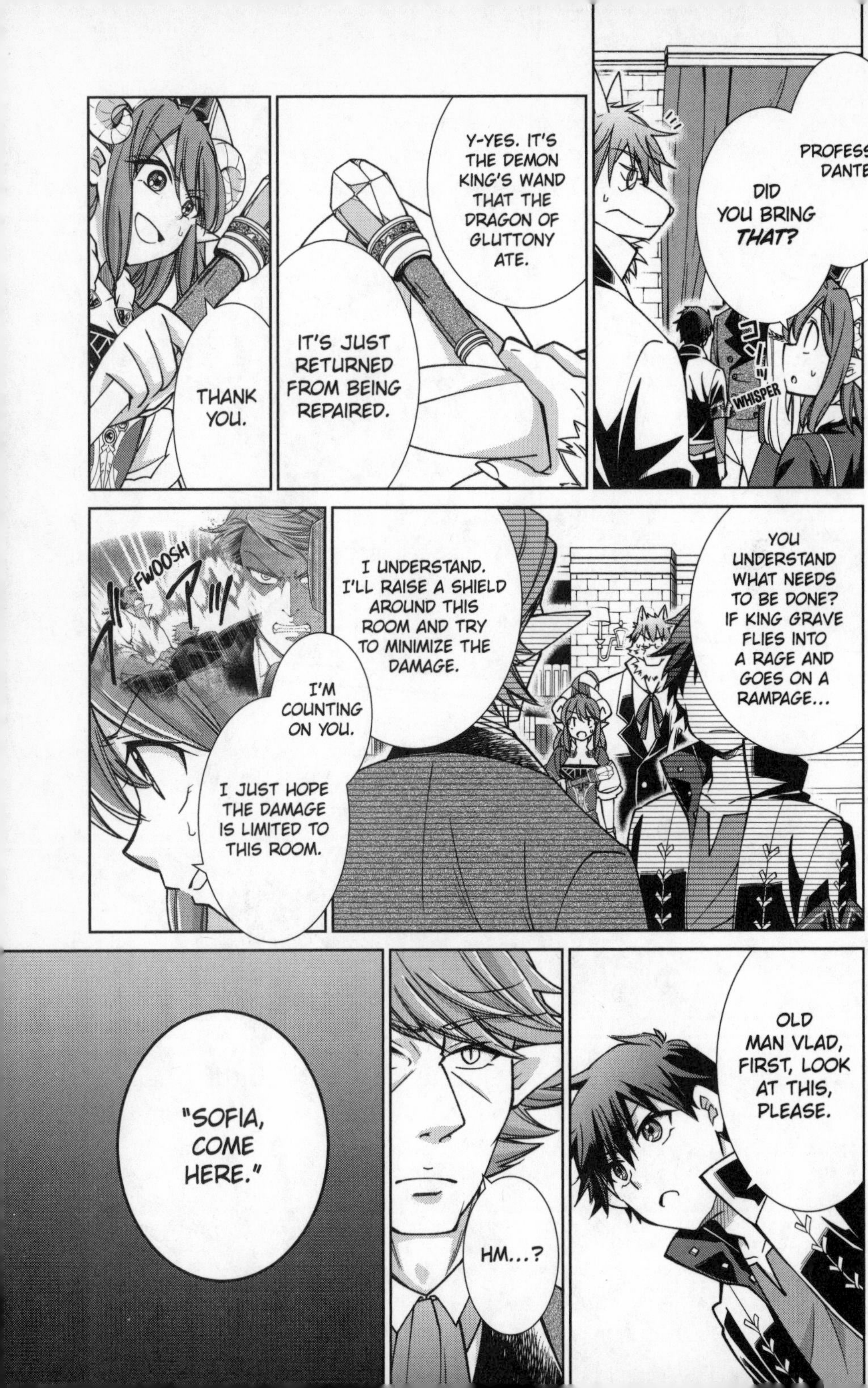
PROFESSOR DANTE,
DID YOU BRING THAT?
WHISPER
Y-YES. IT'S THE DEMON KING'S WAND THAT THE DRAGON OF GLUTTONY ATE.
IT'S JUST RETURNED FROM BEING REPAIRED.
THANK YOU.
YOU UNDERSTAND WHAT NEEDS TO BE DONE? IF KING GRAVE FLIES INTO A RAGE AND GOES ON A RAMPAGE...
I UNDERSTAND. I'LL RAISE A SHIELD AROUND THIS ROOM AND TRY TO MINIMIZE THE DAMAGE.
I'M COUNTING ON YOU.
FWOOSH
I JUST HOPE THE DAMAGE IS LIMITED TO THIS ROOM.
OLD MAN VLAD, FIRST, LOOK AT THIS, PLEASE.
HM...?
"SOFIA, COME HERE."

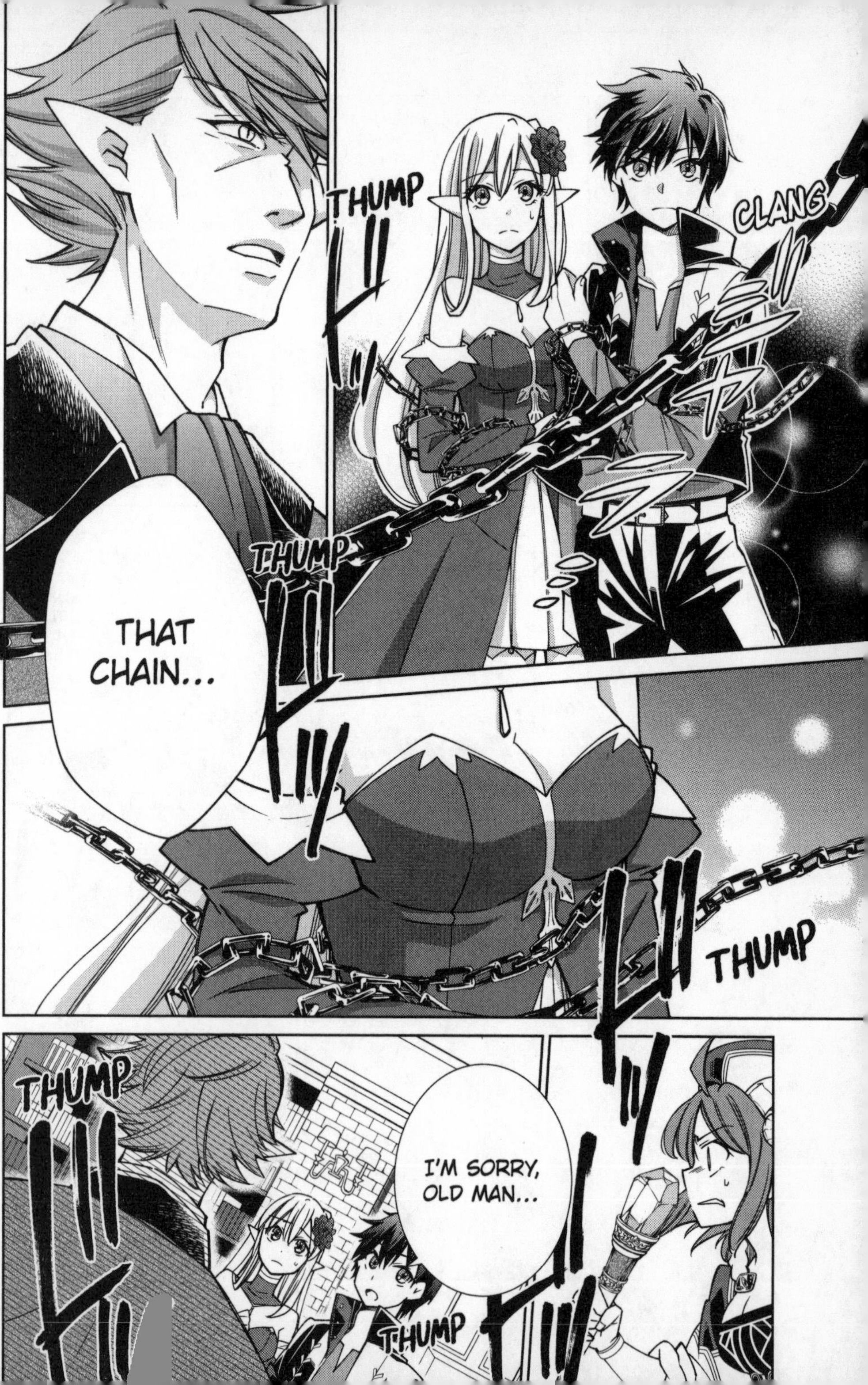
THUMP
CLANG
THUMP
THAT CHAIN...
THUMP
I'M SORRY, OLD MAN...
THUMP
THUMP

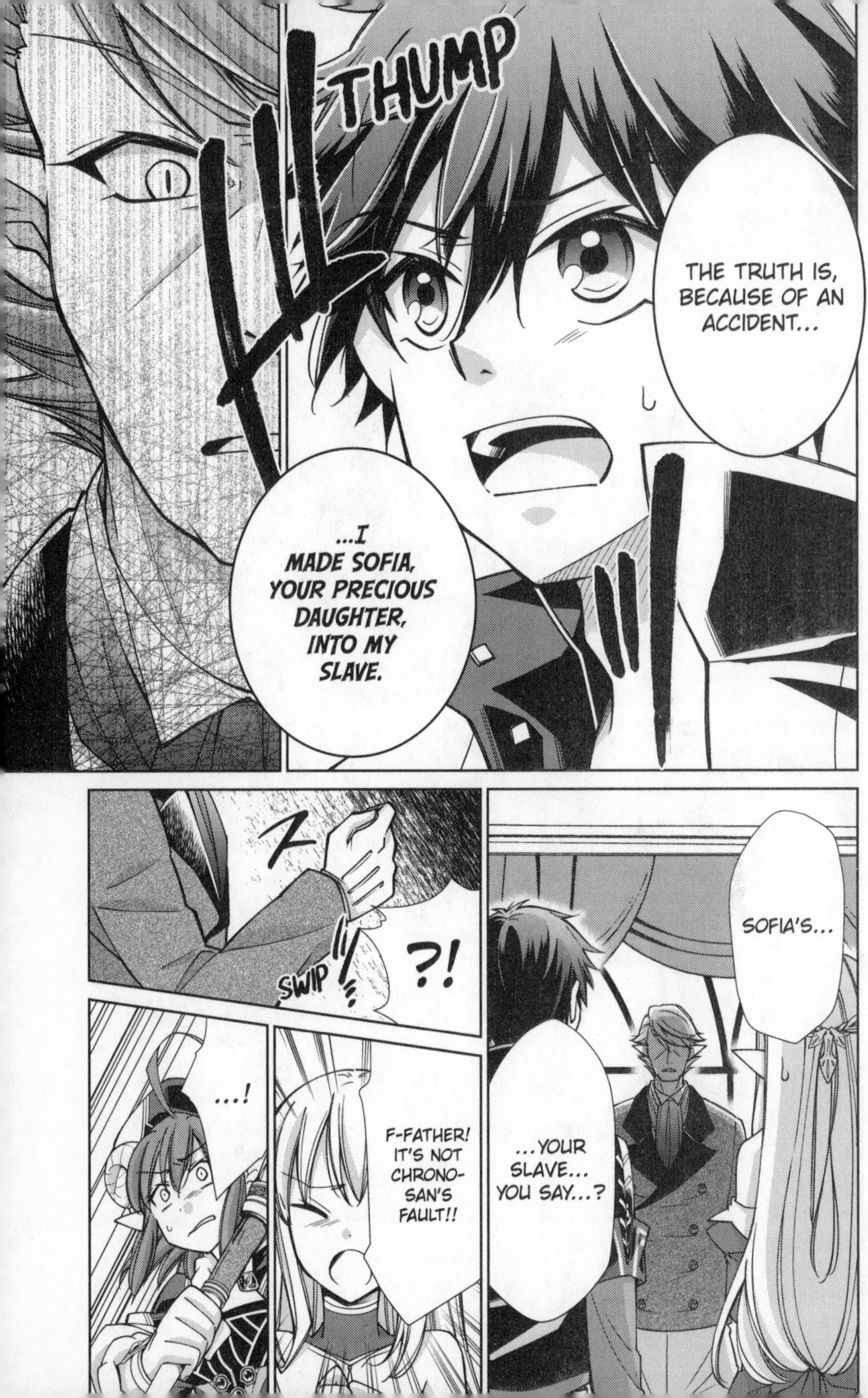
THE TRUTH IS, BECAUSE OF AN ACCIDENT...
...I MADE SOFIA, YOUR PRECIOUS DAUGHTER, INTO MY SLAVE.
THUMP
SOFIA'S...
...YOUR SLAVE... YOU SAY...?
Z
SWIP
?!
F-FATHER! IT'S NOT CHRONO-SAN'S FAULT!!
...!

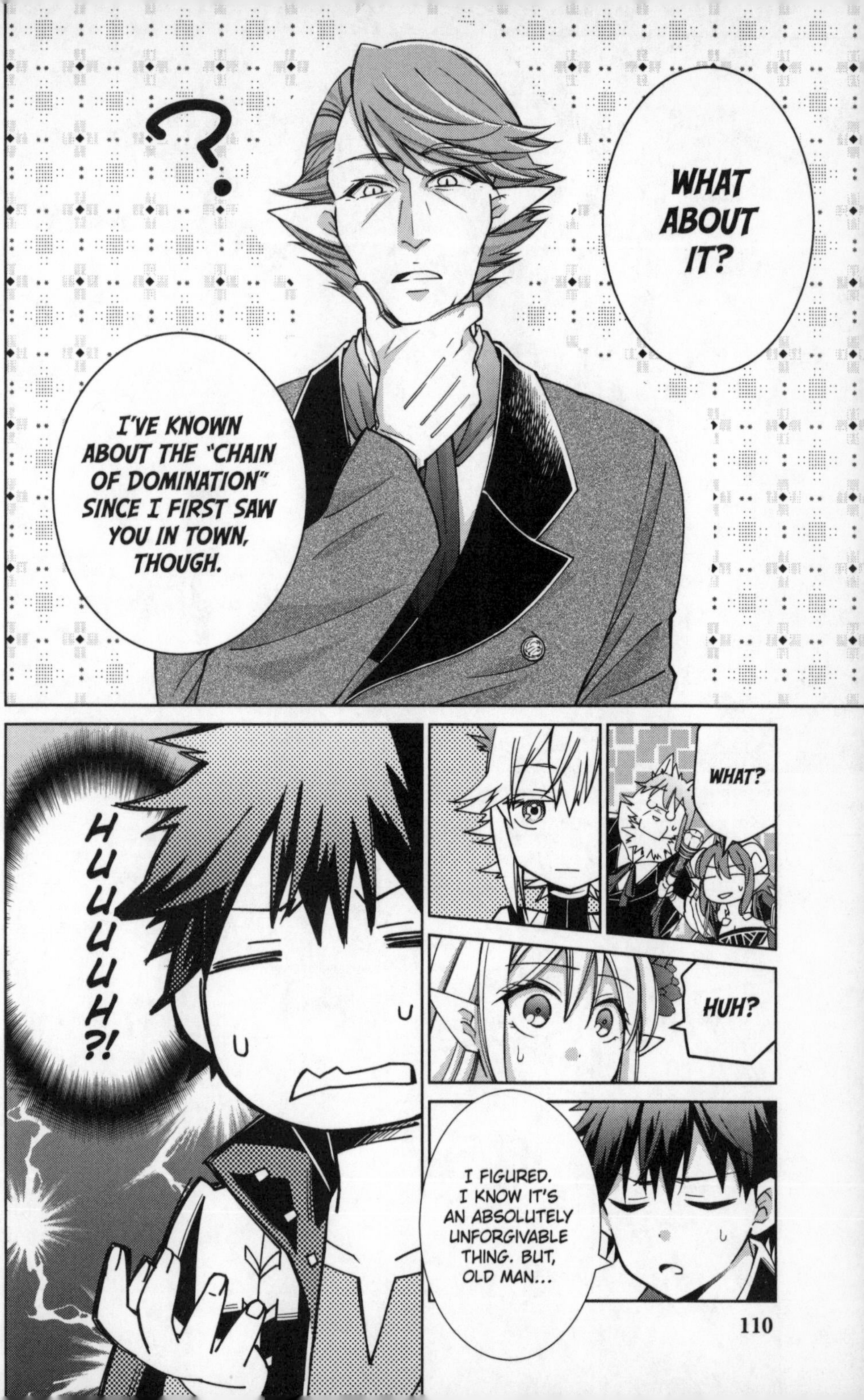

?
WHAT ABOUT IT?
I'VE KNOWN ABOUT THE "CHAIN OF DOMINATION" SINCE I FIRST SAW YOU IN TOWN, THOUGH.
WHAT?
HUH?
I FIGURED. I KNOW IT'S AN ABSOLUTELY UNFORGIVABLE THING. BUT, OLD MAN...
HUUUUUH?!

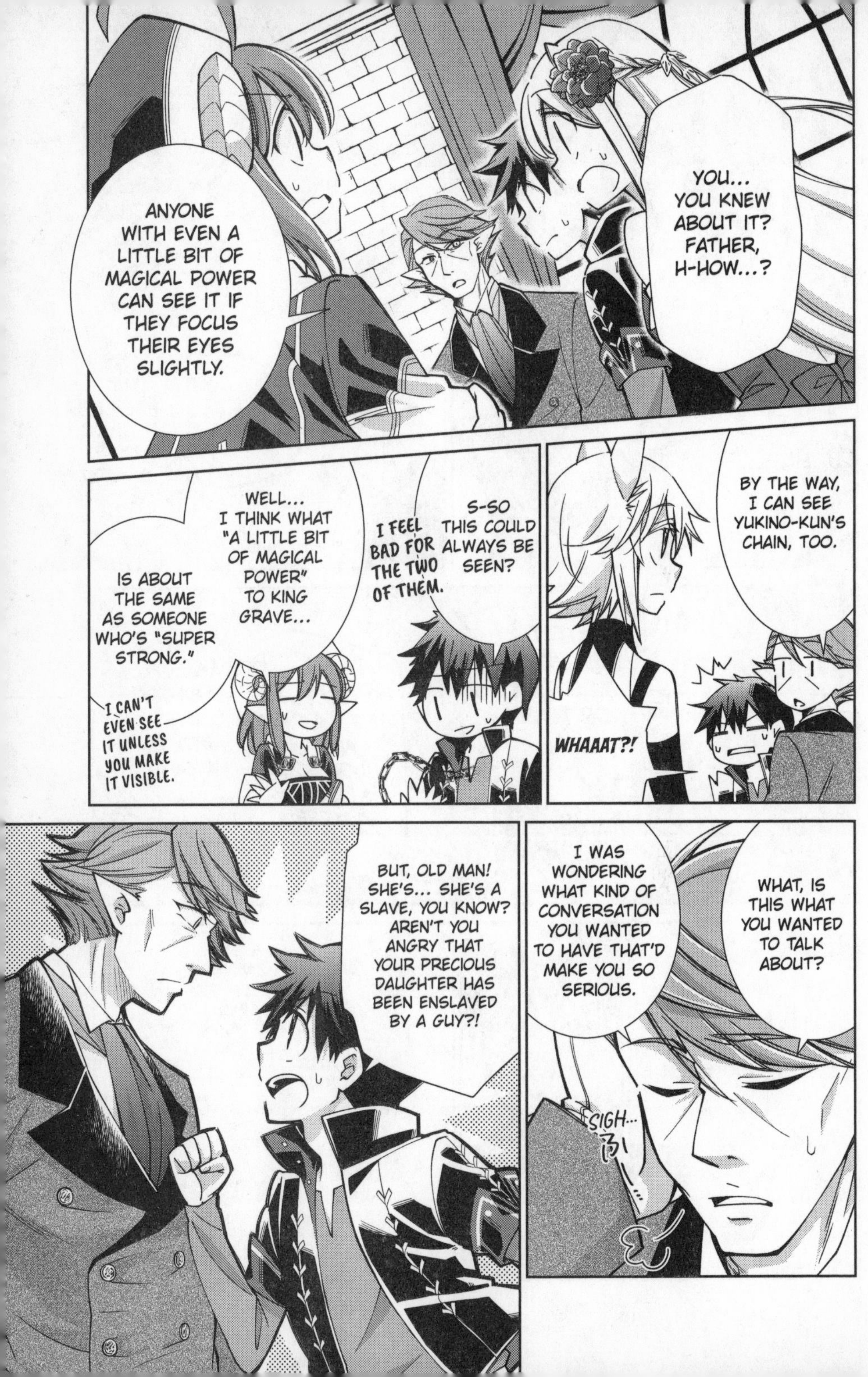
YOU... YOU KNEW ABOUT IT? FATHER, H-HOW...?
ANYONE WITH EVEN A LITTLE BIT OF MAGICAL POWER CAN SEE IT IF THEY FOCUS THEIR EYES SLIGHTLY.
BY THE WAY, I CAN SEE YUKINO-KUN'S CHAIN, TOO.
WHAAAT?!
S-SO THIS COULD ALWAYS BE SEEN?
I FEEL BAD FOR THE TWO OF THEM.
WELL... I THINK WHAT "A LITTLE BIT OF MAGICAL POWER" TO KING GRAVE...
IS ABOUT THE SAME AS SOMEONE WHO'S "SUPER STRONG."
I CAN'T EVEN SEE IT UNLESS YOU MAKE IT VISIBLE.
WHAT, IS THIS WHAT YOU WANTED TO TALK ABOUT?
I WAS WONDERING WHAT KIND OF CONVERSATION YOU WANTED TO HAVE THAT'D MAKE YOU SO SERIOUS.
SIGH...
BUT, OLD MAN! SHE'S... SHE'S A SLAVE, YOU KNOW? AREN'T YOU ANGRY THAT YOUR PRECIOUS DAUGHTER HAS BEEN ENSLAVED BY A GUY?!

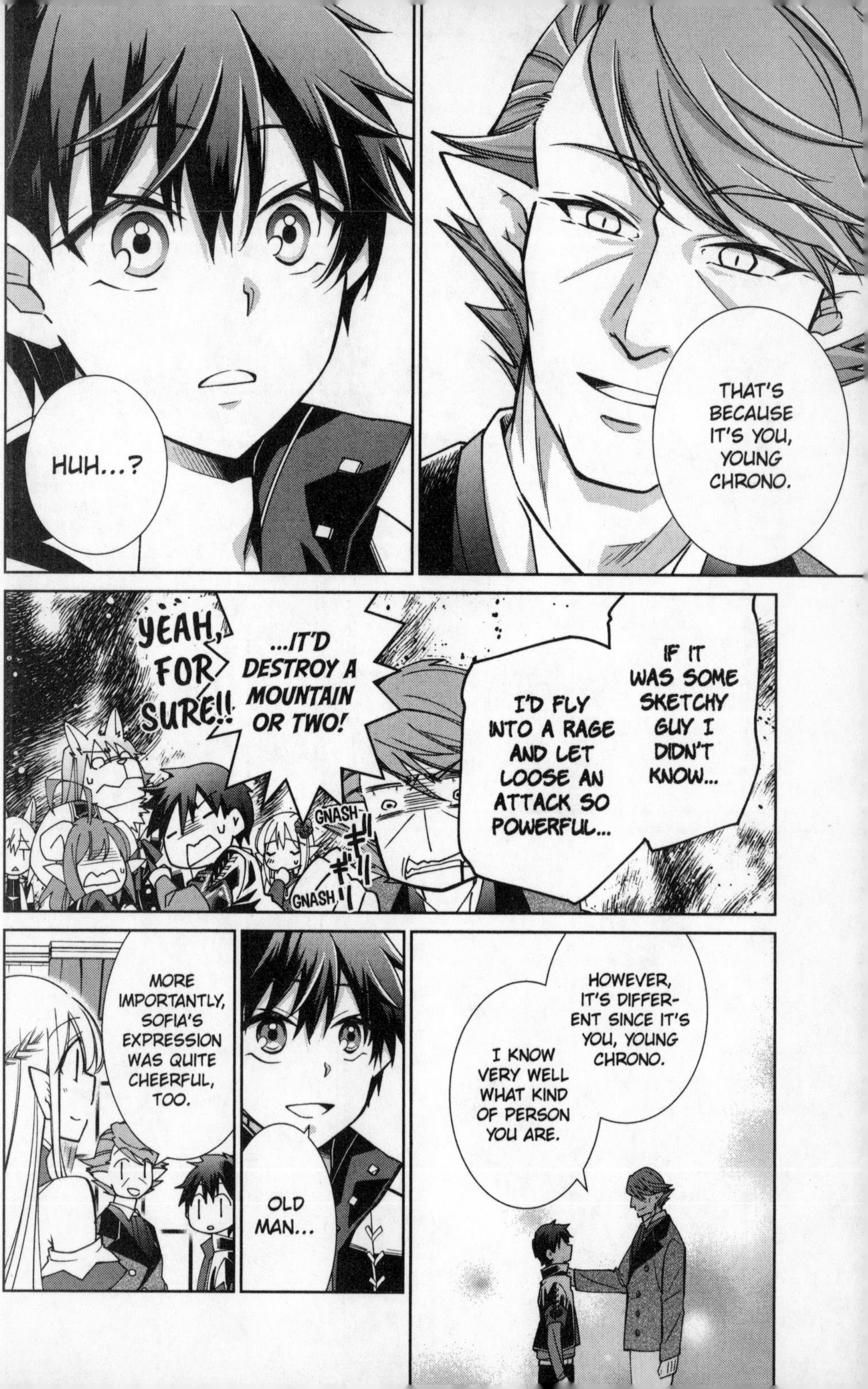
THAT'S BECAUSE IT'S YOU, YOUNG CHRONO.
HUH...?
IF IT WAS SOME SKETCHY GUY I DIDN'T KNOW...
I'D FLY INTO A RAGE AND LET LOOSE AN ATTACK SO POWERFUL...
...IT'D DESTROY A MOUNTAIN OR TWO!
YEAH, FOR SURE!!
GNASH
GNASH
HOWEVER, IT'S DIFFER-ENT SINCE IT'S YOU, YOUNG CHRONO.
I KNOW VERY WELL WHAT KIND OF PERSON YOU ARE.
OLD MAN...
MORE IMPORTANTLY, SOFIA'S EXPRESSION WAS QUITE CHEERFUL, TOO.

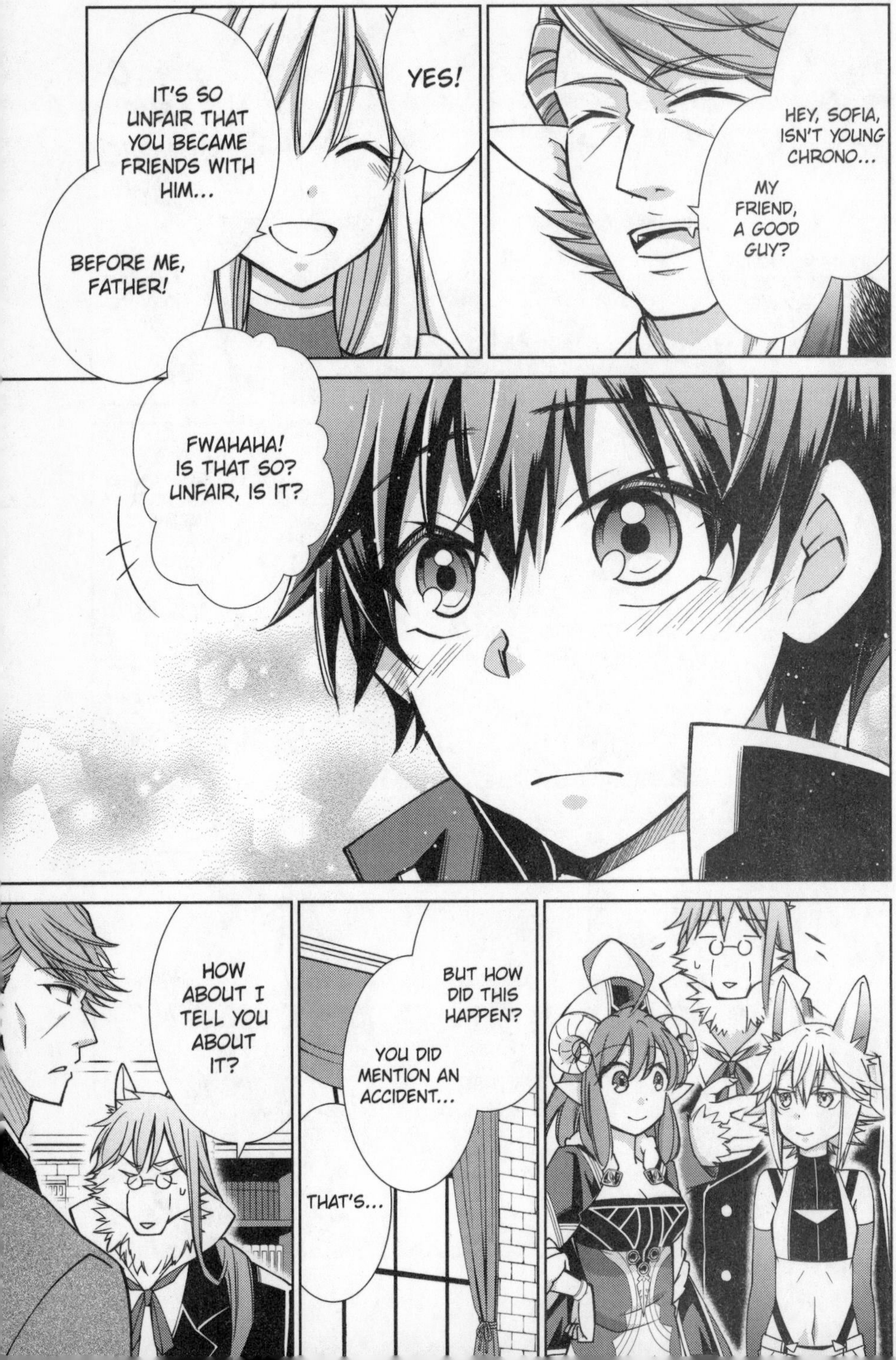
HEY, SOFIA, ISN'T YOUNG CHRONO...
MY FRIEND, A GOOD GUY?
YES!
IT'S SO UNFAIR THAT YOU BECAME FRIENDS WITH HIM...
BEFORE ME, FATHER!
FWAHAHA! IS THAT SO? UNFAIR, IS IT?
BUT HOW DID THIS HAPPEN?
YOU DID MENTION AN ACCIDENT...
THAT'S...
HOW ABOUT I TELL YOU ABOUT IT?

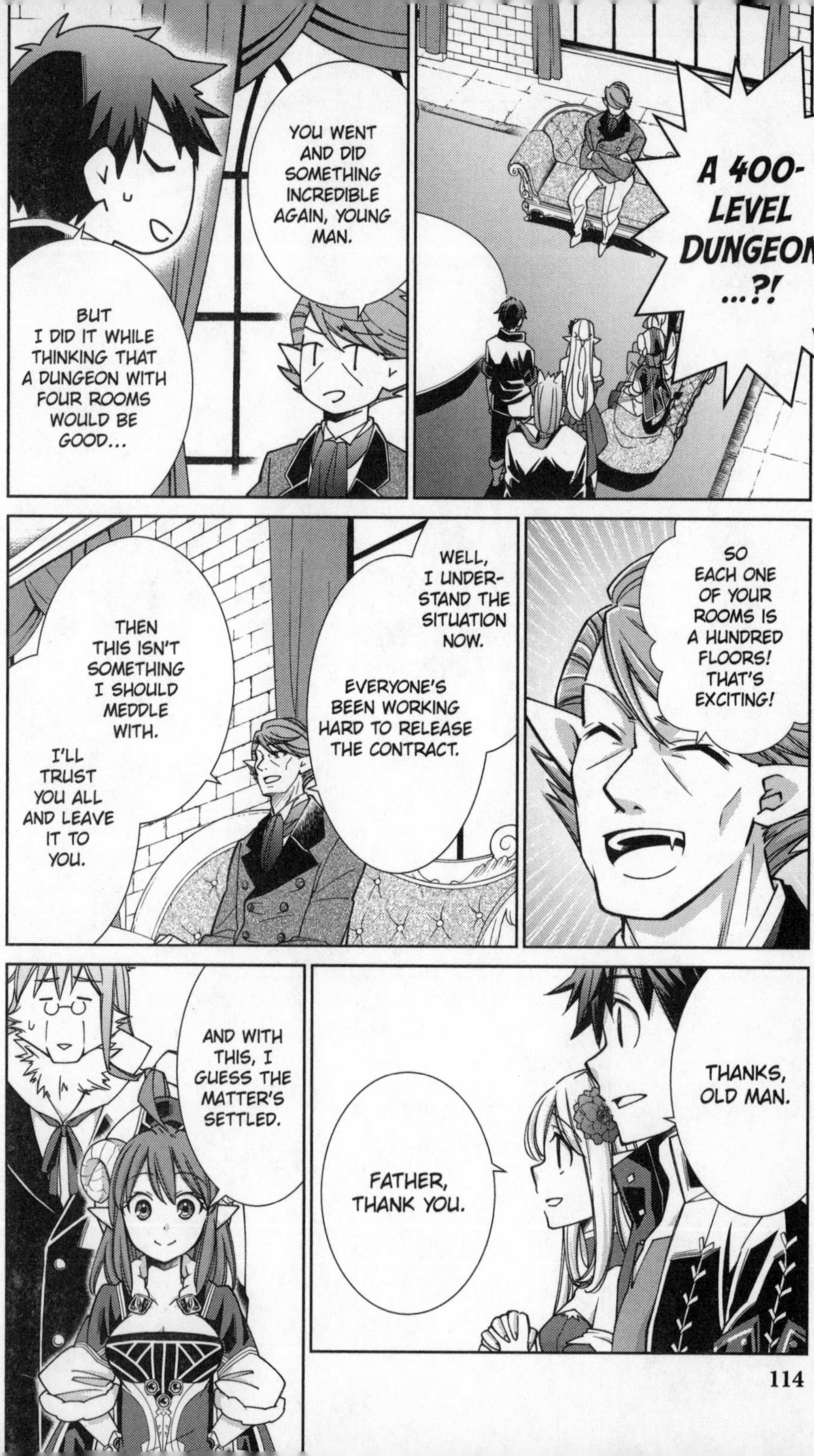
A 400-LEVEL DUNGEON ...?!
YOU WENT AND DID SOMETHING INCREDIBLE AGAIN, YOUNG MAN.
BUT I DID IT WHILE THINKING THAT A DUNGEON WITH FOUR ROOMS WOULD BE GOOD...
SO EACH ONE OF YOUR ROOMS IS A HUNDRED FLOORS! THAT'S EXCITING!
WELL, I UNDER-STAND THE SITUATION NOW.
EVERYONE'S BEEN WORKING HARD TO RELEASE THE CONTRACT.
THEN THIS ISN'T SOMETHING I SHOULD MEDDLE WITH.
I'LL TRUST YOU ALL AND LEAVE IT TO YOU.
THANKS, OLD MAN.
FATHER, THANK YOU.
AND WITH THIS, I GUESS THE MATTER'S SETTLED.

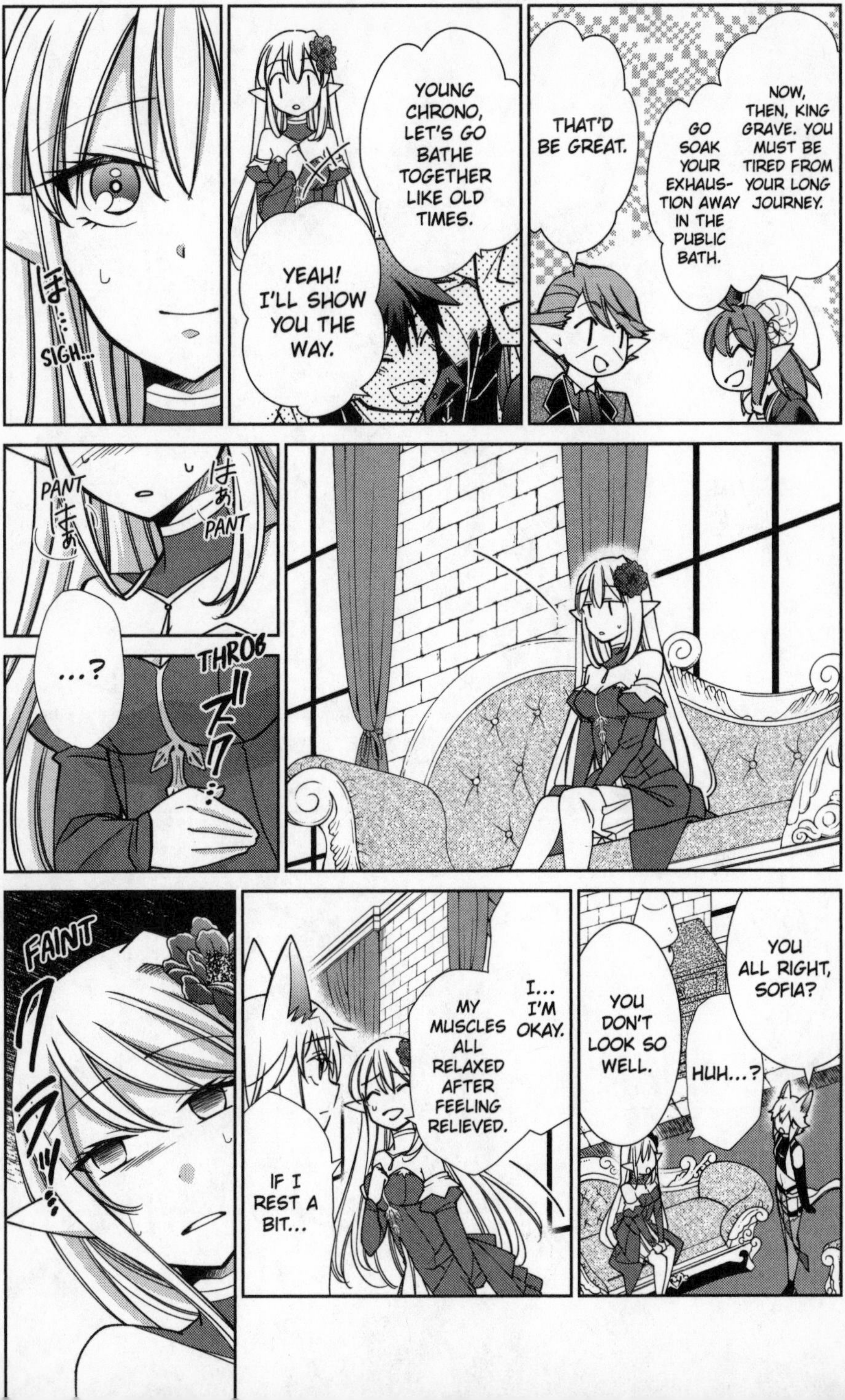
NOW, THEN, KING GRAVE. YOU MUST BE TIRED FROM YOUR LONG JOURNEY.
GO SOAK YOUR EXHAUSTION AWAY IN THE PUBLIC BATH.
THAT'D BE GREAT.
YOUNG CHRONO, LET'S GO BATHE TOGETHER LIKE OLD TIMES.
YEAH! I'LL SHOW YOU THE WAY.
SIGH...
PANT PANT
...?
THROB
YOU ALL RIGHT, SOFIA?
HUH...?
YOU DON'T LOOK SO WELL.
I... I'M OKAY.
MY MUSCLES ALL RELAXED AFTER FEELING RELIEVED.
IF I REST A BIT...
FAINT

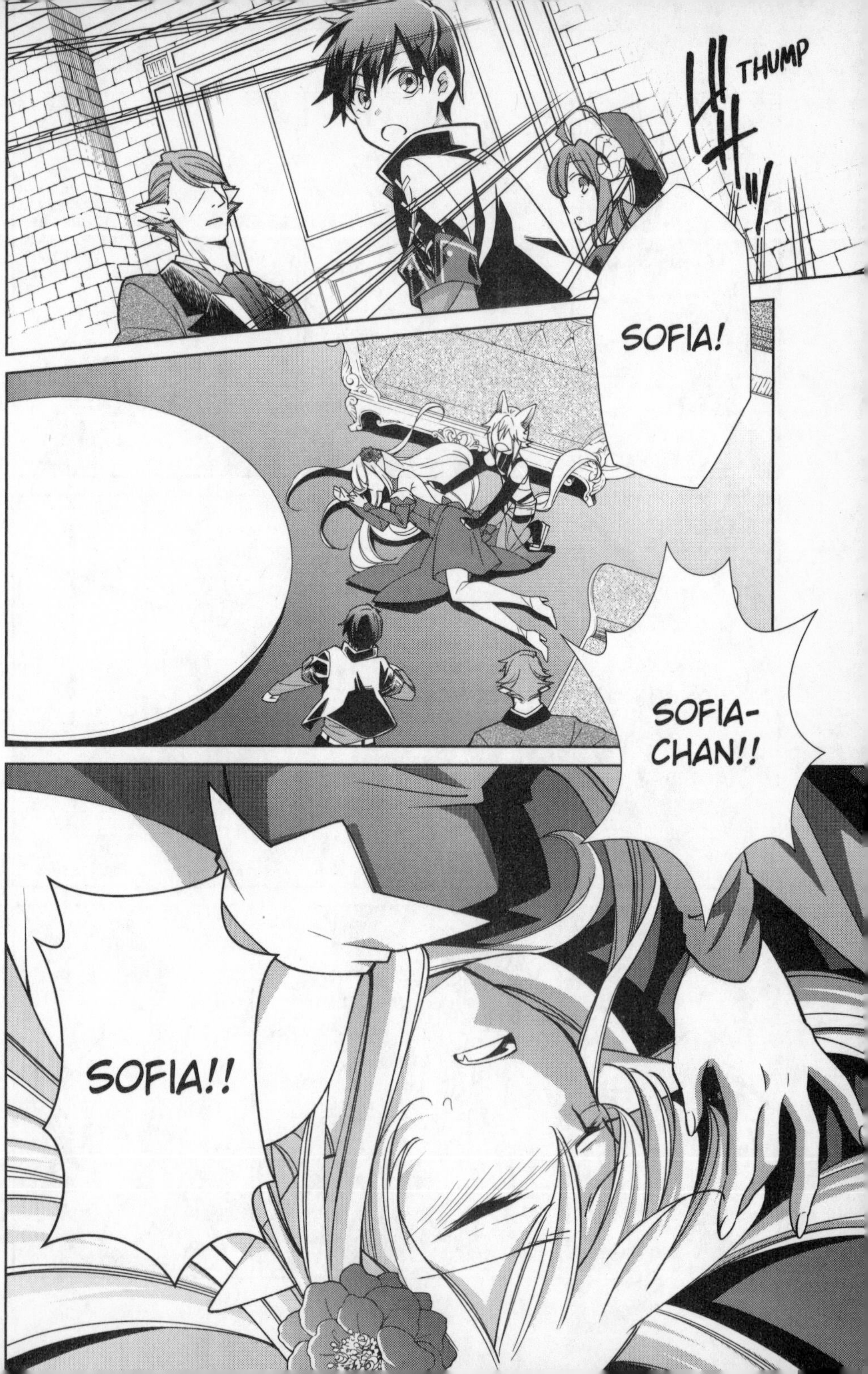
THUMP
SOFIA!
SOFIA-CHAN!!
SOFIA!!

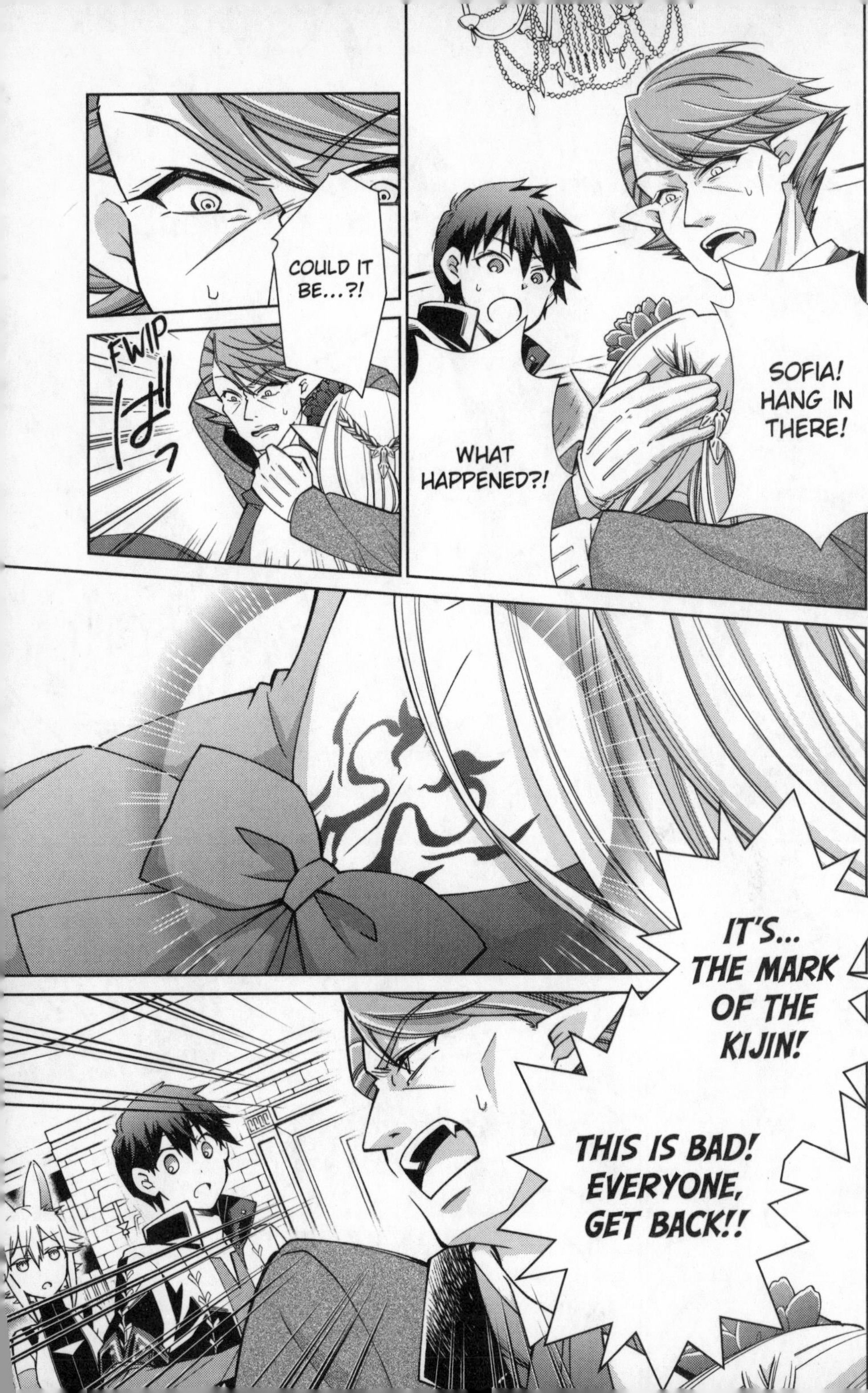
SOFIA! HANG IN THERE!
WHAT HAPPENED?!
COULD IT BE...?!
FWIP
IT'S... THE MARK OF THE KIJIN!
THIS IS BAD! EVERYONE, GET BACK!!

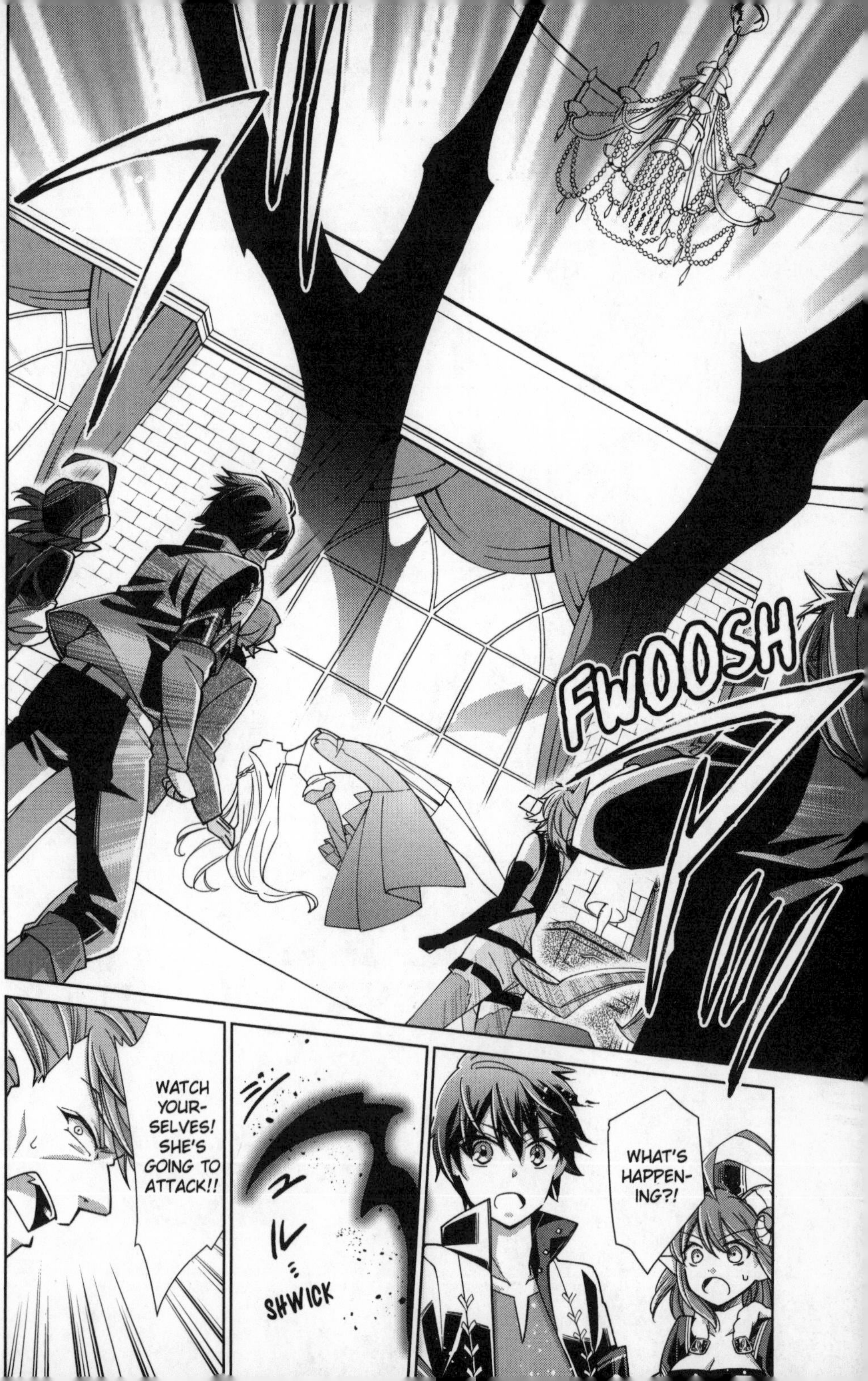
FWOOSH
WHAT'S HAPPEN-ING?!
SHWICK
WATCH YOUR-SELVES! SHE'S GOING TO ATTACK!!

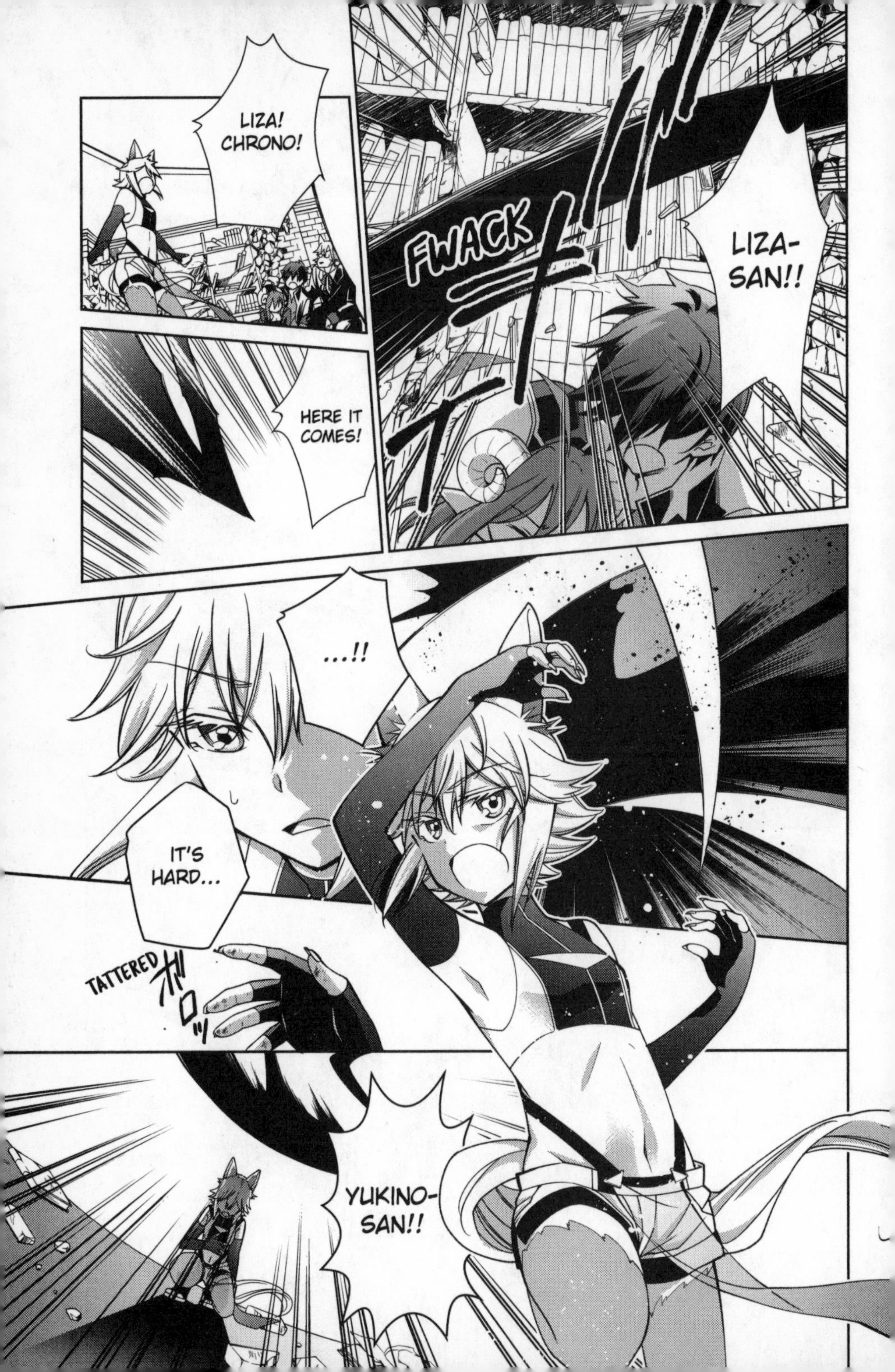
LIZA-SAN!!
FWACK
LIZA! CHRONO!
HERE IT COMES!
...!!
IT'S HARD...
TATTERED
YUKINO-SAN!!

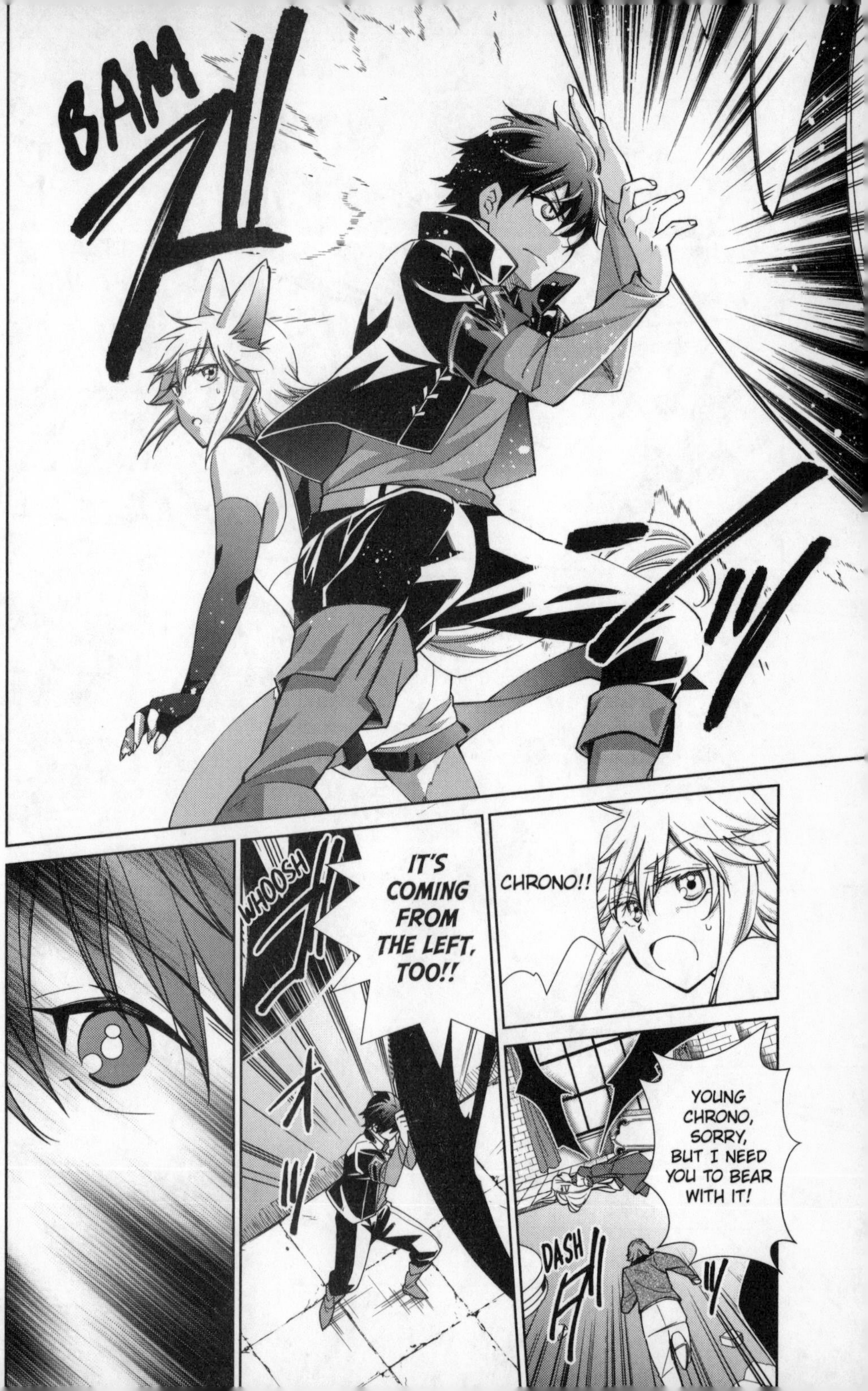
BAM
CHRONO!!
YOUNG CHRONO, SORRY, BUT I NEED YOU TO BEAR WITH IT!
DASH
WHOOSH
IT'S COMING FROM THE LEFT, TOO!!

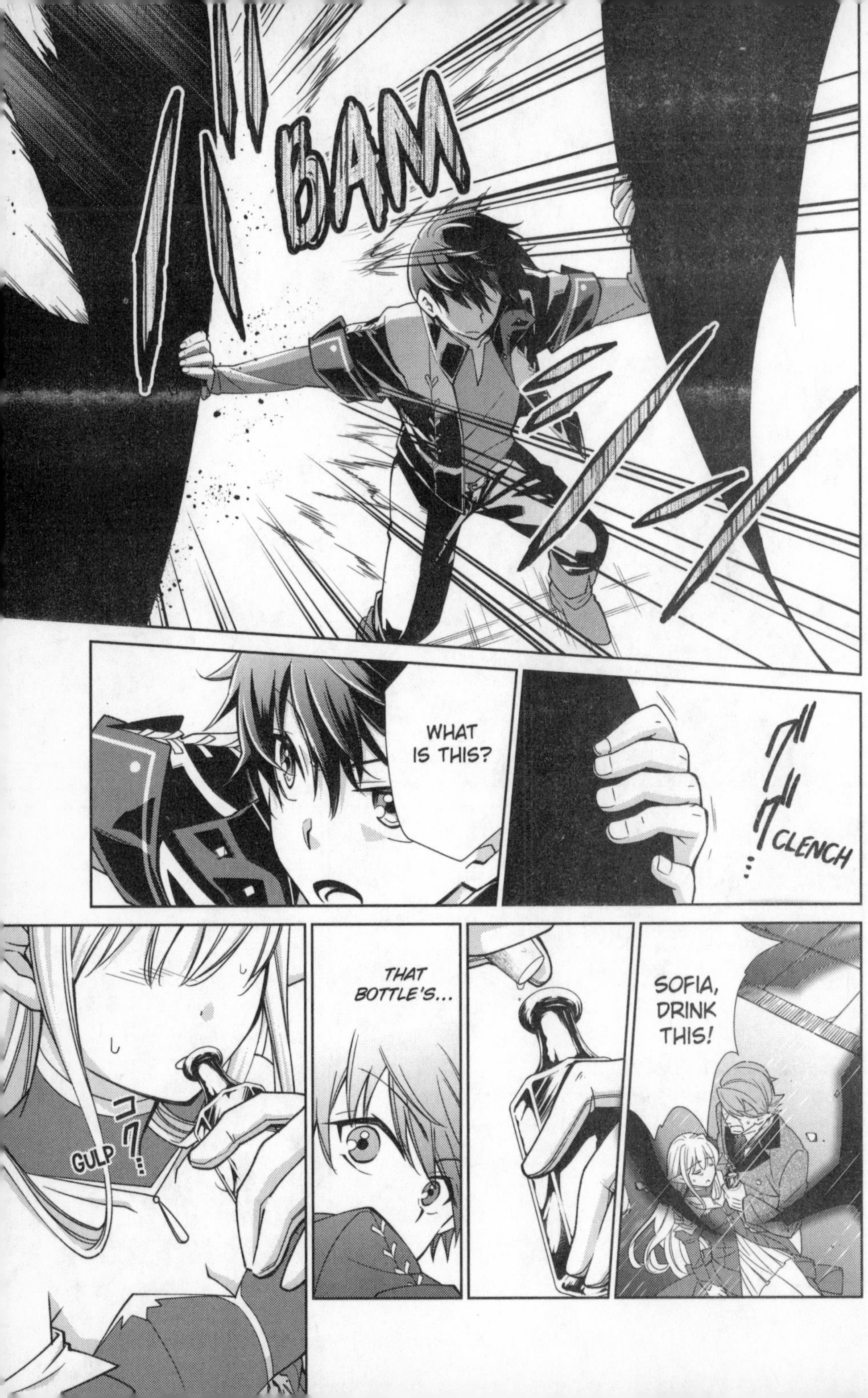
BAM
CLENCH
WHAT IS THIS?
SOFIA, DRINK THIS!
THAT BOTTLE'S...
GULP

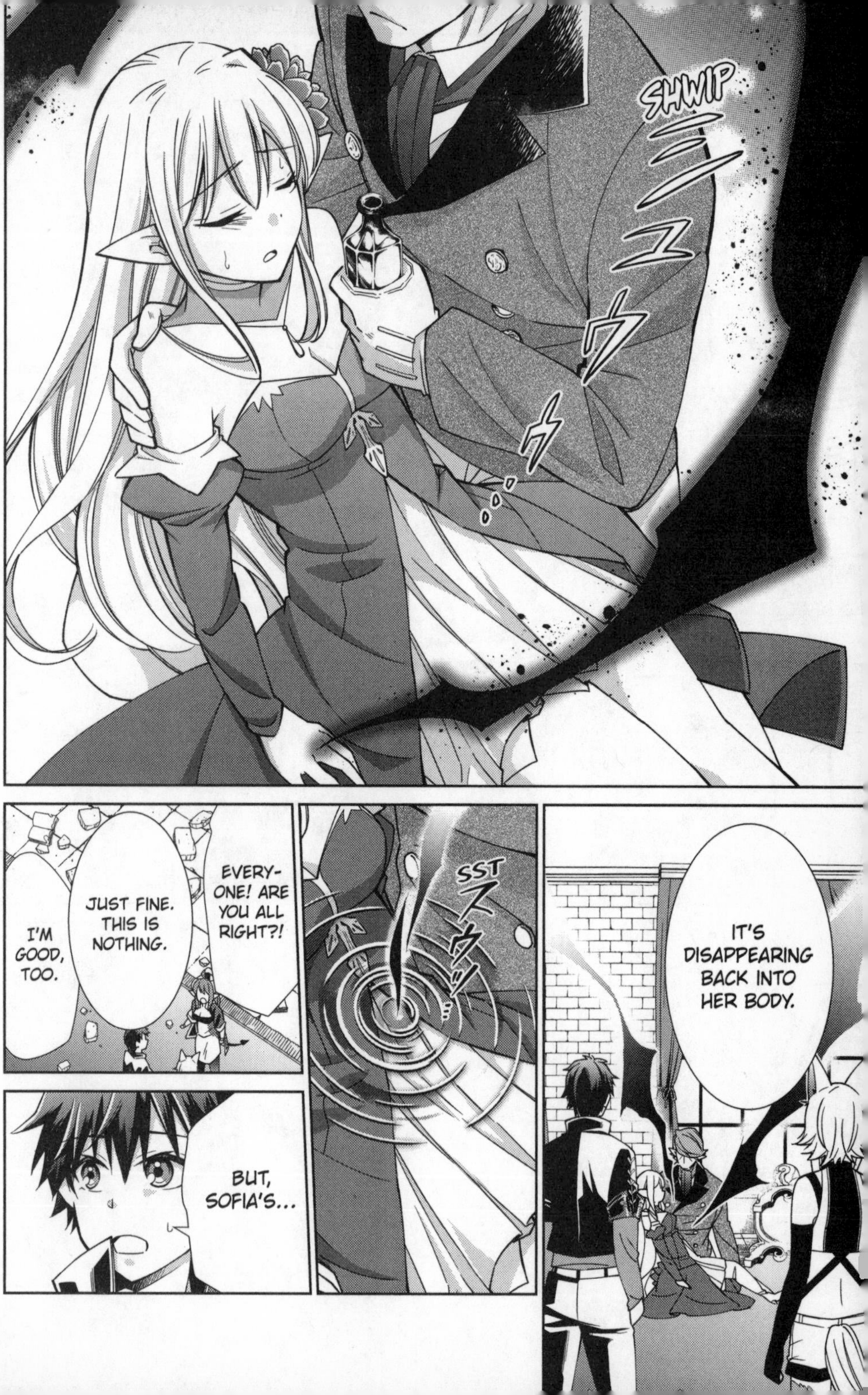
SHWIP
IT'S DISAPPEARING BACK INTO HER BODY.
SST
EVERY-ONE! ARE YOU ALL RIGHT?!
JUST FINE. THIS IS NOTHING.
I'M GOOD, TOO.
BUT, SOFIA'S...

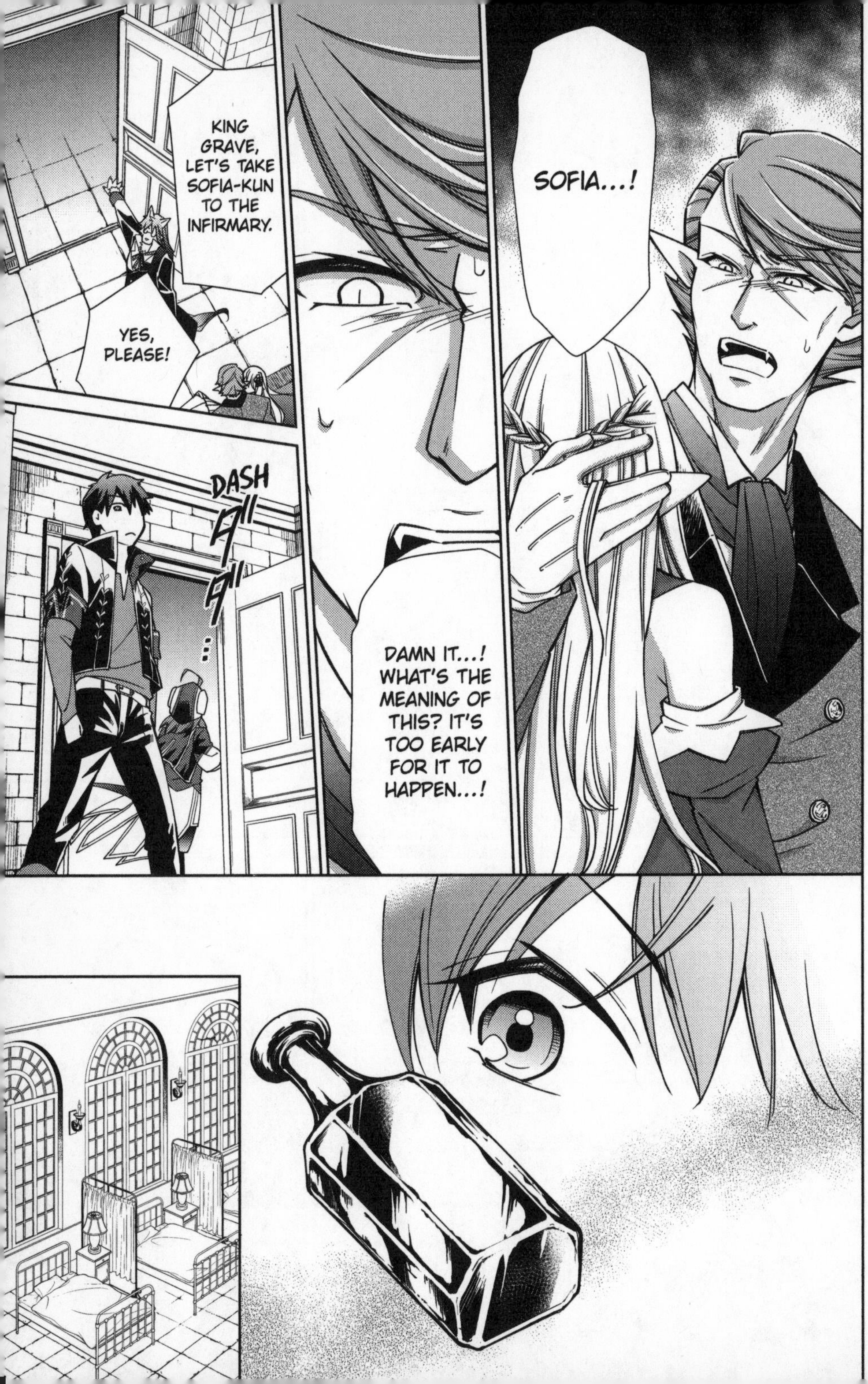

SOFIA...!
DAMN IT...! WHAT'S THE MEANING OF THIS? IT'S TOO EARLY FOR IT TO HAPPEN...!
KING GRAVE, LET'S TAKE SOFIA-KUN TO THE INFIRMARY.
YES, PLEASE!
DASH
...

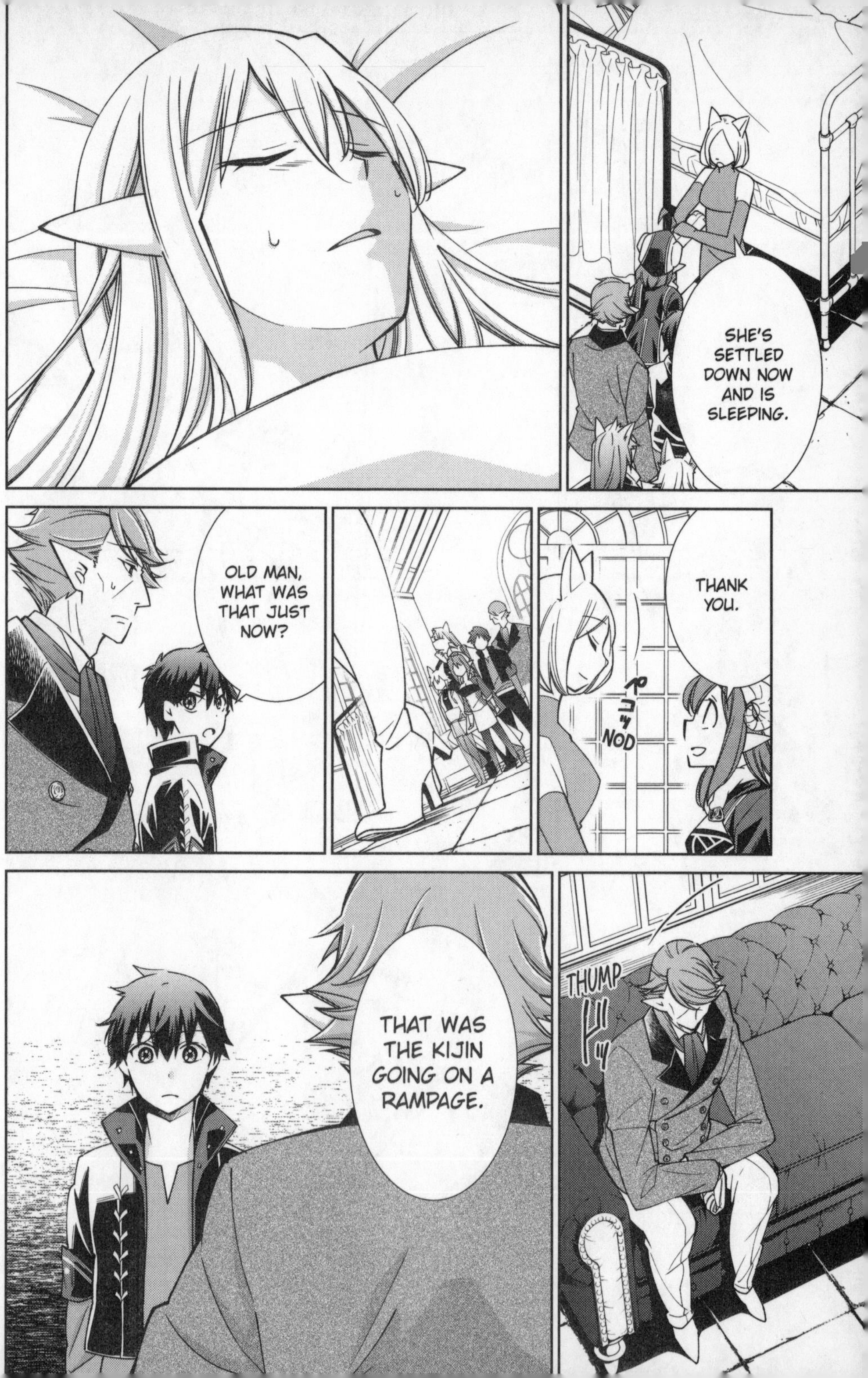
SHE'S SETTLED DOWN NOW AND IS SLEEPING.
THANK YOU.
ペコッ
NOD
OLD MAN, WHAT WAS THAT JUST NOW?
THUMP
ドッ
THAT WAS THE KIJIN GOING ON A RAMPAGE.

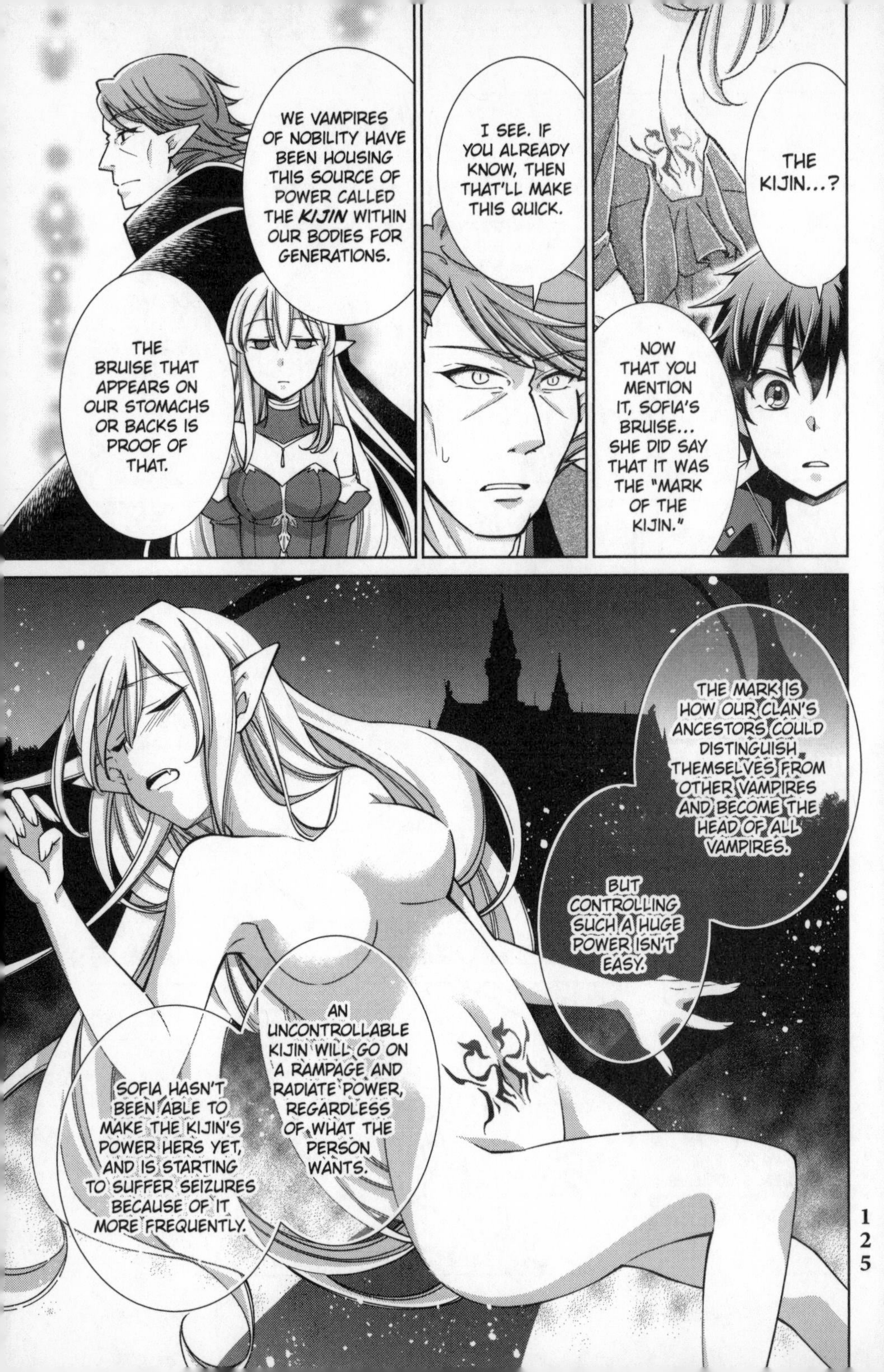
THE KIJIN...?
NOW THAT YOU MENTION IT, SOFIA'S BRUISE... SHE DID SAY THAT IT WAS THE "MARK OF THE KIJIN."
I SEE. IF YOU ALREADY KNOW, THEN THAT'LL MAKE THIS QUICK.
WE VAMPIRES OF NOBILITY HAVE BEEN HOUSING THIS SOURCE OF POWER CALLED THE *KIJIN* WITHIN OUR BODIES FOR GENERATIONS.
THE BRUISE THAT APPEARS ON OUR STOMACHS OR BACKS IS PROOF OF THAT.
THE MARK IS HOW OUR CLAN'S ANCESTORS COULD DISTINGUISH THEMSELVES FROM OTHER VAMPIRES AND BECOME THE HEAD OF ALL VAMPIRES.
BUT CONTROLLING SUCH A HUGE POWER ISN'T EASY.
AN UNCONTROLLABLE KIJIN WILL GO ON A RAMPAGE AND RADIATE POWER, REGARDLESS OF WHAT THE PERSON WANTS.
SOFIA HASN'T BEEN ABLE TO MAKE THE KIJIN'S POWER HERS YET, AND IS STARTING TO SUFFER SEIZURES BECAUSE OF IT MORE FREQUENTLY.

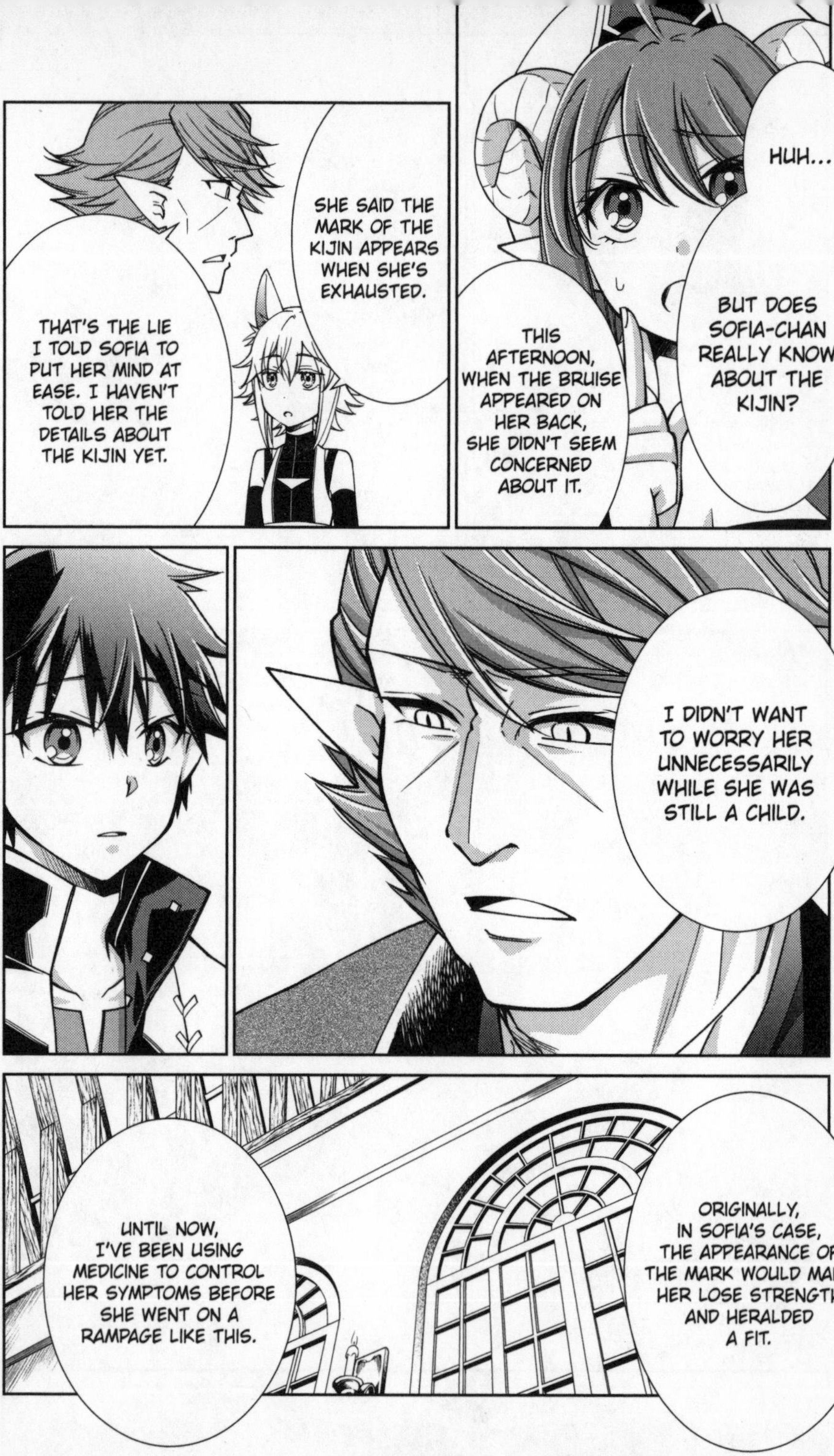
HUH...?
BUT DOES SOFIA-CHAN REALLY KNOW ABOUT THE KIJIN?
THIS AFTERNOON, WHEN THE BRUISE APPEARED ON HER BACK, SHE DIDN'T SEEM CONCERNED ABOUT IT.
SHE SAID THE MARK OF THE KIJIN APPEARS WHEN SHE'S EXHAUSTED.
THAT'S THE LIE I TOLD SOFIA TO PUT HER MIND AT EASE. I HAVEN'T TOLD HER THE DETAILS ABOUT THE KIJIN YET.
I DIDN'T WANT TO WORRY HER UNNECESSARILY WHILE SHE WAS STILL A CHILD.
ORIGINALLY, IN SOFIA'S CASE, THE APPEARANCE OF THE MARK WOULD MAKE HER LOSE STRENGTH AND HERALDED A FIT.
UNTIL NOW, I'VE BEEN USING MEDICINE TO CONTROL HER SYMPTOMS BEFORE SHE WENT ON A RAMPAGE LIKE THIS.

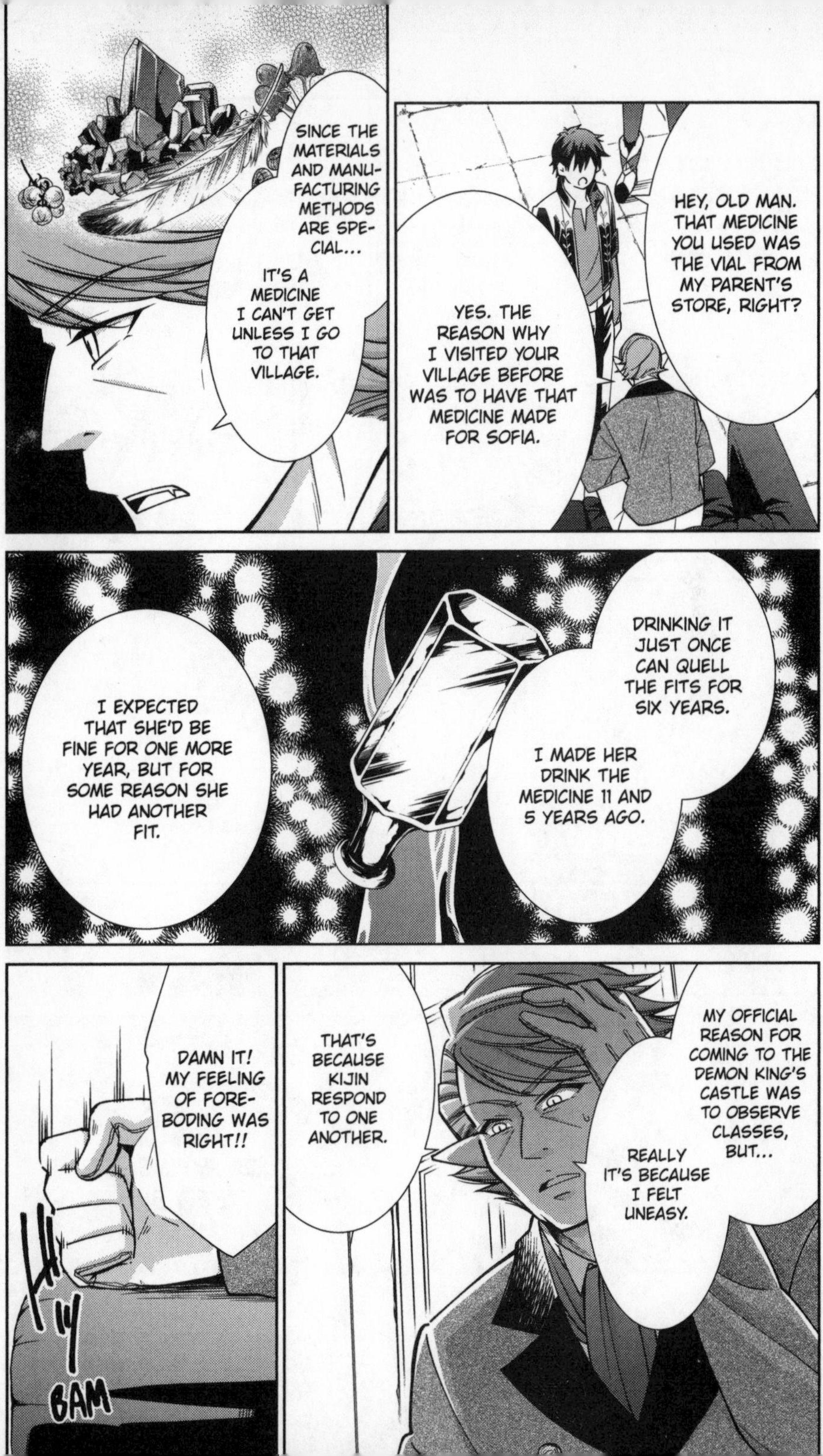
HEY, OLD MAN. THAT MEDICINE YOU USED WAS THE VIAL FROM MY PARENT'S STORE, RIGHT?
YES. THE REASON WHY I VISITED YOUR VILLAGE BEFORE WAS TO HAVE THAT MEDICINE MADE FOR SOFIA.
SINCE THE MATERIALS AND MANU-FACTURING METHODS ARE SPE-CIAL...
IT'S A MEDICINE I CAN'T GET UNLESS I GO TO THAT VILLAGE.
DRINKING IT JUST ONCE CAN QUELL THE FITS FOR SIX YEARS.
I MADE HER DRINK THE MEDICINE 11 AND 5 YEARS AGO.
I EXPECTED THAT SHE'D BE FINE FOR ONE MORE YEAR, BUT FOR SOME REASON SHE HAD ANOTHER FIT.
MY OFFICIAL REASON FOR COMING TO THE DEMON KING'S CASTLE WAS TO OBSERVE CLASSES, BUT...
REALLY IT'S BECAUSE I FELT UNEASY.
THAT'S BECAUSE KIJIN RESPOND TO ONE ANOTHER.
DAMN IT! MY FEELING OF FORE-BODING WAS RIGHT!!
BAM

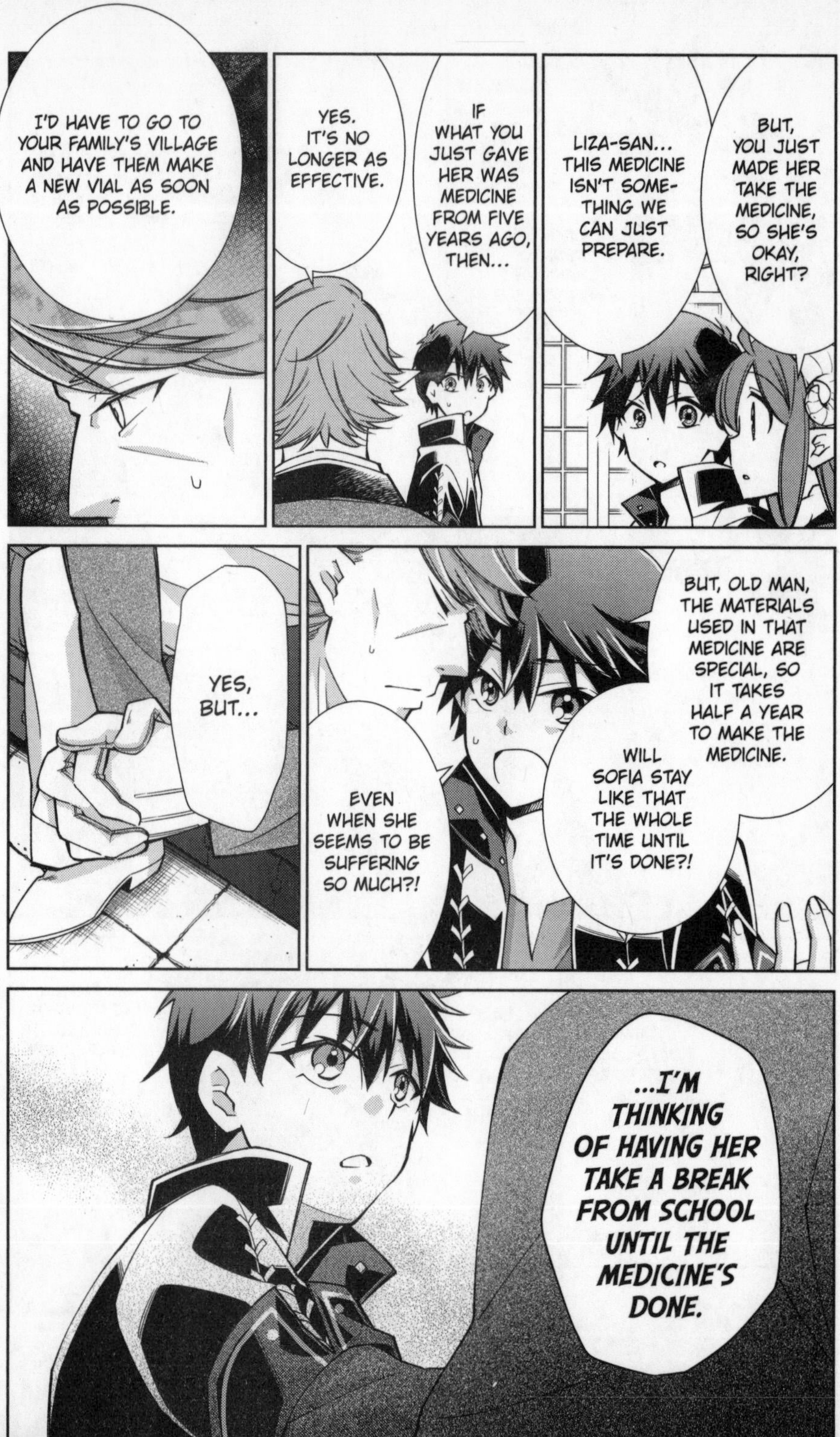
BUT, YOU JUST MADE HER TAKE THE MEDICINE, SO SHE'S OKAY, RIGHT?
LIZA-SAN... THIS MEDICINE ISN'T SOME-THING WE CAN JUST PREPARE.
IF WHAT YOU JUST GAVE HER WAS MEDICINE FROM FIVE YEARS AGO, THEN...
YES. IT'S NO LONGER AS EFFECTIVE.
I'D HAVE TO GO TO YOUR FAMILY'S VILLAGE AND HAVE THEM MAKE A NEW VIAL AS SOON AS POSSIBLE.
BUT, OLD MAN, THE MATERIALS USED IN THAT MEDICINE ARE SPECIAL, SO IT TAKES HALF A YEAR TO MAKE THE MEDICINE.
WILL SOFIA STAY LIKE THAT THE WHOLE TIME UNTIL IT'S DONE?!
EVEN WHEN SHE SEEMS TO BE SUFFERING SO MUCH?!
YES, BUT...
...I'M THINKING OF HAVING HER TAKE A BREAK FROM SCHOOL UNTIL THE MEDICINE'S DONE.

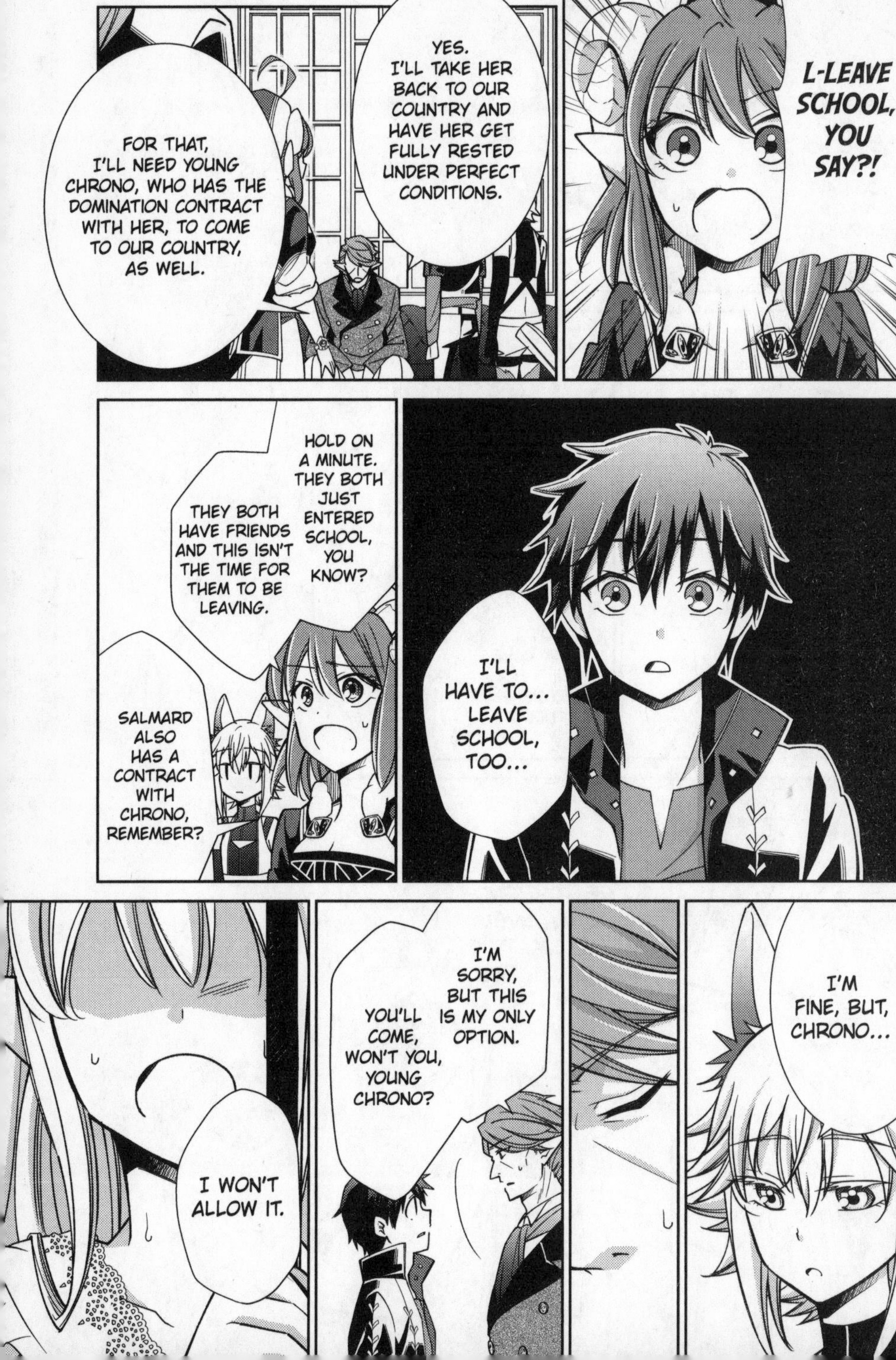
L-LEAVE SCHOOL, YOU SAY?!
YES. I'LL TAKE HER BACK TO OUR COUNTRY AND HAVE HER GET FULLY RESTED UNDER PERFECT CONDITIONS.
FOR THAT, I'LL NEED YOUNG CHRONO, WHO HAS THE DOMINATION CONTRACT WITH HER, TO COME TO OUR COUNTRY, AS WELL.
I'LL HAVE TO... LEAVE SCHOOL, TOO...
HOLD ON A MINUTE. THEY BOTH JUST ENTERED SCHOOL, YOU KNOW?
THEY BOTH HAVE FRIENDS AND THIS ISN'T THE TIME FOR THEM TO BE LEAVING.
SALMARD ALSO HAS A CONTRACT WITH CHRONO, REMEMBER?
I'M FINE, BUT, CHRONO...
I'M SORRY, BUT THIS IS MY ONLY OPTION.
YOU'LL COME, WON'T YOU, YOUNG CHRONO?
I WON'T ALLOW IT.

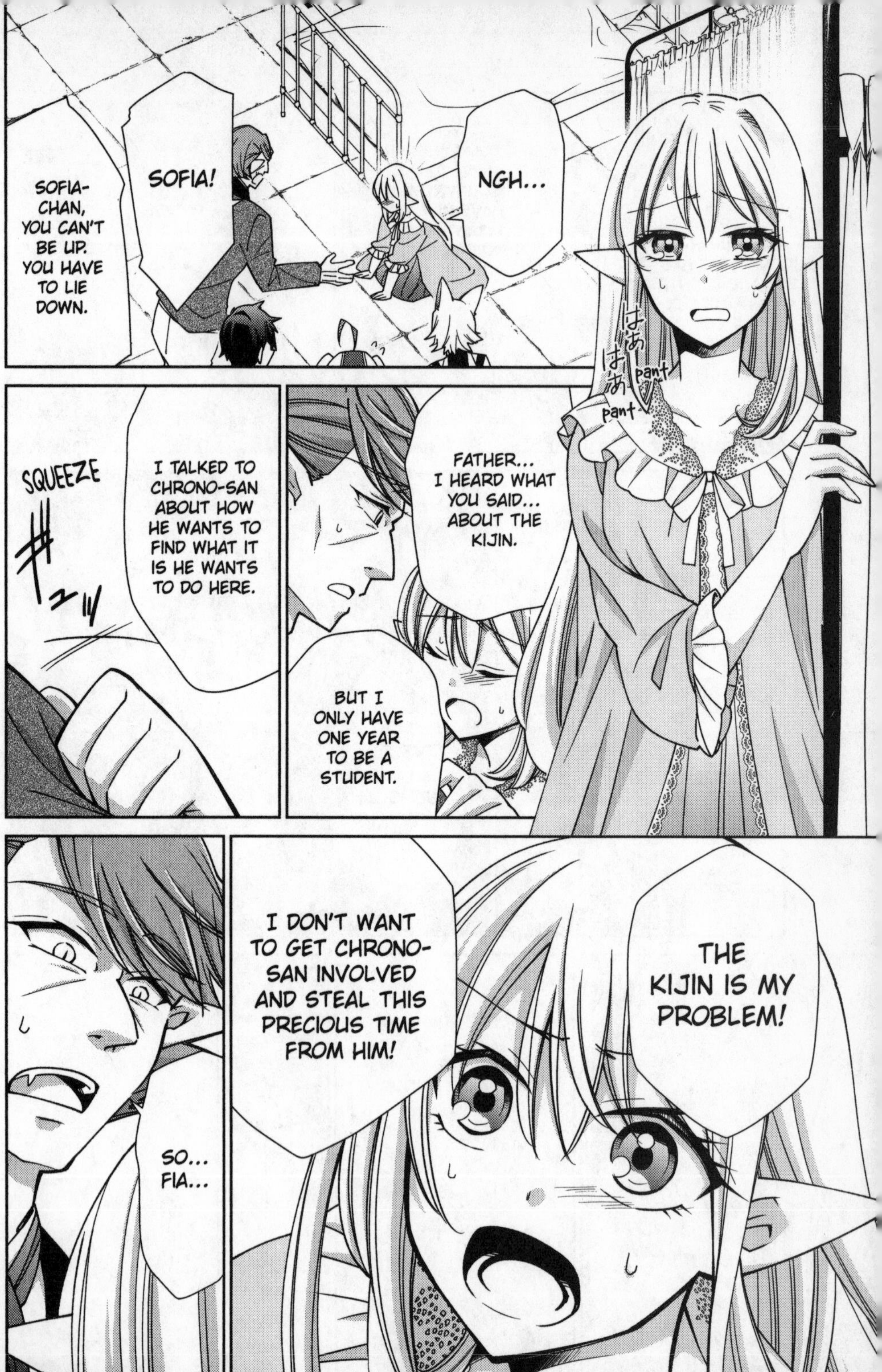
はあ はあ
pant
pant
NGH...
SOFIA!
SOFIA-CHAN, YOU CAN'T BE UP. YOU HAVE TO LIE DOWN.
FATHER... I HEARD WHAT YOU SAID... ABOUT THE KIJIN.
BUT I ONLY HAVE ONE YEAR TO BE A STUDENT.
I TALKED TO CHRONO-SAN ABOUT HOW HE WANTS TO FIND WHAT IT IS HE WANTS TO DO HERE.
SQUEEZE
THE KIJIN IS MY PROBLEM!
I DON'T WANT TO GET CHRONO-SAN INVOLVED AND STEAL THIS PRECIOUS TIME FROM HIM!
SO... FIA...

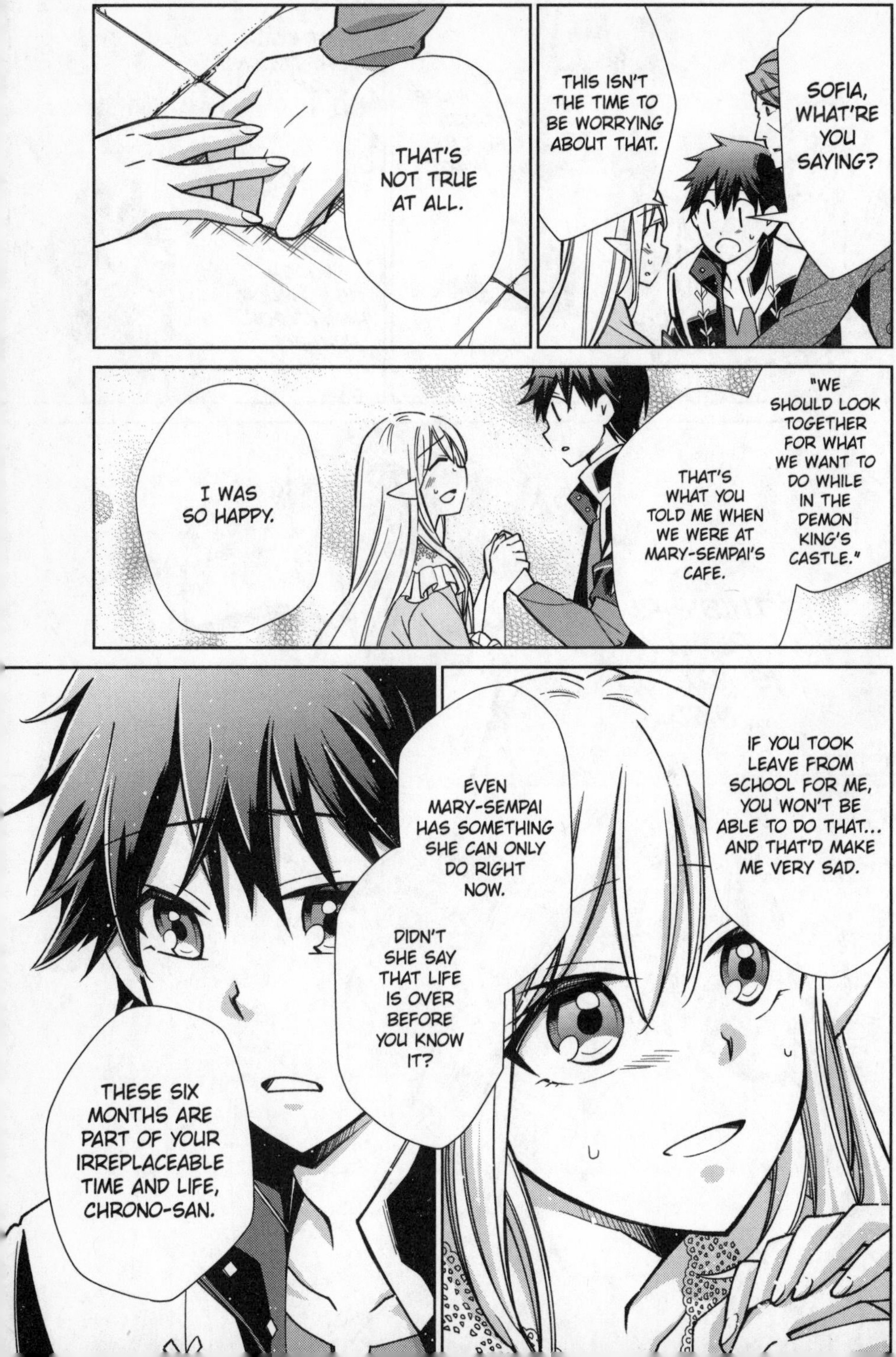
SOFIA, WHAT'RE YOU SAYING?
THIS ISN'T THE TIME TO BE WORRYING ABOUT THAT.
THAT'S NOT TRUE AT ALL.
"WE SHOULD LOOK TOGETHER FOR WHAT WE WANT TO DO WHILE IN THE DEMON KING'S CASTLE."
THAT'S WHAT YOU TOLD ME WHEN WE WERE AT MARY-SEMPAI'S CAFE.
I WAS SO HAPPY.
IF YOU TOOK LEAVE FROM SCHOOL FOR ME, YOU WON'T BE ABLE TO DO THAT... AND THAT'D MAKE ME VERY SAD.
EVEN MARY-SEMPAI HAS SOMETHING SHE CAN ONLY DO RIGHT NOW.
DIDN'T SHE SAY THAT LIFE IS OVER BEFORE YOU KNOW IT?
THESE SIX MONTHS ARE PART OF YOUR IRREPLACEABLE TIME AND LIFE, CHRONO-SAN.

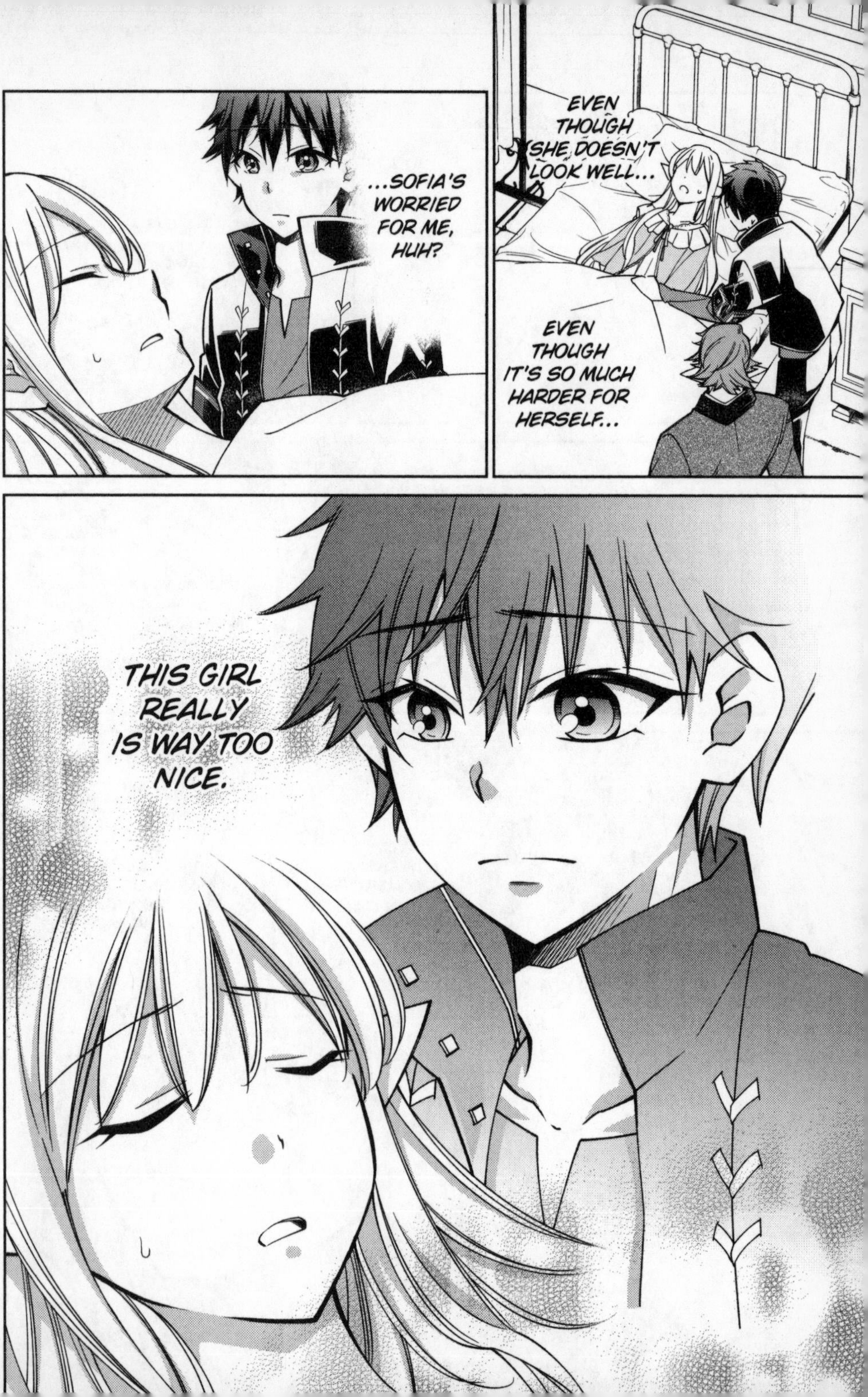
EVEN THOUGH SHE DOESN'T LOOK WELL...
EVEN THOUGH IT'S SO MUCH HARDER FOR HERSELF...
...SOFIA'S WORRIED FOR ME, HUH?
THIS GIRL REALLY IS WAY TOO NICE.

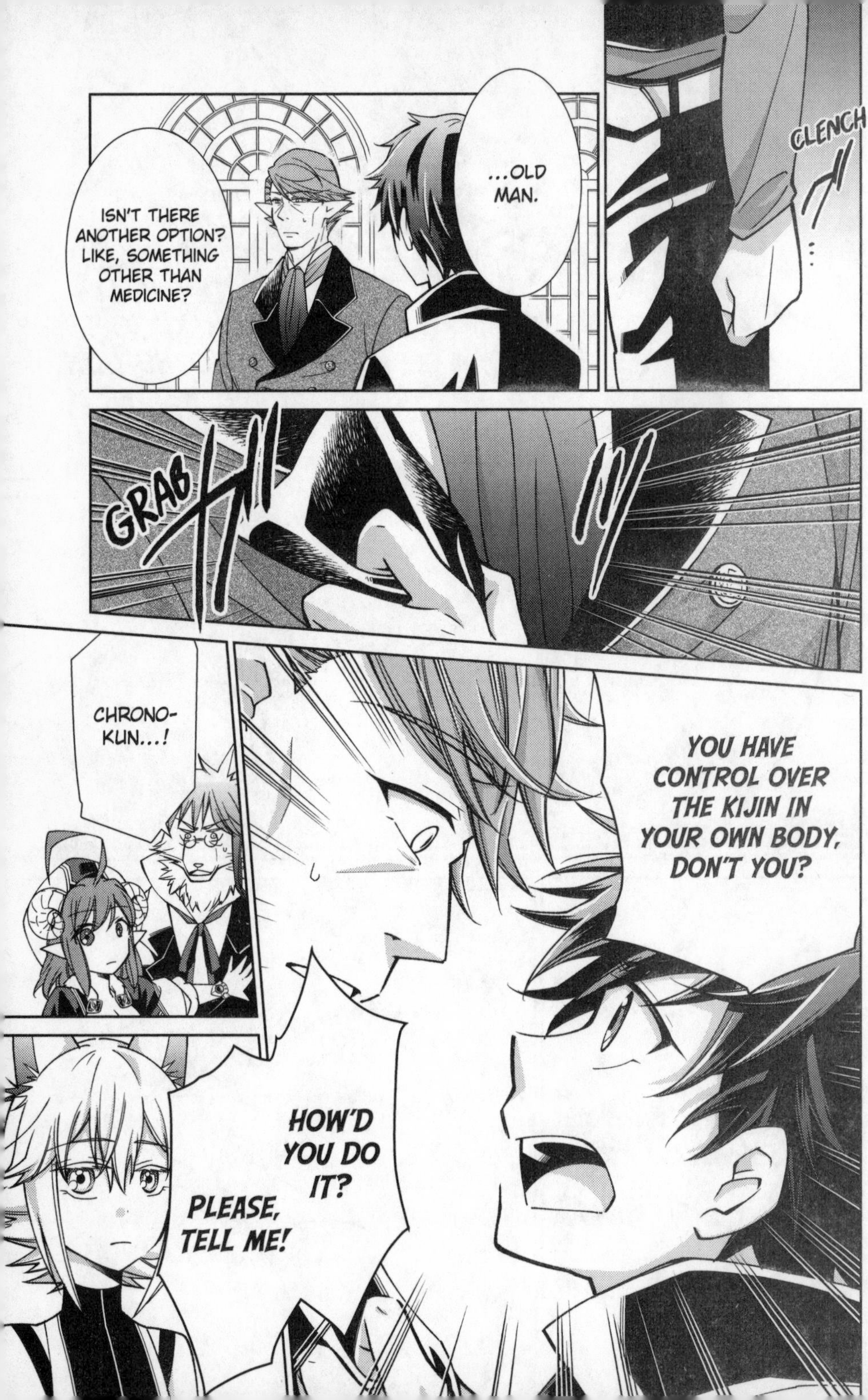
CLENCH
...OLD MAN.
ISN'T THERE ANOTHER OPTION? LIKE, SOMETHING OTHER THAN MEDICINE?
GRAB
YOU HAVE CONTROL OVER THE KIJIN IN YOUR OWN BODY, DON'T YOU?
CHRONO-KUN...!
HOW'D YOU DO IT?
PLEASE, TELL ME!

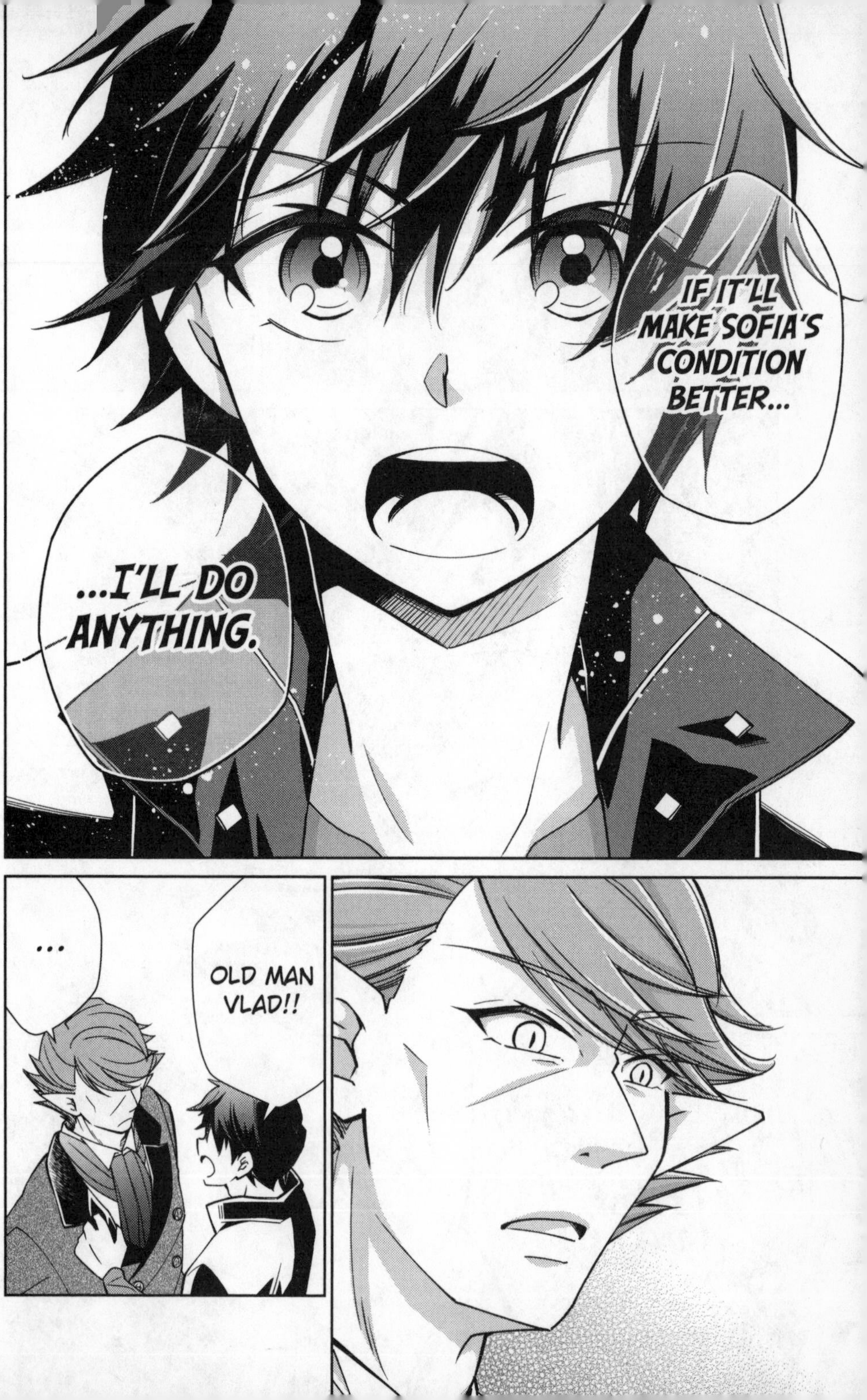
IF IT'LL MAKE SOFIA'S CONDITION BETTER...
...I'LL DO ANYTHING.
OLD MAN VLAD!!
...

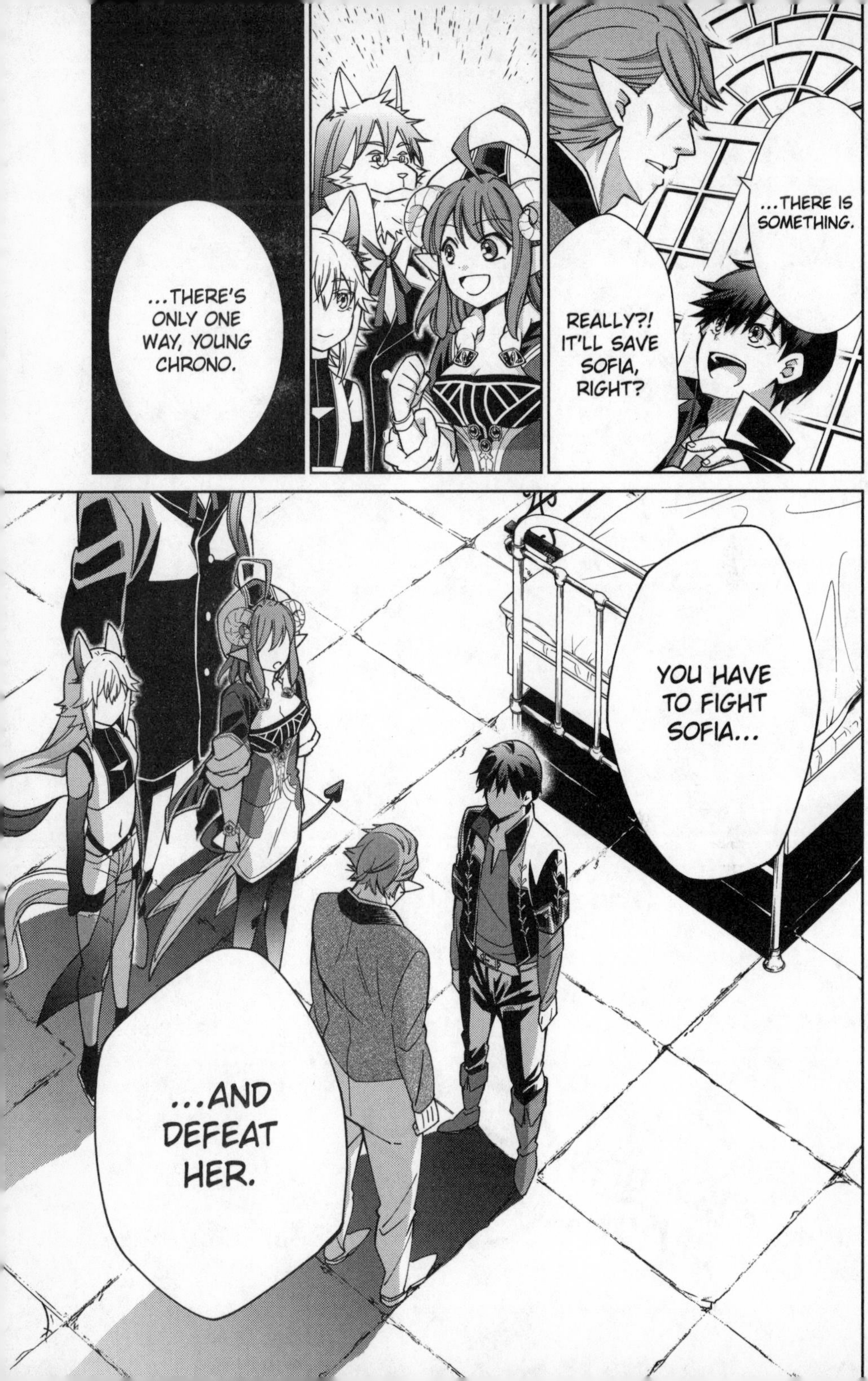
...THERE IS SOMETHING.
REALLY?! IT'LL SAVE SOFIA, RIGHT?
...THERE'S ONLY ONE WAY, YOUNG CHRONO.
YOU HAVE TO FIGHT SOFIA...
...AND DEFEAT HER.

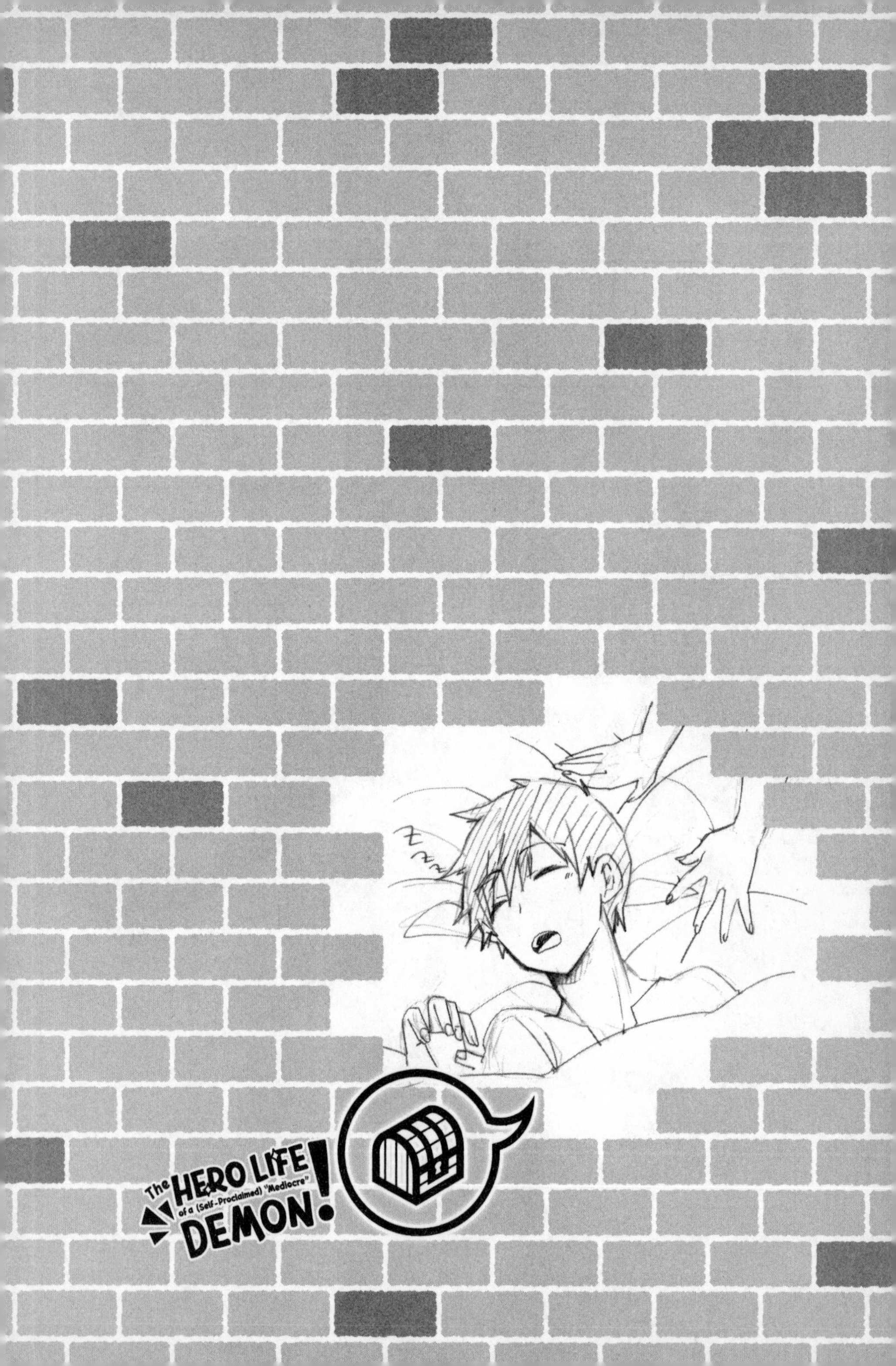
The HERO LIFE of a (Self-Proclaimed) "Mediocre" DEMON!

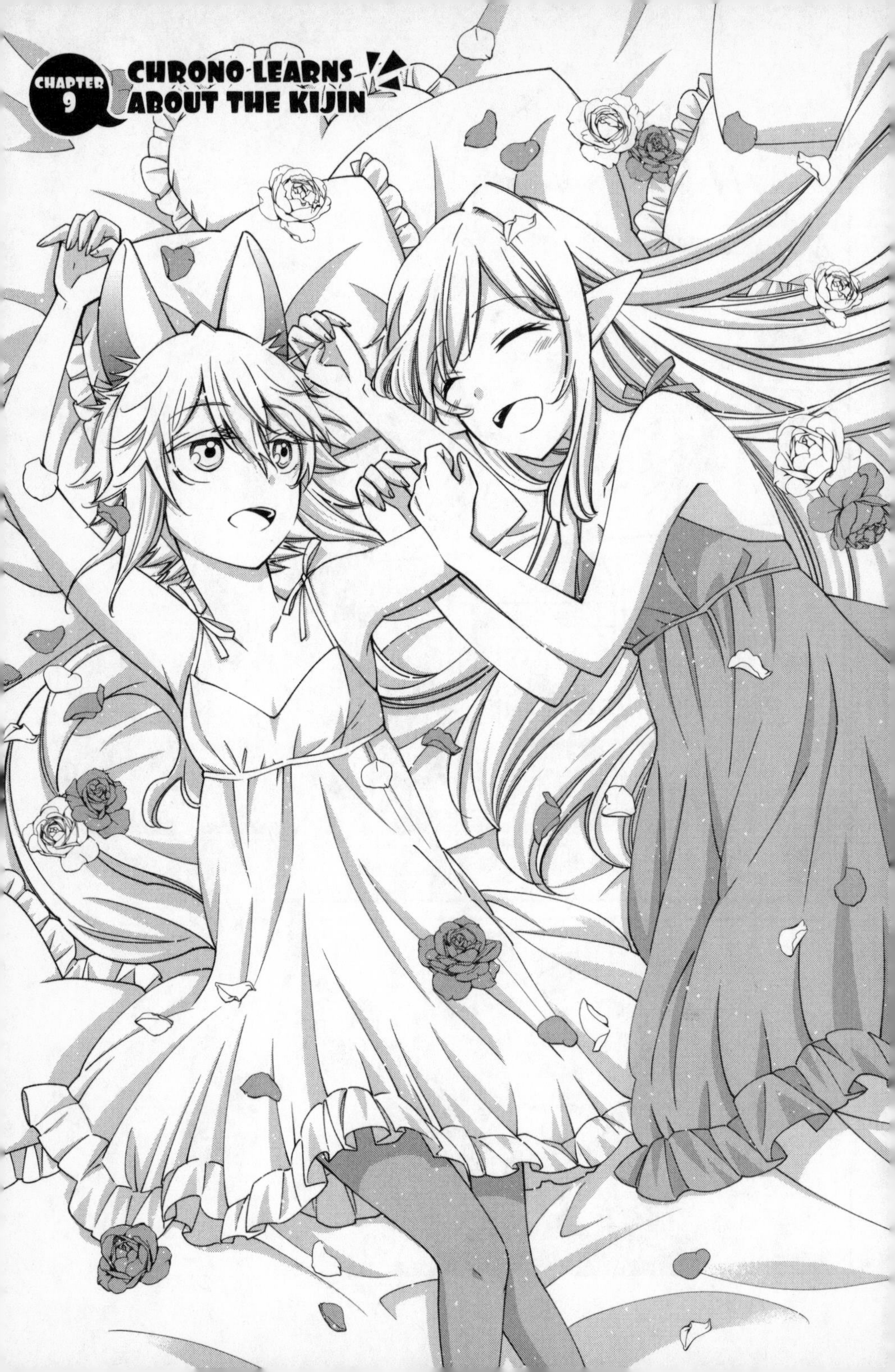
CHAPTER 9
CHRONO LEARNS ABOUT THE KIJIN

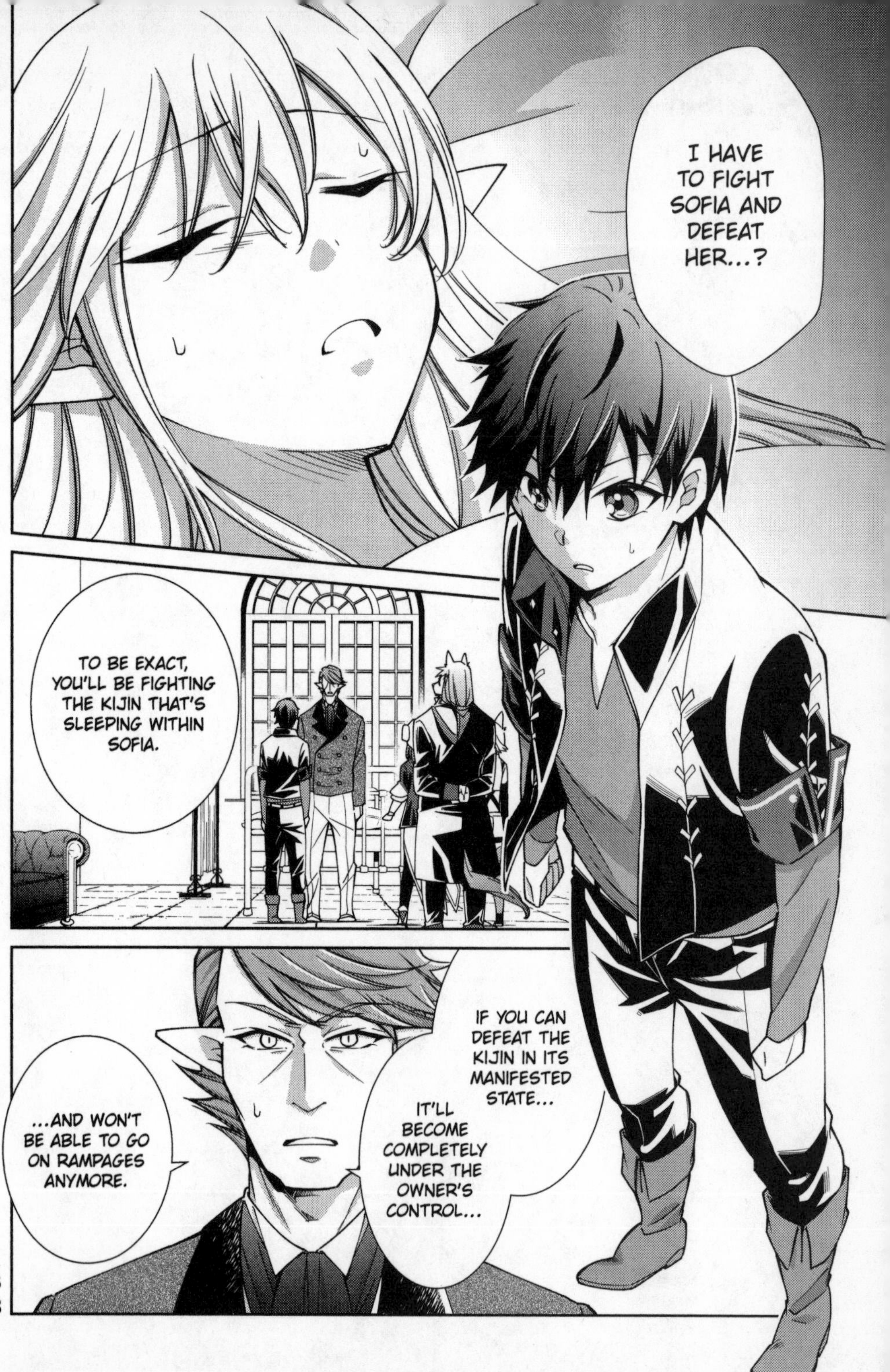
I HAVE TO FIGHT SOFIA AND DEFEAT HER…?
TO BE EXACT, YOU'LL BE FIGHTING THE KIJIN THAT'S SLEEPING WITHIN SOFIA.
IF YOU CAN DEFEAT THE KIJIN IN ITS MANIFESTED STATE…
IT'LL BECOME COMPLETELY UNDER THE OWNER'S CONTROL…
…AND WON'T BE ABLE TO GO ON RAMPAGES ANYMORE.

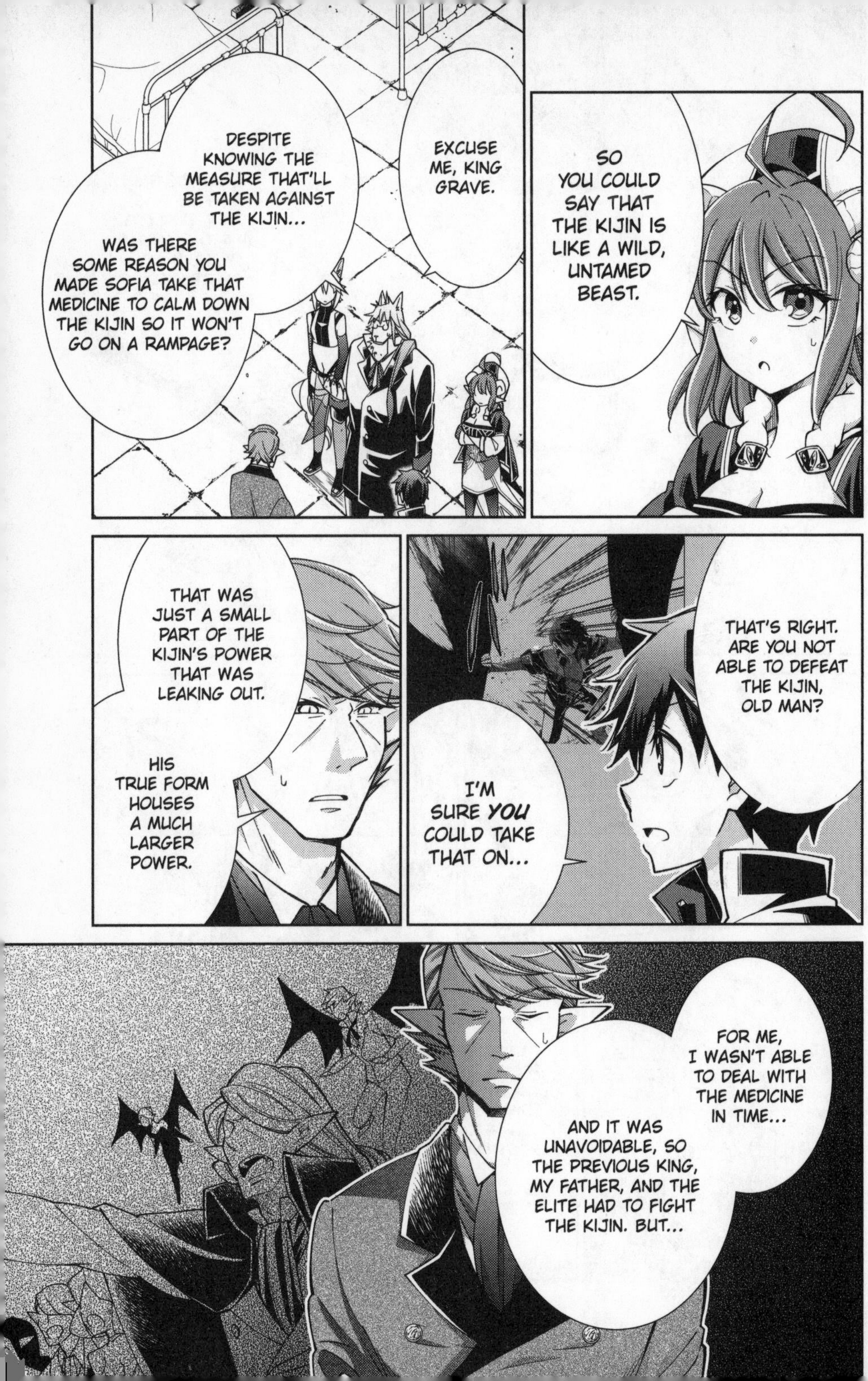

SO YOU COULD SAY THAT THE KIJIN IS LIKE A WILD, UNTAMED BEAST.
EXCUSE ME, KING GRAVE.
DESPITE KNOWING THE MEASURE THAT'LL BE TAKEN AGAINST THE KIJIN...
WAS THERE SOME REASON YOU MADE SOFIA TAKE THAT MEDICINE TO CALM DOWN THE KIJIN SO IT WON'T GO ON A RAMPAGE?
THAT'S RIGHT. ARE YOU NOT ABLE TO DEFEAT THE KIJIN, OLD MAN?
I'M SURE *YOU* COULD TAKE THAT ON...
THAT WAS JUST A SMALL PART OF THE KIJIN'S POWER THAT WAS LEAKING OUT.
HIS TRUE FORM HOUSES A MUCH LARGER POWER.
FOR ME, I WASN'T ABLE TO DEAL WITH THE MEDICINE IN TIME...
AND IT WAS UNAVOIDABLE, SO THE PREVIOUS KING, MY FATHER, AND THE ELITE HAD TO FIGHT THE KIJIN. BUT...

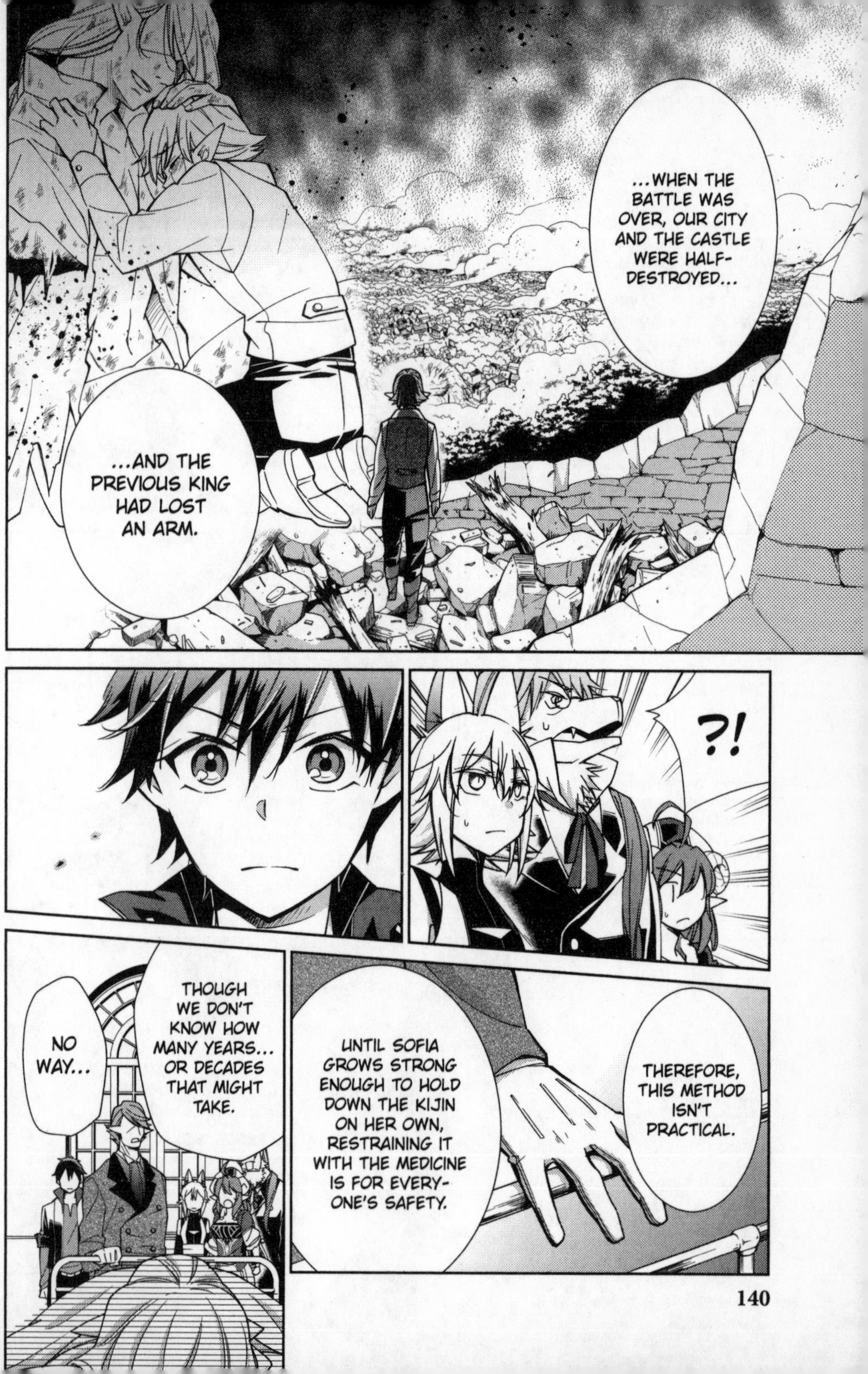
...WHEN THE BATTLE WAS OVER, OUR CITY AND THE CASTLE WERE HALF-DESTROYED...
...AND THE PREVIOUS KING HAD LOST AN ARM.
?!
THEREFORE, THIS METHOD ISN'T PRACTICAL.
UNTIL SOFIA GROWS STRONG ENOUGH TO HOLD DOWN THE KIJIN ON HER OWN, RESTRAINING IT WITH THE MEDICINE IS FOR EVERY-ONE'S SAFETY.
THOUGH WE DON'T KNOW HOW MANY YEARS... OR DECADES THAT MIGHT TAKE.
NO WAY...

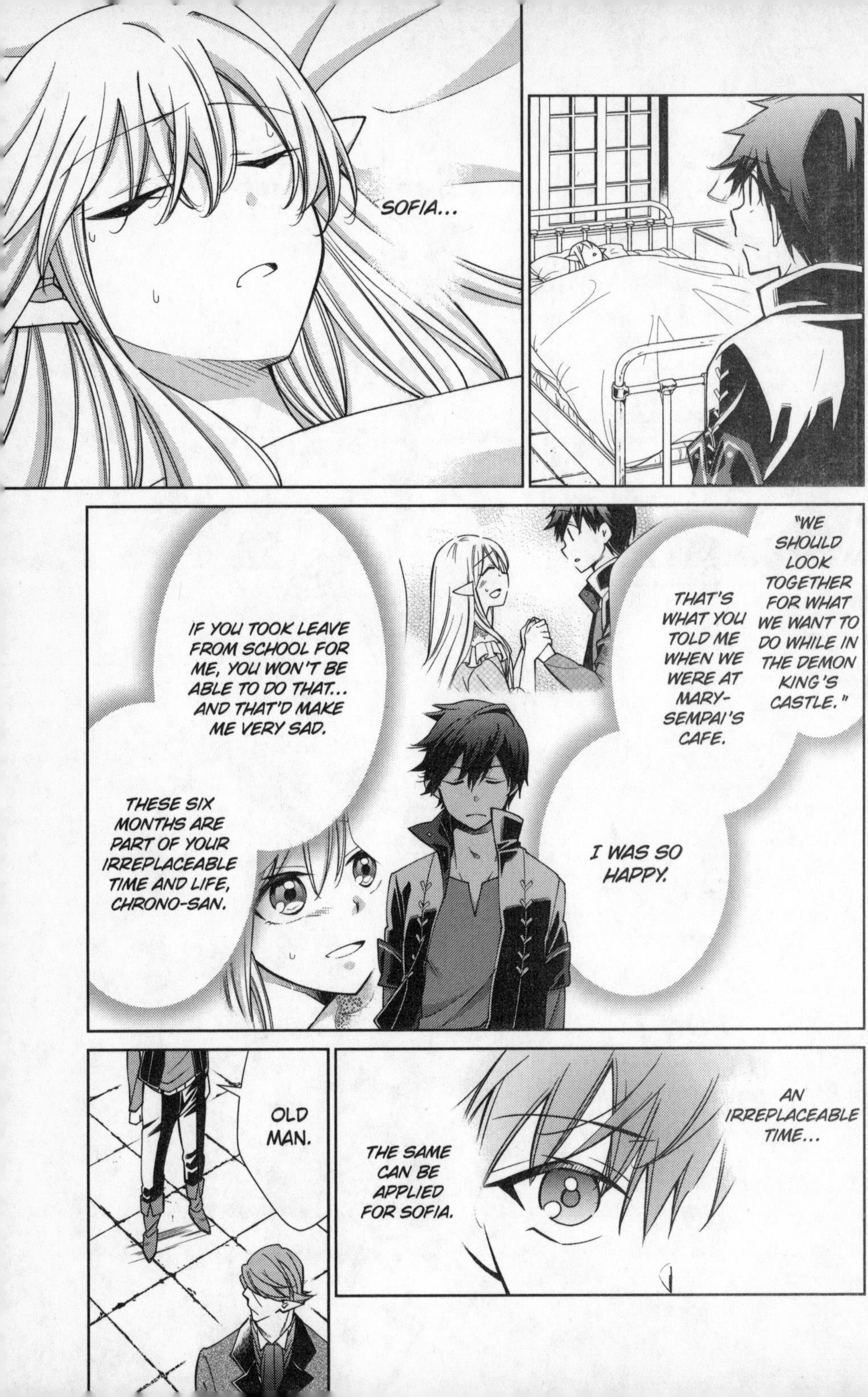
SOFIA...
"WE SHOULD LOOK TOGETHER FOR WHAT WE WANT TO DO WHILE IN THE DEMON KING'S CASTLE."
THAT'S WHAT YOU TOLD ME WHEN WE WERE AT MARY-SEMPAI'S CAFE.
I WAS SO HAPPY.
IF YOU TOOK LEAVE FROM SCHOOL FOR ME, YOU WON'T BE ABLE TO DO THAT... AND THAT'D MAKE ME VERY SAD.
THESE SIX MONTHS ARE PART OF YOUR IRREPLACEABLE TIME AND LIFE, CHRONO-SAN.
AN IRREPLACEABLE TIME...
THE SAME CAN BE APPLIED FOR SOFIA.
OLD MAN.

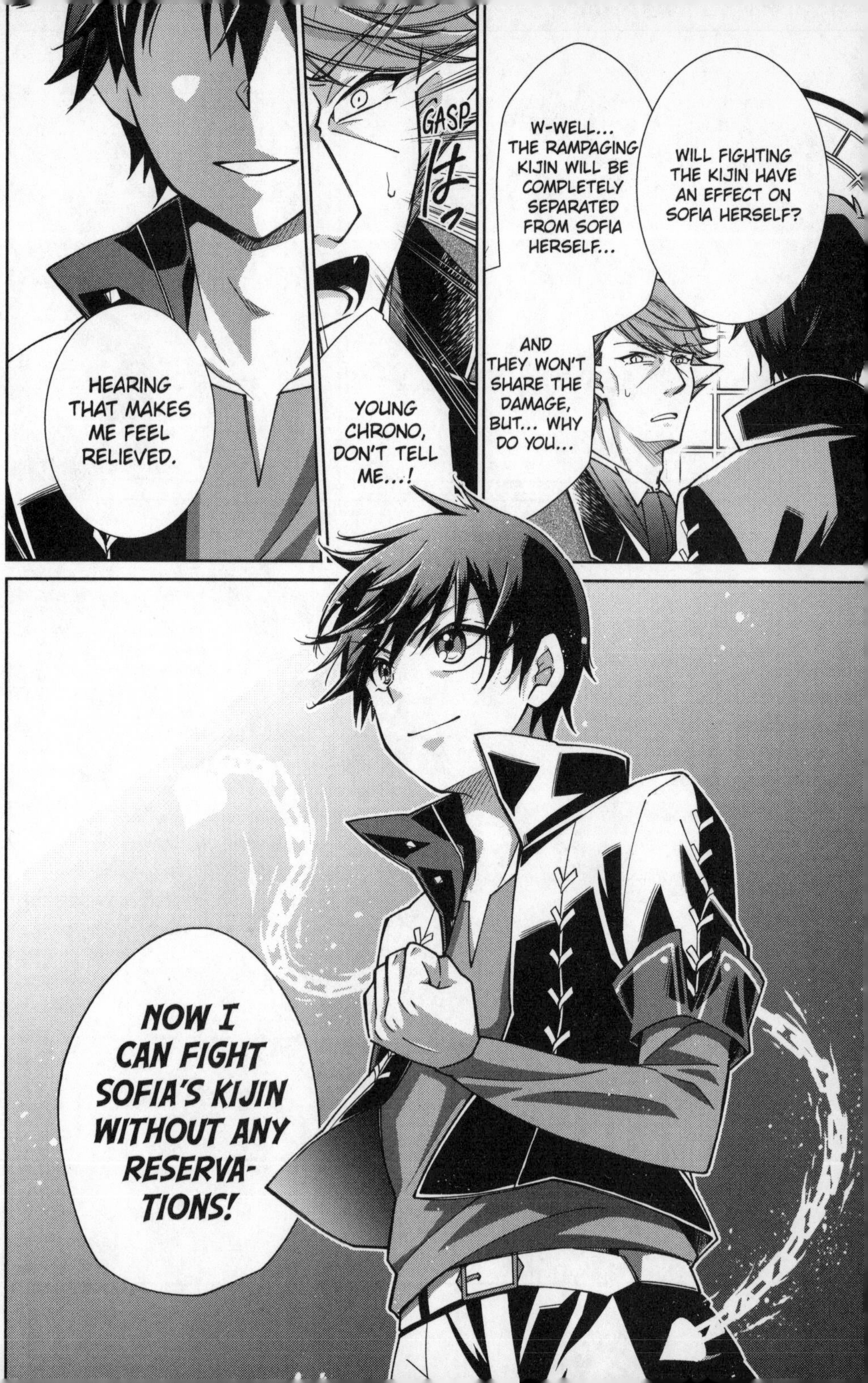
WILL FIGHTING THE KIJIN HAVE AN EFFECT ON SOFIA HERSELF?
W-WELL... THE RAMPAGING KIJIN WILL BE COMPLETELY SEPARATED FROM SOFIA HERSELF...
AND THEY WON'T SHARE THE DAMAGE, BUT... WHY DO YOU...
GASP
はっ
YOUNG CHRONO, DON'T TELL ME...!
HEARING THAT MAKES ME FEEL RELIEVED.
NOW I CAN FIGHT SOFIA'S KIJIN WITHOUT ANY RESERVA-TIONS!

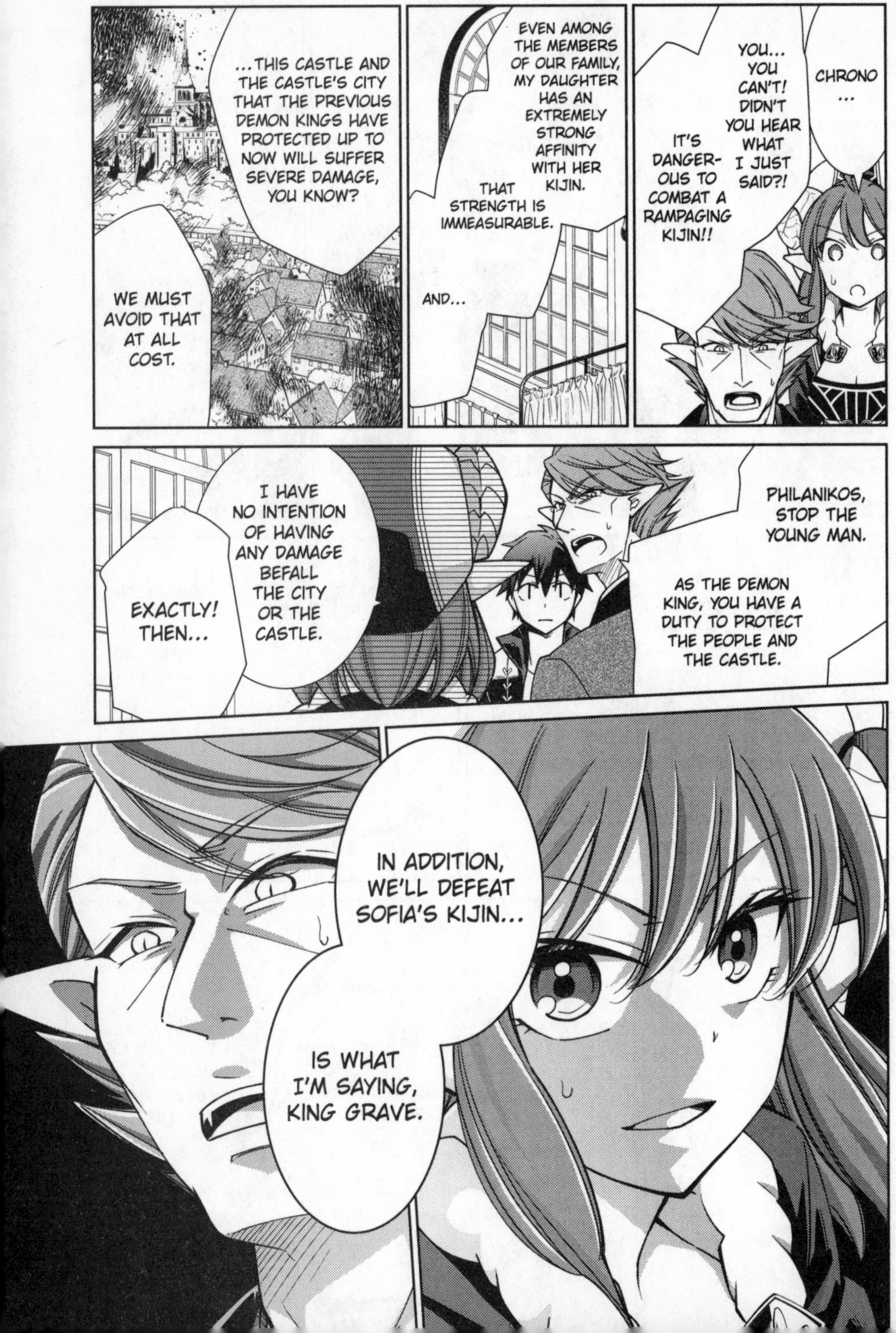
CHRONO ...
YOU... YOU CAN'T! DIDN'T YOU HEAR WHAT I JUST SAID?!
IT'S DANGER-OUS TO COMBAT A RAMPAGING KIJIN!!
EVEN AMONG THE MEMBERS OF OUR FAMILY, MY DAUGHTER HAS AN EXTREMELY STRONG AFFINITY WITH HER KIJIN.
THAT STRENGTH IS IMMEASURABLE.
AND...
...THIS CASTLE AND THE CASTLE'S CITY THAT THE PREVIOUS DEMON KINGS HAVE PROTECTED UP TO NOW WILL SUFFER SEVERE DAMAGE, YOU KNOW?
WE MUST AVOID THAT AT ALL COST.
PHILANIKOS, STOP THE YOUNG MAN.
AS THE DEMON KING, YOU HAVE A DUTY TO PROTECT THE PEOPLE AND THE CASTLE.
I HAVE NO INTENTION OF HAVING ANY DAMAGE BEFALL THE CITY OR THE CASTLE.
EXACTLY! THEN...
IN ADDITION, WE'LL DEFEAT SOFIA'S KIJIN...
IS WHAT I'M SAYING, KING GRAVE.

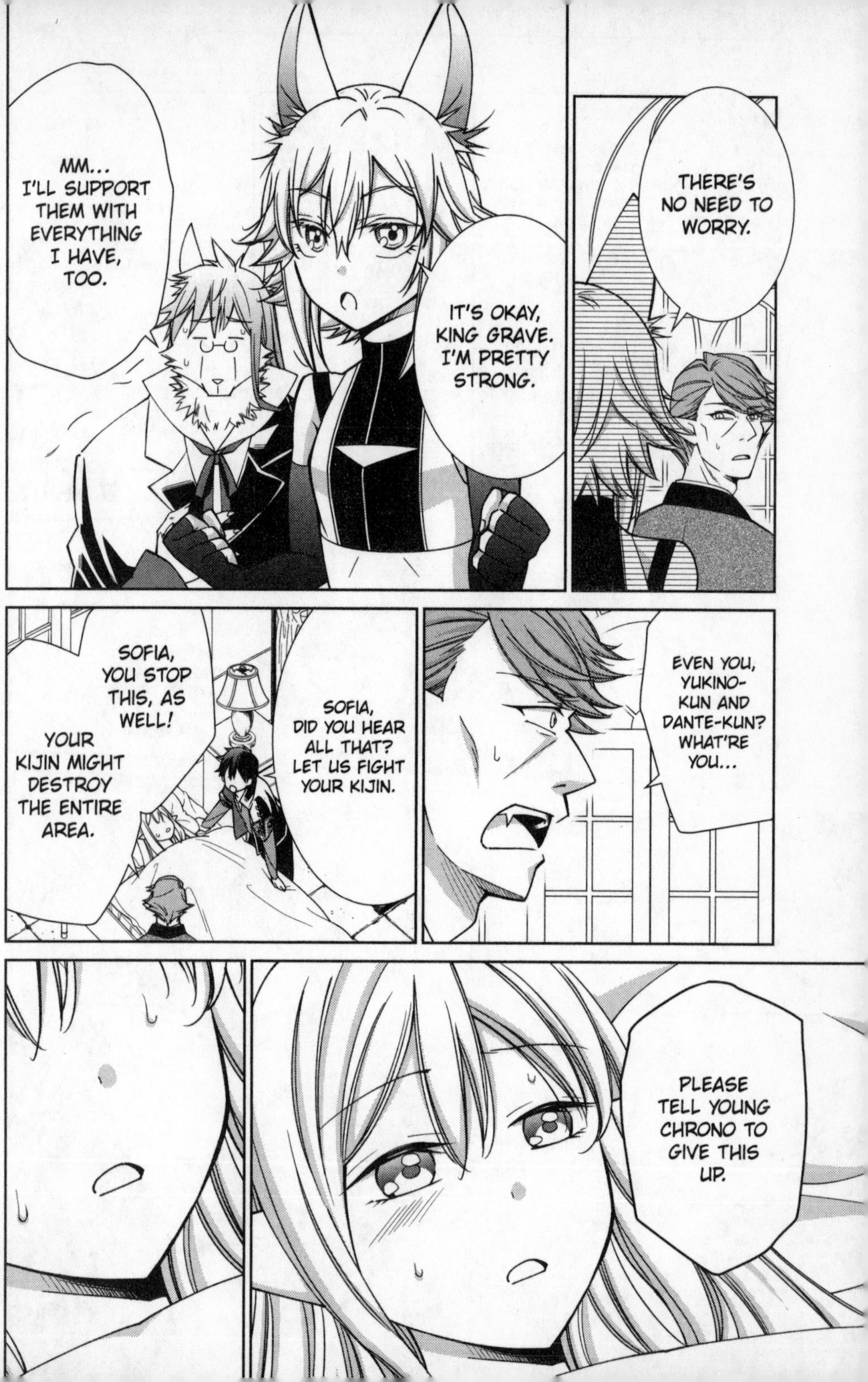
THERE'S NO NEED TO WORRY.
IT'S OKAY, KING GRAVE. I'M PRETTY STRONG.
MM... I'LL SUPPORT THEM WITH EVERYTHING I HAVE, TOO.
EVEN YOU, YUKINO-KUN AND DANTE-KUN? WHAT'RE YOU...
SOFIA, DID YOU HEAR ALL THAT? LET US FIGHT YOUR KIJIN.
SOFIA, YOU STOP THIS, AS WELL!
YOUR KIJIN MIGHT DESTROY THE ENTIRE AREA.
PLEASE TELL YOUNG CHRONO TO GIVE THIS UP.

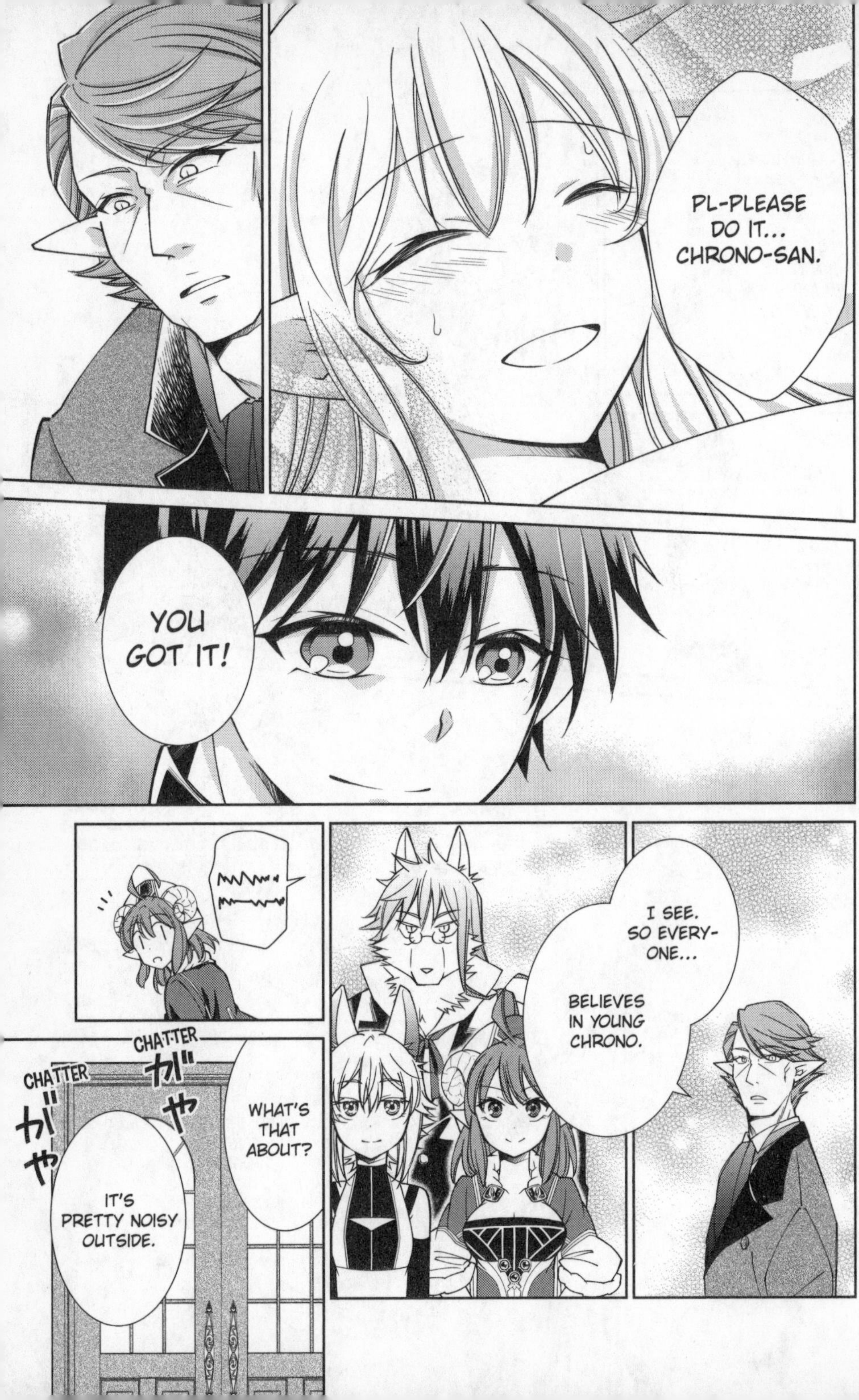
PL-PLEASE DO IT... CHRONO-SAN.
YOU GOT IT!
I SEE. SO EVERY-ONE...
BELIEVES IN YOUNG CHRONO.
CHAT·TER
ガヤ
CHATTER
ガヤ
WHAT'S THAT ABOUT?
IT'S PRETTY NOISY OUTSIDE.

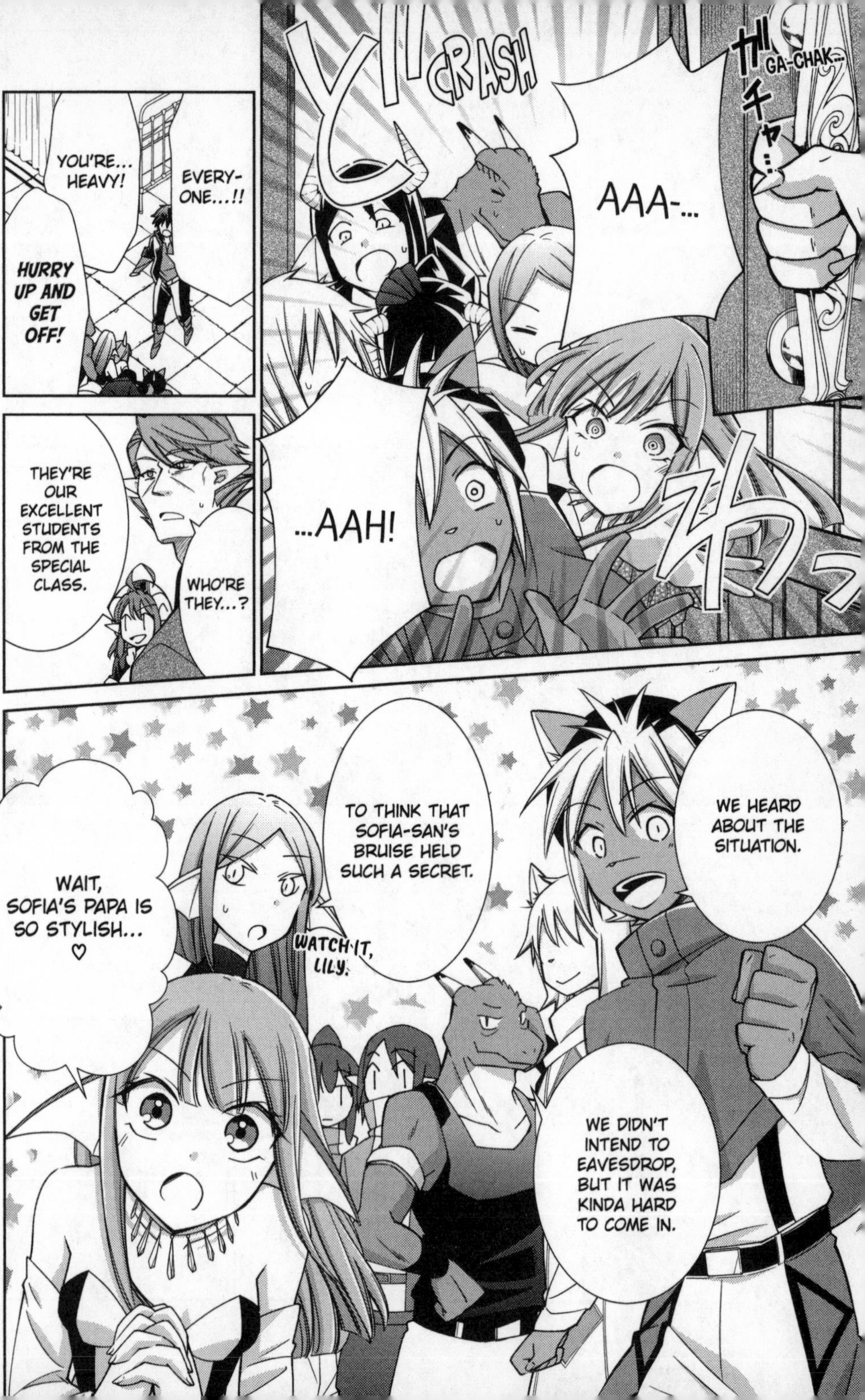
ガチャ…
GA-CHAK...
CRASH
AAA-...
...AAH!
YOU'RE... HEAVY!
EVERY-ONE...!!
HURRY UP AND GET OFF!
WHO'RE THEY...?
THEY'RE OUR EXCELLENT STUDENTS FROM THE SPECIAL CLASS.
WE HEARD ABOUT THE SITUATION.
WE DIDN'T INTEND TO EAVESDROP, BUT IT WAS KINDA HARD TO COME IN.
TO THINK THAT SOFIA-SAN'S BRUISE HELD SUCH A SECRET.
WATCH IT, LILY.
WAIT, SOFIA'S PAPA IS SO STYLISH... ♡

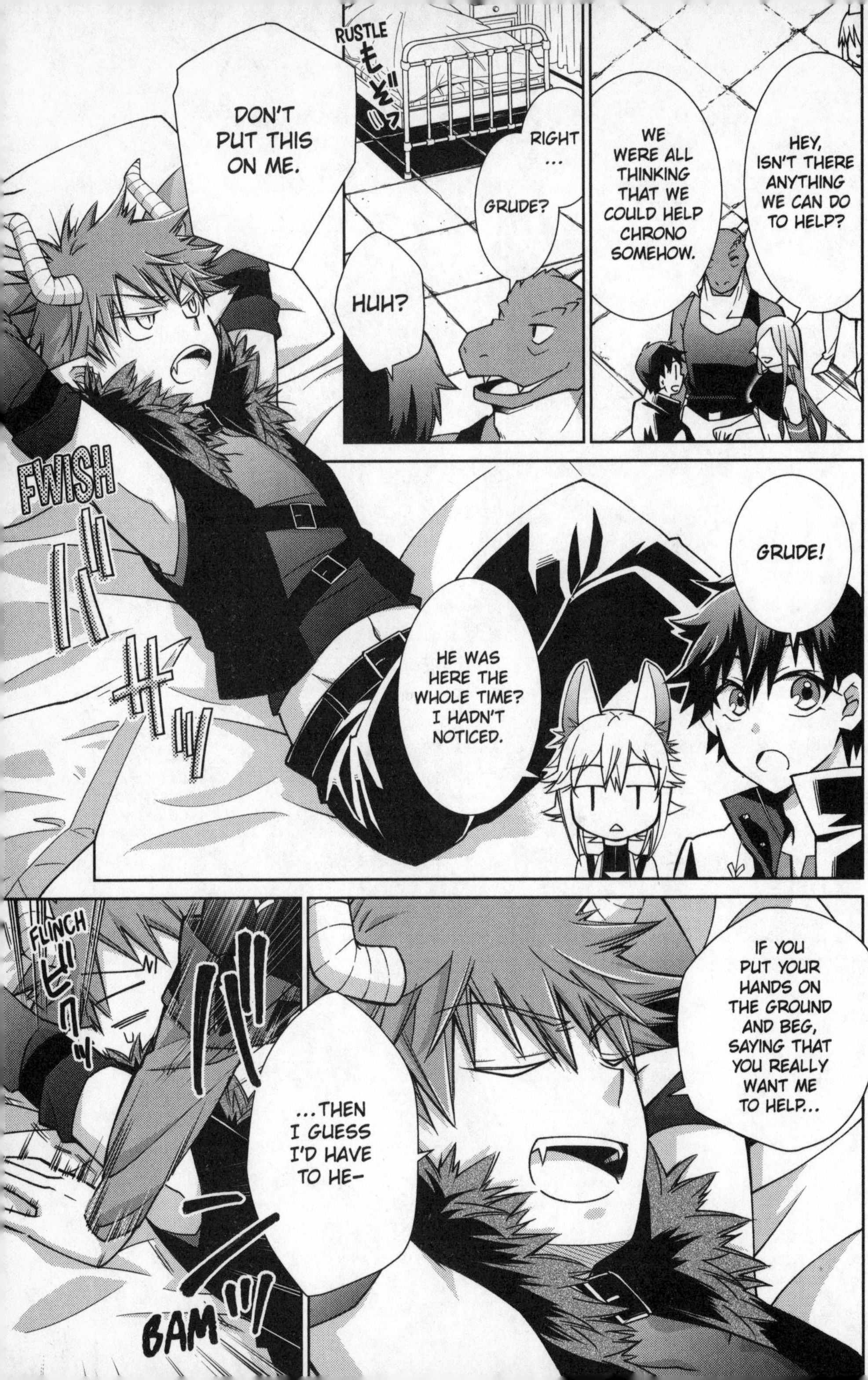
HEY, ISN'T THERE ANYTHING WE CAN DO TO HELP?
WE WERE ALL THINKING THAT WE COULD HELP CHRONO SOMEHOW.
RIGHT ... GRUDE?
HUH?
RUSTLE
DON'T PUT THIS ON ME.
FWISH
GRUDE!
HE WAS HERE THE WHOLE TIME? I HADN'T NOTICED.
IF YOU PUT YOUR HANDS ON THE GROUND AND BEG, SAYING THAT YOU REALLY WANT ME TO HELP...
...THEN I GUESS I'D HAVE TO HE-
FLINCH
BAM

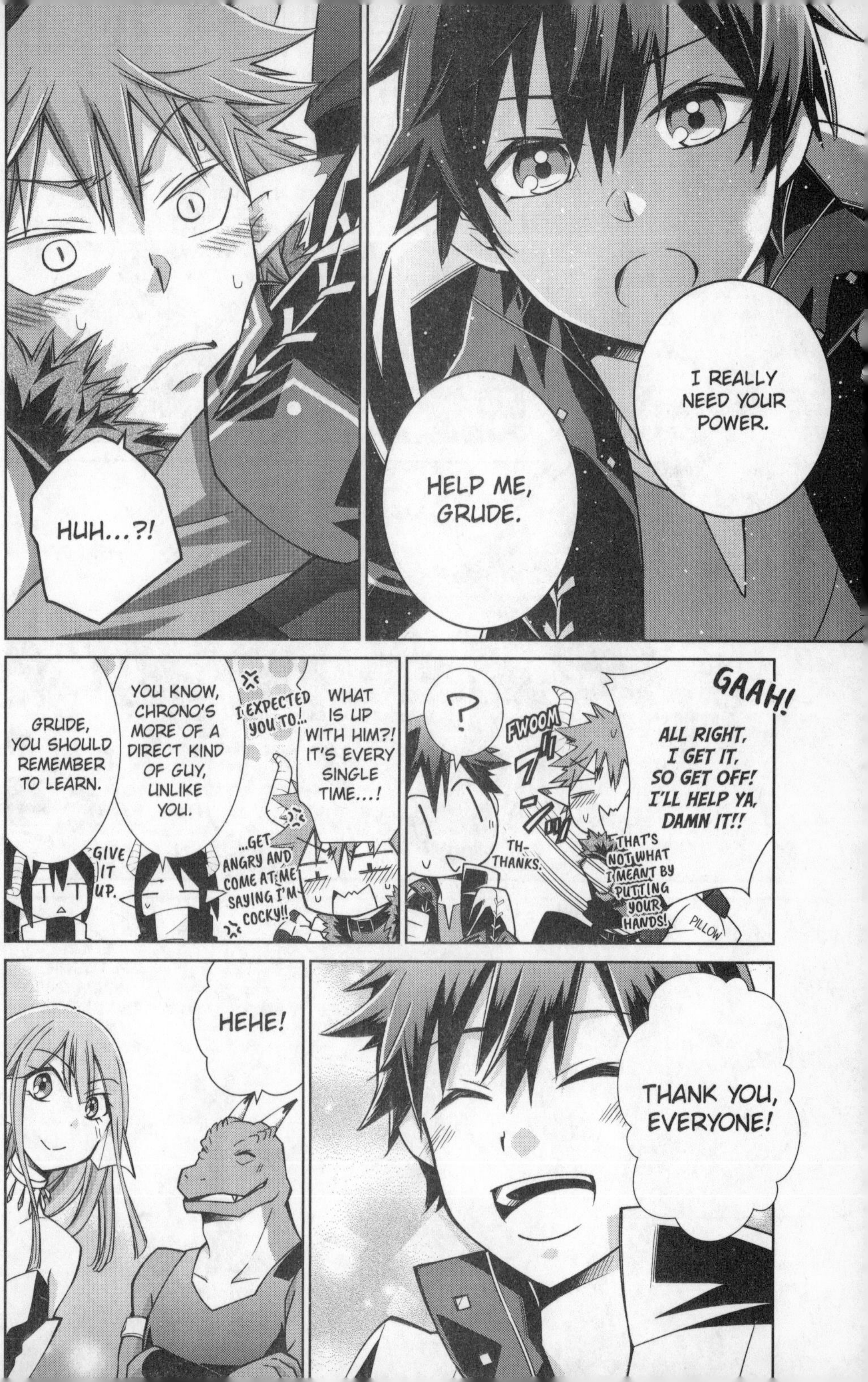
I REALLY NEED YOUR POWER.
HELP ME, GRUDE.
HUH...?!
GAAH!
ALL RIGHT, I GET IT. SO GET OFF! I'LL HELP YA, DAMN IT!!
FWOOM
?
THAT'S NOT WHAT I MEANT BY PUTTING YOUR HANDS!
TH-THANKS.
PILLOW
WHAT IS UP WITH HIM?! IT'S EVERY SINGLE TIME...!
I EXPECTED YOU TO...
...GET ANGRY AND COME AT ME SAYING I'M COCKY!!
YOU KNOW, CHRONO'S MORE OF A DIRECT KIND OF GUY, UNLIKE YOU.
GRUDE, YOU SHOULD REMEMBER TO LEARN.
GIVE IT UP.
THANK YOU, EVERYONE!
HEHE!

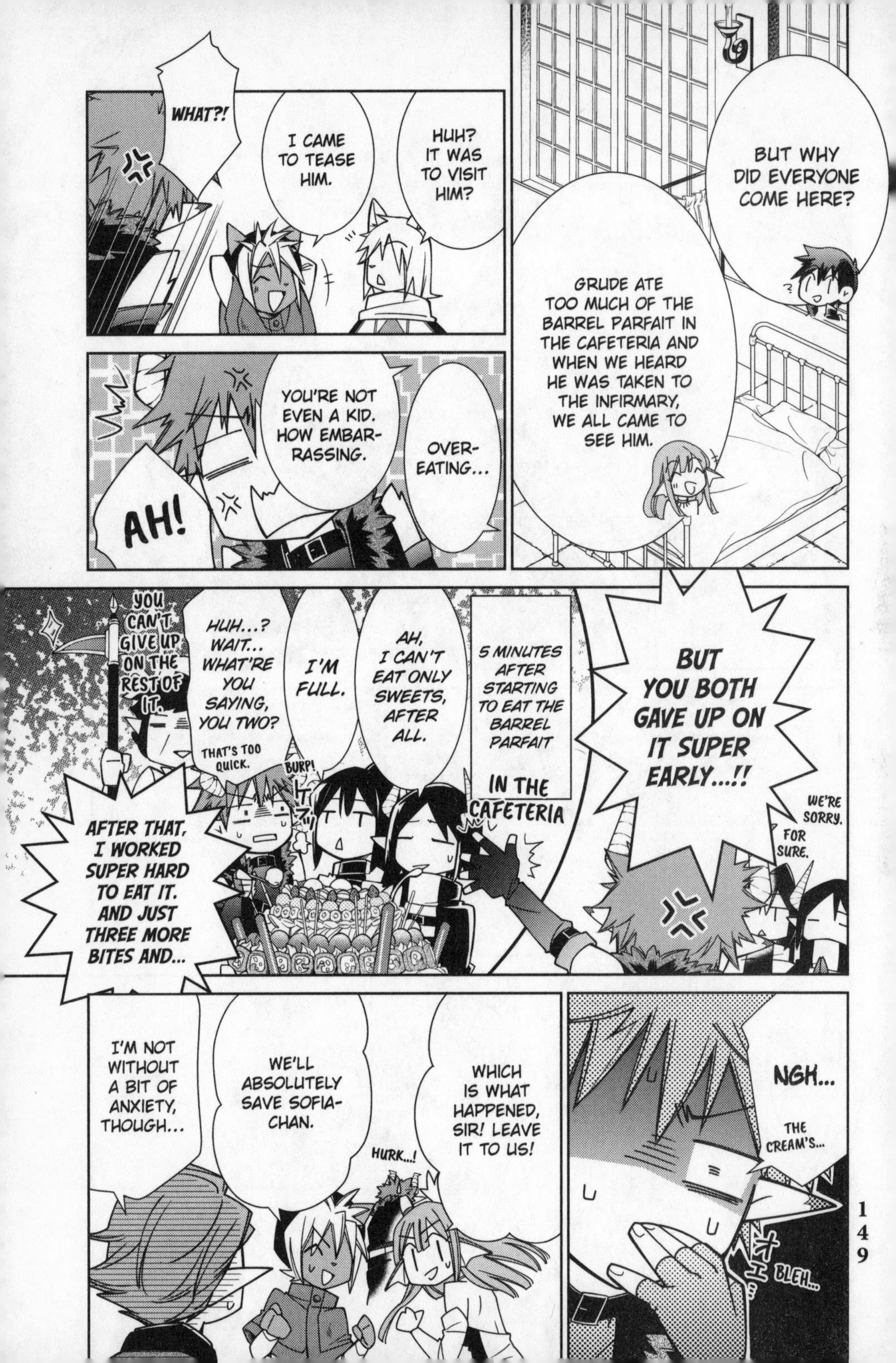
BUT WHY DID EVERYONE COME HERE?
GRUDE ATE TOO MUCH OF THE BARREL PARFAIT IN THE CAFETERIA AND WHEN WE HEARD HE WAS TAKEN TO THE INFIRMARY, WE ALL CAME TO SEE HIM.
HUH? IT WAS TO VISIT HIM?
I CAME TO TEASE HIM.
WHAT?!
OVER-EATING...
YOU'RE NOT EVEN A KID. HOW EMBAR-RASSING.
AH!
BUT YOU BOTH GAVE UP ON IT SUPER EARLY...!!
WE'RE SORRY.
FOR SURE.
5 MINUTES AFTER STARTING TO EAT THE BARREL PARFAIT
IN THE CAFETERIA
AH, I CAN'T EAT ONLY SWEETS, AFTER ALL.
I'M FULL.
HUH...? WAIT... WHAT'RE YOU SAYING, YOU TWO?
THAT'S TOO QUICK.
BURP!
YOU CAN'T GIVE UP ON THE REST OF IT.
AFTER THAT, I WORKED SUPER HARD TO EAT IT. AND JUST THREE MORE BITES AND...
NGH...
THE CREAM'S...
BLEH...
WHICH IS WHAT HAPPENED, SIR! LEAVE IT TO US!
HURK...!
WE'LL ABSOLUTELY SAVE SOFIA-CHAN.
I'M NOT WITHOUT A BIT OF ANXIETY, THOUGH...

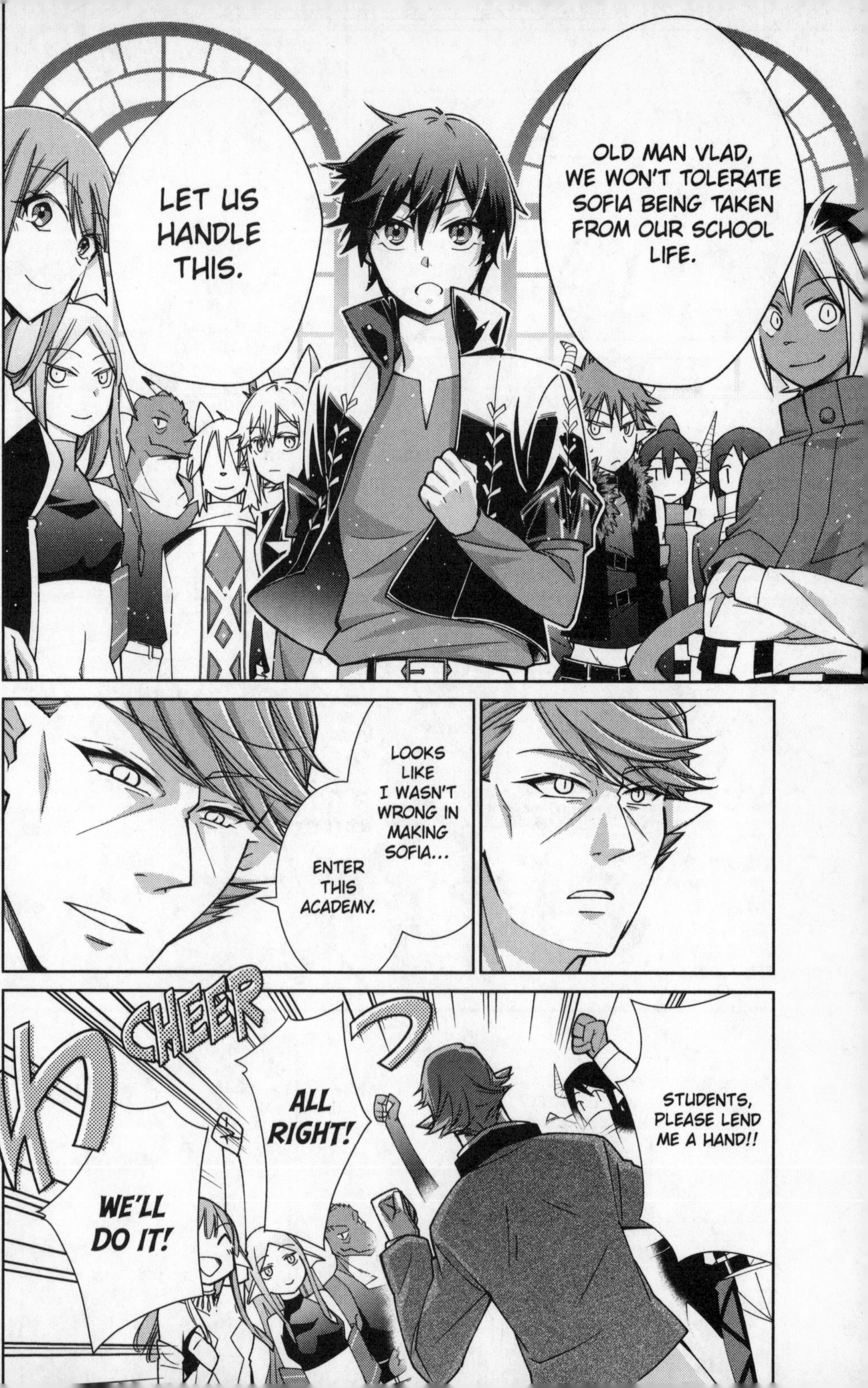
OLD MAN VLAD, WE WON'T TOLERATE SOFIA BEING TAKEN FROM OUR SCHOOL LIFE.
LET US HANDLE THIS.
LOOKS LIKE I WASN'T WRONG IN MAKING SOFIA...
ENTER THIS ACADEMY.
STUDENTS, PLEASE LEND ME A HAND!!
ALL RIGHT!
CHEER
WE'LL DO IT!

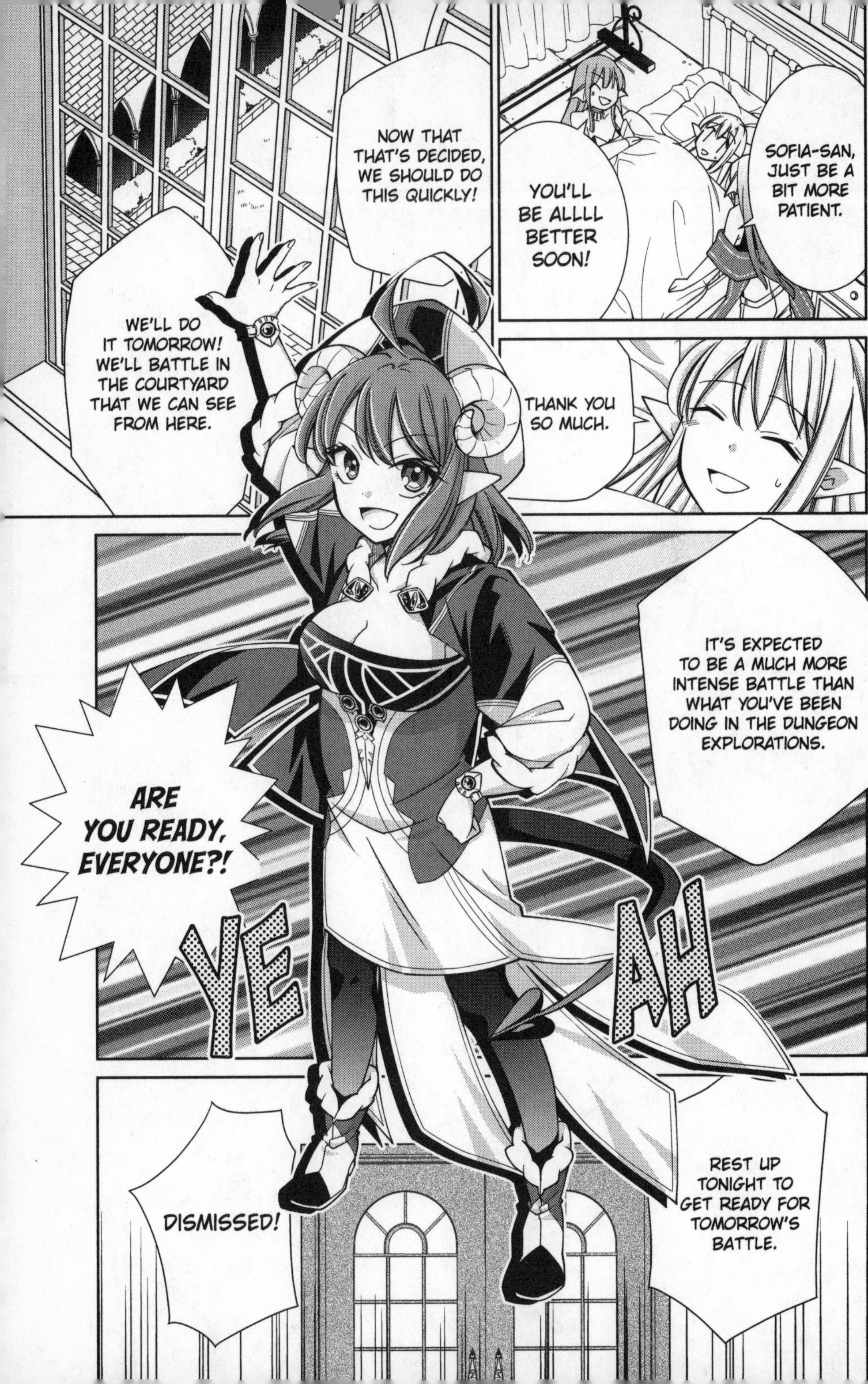

SOFIA-SAN, JUST BE A BIT MORE PATIENT.
YOU'LL BE ALLLL BETTER SOON!
THANK YOU SO MUCH.
NOW THAT THAT'S DECIDED, WE SHOULD DO THIS QUICKLY!
WE'LL DO IT TOMORROW! WE'LL BATTLE IN THE COURTYARD THAT WE CAN SEE FROM HERE.
IT'S EXPECTED TO BE A MUCH MORE INTENSE BATTLE THAN WHAT YOU'VE BEEN DOING IN THE DUNGEON EXPLORATIONS.
ARE YOU READY, EVERYONE?!
YE AH
REST UP TONIGHT TO GET READY FOR TOMORROW'S BATTLE.
DISMISSED!

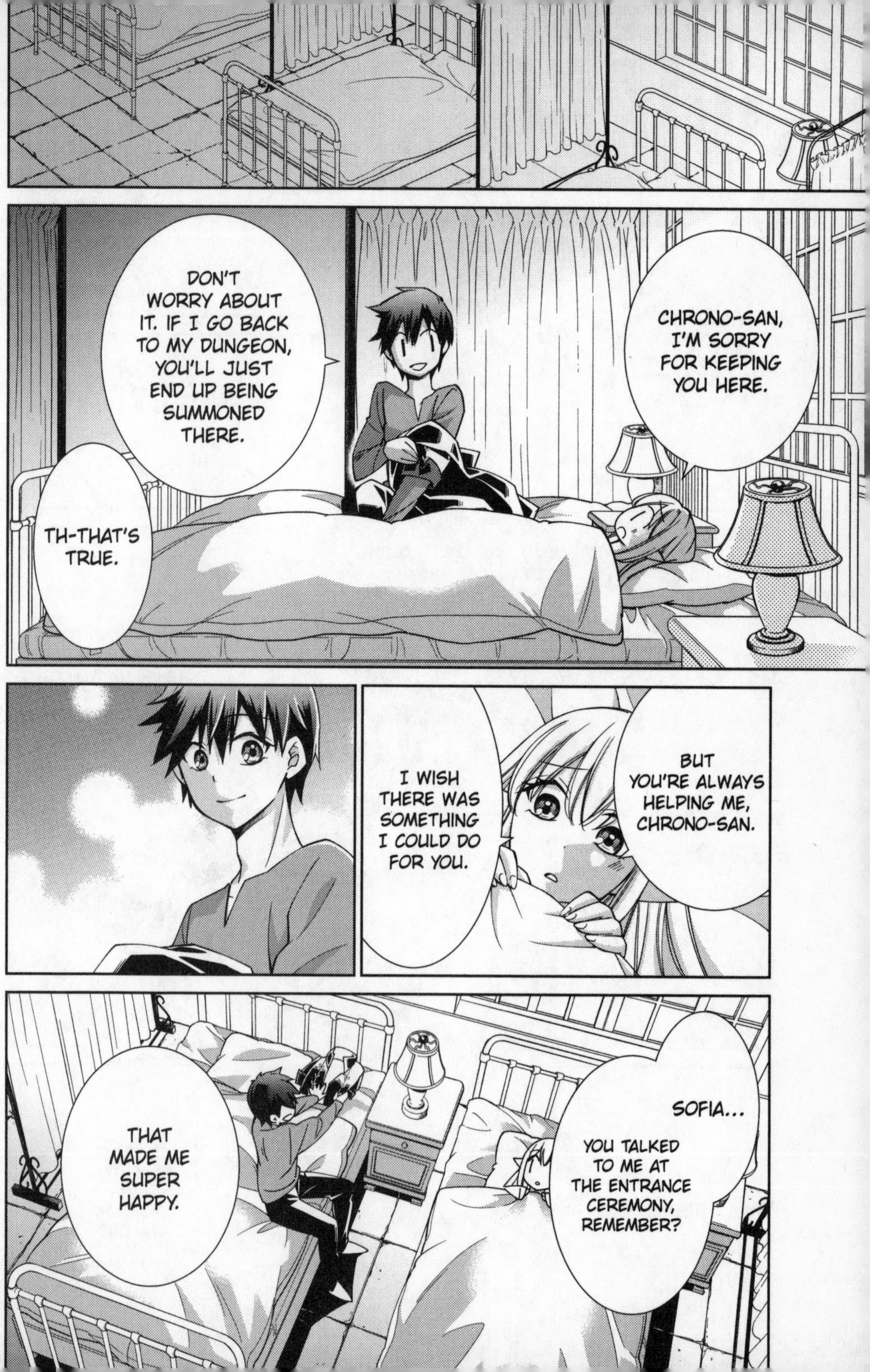
CHRONO-SAN, I'M SORRY FOR KEEPING YOU HERE.
DON'T WORRY ABOUT IT. IF I GO BACK TO MY DUNGEON, YOU'LL JUST END UP BEING SUMMONED THERE.
TH-THAT'S TRUE.
BUT YOU'RE ALWAYS HELPING ME, CHRONO-SAN.
I WISH THERE WAS SOMETHING I COULD DO FOR YOU.
SOFIA...
YOU TALKED TO ME AT THE ENTRANCE CEREMONY, REMEMBER?
THAT MADE ME SUPER HAPPY.

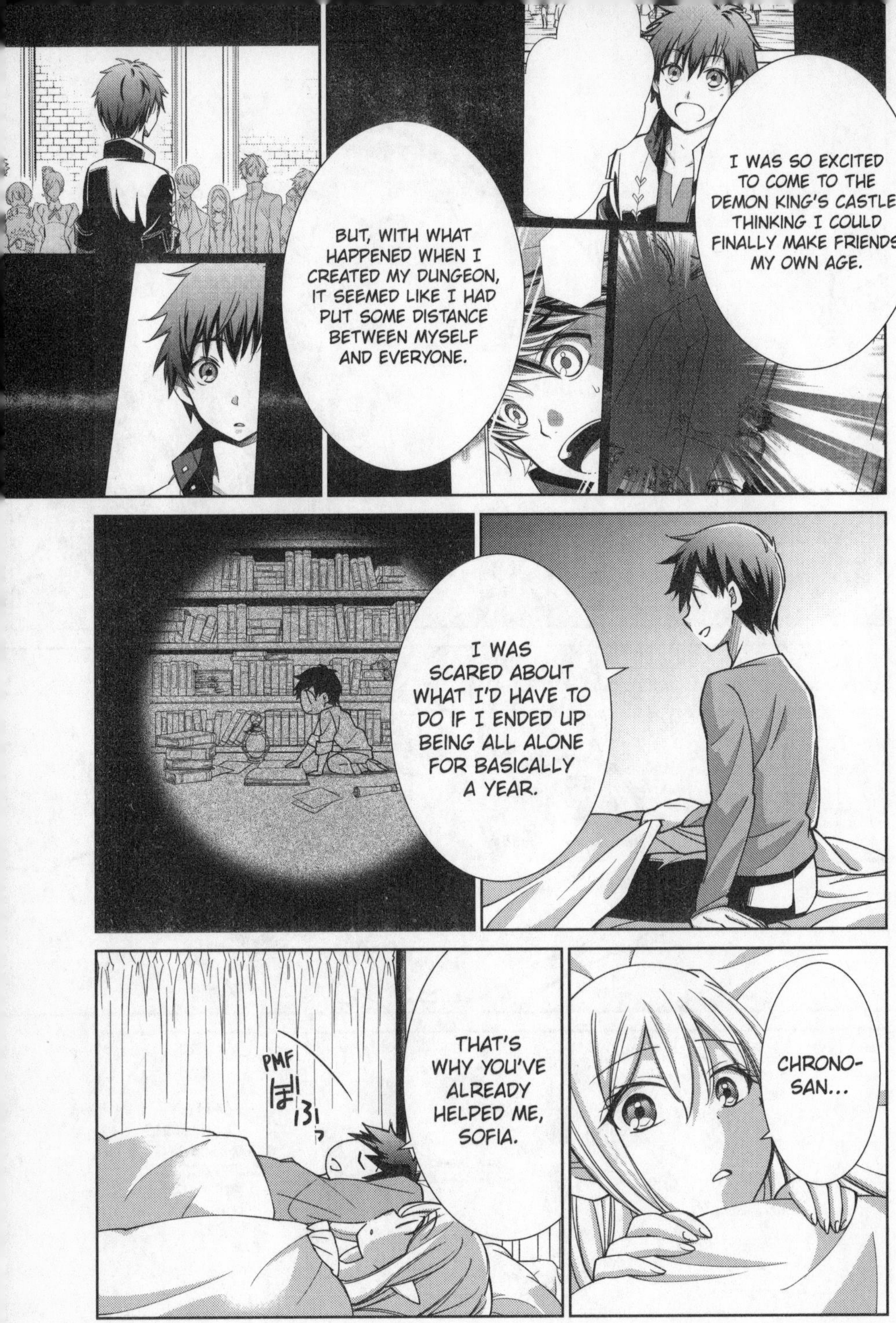
I WAS SO EXCITED TO COME TO THE DEMON KING'S CASTLE, THINKING I COULD FINALLY MAKE FRIENDS MY OWN AGE.
BUT, WITH WHAT HAPPENED WHEN I CREATED MY DUNGEON, IT SEEMED LIKE I HAD PUT SOME DISTANCE BETWEEN MYSELF AND EVERYONE.
I WAS SCARED ABOUT WHAT I'D HAVE TO DO IF I ENDED UP BEING ALL ALONE FOR BASICALLY A YEAR.
CHRONO-SAN...
THAT'S WHY YOU'VE ALREADY HELPED ME, SOFIA.
PMF
ぼふっ

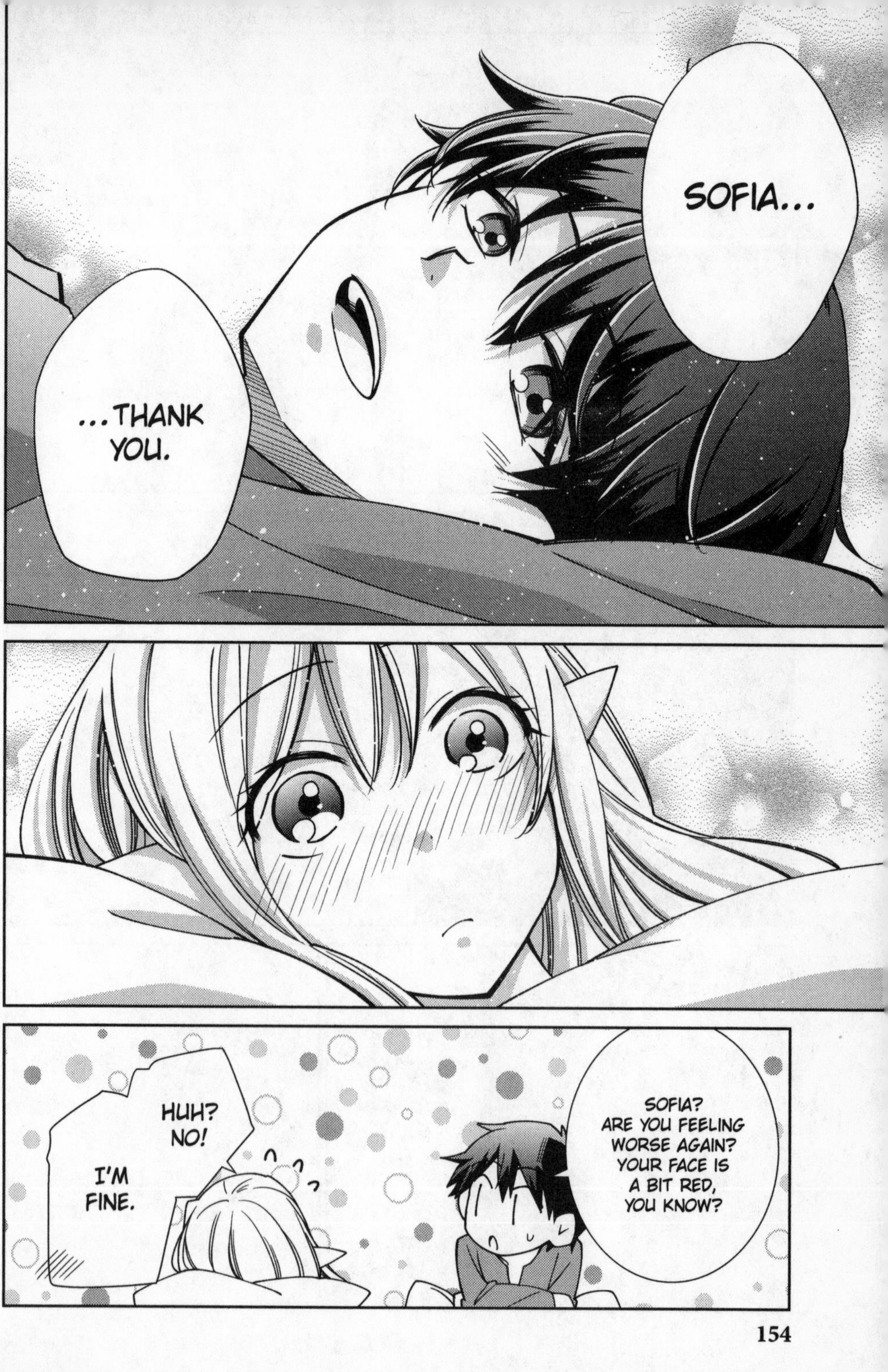
SOFIA...
...THANK YOU.
SOFIA? ARE YOU FEELING WORSE AGAIN? YOUR FACE IS A BIT RED, YOU KNOW?
HUH? NO!
I'M FINE.

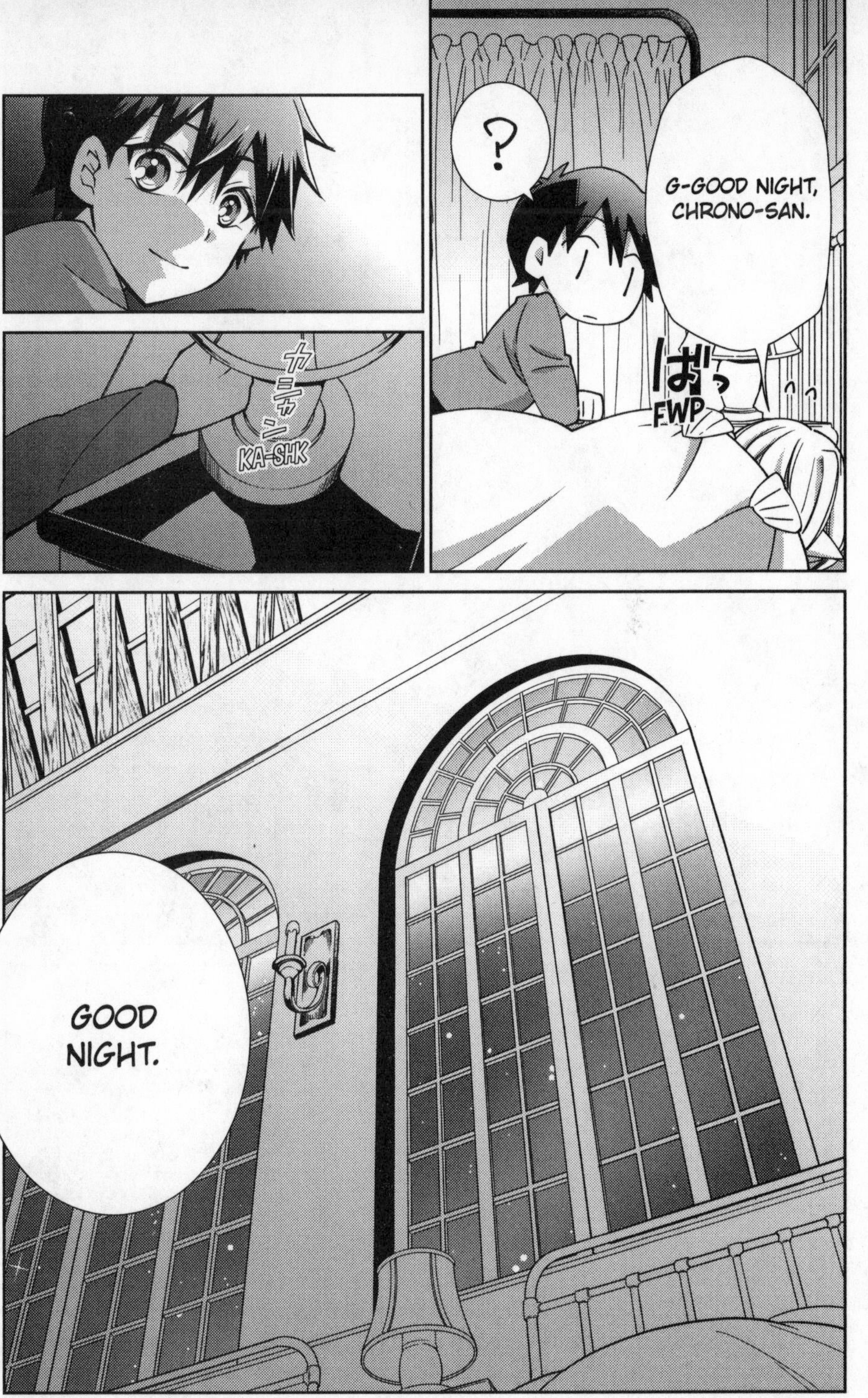
?
G-GOOD NIGHT, CHRONO-SAN.
ぱっ
FWP
カシャン
KA-SHK
GOOD NIGHT.

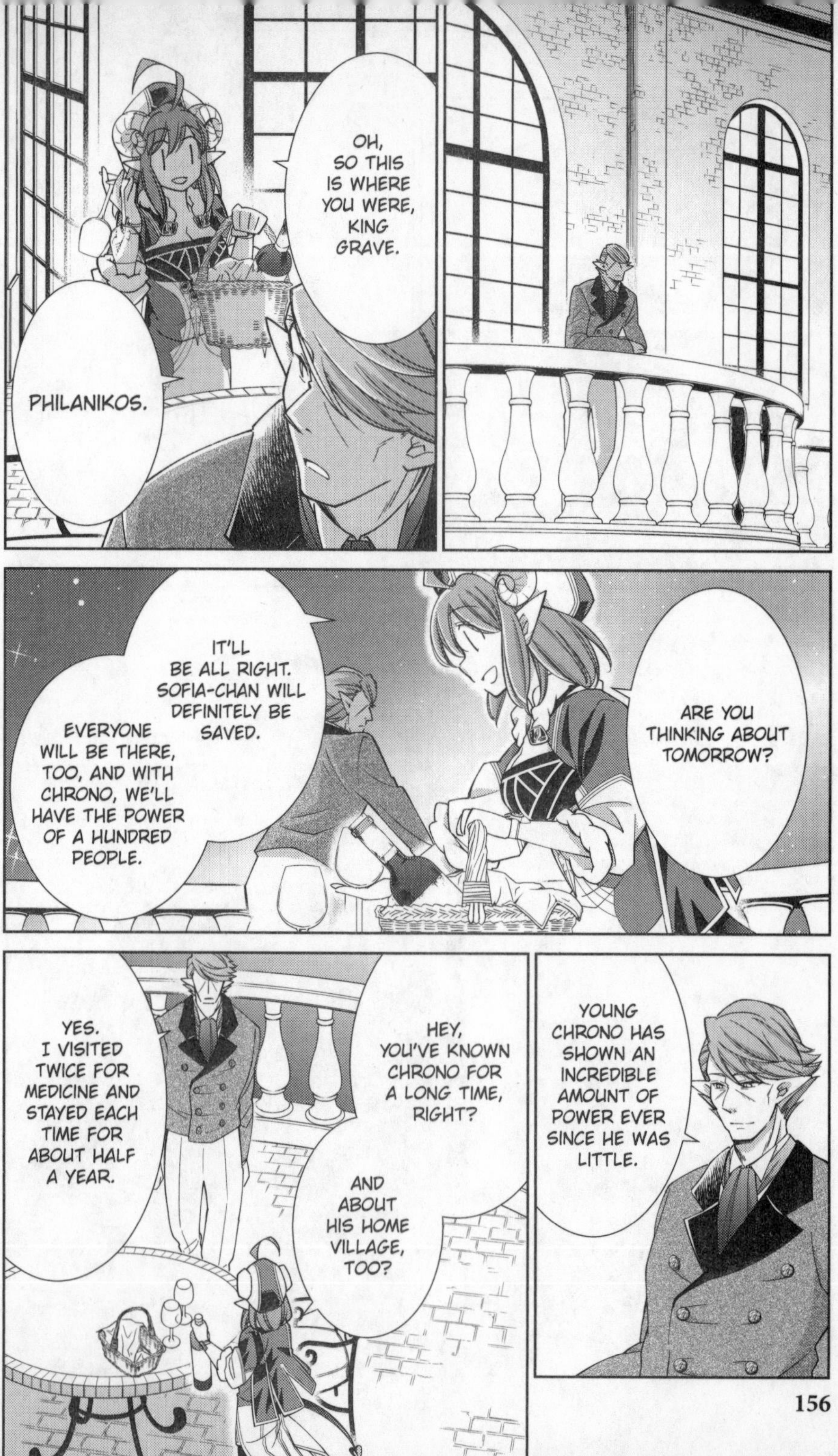
OH, SO THIS IS WHERE YOU WERE, KING GRAVE.
PHILANIKOS.
ARE YOU THINKING ABOUT TOMORROW?
IT'LL BE ALL RIGHT. SOFIA-CHAN WILL DEFINITELY BE SAVED.
EVERYONE WILL BE THERE, TOO, AND WITH CHRONO, WE'LL HAVE THE POWER OF A HUNDRED PEOPLE.
YOUNG CHRONO HAS SHOWN AN INCREDIBLE AMOUNT OF POWER EVER SINCE HE WAS LITTLE.
HEY, YOU'VE KNOWN CHRONO FOR A LONG TIME, RIGHT?
AND ABOUT HIS HOME VILLAGE, TOO?
YES. I VISITED TWICE FOR MEDICINE AND STAYED EACH TIME FOR ABOUT HALF A YEAR.

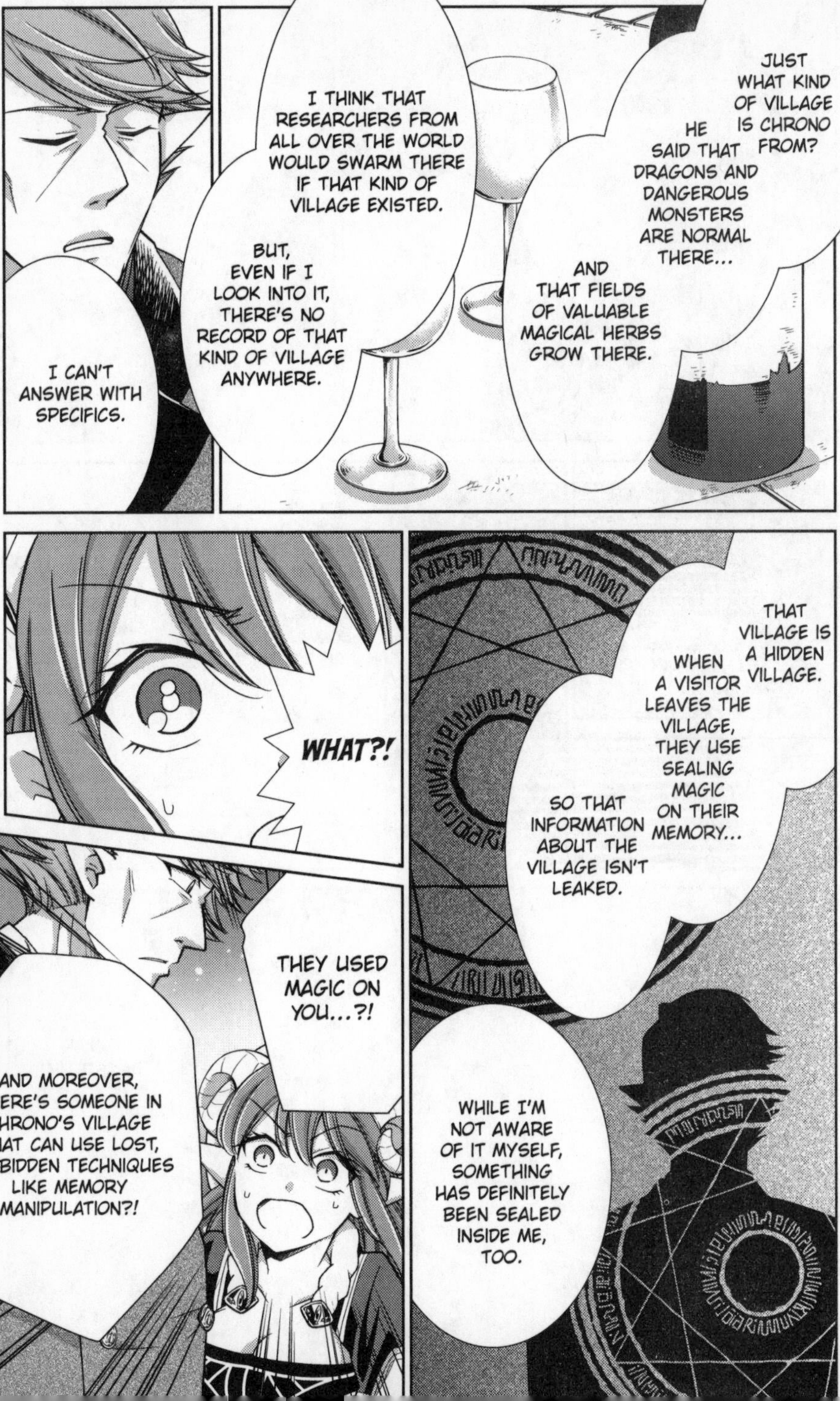
JUST WHAT KIND OF VILLAGE IS CHRONO FROM?
HE SAID THAT DRAGONS AND DANGEROUS MONSTERS ARE NORMAL THERE...
AND THAT FIELDS OF VALUABLE MAGICAL HERBS GROW THERE.
I THINK THAT RESEARCHERS FROM ALL OVER THE WORLD WOULD SWARM THERE IF THAT KIND OF VILLAGE EXISTED.
BUT, EVEN IF I LOOK INTO IT, THERE'S NO RECORD OF THAT KIND OF VILLAGE ANYWHERE.
I CAN'T ANSWER WITH SPECIFICS.
THAT VILLAGE IS A HIDDEN VILLAGE.
WHEN A VISITOR LEAVES THE VILLAGE, THEY USE SEALING MAGIC ON THEIR MEMORY...
SO THAT INFORMATION ABOUT THE VILLAGE ISN'T LEAKED.
WHILE I'M NOT AWARE OF IT MYSELF, SOMETHING HAS DEFINITELY BEEN SEALED INSIDE ME, TOO.
WHAT?!
THEY USED MAGIC ON YOU...?!
AND MOREOVER, THERE'S SOMEONE IN CHRONO'S VILLAGE THAT CAN USE LOST, FORBIDDEN TECHNIQUES LIKE MEMORY MANIPULATION?!

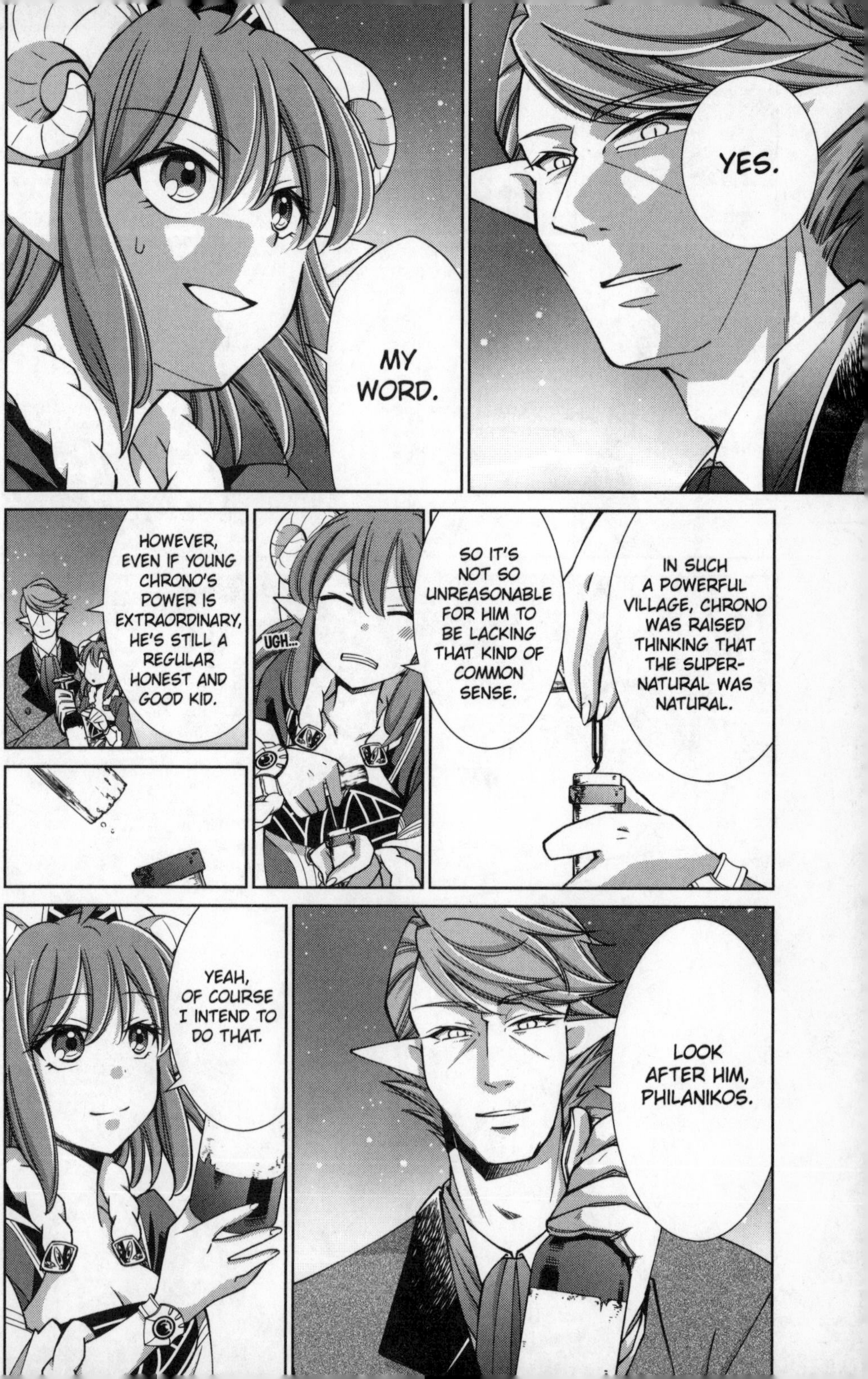
YES.
MY WORD.
IN SUCH A POWERFUL VILLAGE, CHRONO WAS RAISED THINKING THAT THE SUPER-NATURAL WAS NATURAL.
SO IT'S NOT SO UNREASONABLE FOR HIM TO BE LACKING THAT KIND OF COMMON SENSE.
UGH...
HOWEVER, EVEN IF YOUNG CHRONO'S POWER IS EXTRAORDINARY, HE'S STILL A REGULAR HONEST AND GOOD KID.
LOOK AFTER HIM, PHILANIKOS.
YEAH, OF COURSE I INTEND TO DO THAT.

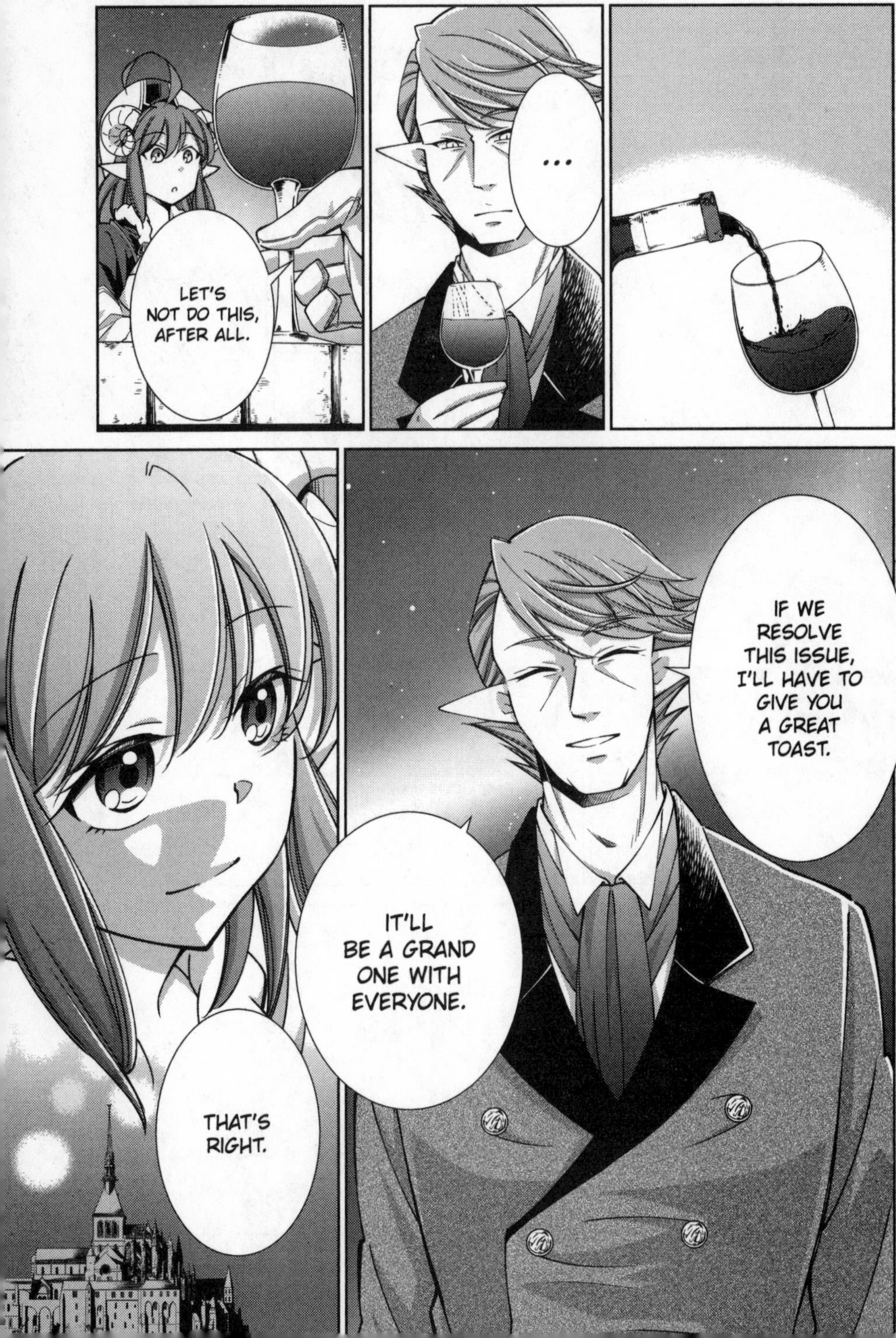
...
LET'S NOT DO THIS, AFTER ALL.
IF WE RESOLVE THIS ISSUE, I'LL HAVE TO GIVE YOU A GREAT TOAST.
IT'LL BE A GRAND ONE WITH EVERYONE.
THAT'S RIGHT.

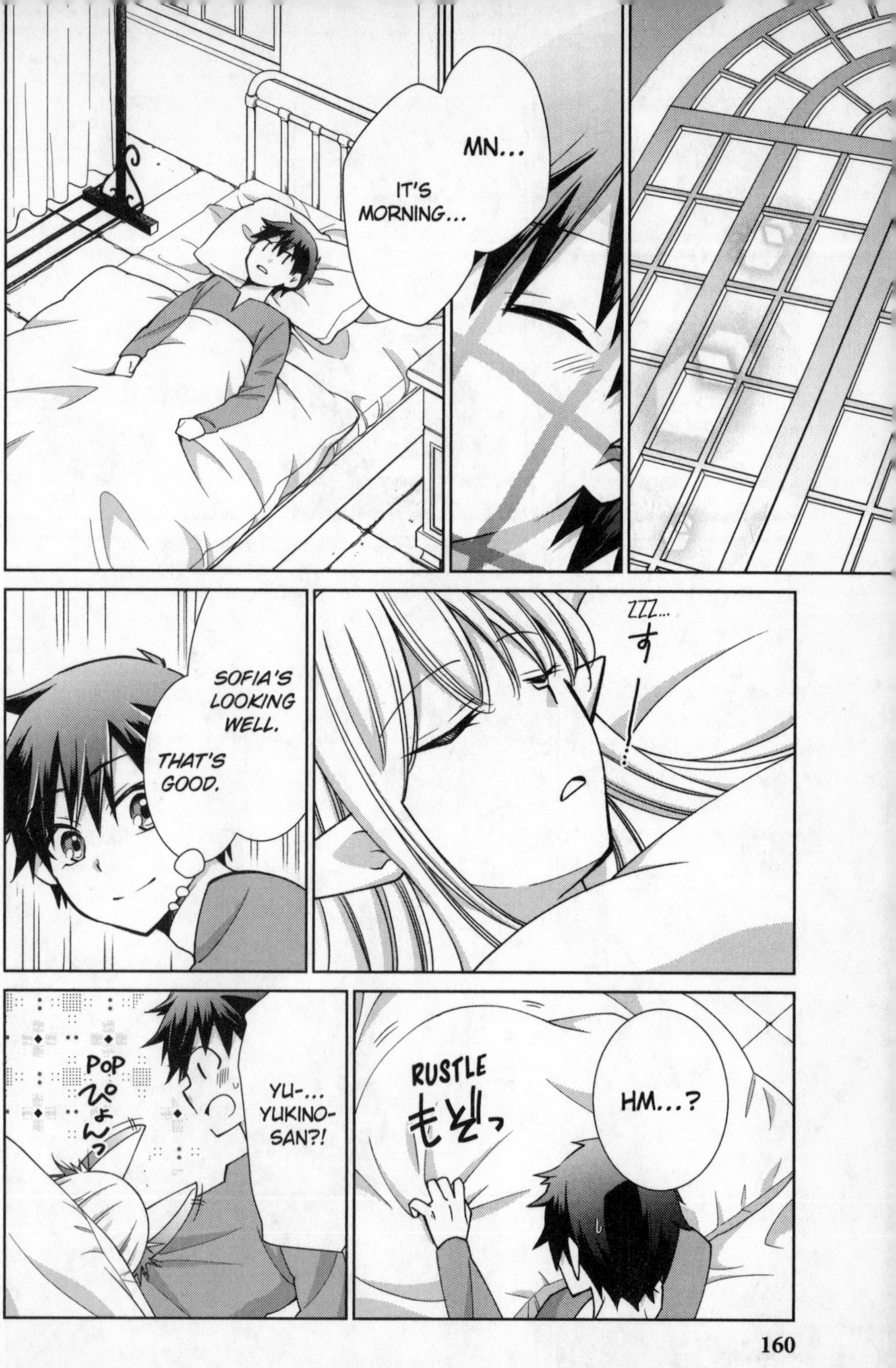
MN...
IT'S MORNING...
ZZZ...
す—!...
SOFIA'S LOOKING WELL.
THAT'S GOOD.
HM...?
RUSTLE
もぞっ
YU-... YUKINO-SAN?!
POP
ぴょんっ

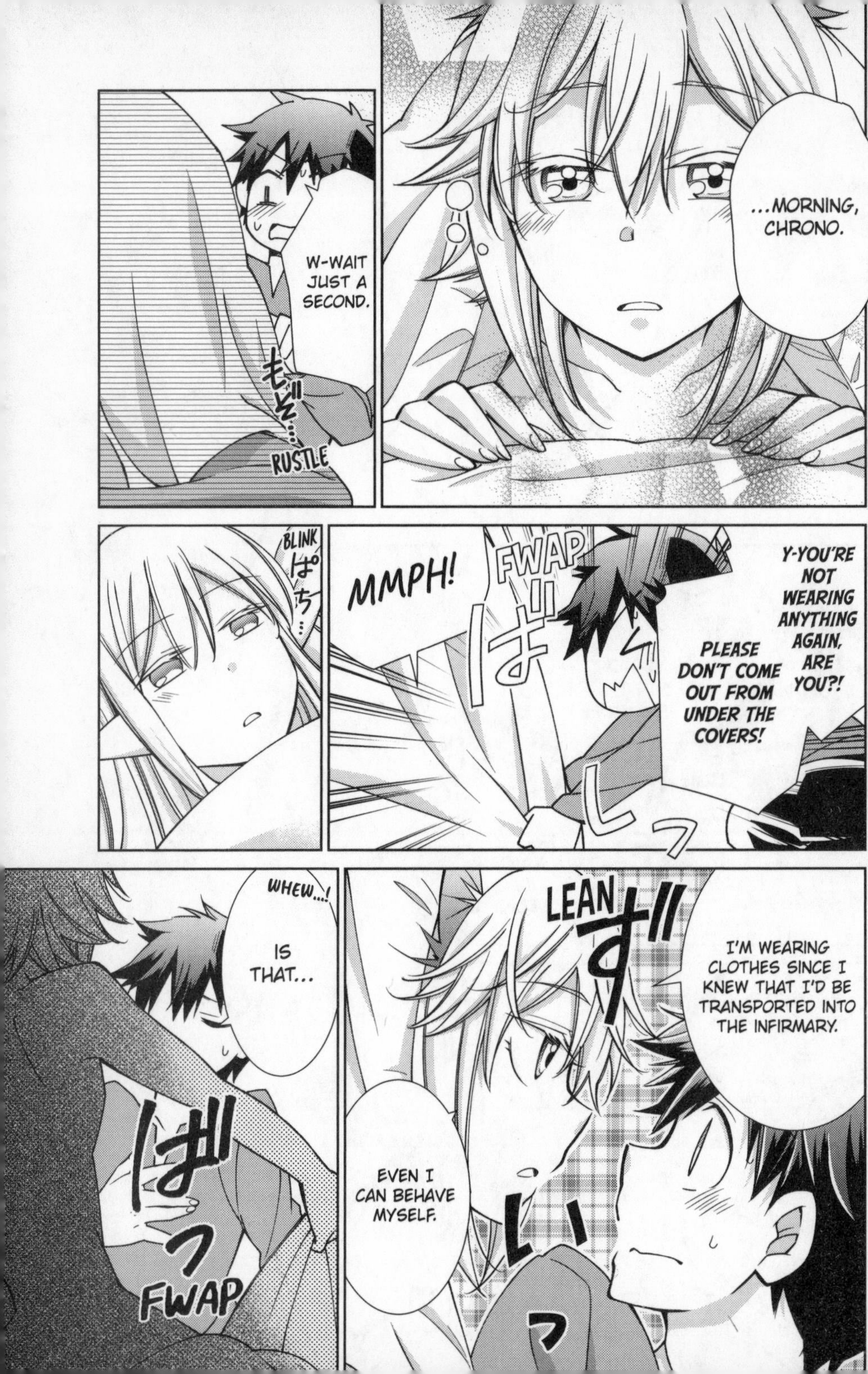
...MORNING, CHRONO.
W-WAIT JUST A SECOND.
もぞ…
RUSTLE
FWAP
ばっ
MMPH!
Y-YOU'RE NOT WEARING ANYTHING AGAIN, ARE YOU?!
PLEASE DON'T COME OUT FROM UNDER THE COVERS!
BLINK
ぱち…
LEAN
ずい
I'M WEARING CLOTHES SINCE I KNEW THAT I'D BE TRANSPORTED INTO THE INFIRMARY.
EVEN I CAN BEHAVE MYSELF.
WHEW...!
IS THAT...
ばっ
FWAP

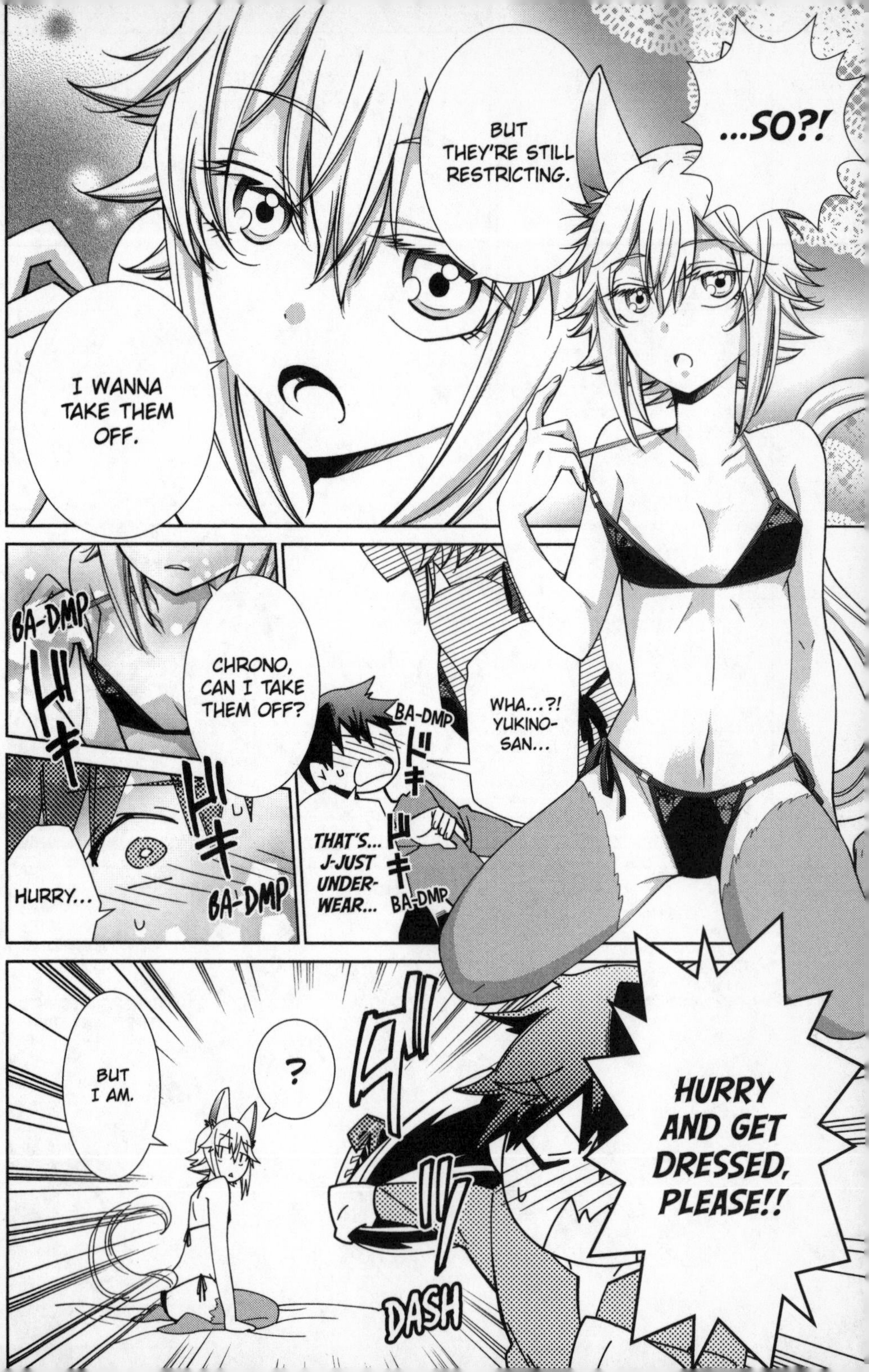
...SO?!
BUT THEY'RE STILL RESTRICTING.
I WANNA TAKE THEM OFF.
WHA...?! YUKINO-SAN...
BA-DMP
THAT'S... J-JUST UNDER-WEAR...
BA-DMP
CHRONO, CAN I TAKE THEM OFF?
BA-DMP
HURRY...
BA-DMP
HURRY AND GET DRESSED, PLEASE!!
DASH
?
BUT I AM.

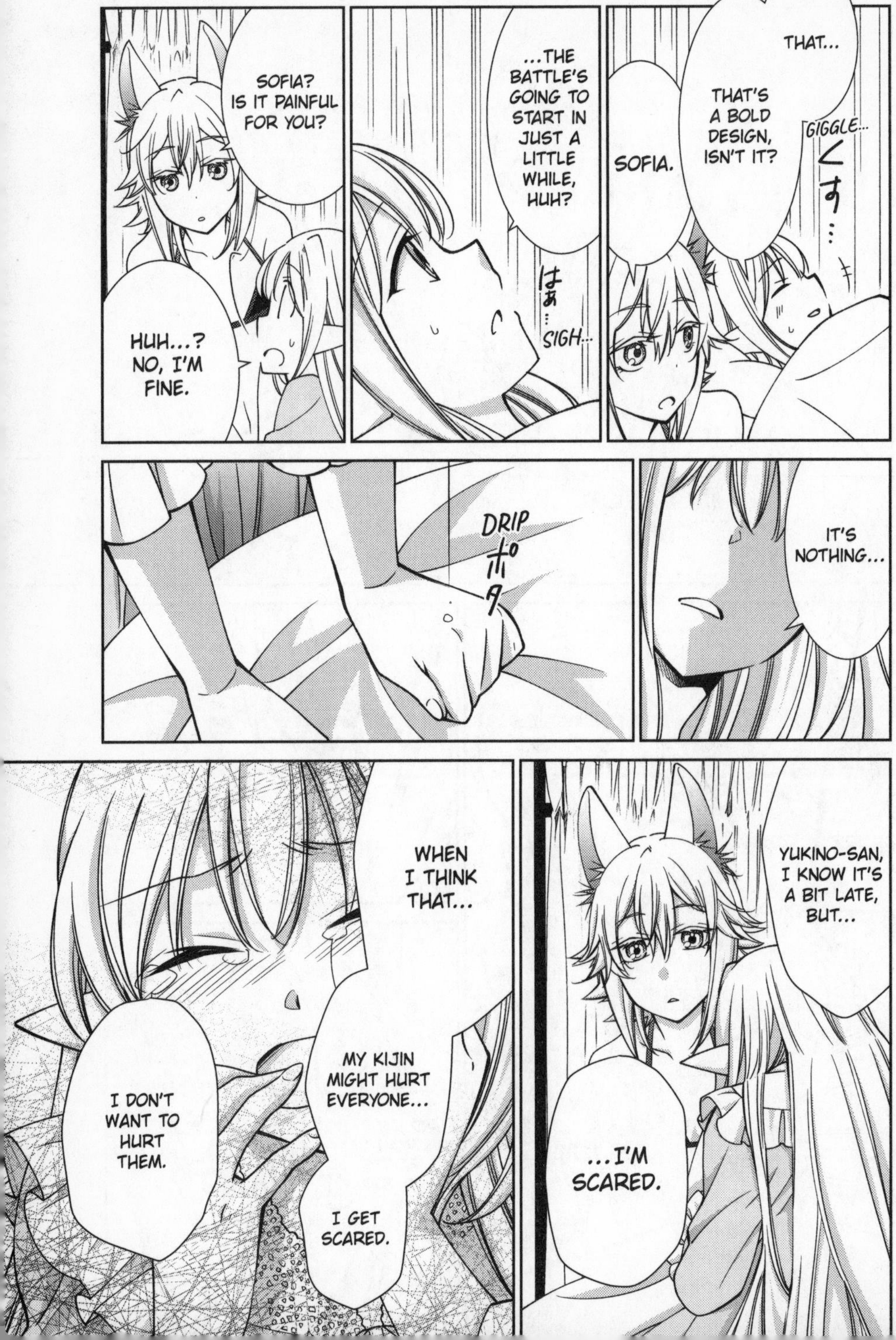
THAT...
THAT'S A BOLD DESIGN, ISN'T IT?
GIGGLE... くす…
SOFIA.
...THE BATTLE'S GOING TO START IN JUST A LITTLE WHILE, HUH?
はぁ… SIGH...
SOFIA? IS IT PAINFUL FOR YOU?
HUH...? NO, I'M FINE.
IT'S NOTHING...
DRIP ポタ
YUKINO-SAN, I KNOW IT'S A BIT LATE, BUT...
...I'M SCARED.
WHEN I THINK THAT...
MY KIJIN MIGHT HURT EVERYONE...
I GET SCARED.
I DON'T WANT TO HURT THEM.

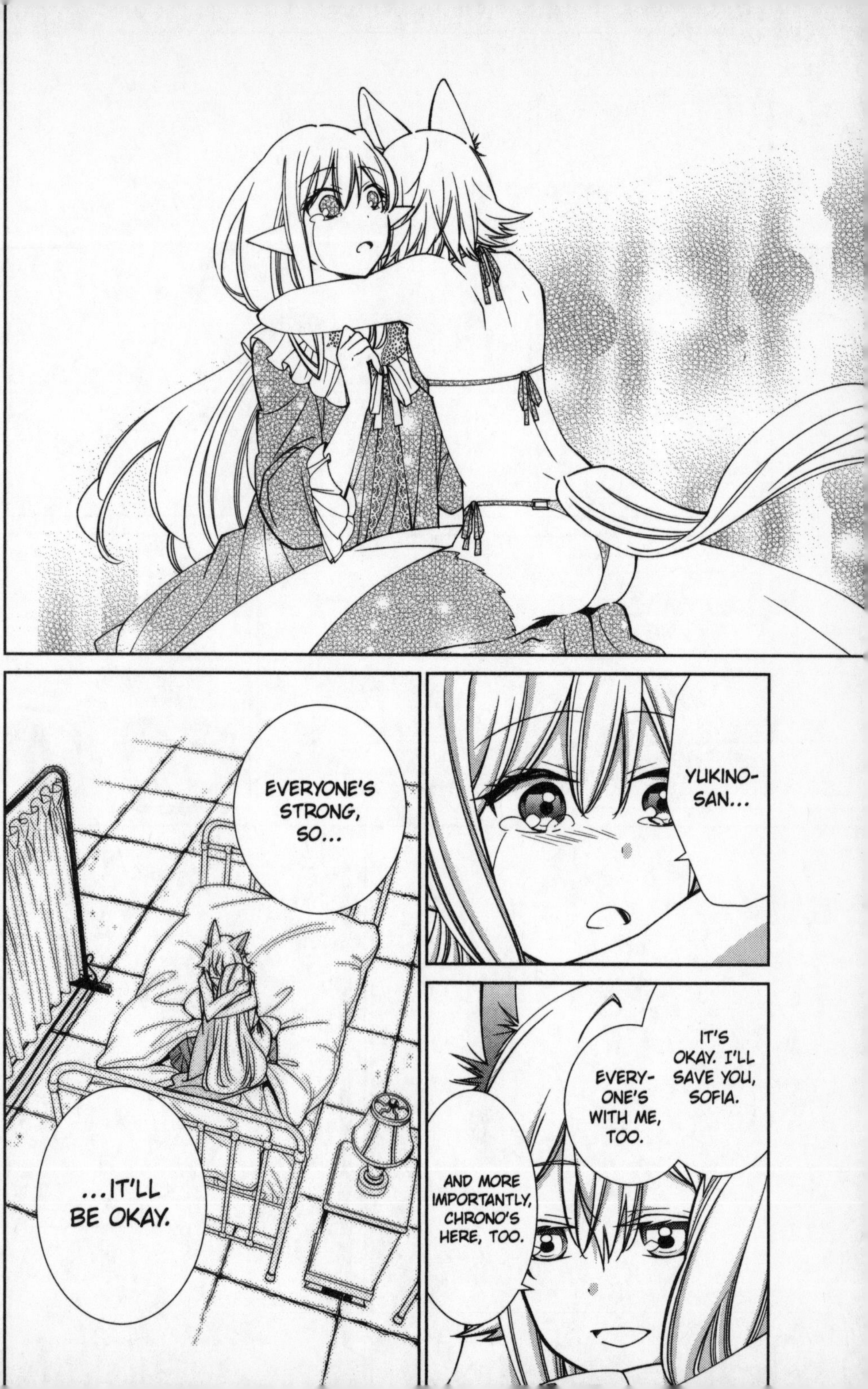
YUKINO-SAN...
IT'S OKAY. I'LL SAVE YOU, SOFIA.
EVERY-ONE'S WITH ME, TOO.
AND MORE IMPORTANTLY, CHRONO'S HERE, TOO.
EVERYONE'S STRONG, SO...
...IT'LL BE OKAY.

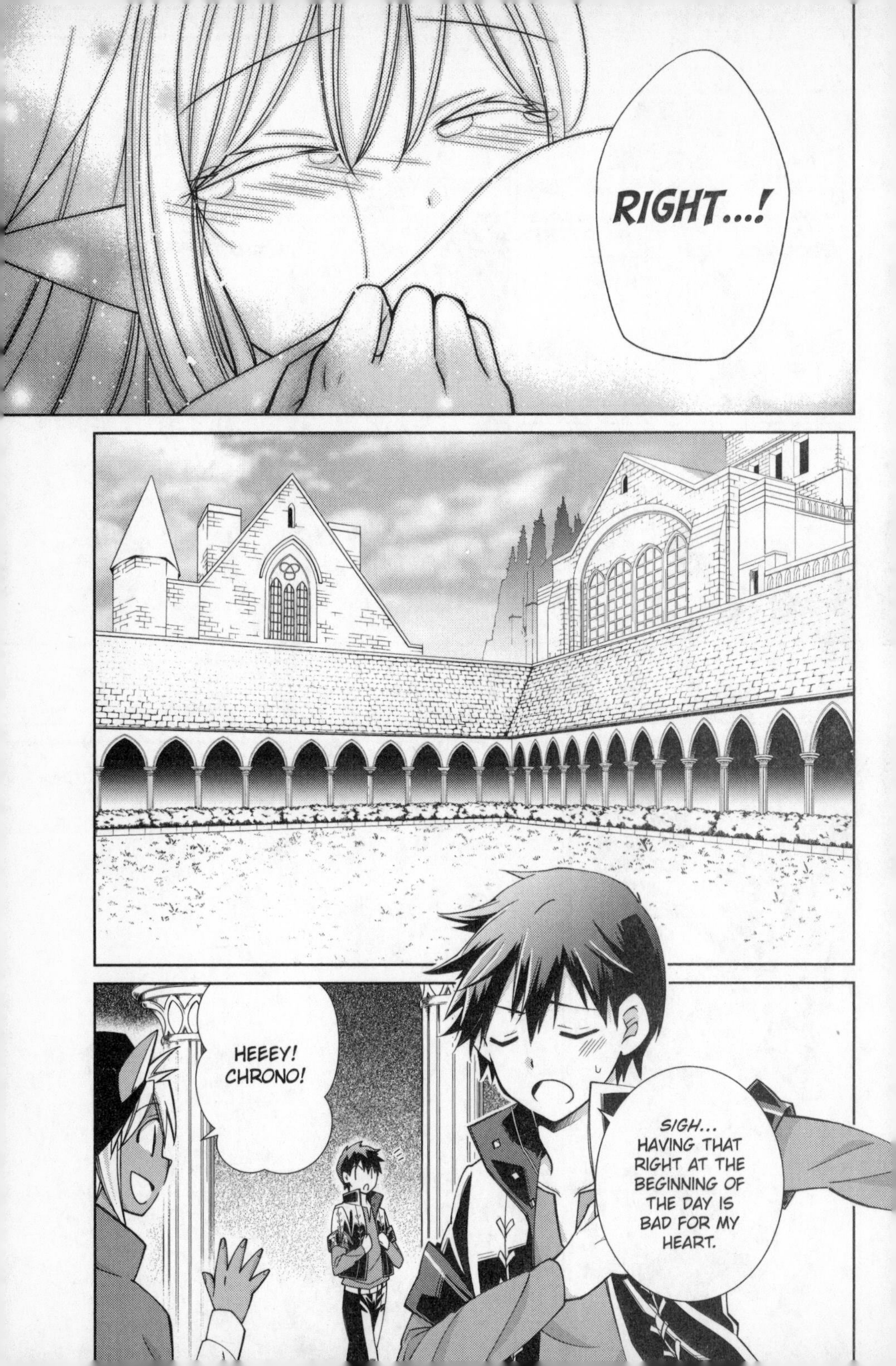
RIGHT...!
HEEEY! CHRONO!
SIGH... HAVING THAT RIGHT AT THE BEGINNING OF THE DAY IS BAD FOR MY HEART.

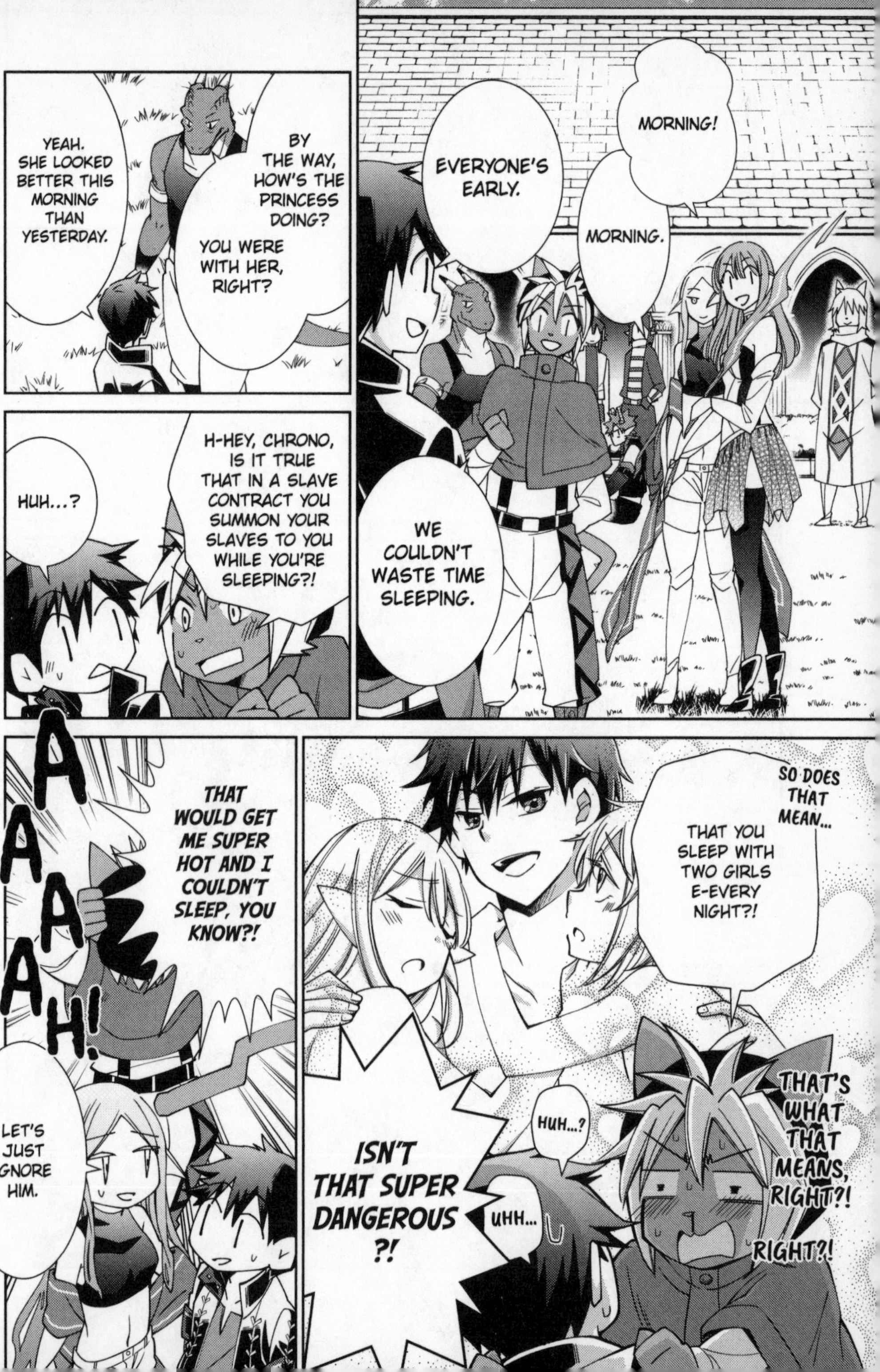
MORNING!
MORNING.
EVERYONE'S EARLY.
WE COULDN'T WASTE TIME SLEEPING.
BY THE WAY, HOW'S THE PRINCESS DOING?
YOU WERE WITH HER, RIGHT?
YEAH. SHE LOOKED BETTER THIS MORNING THAN YESTERDAY.
H-HEY, CHRONO, IS IT TRUE THAT IN A SLAVE CONTRACT YOU SUMMON YOUR SLAVES TO YOU WHILE YOU'RE SLEEPING?!
HUH...?
SO DOES THAT MEAN...
THAT YOU SLEEP WITH TWO GIRLS E-EVERY NIGHT?!
THAT'S WHAT THAT MEANS, RIGHT?!
RIGHT?!
HUH...?
UHH...
ISN'T THAT SUPER DANGEROUS?!
THAT WOULD GET ME SUPER HOT AND I COULDN'T SLEEP, YOU KNOW?!
AAAAH!
LET'S JUST IGNORE HIM.

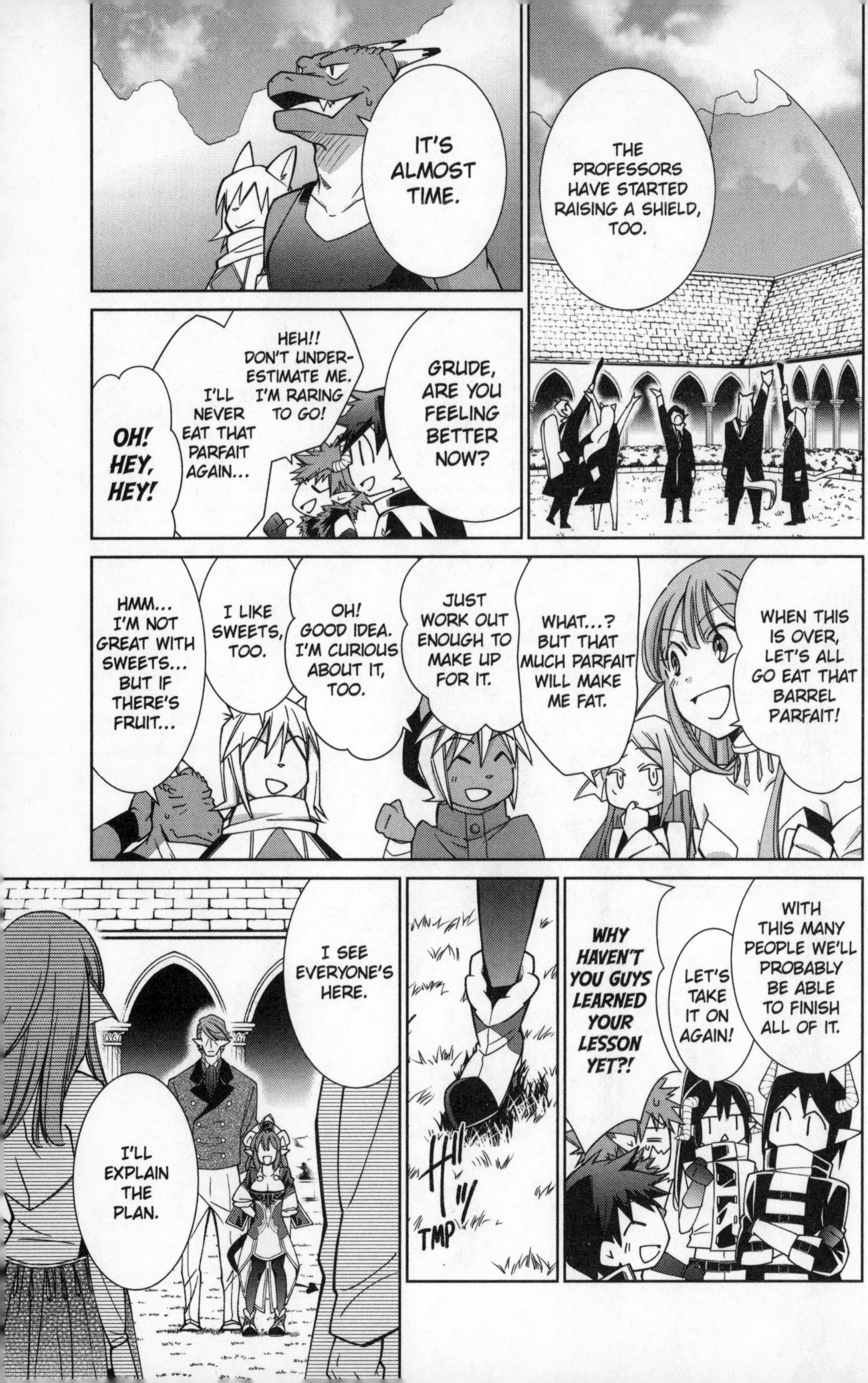
THE PROFESSORS HAVE STARTED RAISING A SHIELD, TOO.
IT'S ALMOST TIME.
GRUDE, ARE YOU FEELING BETTER NOW?
HEH!! DON'T UNDER-ESTIMATE ME. I'M RARING TO GO!
I'LL NEVER EAT THAT PARFAIT AGAIN...
OH! HEY, HEY!
WHEN THIS IS OVER, LET'S ALL GO EAT THAT BARREL PARFAIT!
WHAT...? BUT THAT MUCH PARFAIT WILL MAKE ME FAT.
JUST WORK OUT ENOUGH TO MAKE UP FOR IT.
OH! GOOD IDEA. I'M CURIOUS ABOUT IT, TOO.
I LIKE SWEETS, TOO.
HMM... I'M NOT GREAT WITH SWEETS... BUT IF THERE'S FRUIT...
WITH THIS MANY PEOPLE WE'LL PROBABLY BE ABLE TO FINISH ALL OF IT.
LET'S TAKE IT ON AGAIN!
WHY HAVEN'T YOU GUYS LEARNED YOUR LESSON YET?!
TMP
I SEE EVERYONE'S HERE.
I'LL EXPLAIN THE PLAN.

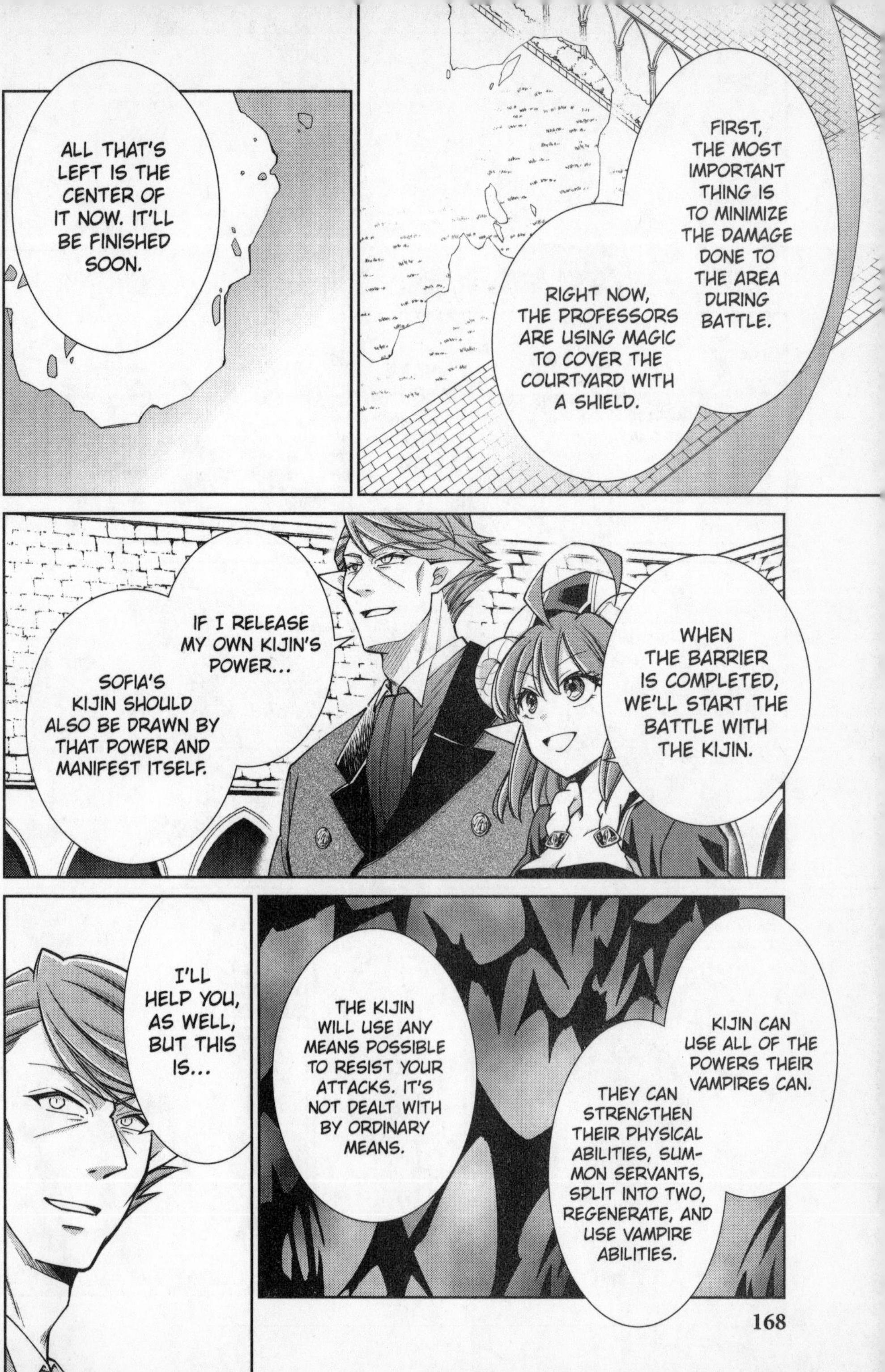
FIRST, THE MOST IMPORTANT THING IS TO MINIMIZE THE DAMAGE DONE TO THE AREA DURING BATTLE.
RIGHT NOW, THE PROFESSORS ARE USING MAGIC TO COVER THE COURTYARD WITH A SHIELD.
ALL THAT'S LEFT IS THE CENTER OF IT NOW. IT'LL BE FINISHED SOON.
WHEN THE BARRIER IS COMPLETED, WE'LL START THE BATTLE WITH THE KIJIN.
IF I RELEASE MY OWN KIJIN'S POWER...
SOFIA'S KIJIN SHOULD ALSO BE DRAWN BY THAT POWER AND MANIFEST ITSELF.
KIJIN CAN USE ALL OF THE POWERS THEIR VAMPIRES CAN.
THEY CAN STRENGTHEN THEIR PHYSICAL ABILITIES, SUM-MON SERVANTS, SPLIT INTO TWO, REGENERATE, AND USE VAMPIRE ABILITIES.
THE KIJIN WILL USE ANY MEANS POSSIBLE TO RESIST YOUR ATTACKS. IT'S NOT DEALT WITH BY ORDINARY MEANS.
I'LL HELP YOU, AS WELL, BUT THIS IS...

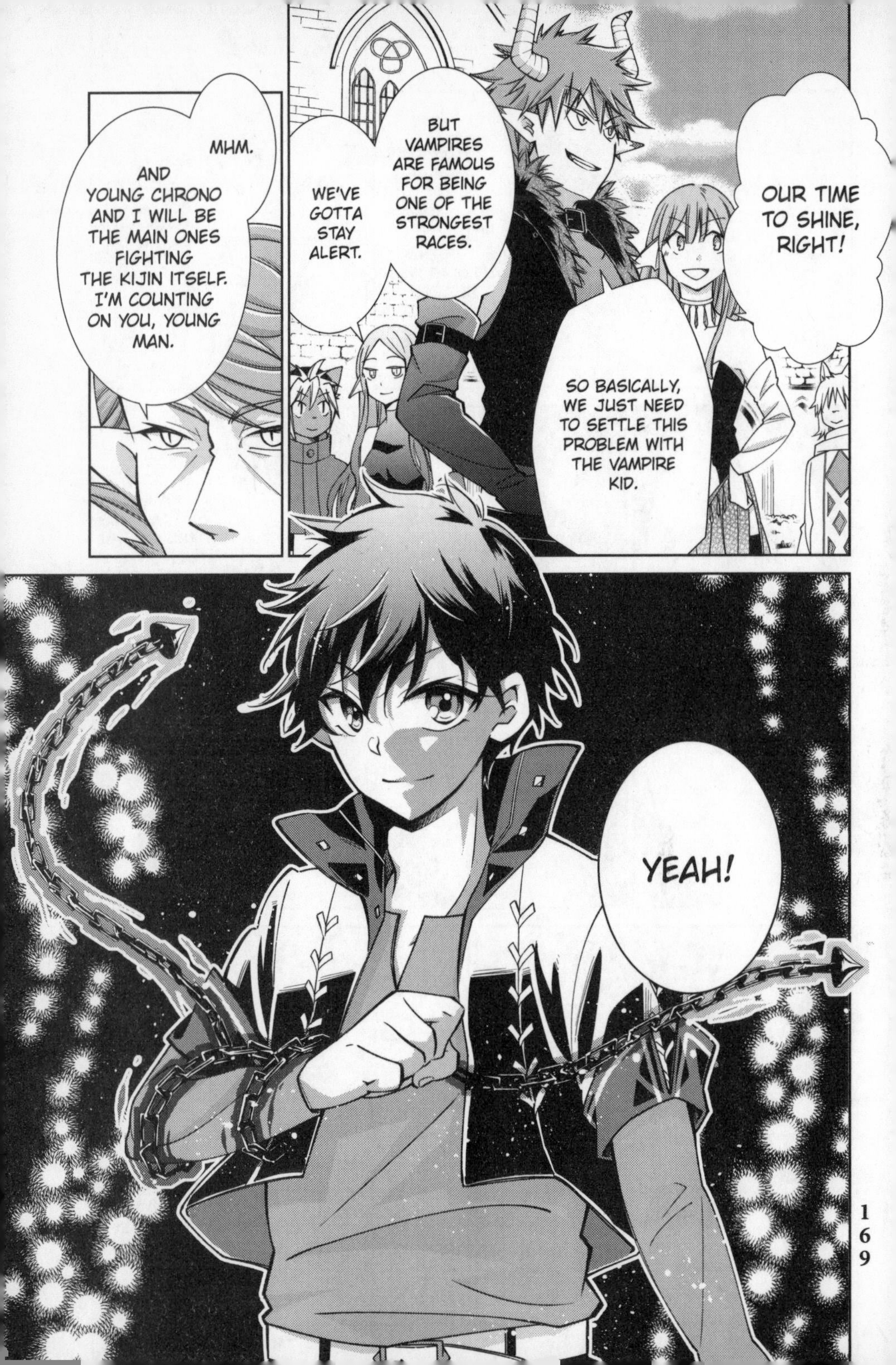
OUR TIME TO SHINE, RIGHT!
SO BASICALLY, WE JUST NEED TO SETTLE THIS PROBLEM WITH THE VAMPIRE KID.
BUT VAMPIRES ARE FAMOUS FOR BEING ONE OF THE STRONGEST RACES.
WE'VE GOTTA STAY ALERT.
MHM.
AND YOUNG CHRONO AND I WILL BE THE MAIN ONES FIGHTING THE KIJIN ITSELF. I'M COUNTING ON YOU, YOUNG MAN.
YEAH!

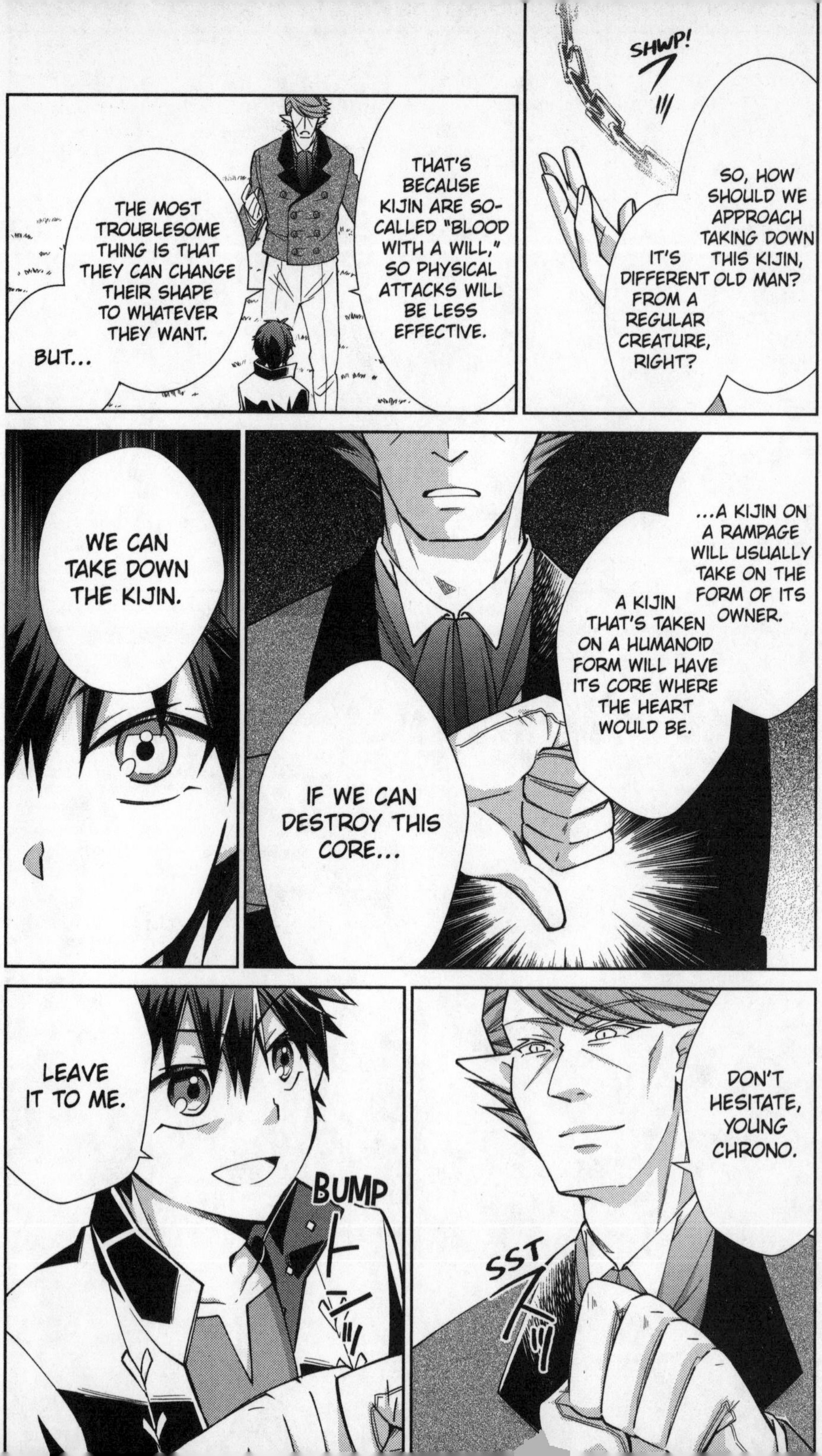
SHWP!
SO, HOW SHOULD WE APPROACH TAKING DOWN THIS KIJIN, OLD MAN?
IT'S DIFFERENT FROM A REGULAR CREATURE, RIGHT?
THAT'S BECAUSE KIJIN ARE SO-CALLED "BLOOD WITH A WILL," SO PHYSICAL ATTACKS WILL BE LESS EFFECTIVE.
THE MOST TROUBLESOME THING IS THAT THEY CAN CHANGE THEIR SHAPE TO WHATEVER THEY WANT.
BUT...
...A KIJIN ON A RAMPAGE WILL USUALLY TAKE ON THE FORM OF ITS OWNER.
A KIJIN THAT'S TAKEN ON A HUMANOID FORM WILL HAVE ITS CORE WHERE THE HEART WOULD BE.
IF WE CAN DESTROY THIS CORE...
WE CAN TAKE DOWN THE KIJIN.
DON'T HESITATE, YOUNG CHRONO.
SST
LEAVE IT TO ME.
BUMP

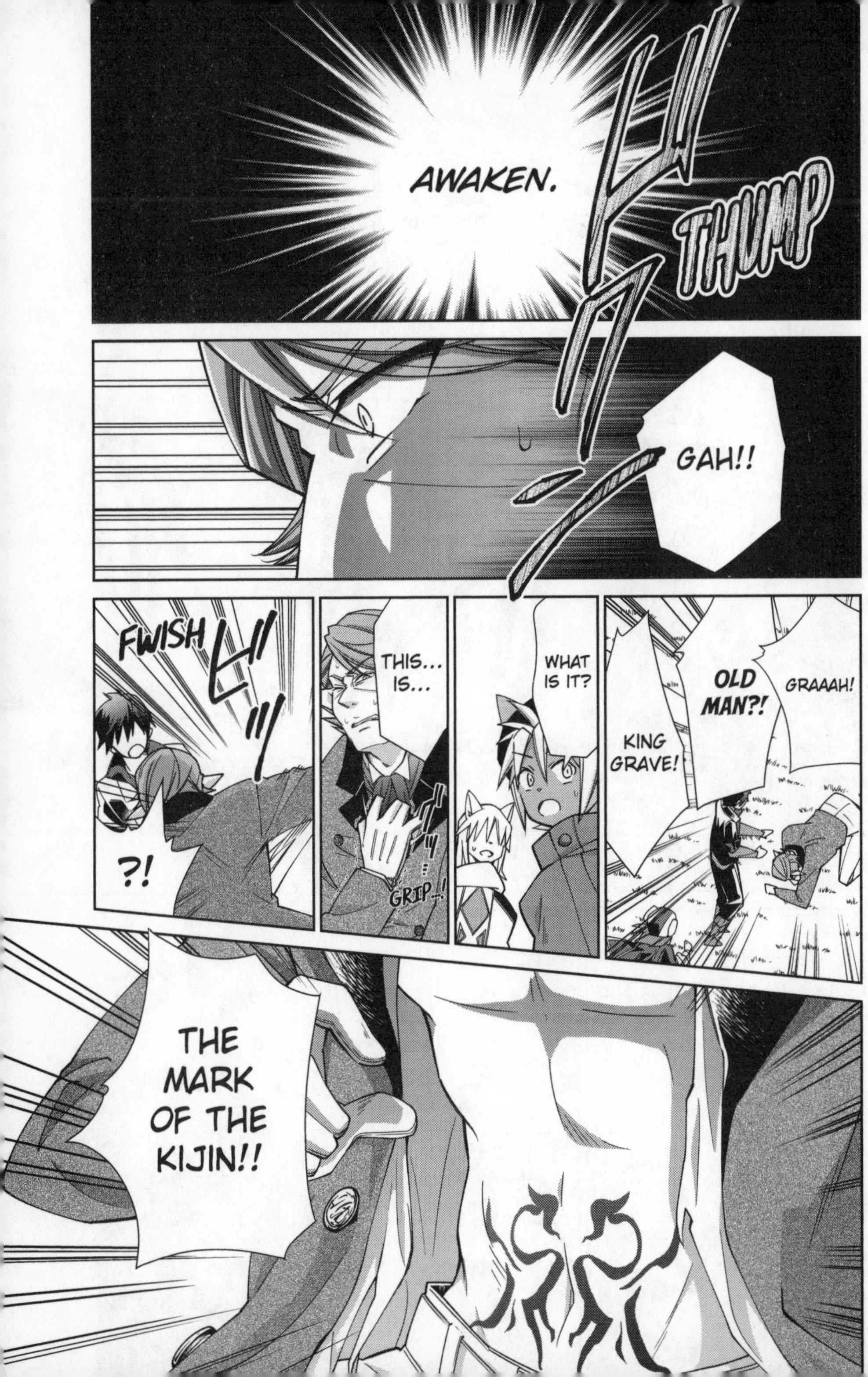
THUMP
AWAKEN.
GAH!!
GRAAAH!
OLD MAN?!
KING GRAVE!
WHAT IS IT?
THIS... IS...
GRIP...!
FWISH
?!
THE MARK OF THE KIJIN!!

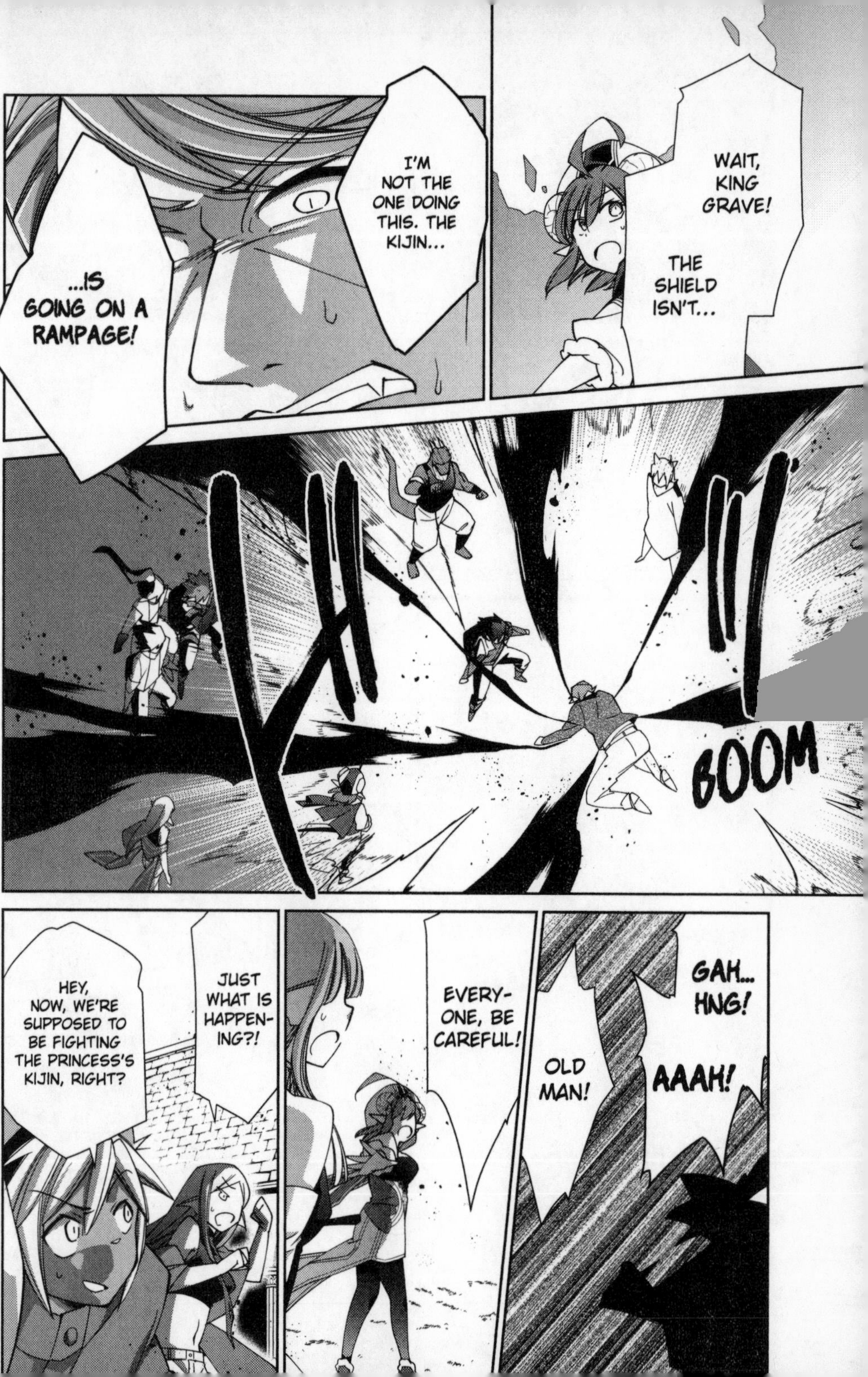
WAIT, KING GRAVE!
THE SHIELD ISN'T...
I'M NOT THE ONE DOING THIS. THE KIJIN...
...IS GOING ON A RAMPAGE!
BOOM
GAH... HNG!
AAAH!
OLD MAN!
EVERY-ONE, BE CAREFUL!
JUST WHAT IS HAPPEN-ING?!
HEY, NOW, WE'RE SUPPOSED TO BE FIGHTING THE PRINCESS'S KIJIN, RIGHT?

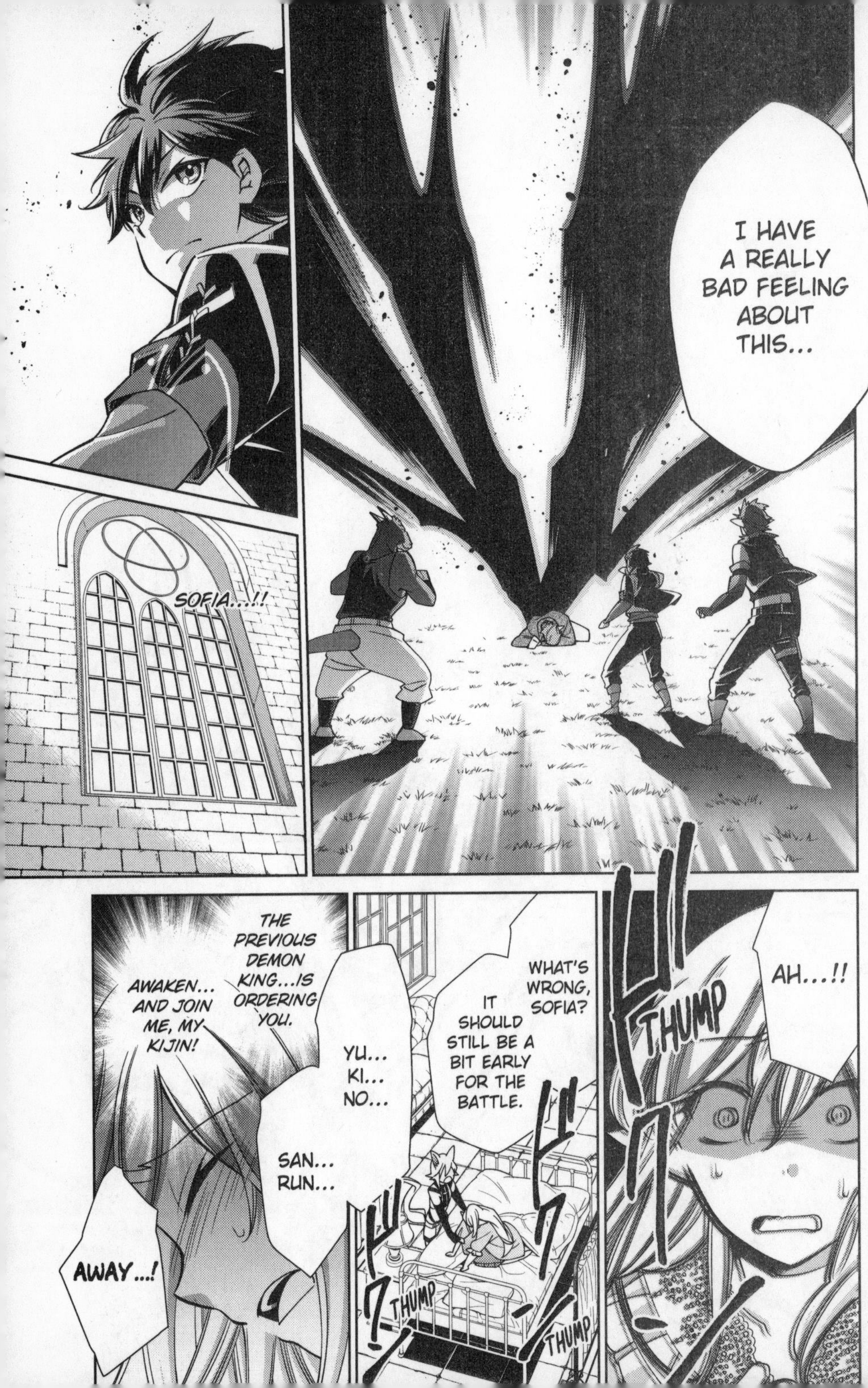
I HAVE A REALLY BAD FEELING ABOUT THIS...
SOFIA...!!
AH...!!
THUMP
WHAT'S WRONG, SOFIA?
IT SHOULD STILL BE A BIT EARLY FOR THE BATTLE.
THUMP
THUMP
THE PREVIOUS DEMON KING...IS ORDERING YOU.
AWAKEN... AND JOIN ME, MY KIJIN!
YU... KI... NO...
SAN... RUN...
AWAY...!

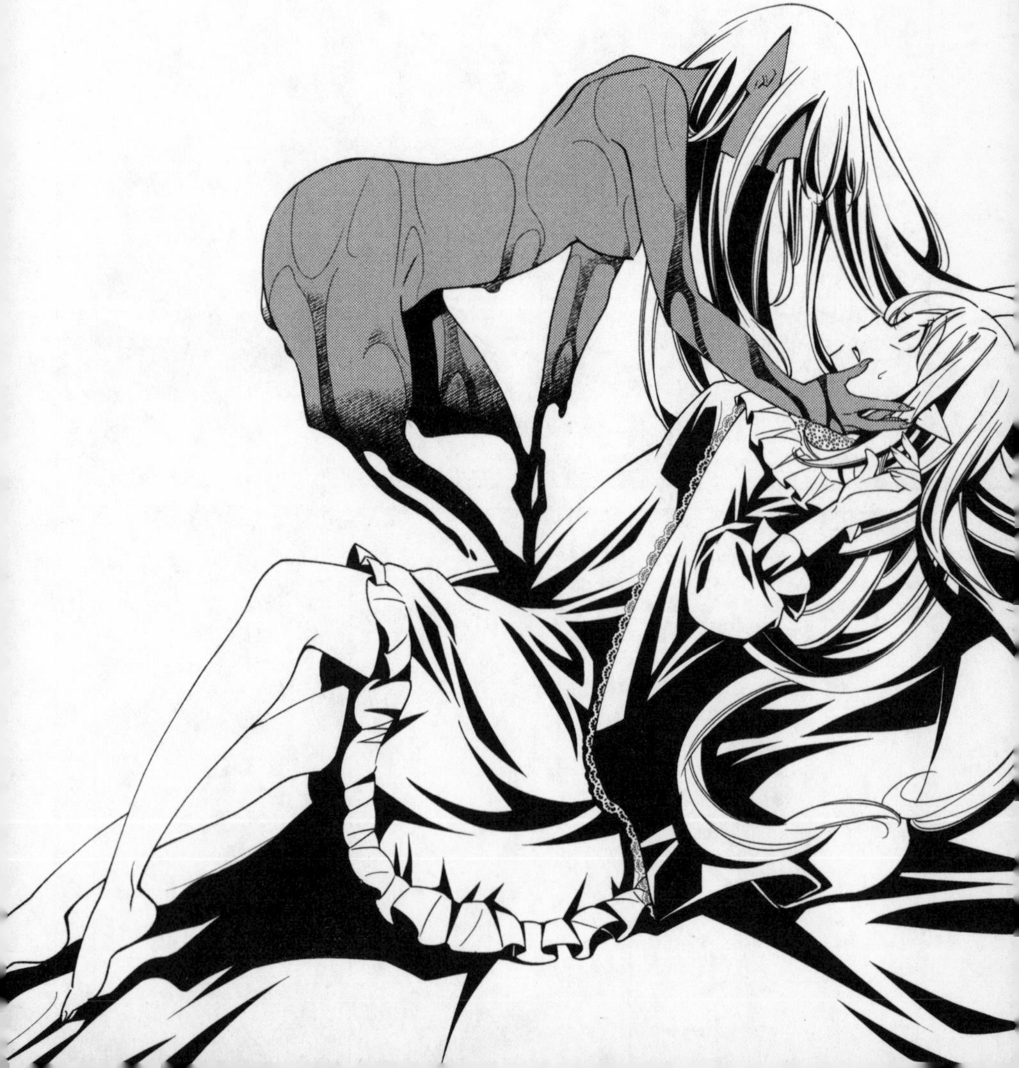

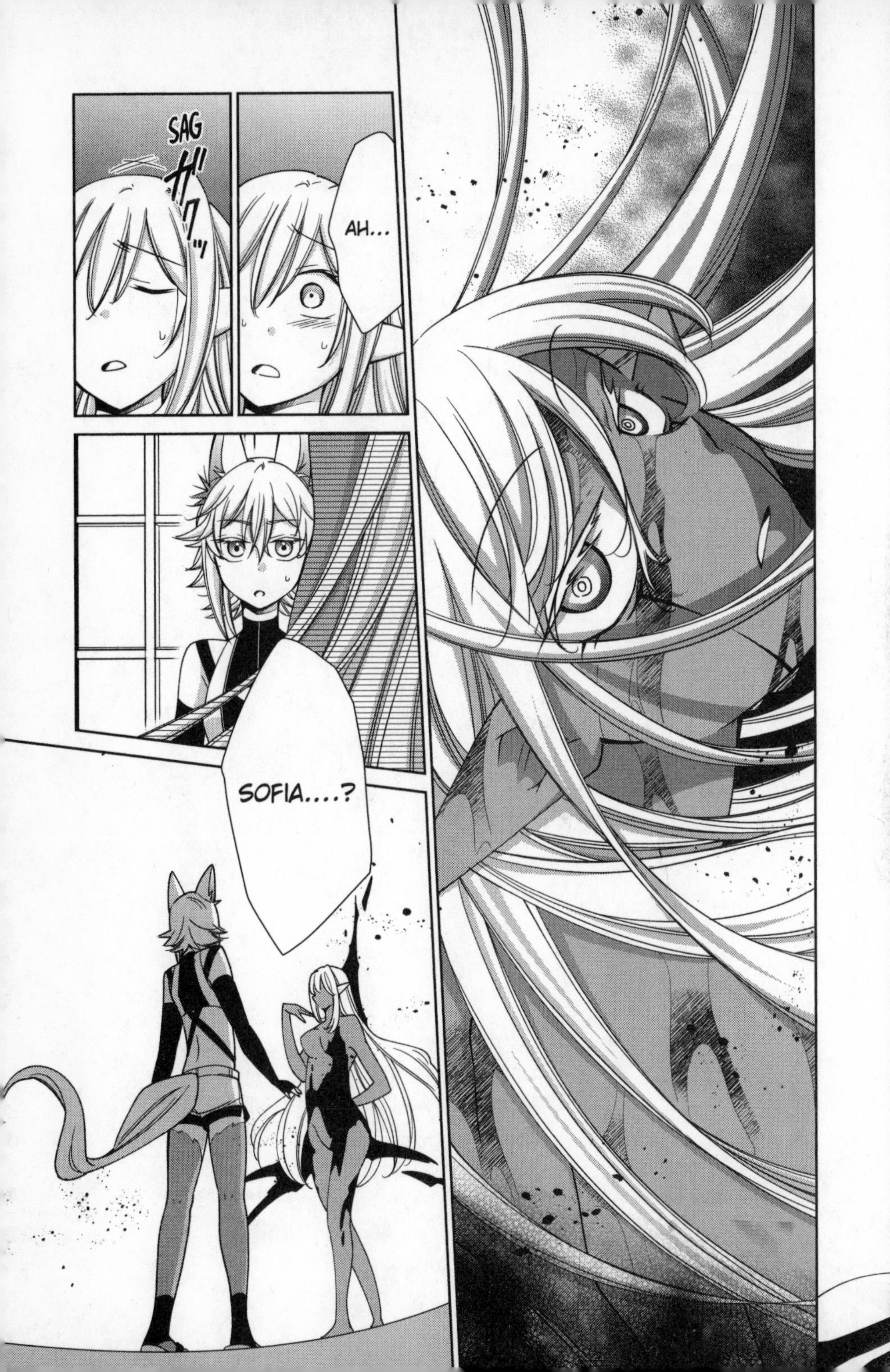
AH...
SAG
ガクッ
SOFIA....?

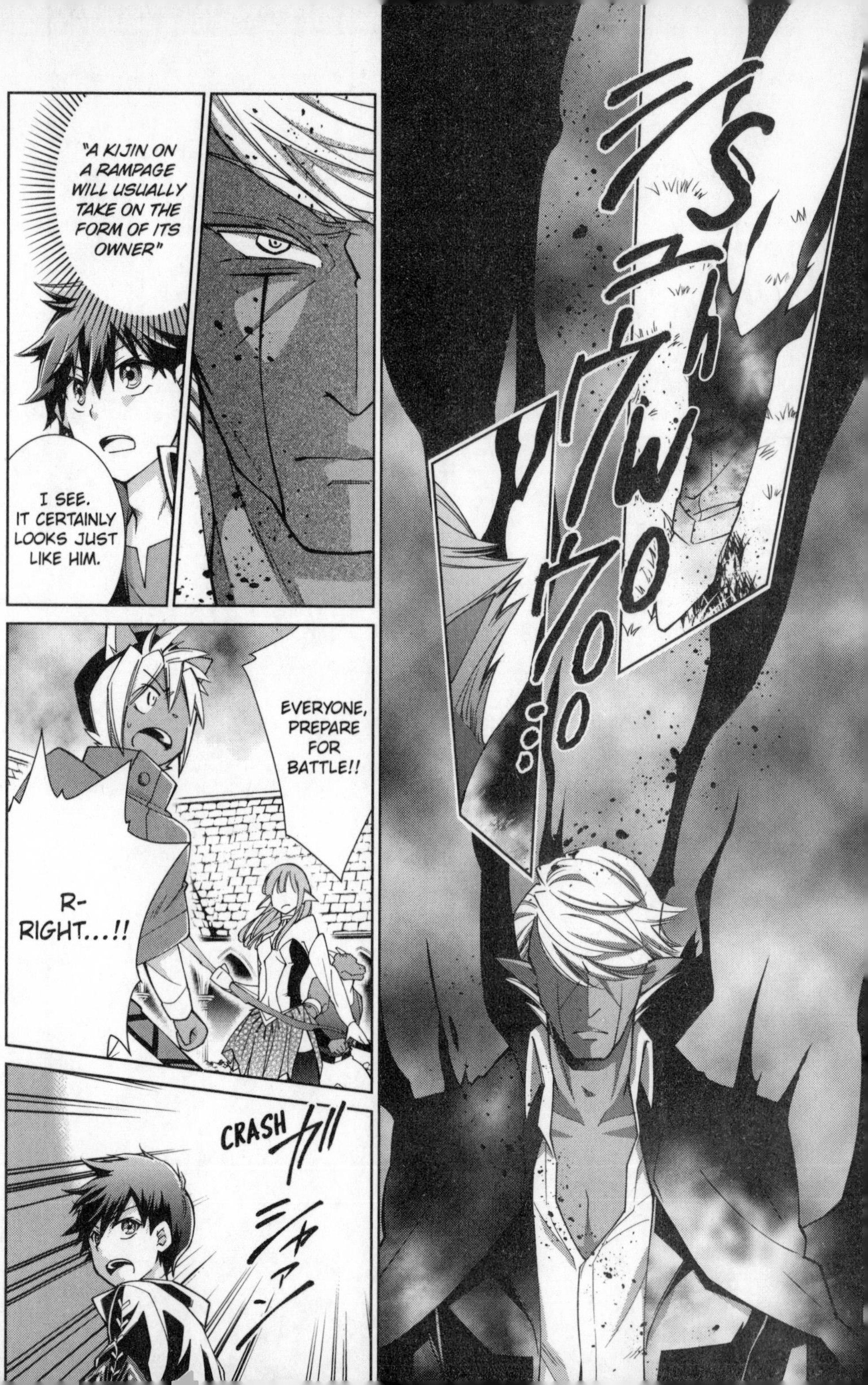
SWOOO...
"A KIJIN ON A RAMPAGE WILL USUALLY TAKE ON THE FORM OF ITS OWNER"
I SEE. IT CERTAINLY LOOKS JUST LIKE HIM.
EVERYONE, PREPARE FOR BATTLE!!
R-RIGHT...!!
CRASH

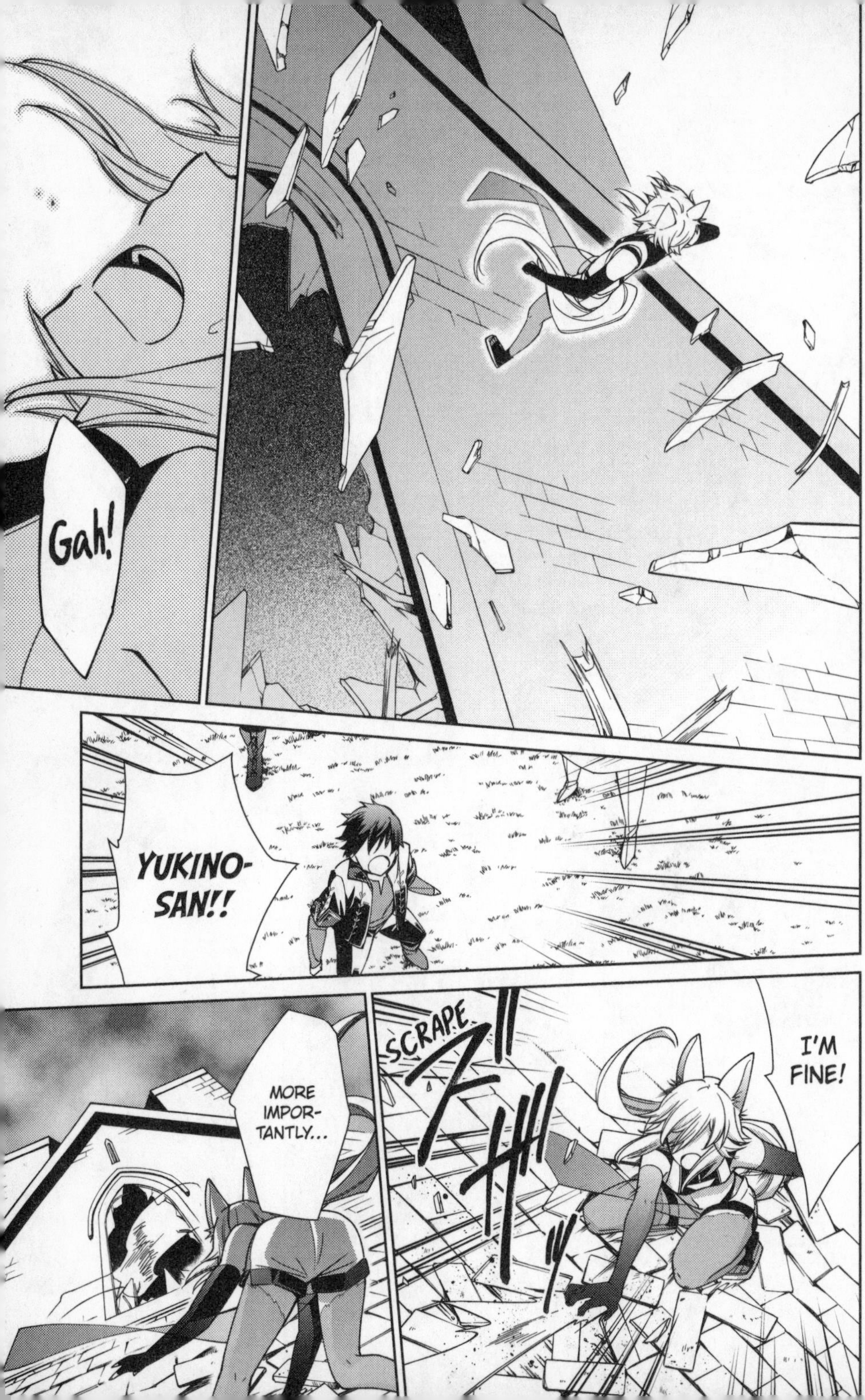
Gah!
YUKINO-SAN!!
I'M FINE!
SCRAPE
MORE IMPORTANTLY...

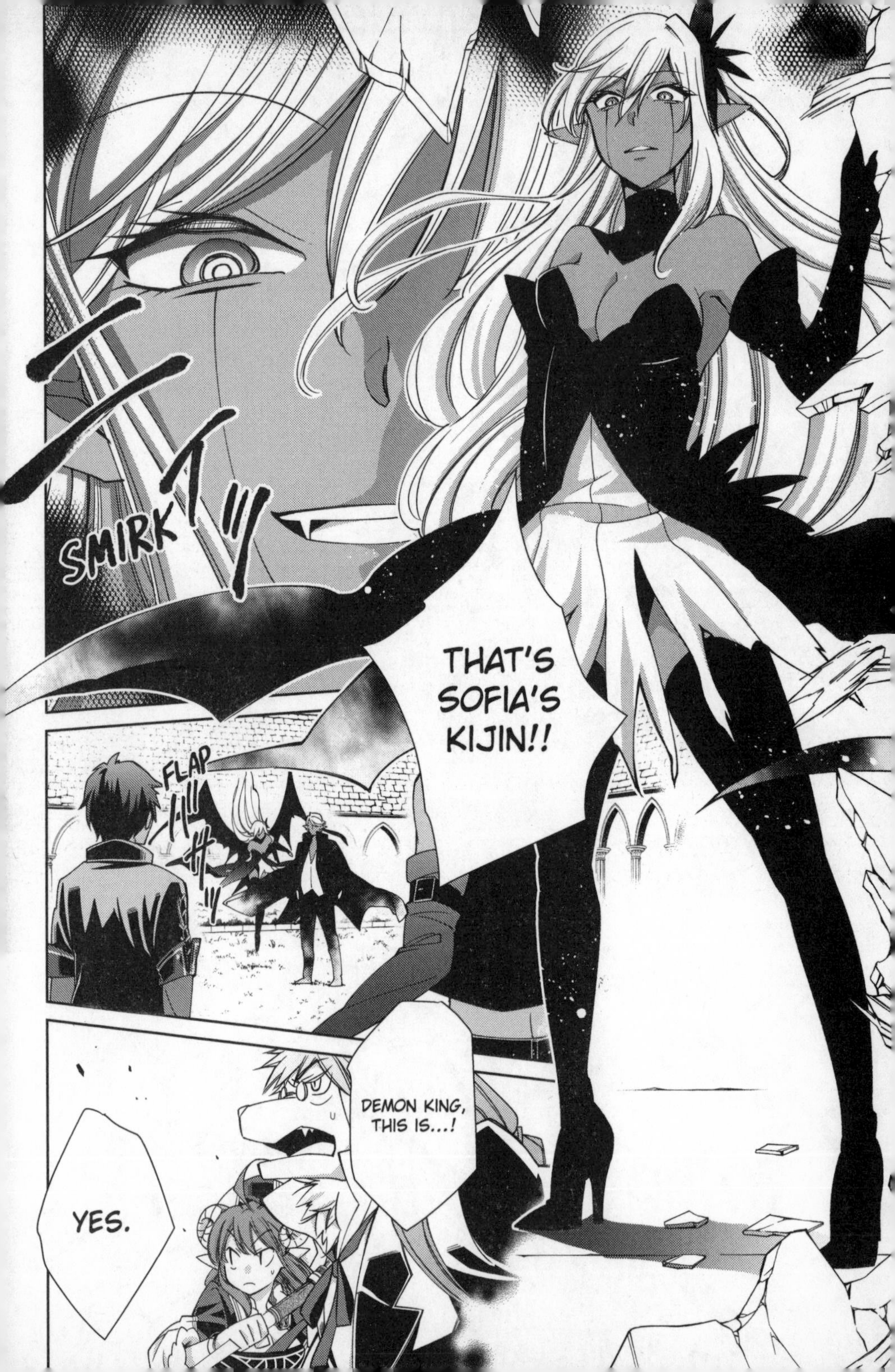
SMIRK
THAT'S SOFIA'S KIJIN!!
FLAP
DEMON KING, THIS IS...!
YES.

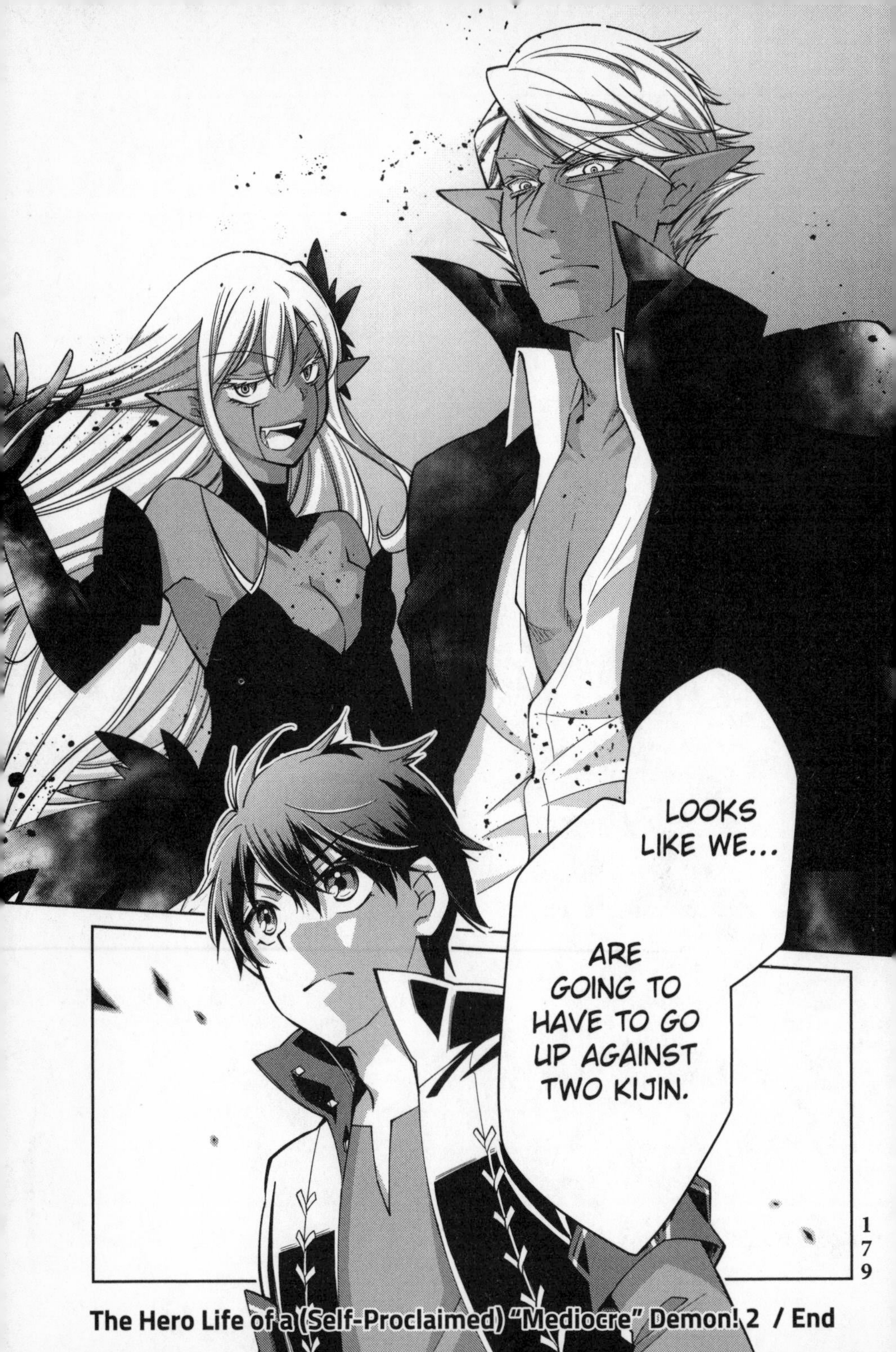
LOOKS LIKE WE...
ARE GOING TO HAVE TO GO UP AGAINST TWO KIJIN.

The Hero Life of a (Self-Proclaimed) "Mediocre" Demon! 2 / End

Bonus Comic 1 - Lily and Akue Shopping

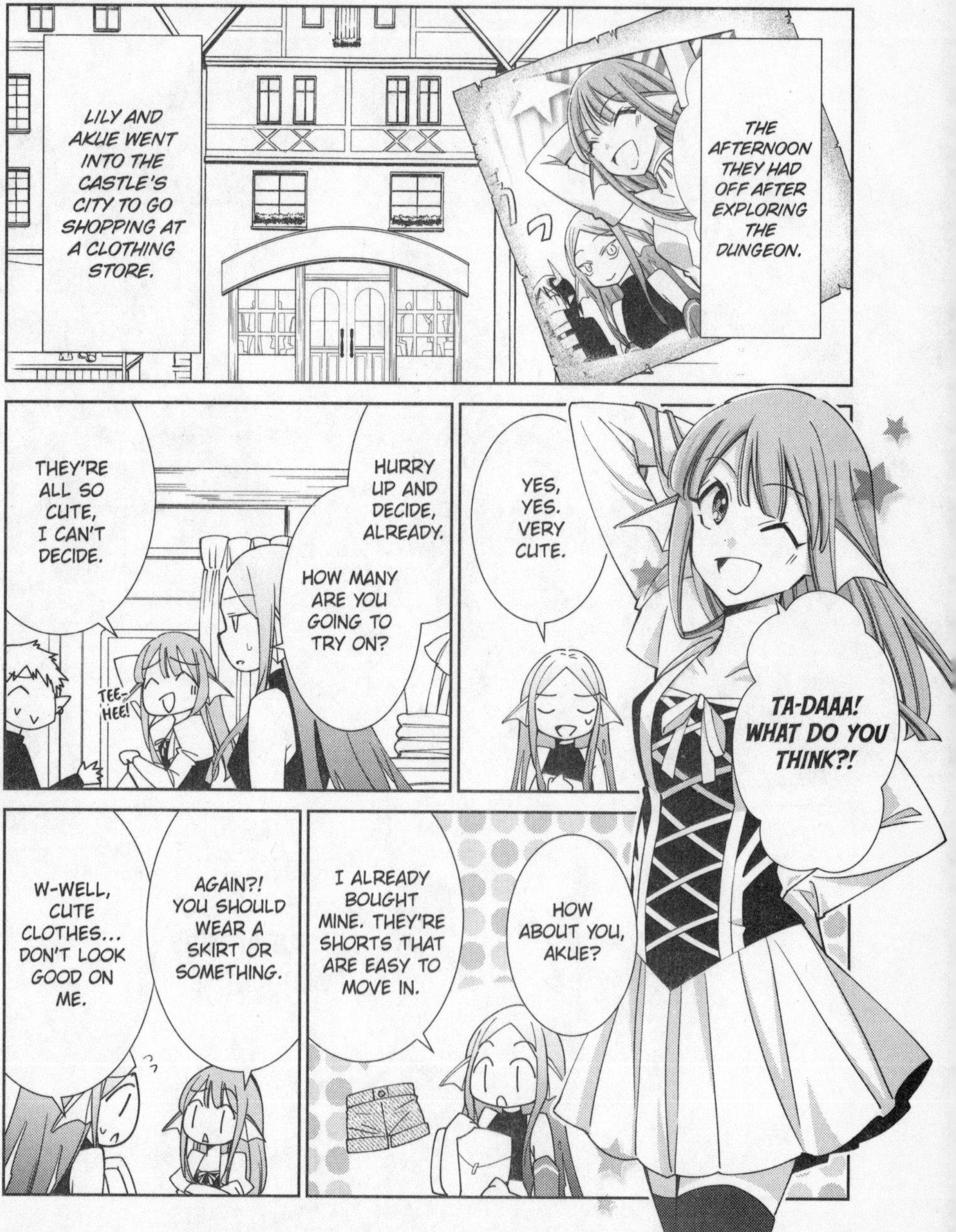

THE AFTERNOON THEY HAD OFF AFTER EXPLORING THE DUNGEON.
LILY AND AKUE WENT INTO THE CASTLE'S CITY TO GO SHOPPING AT A CLOTHING STORE.
TA-DAAA! WHAT DO YOU THINK?!
YES, YES. VERY CUTE.
HURRY UP AND DECIDE, ALREADY.
HOW MANY ARE YOU GOING TO TRY ON?
THEY'RE ALL SO CUTE, I CAN'T DECIDE.
TEE-HEE!
HOW ABOUT YOU, AKUE?
I ALREADY BOUGHT MINE. THEY'RE SHORTS THAT ARE EASY TO MOVE IN.
AGAIN?! YOU SHOULD WEAR A SKIRT OR SOMETHING.
W-WELL, CUTE CLOTHES... DON'T LOOK GOOD ON ME.

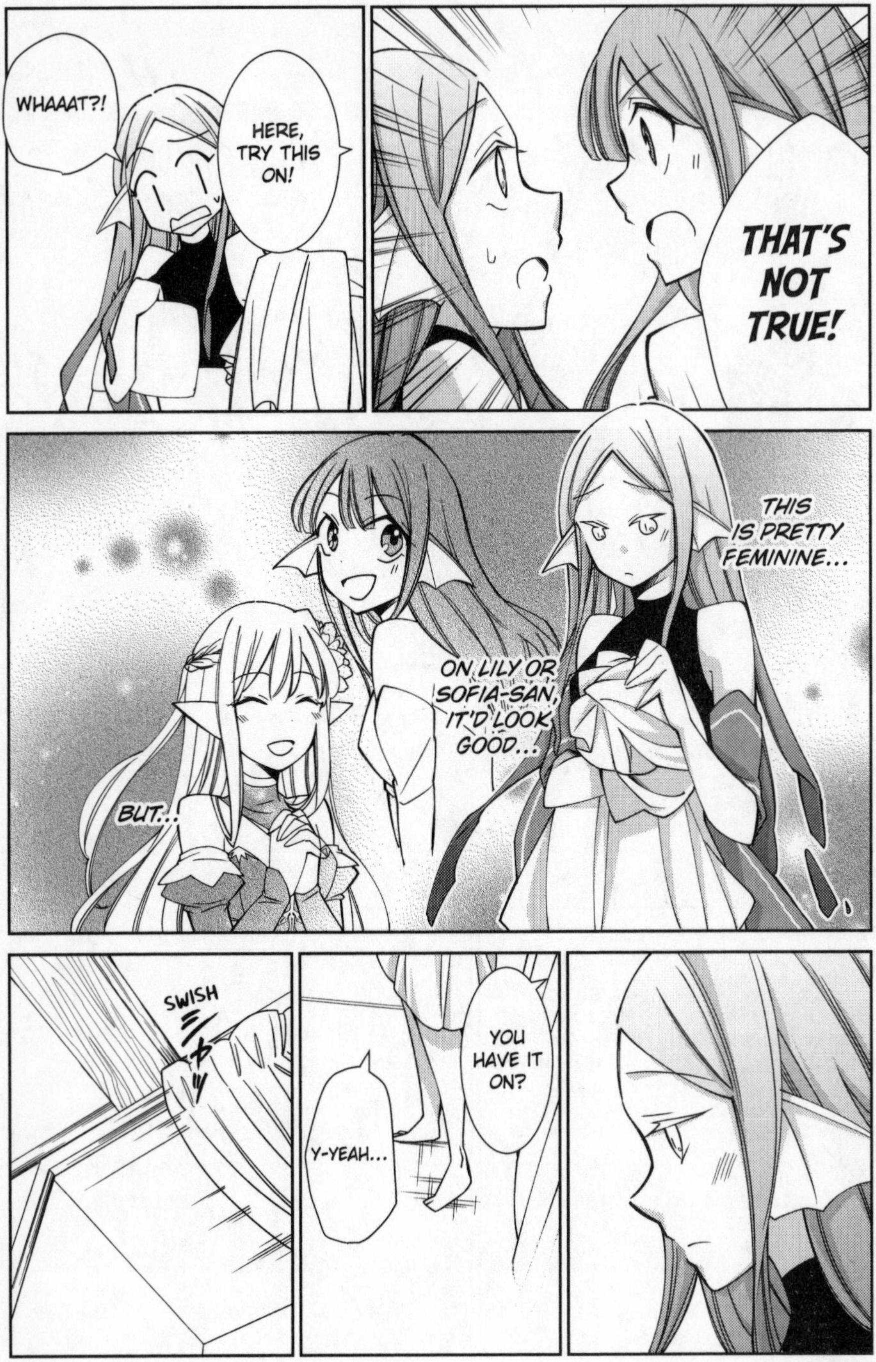
THAT'S NOT TRUE!
HERE, TRY THIS ON!
WHAAAT?!
THIS IS PRETTY FEMININE...
ON LILY OR SOFIA-SAN, IT'D LOOK GOOD...
BUT...
YOU HAVE IT ON?
Y-YEAH...
SWISH

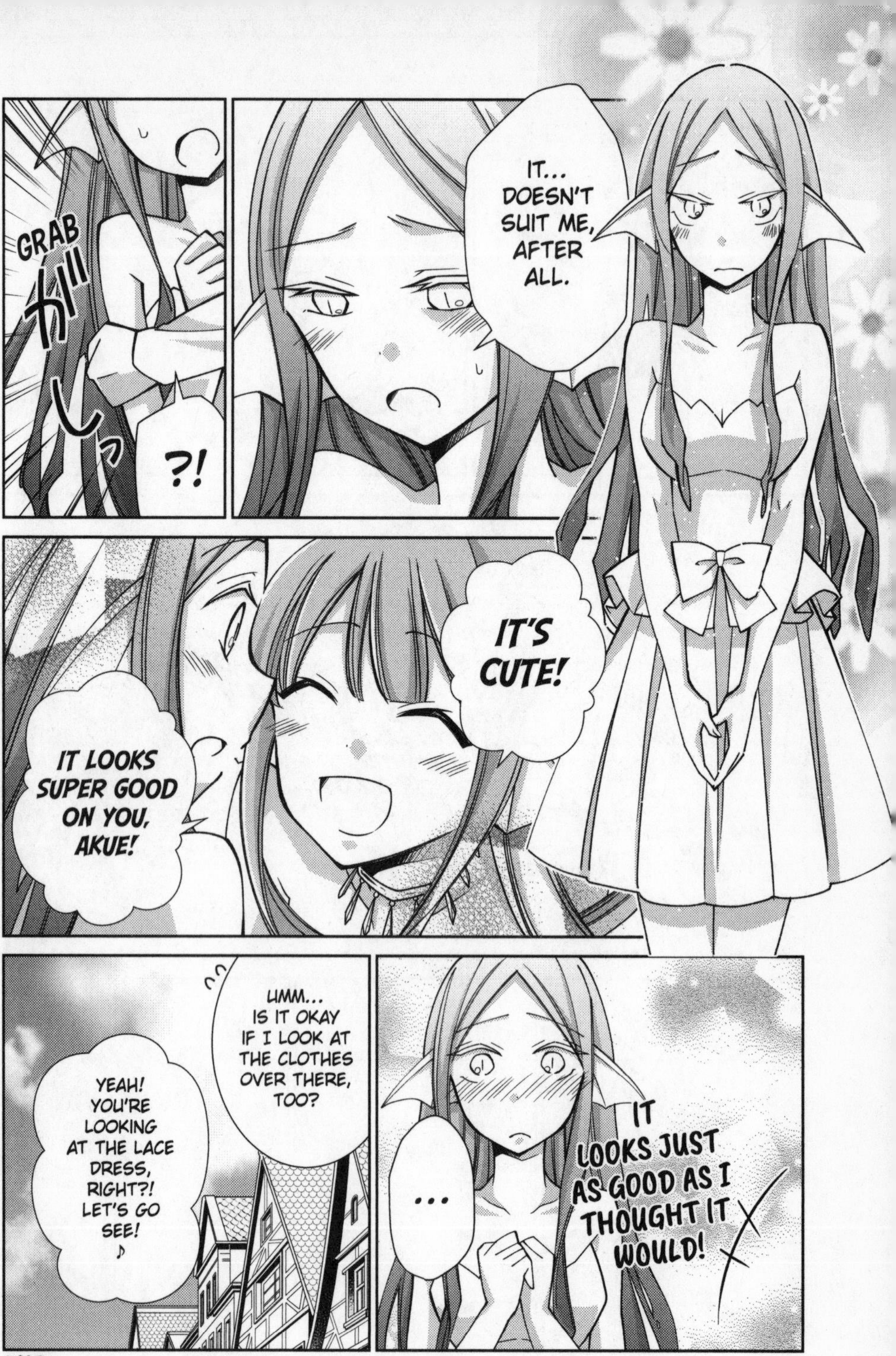
IT... DOESN'T SUIT ME, AFTER ALL.
GRAB
ガシッ
?!
IT'S CUTE!
IT LOOKS SUPER GOOD ON YOU, AKUE!
IT LOOKS JUST AS GOOD AS I THOUGHT IT WOULD!
...
UMM... IS IT OKAY IF I LOOK AT THE CLOTHES OVER THERE, TOO?
YEAH! YOU'RE LOOKING AT THE LACE DRESS, RIGHT?! LET'S GO SEE! ♪

END

Bonus Comic 2 - What Happened With Grude and Friends After Dismissal in Chapter 9

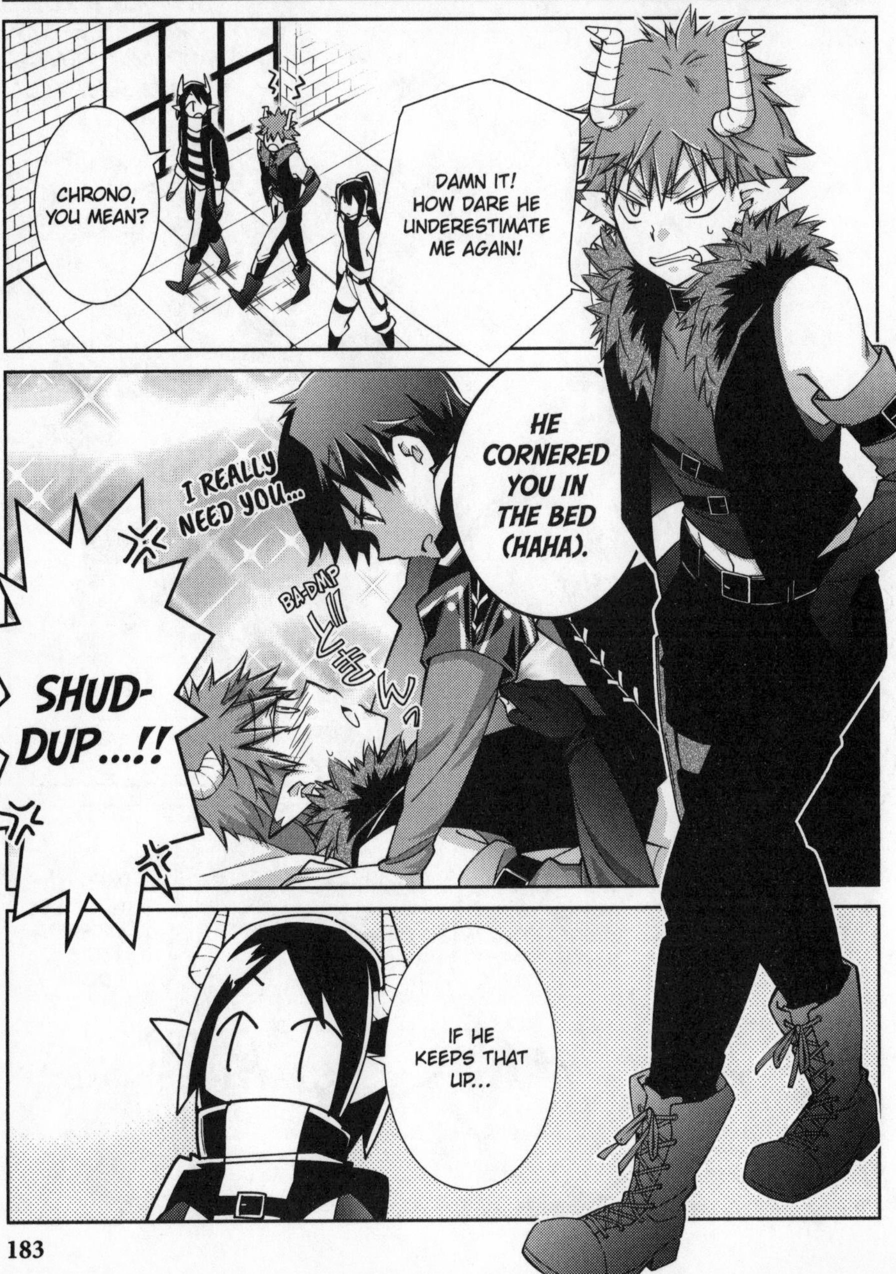
DAMN IT! HOW DARE HE UNDERESTIMATE ME AGAIN!
CHRONO, YOU MEAN?
HE CORNERED YOU IN THE BED (HAHA).
I REALLY NEED YOU...
BA-DMP
SHUD-DUP...!!
IF HE KEEPS THAT UP...

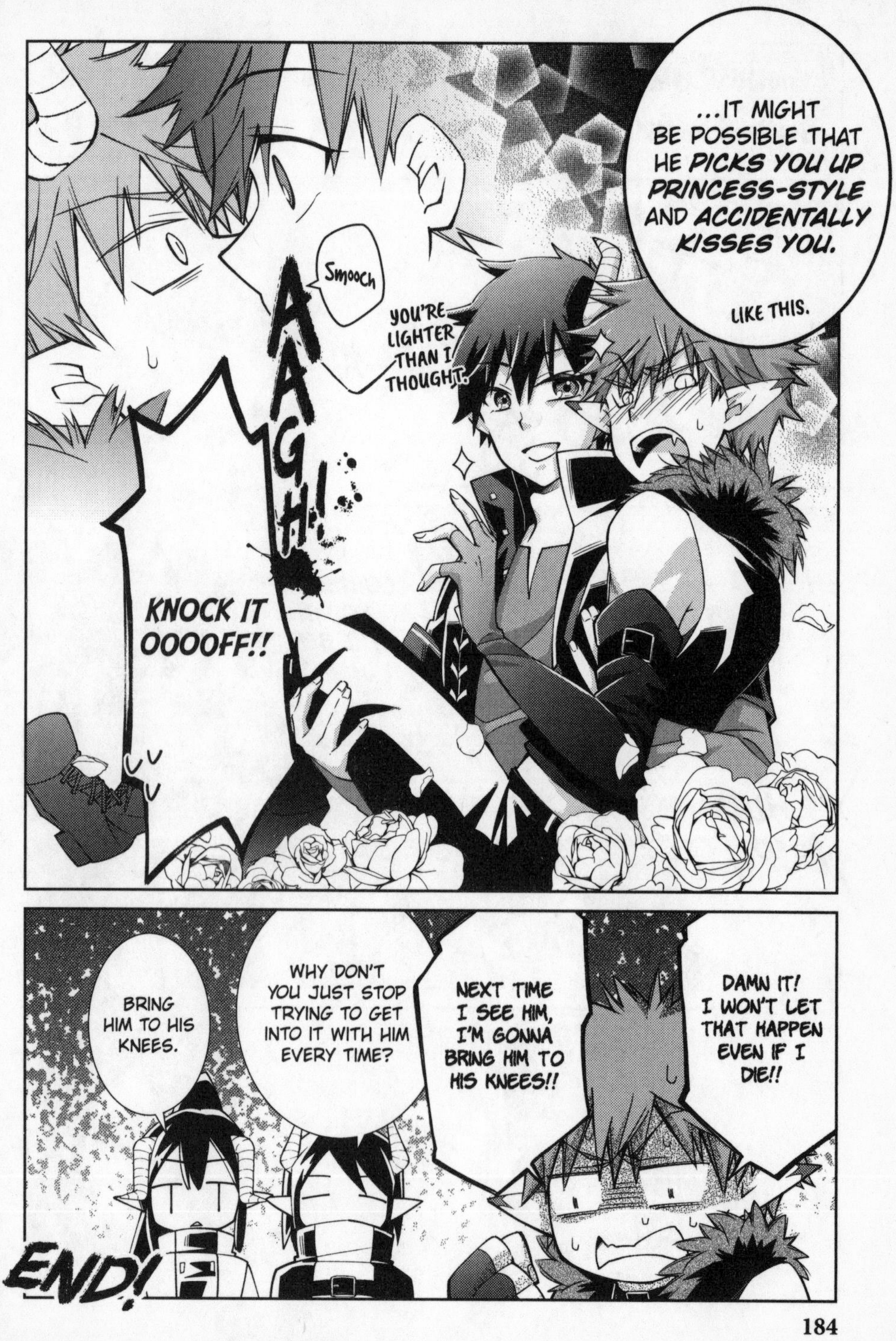
...IT MIGHT BE POSSIBLE THAT HE PICKS YOU UP PRINCESS-STYLE AND ACCIDENTALLY KISSES YOU.
LIKE THIS.
YOU'RE LIGHTER THAN I THOUGHT.
Smooch
AAGH!!
KNOCK IT OOOOFF!!
DAMN IT! I WON'T LET THAT HAPPEN EVEN IF I DIE!!
NEXT TIME I SEE HIM, I'M GONNA BRING HIM TO HIS KNEES!!
WHY DON'T YOU JUST STOP TRYING TO GET INTO IT WITH HIM EVERY TIME?
BRING HIM TO HIS KNEES.
END!

The HERO LIFE of a (Self-Proclaimed) "Mediocre" DEMON!

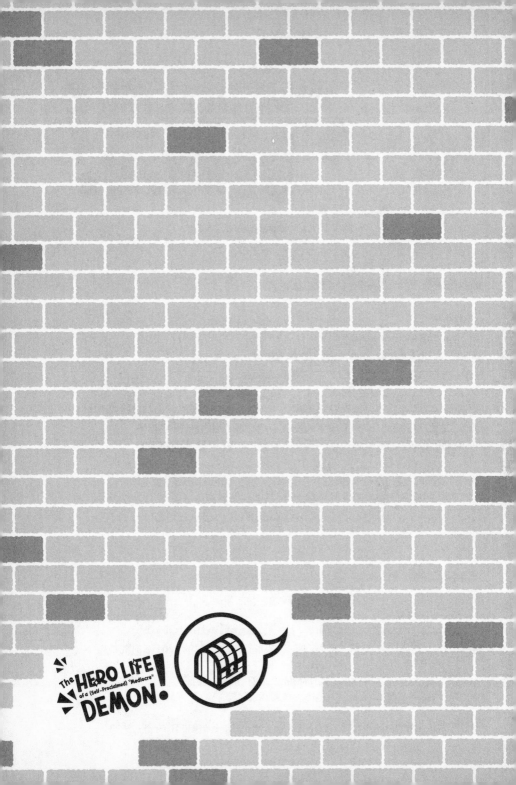

 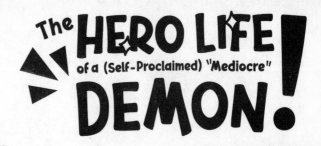

The HERO LIFE of a (Self-Proclaimed) "Mediocre" DEMON!

SPECIAL COMMENTS PAGE

AUTHOR ⬚ SHIROICHI AMAUI

HELLO.
I'M THE AUTHOR, SHIROICHI AMAUI.
THANK YOU SO MUCH FOR PURCHASING THE SECOND VOLUME OF "THE HERO LIFE OF A (SELF-PROCLAIMED) 'MEDIOCRE' DEMON!"

THIS TIME, A LOT OF DIFFERENT EVENTS HAPPENED INSIDE AND OUTSIDE OF THE DEMON KING CASTLE. EVEN IF IT'S SOMETHING THAT'S OUTRAGEOUS FOR ORDINARY PEOPLE AND DEMONS, TO CHRONO, WHOSE HOMETOWN IS PRETTY RIDICULOUS, IT SEEMS TO BE "COMMON."

I HOPE THAT YOU WILL LOOK FORWARD TO SEEING CHRONO, WHO BELIEVES HIS ABILITIES ARE JUST ORDINARY, AND CONTINUE TO ENJOY WATCHING HIM GO ON ADVENTURES WITH HIS FRIENDS AND TAKE ON A VARIETY OF NEW CHALLENGES.

CHARACTER DESIGN ⬚ TAMAGONOKIMI-SENSEI

CONGRATULATIONS ON THE SECOND VOLUME'S RELEASE!

FIRST OF ALL, ALLOW ME TO TELL KONEKONEKO-SAMA "I'M SO SORRY FOR THE TROUBLESOME CHARACTER DESIGNS!" PLEASE DON'T WORRY ABOUT THE DESIGN AND KEEP ON OMITTING SOME OF IT!

BOTH THE CONTENT AND CHRONO ARE BEING DRAWN SO CUTELY AND I TAKE OFF MY HAT TO YOU FOR GIVING IT MORE CHARM THAN WHAT I COULD DO.

I'M EXPECTING GOOD THINGS TO COME FROM THIS SERIES, SO PLEASE CONTINUE TO DO YOUR BEST!

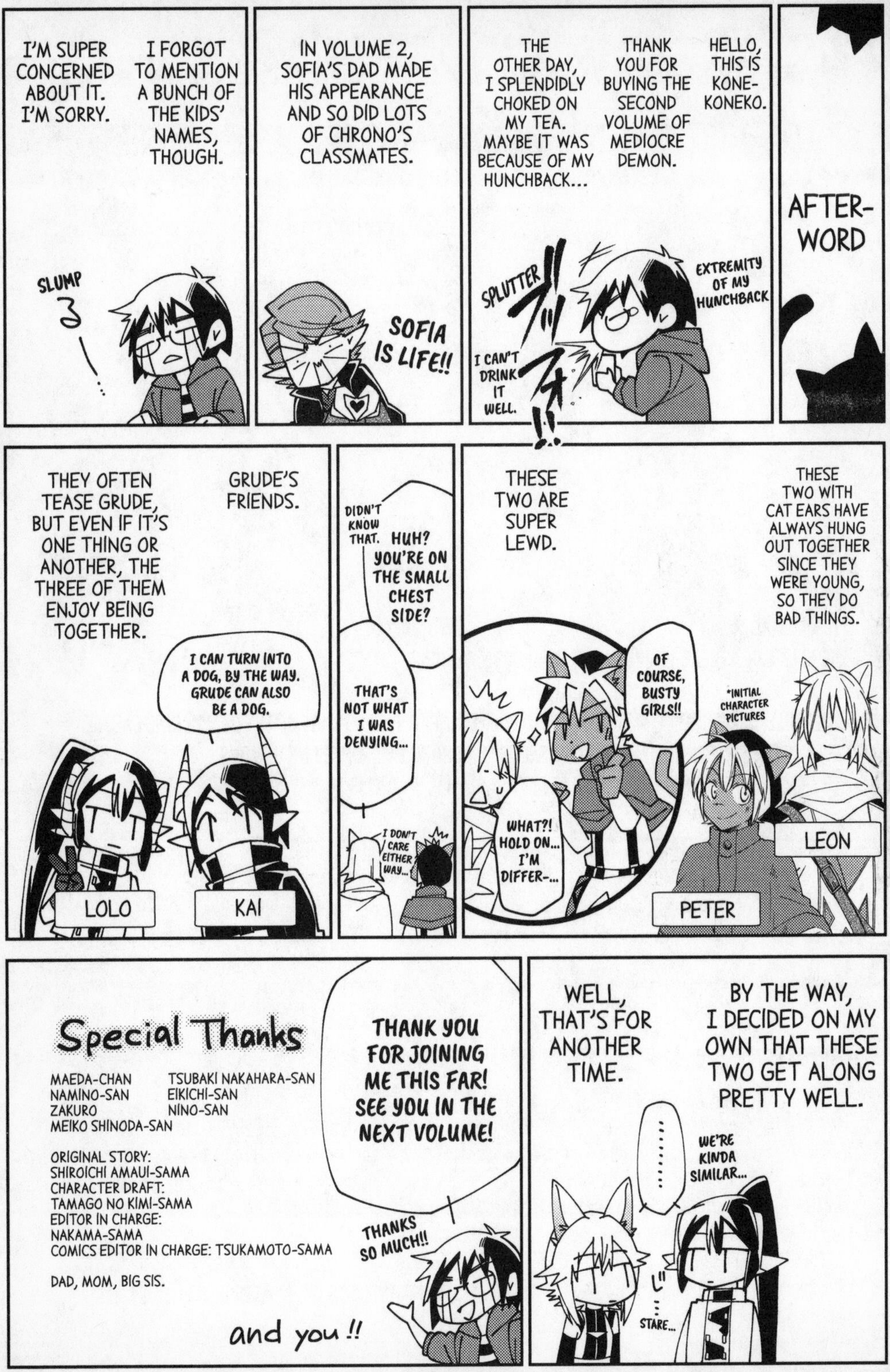
AFTER-WORD
HELLO, THIS IS KONE-KONEKO.
THANK YOU FOR BUYING THE SECOND VOLUME OF MEDIOCRE DEMON.
THE OTHER DAY, I SPLENDIDLY CHOKED ON MY TEA. MAYBE IT WAS BECAUSE OF MY HUNCHBACK...
EXTREMITY OF MY HUNCHBACK
SPLUTTER
ブッフォ!!
I CAN'T DRINK IT WELL.
IN VOLUME 2, SOFIA'S DAD MADE HIS APPEARANCE AND SO DID LOTS OF CHRONO'S CLASSMATES.
SOFIA IS LIFE!!
I FORGOT TO MENTION A BUNCH OF THE KIDS' NAMES, THOUGH.
I'M SUPER CONCERNED ABOUT IT. I'M SORRY.
SLUMP
THESE TWO WITH CAT EARS HAVE ALWAYS HUNG OUT TOGETHER SINCE THEY WERE YOUNG, SO THEY DO BAD THINGS.
THESE TWO ARE SUPER LEWD.
*INITIAL CHARACTER PICTURES
OF COURSE, BUSTY GIRLS!!
LEON
PETER
WHAT?! HOLD ON... I'M DIFFER-...
HUH? YOU'RE ON THE SMALL CHEST SIDE?
DIDN'T KNOW THAT.
THAT'S NOT WHAT I WAS DENYING...
I DON'T CARE EITHER WAY...
GRUDE'S FRIENDS.
THEY OFTEN TEASE GRUDE, BUT EVEN IF IT'S ONE THING OR ANOTHER, THE THREE OF THEM ENJOY BEING TOGETHER.
I CAN TURN INTO A DOG, BY THE WAY. GRUDE CAN ALSO BE A DOG.
KAI
LOLO
BY THE WAY, I DECIDED ON MY OWN THAT THESE TWO GET ALONG PRETTY WELL.
WELL, THAT'S FOR ANOTHER TIME.
......
WE'RE KINDA SIMILAR...
じ...
STARE...
THANK YOU FOR JOINING ME THIS FAR! SEE YOU IN THE NEXT VOLUME!
THANKS SO MUCH!!
Special Thanks
MAEDA-CHAN
NAMINO-SAN
ZAKURO
MEIKO SHINODA-SAN
TSUBAKI NAKAHARA-SAN
EIKICHI-SAN
NINO-SAN
ORIGINAL STORY: SHIROICHI AMAUI-SAMA
CHARACTER DRAFT: TAMAGO NO KIMI-SAMA
EDITOR IN CHARGE: NAKAMA-SAMA
COMICS EDITOR IN CHARGE: TSUKAMOTO-SAMA
DAD, MOM, BIG SIS.
and you !!

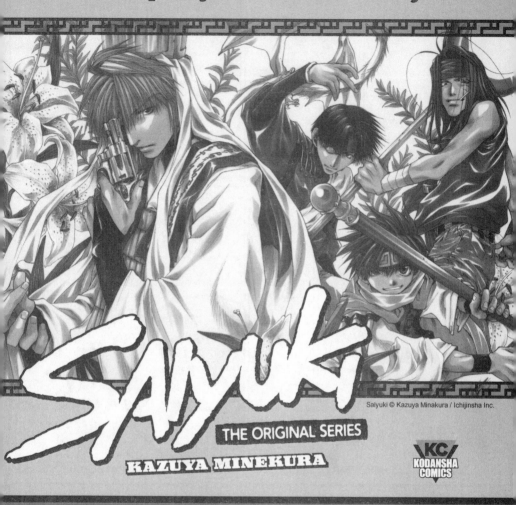

The adorable new odd-couple cat comedy manga from the creator of the beloved *Chi's Sweet Home*, in full color!

Sue & Tai-chan

Konami Kanata

Sue is an aging housecat who's looking forward to living out her life in peace... but her plans change when the mischievous black tomcat Tai-chan enters the picture! Hey! Sue never signed up to be a catsitter! *Sue & Tai-chan* is the latest from the reigning meow-narch of cute kitty comics, Konami Kanata.

KC KODANSHA COMICS

THE SWEET SCENT OF LOVE IS IN THE AIR! FOR FANS OF OFFBEAT ROMANCES LIKE *WOTAKOI*

Sweat and Soap © Kintetsu Yamada / Kodansha Ltd.

In an office romance, there's a fine line between sexy and awkward... and that line is where Asako — a woman who sweats copiously — meets Koutarou — a perfume developer who can't get enough of Asako's, er, scent. Don't miss a romcom manga like no other!

Young characters and steampunk setting, like *Howl's Moving Castle* and *Battle Angel Alita*

A boy with a talent for machines and a mysterious girl whose wings he's fixed will take you beyond the clouds! In the tradition of the high-flying, resonant adventure stories of Studio Ghibli comes a gorgeous tale about the longing of young hearts for adventure and friendship!

A Kodansha Trade Paperback Original

The Hero Life of a (Self-Proclaimed) Mediocre Demon! 2 copyright © 2019 Shiroichi Amaui / Konekoneko / Tamagonokimi
English translation copyright © 2021 Shiroichi Amaui / Konekoneko / Tamagonokimi

Published in the United States by
Kodansha USA Publishing, LLC, New York.

Publication rights for this English edition arranged through
Kodansha Ltd., Tokyo.

First published in Japan in 2019 by Kodansha Ltd., Tokyo as
Jishō! Heibon mazoku no eiyū raifu 2.

ISBN 978-1-64651-335-2

Printed in the United States of America.

1st Printing

Translation: Jessica Latherow / amimaru
Lettering: Chris Burgener / amimaru
Additional Lettering: Phil Christie
Editing: David Yoo
Kodansha USA Publishing edition cover design by Matt Akuginow

Publisher: Kiichiro Sugawara

Director of Publishing Services: Ben Applegate
Associate Director, Publishing Operations: Stephen Pakula
Publishing Services Managing Editors: Madison Salters, Alanna Ruse
Production Managers: Emi Lotto, Angela Zurlo

KODANSHA.US

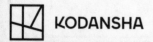

KODANSHA